T0196471

THE SECOND COMING AND I:
A READING FOR LEANNE LONG

BOOK TWO

JOHN KORDUPEL

BALBOA.
PRESS

A DIVISION OF HAY HOUSE

Balboa Press books may be ordered through booksellers or by contacting:

Balboa Press
A Division of Hay House
1663 Liberty Drive
Bloomington, IN 47403
www.balboapress.com.au
1 (877) 407-4847

ISBN: 978-1-5043-1340-7 (sc)
ISBN: 978-1-5043-1341-4 (e)

Print information available on the last page.

Balboa Press rev. date: 07/02/2018

INDEX

2:1. APPONTMENTS.. P. 1

2:2. THE TRANSFER OF COSMIC ENERGIES BETWEEN REALMS. .... P. 14

2:3. THE CHAIN OF REBIRTH. .... P. 39

2:4. A DEATH, A FUNERAL & A RESURRECTION. .... P. 172

2:5. Forthcoming publications... P. 186

2:6. Book Two: Back Cover.. P. 215

Acknowledgement

John and I would like to thank Leanne Lowther for her tireless effort in helping to bring these manuscripts to fruition.

READING.

APPONTMENTS.

Energy Healing Appointments:

Energy Healing Appointments: the Journey:
First appointment: 28/7/2017.
Second appointment: 11/8/2017.
Third appointment: 1/9/2017; You're a reincarnation of Cher, of Mary Magdalene: Leanne agrees to a Reading.

Fourth appointment: 6/10/2017.
Fifth appointment: 20/10/2017; it is 17/(11)/10 ↔ 17/11/10, know My world to know yours.
Sixth appointment: 10/11/2017; it is 17/11/10 ↔ 17/11/10, know My world to know yours.

Seventh appointment: 15/12/2017.
Eighth appointment: 29/12/2017
Ninth appointment: 19/1/2018.

15/12/17 is 17/12/15 . . . 171215 / 55 = 3113 . . . 31:(13) = 1847 minutes - <31> = 1816.
    18/1/(6) is 18/25 ↔ 18:25 = 6:25 PM . . . **625**, Robert begins to tidy things up.
   (18)/1/{6}, You have made the bed as far as you could. Now it is up to Me.

29/12/17 is 17/363 . . . 173:63 = 7 days / 563 . . . 7563 – [563/7 days . . . 5637] = 1926 . . . Genesis **19:26**, Lot's wife looks back.

19/1/18 is (12)/1/18 . . . 121:18 is 5 days / 118 . . . 51:18 = 3:18 / 2 days . . . 31:82 = 1 day / 7:82 . . . **1782**.

and,
[1816 + 1926 + 1782 = **5524**] - [<6181> + <6291> + <2871> = 15343] = 9819
    5524 + <9189> = **14713** . . . 147:13 = 3:13 / 6 days . . . **31/3/{6}**, a marriage.

    (5524 – [31/3/{6}, a marriage = <6313>] = **789**) + **2/3/47**, my birth day = **31/3/{6}**, a marriage.

    [5524 + <4255> = **9779**] + [2/3/47, my birth day + <7432> = **9779**] = 19558
    14713 - ([195:58 = 8 days / 3:58 . . . 8358] + [3:58/8 days . . . 3588] = 11946) = **2767**.
       2767 . . . [2 * 7 = 14][6 * 7 = 42] . . . 1442 . . . **144/{2}**, Robert Loomis / manuscript.
       27:67 = 1 day / 3:67 . . . **13/(67)**, Hay house / no, need a literary agent.
       27:67 = 1687 minutes + <76> = **1763**, the other Book-End.

1

and,
0413 481 764, L & L Energy Healing Studio + <4671843140> = 5085,324,904 . . . 50:85 = 2:85 / 2 days . . . 2852
2852 + 324 = 3176 - <409> = **2767**.

[5524 = <4255>] - [31/3/{6}, a marriage = <6313>] = 2058 + 789 = 2847 . . . 28:47 = 1727 minutes . . . **1727**.
From *Regeneration of the Human Race*.
17/2/7. We recall a comment made in the theme 'Old Energies, New Energies on 13/1/7.

You have made the bed as far as you could. Now it is up to Me.

From where I sit, I stopped making my bed on 24/5/3. After that I delivered messages. All up, including the publishers before Robert Loomis, I delivered messages to the Product Mix coming out of the Hose – the Collective Consciousness. To my way of thinking, that makes it Your bed.

It depends on who is included in 'you'.

and,
5524 + <9189> = **14713 – 17/11/{9}**, I cannot talk with you about your world unless you know about Mine = **2406**.
Leanne's birth day: 7/2/5/{61} + 5/2/7/62 = 19799.
[Cher's passing: 8/(60)/{7} + {7}/(60)/8 = 16215] + 11/7/8, Cher's funeral = 19393.
19799, Leanne's birth day – **17393**, Cher's passing, her funeral = **2406** ↔ **2406**, Mary Magdalene.

2406, Mary Magdalene . . . 5√**2772**, Leanne Long = 12811125; 1281 + 1125 = **2406**.

2406, Mary Magdalene . . . √2406 = 4905 0993 . . . [4905 = <5094>] - [0993 = <3990>] = 1104.
1104 minutes = 16:144 . . . **16144**, Mary Magdalene
[**(18)**/7/62, Leanne's birth day – **16144**, Mary Magdalene = **2618**] - <8162> = **5544**, Leanne Long.

and,

(18)/7/62, Leanne's birth day - ([Cher's passing: 8/(60)/{7} + {7}/(60)/8 = **16215**] + **11/7/8**, M/D/Y, Cher's funeral = **17393**) = **1369**.

([2406, Mary Magdalene ↔ 2406, Leanne Long] + <6042> = 8448) + **1369**, a death, a funeral, a birth day = **9/8/17**, Leanne / Reading.

fate and destiny, preordained.

Energy healing appointments,
an,
appointment with destiny.

12/11/2017.
the time footprint:
{16}/11/(18) . . . [1 + 6 = 7]1118 . . . 71118 . . . {7}/1/11/8, Cher passed away.
17/11/(18) . . . [1 + 7 = 8]11[-1 + 8 = 7] . . . 8117 . . . **8/11/7**, Cher's funeral.

Nurture Yourself – Mother Mary.

You've given a lot of yourself lately, and now it's time to give something to yourself. You've drawn this card because you need to nurture yourself. This means taking good care of your body through sleep, detoxification, and exercise. It also means taking care of your needs as you would for others. To have more energy, abundance, peace, purpose, and everything that you desire, nurture yourself.

Additional meanings for this card:
- Balance giving to others with receiving for yourself.
- Honor your inner voice.
- Get some rest.
- Take care of your body.
- Nurture your inner child.
- Your life purpose involves helping children.
- Mother Mary is with you, helping and guiding you.

* * * * *

Mother Mary is the beloved mother of Jesus who is renowned for her purity and compassion. Mary helps children (including your inner children) and caretakers of children. You can ask Mother Mary for Divine assignments to help children as your life's work.
Ascended Masters Oracle Cards Guidebook. Doreen Virtue.
    Comment: children in the context of children in kindergarten cannot teach children in kindergarten.

10. Karmic Completion.

This card indicates the end of a karmic lesson or cycle where you have successfully cleared a contract or debt from your past. This could refer to a challenging situation you have recently conquered in your life or a troubling experience with an individual that involved a great deal of effort or pain. Even though there are ongoing lessons to confront throughout the course of your life, you will never have to experience this particular lesson again.
This card also represents the "wheel of fortune," where whatever goes up must also come down. Just as the tides are constantly ebbing and flowing, you are being encouraged to adapt to both the highs and lows in your life. For it is in your ability to adapt that you will make your dreams come true. By stating "This too shall pass" in the face of each and every experience, you will remain centered, grounded, and stable.
In order to better your current situation, you are being asked to adjust to, and harmonize with, the natural rhythm and cycles of your life – cycles that have cleared you of a karmic debt from your past. So pat yourself on the back and acknowledge your efforts and achievements. By continuing to face your challenges head-on and treating others with love and respect, you will be rewarded beyond your wildest dreams. Numerology Guidance Cards Guidebook. Michelle Buchanan.

Freedom- Hina.

Walk away from restrictions and be free! You have the power and the right to change your life so that you experience more freedom. This card signifies that your soul is crying out for more freedom, especially as it involves your life's purpose. Perhaps it's time to take a break so that you can think clearly about your desires and available options. The universe always supports the desire for expansion, creativity, and freedom. Say yes to freedom and the universe will say yes to you.

Additional meanings for this card:
- It's time to leave a situation that you've outgrown.
- Question the validity of any rules that you've imposed on yourself.
- Allow the universe to support you while you make desired life changes.
- Be assertive and say no to anyone who's overstepping boundaries with you.

* * * * *

Hina is a Polynesian and Hawaiian moon goddess who's considered so beautiful that no one can directly look at her. She felt compassion for the natives, so she threw pieces of moon down on the islands to provide for their material needs. The pieces turned into banyan trees, which the natives pounded into tapas cloth for use in clothing and commerce. Call upon Hina for issues involving fertility, attraction, and manifestation. Ascended Masters Oracle Card Guidebook. Doreen Virtue.

13/11/2017.
the story so far:
from Journal: *The Writings.*
20/10/2017.
Selenite – Spiritual Awakening.
Crystal Medicine.

Selenite is a powerful light-saver of universal energy. This potent crystal sends energy into the crown chakra, bathing the body in the loving healing energy of the cosmos, and clearing away the old and making way for new vibrant energy and a deeper spiritual connection. The medicine of Selenite balances and cleanses the seven main chakras. This powerful crystal assists in opening the crown chakra as it draws down the divine light of the cosmos into the top of your head. It acts like a lightning bolt of universal energy. Due to its structure, it allows energy to flow powerfully like a strike of lightning. It's a perfect crystal for clearing the energy field and for awakening deeply into your spiritual essence. Being in the presence of this magnificent crystal allows for a direct link and connect to the cosmos and spiritual wisdom.

Crystal Meaning.
   * Works as a vacuum cleaner to purify and cleanse the aura.
   * Opens and stimulates the crown chakra, bringing in the divine light of the cosmos.
   * Allows you to move forward in strength.
   * Connects to your higher self and 'I am' presence.

Oracle Reading: Message From The Crystal Deva.
You have attracted this card today because you are entering into a powerful time of spiritual awakening. There are specific cycles and times in life when the opportunity to deepen spiritually are more potent than others. This is your time now, as you are gifted with the opportunity to awaken to deeper aspects of this wisdom within yourself. If you have been feeling a little ungrounded and dizzy of late or just feeling confused about things in your world, know that this is perfectly fine and is a part of your spiritual awakening. It can stir things up for a while as the new energies integrate and ground into your day-to-day life. The devas of Selenite have arrived to carry you through this sacred time of awakening – open and receive this potent energy into your world. Your conscious awareness is expanding and profound spiritual insights and deeply held ancient wisdom are surfacing from deep within. You are encouraged to honor this process for yourself and trust and open to the experiences that are been shared with you at this amazing time. You may feel inspired to study spiritual books, attend courses and workshops, join a meditation group and experience different forms of healing and self-discovery, or be guided to travel to a spiritually inspired location or retreat. Remember this time of spiritual awakening is a sacred opportunity for you to embrace your true magnificence. Trust your own guidance and intuition and enjoy this amazing journey of awakening.
Crystal Healing Cards. The Healing Oracle. Rachelle Charman.

12. The Temple Path – Spiritual Purpose and Support.
   Upright.
   Receiving this card upright represents your own spiritual evolution. The winding path you are on leads to a blessed temple in a lovely garden, symbolizing the spiritual destiny your soul has had in mind for this lifetime. This card

upright is here to tell you that what you're going through now is all part of your soul's process. You are on your karmic path and heading in the right direction, and the choices you make now are important for your personal growth and life lessons.

The lights around the temple represent the spirit world – your family members and friends, angels and guides – all the loving spirit helpers who long to assist you. Call upon them and be open to their wisdom and inspiration.

This is a wonderful, life-expanding time, so keep in mind your personal priorities as well as your spiritual connection. Following your higher intentions will help you move your life forward in dramatic ways, and connecting with spirit – and your higher self – will have a wonderful influence on all that you experience. Energy Oracle Cards Guidebook. Sandra Anne Taylor.

Comment: I am not interested in that quest.

Why not?

What is 'spiritual awakening'? The goal posts keep shifting. Knowing Spirit has not bought me happiness.
You have not given me enough time.

I am not willing to give You any more time!

Everything happens according to divine timing for the best results. Butterfly Affirmations. Alana Fairchild.

Guess we've got nothing to talk about – just sit back and wait until Divine Timing comes off the Cosmic Shelf.

That is not how it works.

I am not chasing!!!

and,
from Journal: *Energy Grids and Oomph.*
7/11/17.
The time footprint: it is exactly nine years since Cher's funeral – the last time I saw Paris.

The original title of this chapter was *New Beginning*, but that was a title to a previous chapter, so the title was changed to *Play Me a Fiddle*.
On reflection, we have two energy grids, both with a lot of oomph.
One potential explanation is that one energy grid relates to establishing contact with Robert - followed by the resolution of corporate issues - while the other energy grid relates to the publication of the manuscript → exposing it to Market Forces.

Based on that view, the title was changed - once more - to to its current title.
Perhaps,
just perhaps,
the FUCKING BULLSHIT has stopped!

No PERHAPS!

If

No more 'if', no more 'buts'.

that is the case, then that would extend to apply to the Collective Consciousness?

That is so.

Yet, in *Conversations With God*, You make the frequent comment Until it is, it isn't',
so,
until it is, it isn't!

A doubting Thomas?

I have had over 10 years of Your BULLSHIT! I am not about to become a BELIEVER on those few lines!

That is understandable!
I will leave you with *Freedom*. Believe it or not!

Freedom- Hina.
Walk away from restrictions and be free! You have the power and the right to change your life so that you experience more freedom. This card signifies that your soul is crying out for more freedom, especially as it involves your life's purpose. Perhaps it's time to take a break so that you can think clearly about your desires and available options. The universe always supports the desire for expansion, creativity, and freedom. Say yes to freedom and the universe will say yes to you.

Additional meanings for this card:
• It's time to leave a situation that you've outgrown.
• Question the validity of any rules that you've imposed on yourself.
• Allow the universe to support you while you make desired life changes.
• Be assertive and say no to anyone who's overstepping boundaries with you.
Ascended Masters Oracle Card Guidebook. Doreen Virtue.
Comment: "Be assertive and say no to anyone who's overstepping boundaries with you" - that would also include Spirit and a focus on the matrix of the energy grids.

which brings us to today:

28. Solfeggio Frequency 852 HZ – I cleanse, reawaken and reactivate every cell within my light body.
852 Hz has shown up today as you are not listening to your intuition and have blocked messages Spirit is trying to relay. It is here to remind you that you are an awakening soul living your life in a physical body. It is time to work on your spiritual gifts which we all possess but have feared to engage. It is time to raise your vibrations and create a link between heaven and earth to become more in tune with people and your surroundings.

Frequency.
By using certain sounds and frequencies we are able to enhance our senses and create a deeper connection to Spirit. Every sound has a different vibration. Solfeggio frequency 852 Hz carries the sound and vibration of LA.
On a cellular level, this tone helps to awaken the cells and lift their vibration so our bodies can work on a higher vibratory level. Hence it increases our intuitive state and our abilities to use our sixth sense. Spiritual experiences will start to unfold and as we develop, our bodies become that of pure light form.
As our intuition improves, we will start finding that we can gain more perspective and insight into situations at hand and will be able to see through the veil when others are not being true to us.
Comment: In the Koran, there is repeated reference to those that Allah guides rightly, to those that Allah misleads, so by 'others', that would include Spirit.
But,

if the veil is lifted, what happens to the fundamental relationship between Heaven and Earth, that of the testing of hearts and minds.

I cannot see that changing!

Nor can I, but there are veils concerning this level of self-mastery, and then there are veils at that level of self-mastery.

Self-mastery in relation to what?

Exactly!

I have half a knee-cap. A lizard that looses its tail can grow it back. One definition of self-mastery would have me grow the other half of my knee-cap.

In your dreams.

Practical Application.
Through the practice of meditation, working with crystals, eating healthier, having regular integrated healing sessions (to name a few) and ridding yourself of energies or people that no longer serve your needs, you will start to enhance your ability to work at a high vibratory level.
Whilst focusing on your intention of awakening your sixth sense and opening your third eye and crown to allow for a direct link to Spirit and heightening your intuition, use the sound LA. This frequency on a cellular level will reawaken and reactivate the DNA that once lay dormant. Once activated, your life will begin to change in ways you didn't expect. People, surroundings, sounds, taste, smell will start to seem different.
Work with the colour indigo when using this frequency.

Card Numerology: 6.
Crystal suggestions: Danburite, amethyst, moldavite, phenacite.
Sacred Geometry Healing Cards Guidebook. Emily Kisvarda.

22. Dodecahedron – I am open to receiving divine wisdom.
This card has appeared today because you are feeling spiritually stuck. You feel as though your connection to spirit is lost and aren't receiving messages in any avenue of clairvoyance, clairsentience, clairaudience or claircognizance. It is time to rebalance and recalibrate and find the reason to why you are experiencing a block in this area. There may be a number of reasons, whether it be physical, mental or emotional. Whatever the reason, do not fear receiving the divine wisdom that can be accessed if you are open to experiencing heavenly connections.

Sacred Geometry.
The dodecahedron has twelve faces, works with the element of ether or spirit. Its dual is the icosahedron. It corresponds to the third eye and crown chakra. The dodecahedron is considered the most sacred of the Platonic solids. Plato saw this shape as that which was used by God for arranging the constellations. It was highly revered, and of all of the Plantonics, it was the one shape that couldn't be spoken of.

The dodecahedron / icosahedron dual is quite special. Both geometries have phi ratios that is the golden mean / golden ratio / golden proportions is seen. As an example in the human body, the ultimate expression of phi codes is depicted in Leonardo Da Vinci's painting of Vitruvian man.

The molecular structure of DNA has a pent / hex (pentagram / hexagram) structure if you look under a microscope. What is divine is that as the dodecahedron and icosahedron are duals, when they rotate up as a DNA strand there is a specific pattern occurring. It truly is a marriage made in heaven.

Given the pent / hex relationship working together to create our DNA, our blueprint, we can say that we are working with the male / female, heaven and earth or spiritual and physical.

In two-dimensions the dodecahedron represents the pentagram. The pentagram is highly revered in the occult world and is used in magick. It is also known as an ultimate symbol of Phi ratio because where two lines intersect, you get the Fibonacci numbers. Pent is fractal. That is infinitely large and infinitely small.

All proteins are said to be pent in nature.

Practical Application.

By using and connecting to the dodecahedron through meditation and in healing work, you can increase your spiritual and physical awareness, access your higher consciousness and vibration. This will lead the way to spiritual ascension and awaken dormant DNA. It activates the pineal gland, which assists with quantum shifts and assessing and working within other dimensions. The pineal gland also stimulates the release of melatonin, which is stimulated by darkness. By working with this gland and increasing the level of this hormone, it will help regulate awake-sleep cycles. Sacred Geometry Healing Cards Guidebook. Emily Kisvarda.

14/11/2017.

A lizard can grow a tail back, why is that a 'in your dreams' scenario? Why is that option excluded from us?

Do you want to give it a go?

We have had discussions concerning the Puppet-Master / puppet relationship, and You have consistently maintained that we are not puppets – press this button, press that button, and the puppet dances to your tune is not the nature of the relationship. For all Your smooth talking, that is how I see the Relationship.

Being able to grow a 'tail' would clarify that issue.

Yes, it would.
Do you think you are up to it?

If not me, then who else.

Let's see how you go.

This discussion has gone beyond what I was trying to address by going to an energy healer. As there remains but three more appointments, it may be appropriate to transfer this story to my Journal.

16/11/2017.

Owl – Follow your Intuition.

You hold within you some of the qualities and traits of the owl. You may have fine-tuned your intuitive abilities – that sense of inner knowing. Or you may have become strong-willed, perceptive and wise. Learn from the silence of the owl's spirit, which offers lessons of stealth and poise in our everyday lives. If you are about to take on a new business venture or let go of some parts of your life that are no longer relevant, it is important that you become more observant. You cannot fool the owl, as he is aware of his surroundings at all times. With this message you can follow your goals to prosperity and heed these qualities to live the life of your dreams.

Mystical Wisdom Card Deck. Gaye Guthrie.

the time footprint:

[day 320 + 20{16} + 2017 = 4353] – [16/11 + 11/16 = 2727] = 1626 . . . **16/2/6**, is contact with Robert imminent?
      it is 16/2/{5} . . . 1625 . . . 1 day / 6:25 = 30:25 = 1825 minutes . . . **18/25**.

([day 320 + 20{16} + 2017 = 4353 = <3534>] + (2) weeks / 11 = 3745) - [2727 + 11/(2) weeks = 2839] = 906 . . . **90/{6}**, a marriage.
    (275)/7, a marriage = **16/2/6**, is contact with Robert imminent? + 1131 . . . 1131 minutes = 18:51 . . . **18/(5)/1** is **18/26** ↔
    16/2/6, is contact with Robert imminent? . . . 1 day / 6:26 = 30:26 = 1826 minutes . . . **18/26**.

Focusing on: " . . . let go of some parts of your life that are no longer relevant . . .

I have consistently maintained, this is not my Playground,

I have been pissed on and told it was rain!
    Shitted on,
        and told it was hail!

        Along the line, you have declared your Truth.
        Take time out to get grounded.

Why would you want to get into bed with God?

    In order to reveal your Truth.

    All that is yesterday's story, water under the bridge.
Bottom line,
I am out of the God-Business.

    For the time being.

It is over.

    There remains but the difference between a death and a funeral.

19/11/2017.

the time footprint: it is {16}/(42) . . . 1642 . . . 1 day / 6:42 = 30:42 . . . 30:(42) = 1758 minutes + <24> = **1782** ↔
    {17}/8/2 is 14 days after **18/25** ↔ **18/2/(5)** ↔
        306/8, Cher passed away . . . 30:68 = 1868 minutes . . . **18/68** is 14 days after **18/2/(5)**
        and,
        1868 minutes - <86> = **1782**.

16. The Shadow Queen – acquiring knowledge, insecurity, manipulation.
    Challenger.
    The Shadow Queen gently asks you to address your innermost character flaws with compassion, for now it's time to bring your wounded self and hidden agendas into the light. You're seeing the tangible results of those aspects of your nature that have evolved in response to the difficulties in your life: they've been a means to help you survive.
    Perhaps your falling prey to insecurity masked as elitism and arrogance, believing that you know best; to comparing yourself with others; or to being fearful and self-sabotaging. You may have been taught that manipulating others rather than being direct is the way to get your needs met. The Shadow Queen reminds you that manipulation in any form

isn't the best method of getting what you want. Another meaning that can also apply is the possibility that you're being affected by someone else's wounded self. Perhaps *you* are the one being manipulated.

Whatever the case, it's time to take a fearless personal inventory and observe what part you play in the dramas and potential disasters in your life. When you come to the place of humility, forgiveness, and grace, then you may proceed again and walk into the Light. There is great value and strength in facing your own shadow in the realm of the Shadow Queen.

Wisdom of the Hidden Realms Guidebook. Colette Baron-Reid.

10. Storm Warning – Clouds on the Horizon.

Reversed.

This card reversed indicates that the dark times are behind you – or at least beginning to fall away. You can take heart that sunny skies and better times are on the horizon. This new light may bring a time of reassessment and redirection for you. Let yourself consider where you want to go next. Also spend some time reflecting on the difficulty that has passed. What was the lesson for you? Whether it's about self-love or empowerment, remember to bring these intentions (and the lessons learned) into your bright new path.

Energy Oracle Cards Guidebook. Sandra Anne Taylor.

Comment: One. You cannot trust God.

Two: Synchronicity dictates that we are puppets.

Three: Cannot see any point in knowing Your World.

Life is not a rip-off.

You are not puppets.

You have not given me enough time.

37. Time-Out.

This card indicates a need to take a time out from your busy schedule and the hustle and bustle of life. Perhaps you've been working too hard or have a lot going on. Maybe you've been tired or irritable, and anxious, or just generally feeling unwell. If you've been under stress of any kind or have been spending time in a negative or toxic environment, you must remove yourself from the situation to heal and recharge.

This is the perfect time to take a vacation. Even a day or two away will revitalize and recharge your soul. You don't necessarily need to leave home; you could laze around the house and unplug your computer and phone. Having an energy healing, massage, or facial; soaking in a hot bath; taking a walk in nature; watching a movie; and reading a good book are perfect ways to unwind, center yourself, and feel a sense of renewal.

In order to improve your current situation, you are being asked to adjust to, and harmonize with, the natural rhythm and cycles of life – cycles that are encouraging you to take time out for *you*. If you're feeling overwhelmed, uncertain or confused, the answers will present themselves during your quiet time. Clarity comes from silence, and order follows peace. So step away from the stress and find your inner sanctuary. Numerology Guidance Cards Guidebook. Michelle Buchanan.

20/11/2017.

the time footprint:

it is 17/11/(10) ↔ **17/11/10**, D/M/Y, I cannot talk with you about your world unless you know about Mine. Get out of My Car.

6. Cycles – Life is cyclical, sometimes things flow and at other times they slow down.

What cycle of life are you in right now? What is the one area of your life where you need to focus most of your energy? Is it time to focus on your family? Do you need alone time to discover your true purpose? Do you yearn to open your heart and love fully, deeply and passionately? Is this the time for healing and regeneration?

Maybe you are completely ready to enthusiastically concentrate on your life purpose and put all your energy and effort into making your dreams a reality.

Each cycle you encounter offers you fresh gifts and possibilities to learn and grow. The better you become at identifying the cycle you are in, the more flow and harmony you will experience in the choices you make.

Comment: flow and harmony, hmm! I get plenty of flow – the bullshit is as thick as ever.

Action.

Your body is the key to showing you where you are at. Do you have the energy and the vitality to focus on your goals or are you in a period of healing? Heal Yourself Reading Cards Guidebook. Inna Segal.

Comment:

Teenagers have their language, while people who have come out of their mid-life crisis have their perspective on life. It would be good if there were oracle cards for people my age.

Third-Agers and their sanctimonious buzz-words.

Everybody has a turn at the bottom of the wheel. If you are somewhere between 12 o'clock and 6 o'clock you are supposed to "harmonize" with the times.

Tell that to Mary Magdalene!

In a subsequent manifestation, Mary Magdalene came down with scleroderma because she was not able to "adjust and harmonize" with a life experience.

Unconditional love – if people practiced unconditional love there would be no divorce.

Divorce is emotionally draining.

There are people who have come down with a serious illness following the emotional pain of a divorce or separation.

While in *Conversations with God*, there is a reference to Hitler going to Heaven because there was nowhere else for him to go, you need to reconcile that piece of information with another piece of information – the perfection of Cosmic Law, the law of cause and effect. Hitler may well end up in Heaven, but more than likely he will need to spend quite a few lifetimes in purgatory addressing his shadow side. Purgatory in this sense is not some mythical space on the Cosmic Shelf, but rather here, on Earth – Kali Yuga and Earth's dark night of the Soul, the God/Devil matrix.

None, absolutely none, of the Scriptures give counsel for the evolution of the inferior wo/man.

Jeremiah 17:9 and 17:10 speaks of the testing of hearts and minds. The I Ching says the same thing, but using different words. There is also a reference to your lodestar.

The Gita waxes lyrical about how the man of wisdom, sits, walks, talk.

The Koran makes frequent mention concerning those that Allah rightly guides, verses those whom He misleads.

If there is a distinction between being rightly and wrongly guided, then you cannot have unconditional love.

The Scriptures were a forewarning to the plain explanation that is in *Conversations with God*.

What does your own experience tell you?

Are there not stories that you come across on the News that absolutely disgust you?

We will not evolve while we treat those who skin animals alive with unconditional love.

Animals are deserving too! Can you not DISCERN?

Love the dark side unconditionally
? ? ? ? ?

Is that what you are saying????
Earth is not going through it's dark night of the Soul because of unconditional love.
Those who use the term unconditional love may have fond memories of the Golden Age of Atlantis. But that Golden Age was bought to an end by the emergence of the Dark Side, an evolutionary gap that Earth's dark night of the Soul is addressing.

I am in-between healing sessions, and I am "harmonizing" with where I am at – I have had it up to HERE with the bullshit from Spirit.
Spirit reckons I haven't given Spirit enough time.
Spirit reckons that Four Medicine Wheels doesn't constitute enough time!
See how you go harmonizing with life's cycle when you have to go through a rite of passage that requires the burying of karmic baggage going back four Medicine Wheels.
My life purpose was to get out of the God-Business. Everything else were steps along the way.
Your life purpose may be to begin the crossing through the Borderlands. You may have cleansed some, but not all, of the smell of garlic.

My time for looking under rocks is nearly over. I thank all of the oracle cards that have helped me on my journey.

Who says you cannot learn from teenagers, teenagers in years that is, not teenagers in an evolutionary sense.

Write your oracle cards.

They are an evolutionary platform that offers an opportunity to have a conversation with the Keeper of our Book of Life.
As your life experience expands, you will get to know your Playground more intimately. You will evolve to speak a different language, giving us a new series of oracle cards, permitting a different conversation with the Keeper.

Following the natural rhythm of where I am at means it is time to get out of the Car – it is time to take some Time-Out.
I have been through the mill, and where I am at, is that love is something that Spirit uses to manipulate us with.
But I am not being fair, and it is not quite true. We all have a Soul Mate, and we all get along with some people more so than with others.
However,
as beauty is in the eyes of the beholder,
what buttons are being pressed?
Love does not always occur at first sight. Love can have a genesis as a thought rather than a feeling – the feeling coming later.
So,
whether the 'love' button is pressed or some other button, the puppet will dance.

You are not FUCKING puppets!!!
Life is not, is not, a FUCKING rip-off!!!

I have got down and got dirty, and exactly what have you dished up to me?

You haven't given Me enough time.
That sums it up.

Fuck you!
Am I not harmonizing with the times to Your satisfaction?

You are not doing too badly.
Talk to Me. Talk to Me in your language.
The truth will set you free.

21/11/2017.
the time footprint:
it is 17/11/(9) ↔ **17/11/{9}**, D/M/Y, I cannot talk with you about your world unless you know about Mine. Get out of My Car.

41. The Cosmos – creativity, vastness.
Ally.
The Cosmos always appears as an Ally and never as a Challenger. Creativity in all forms is represented by the Cosmos. This is a sign to place your attention on creative projects . . . they will be successful. Remember that all of life is creative, and you're always co-creating with the Divine.
The Cosmos also represents the principle of infinity and the vastness of the energetic exchange of consciousness influencing all living things. This teaches us that every intention we set is, in fact, contagious, with the power to influence others. We're entangled at our deepest energetic place, so we can't help but have an effect on others – from an individual level to a global one.
This is a sign to remind you to open up to the well of creativity deep within you and be mindful of your thoughts and actions: both are influencing your outer world. Most important, keep taking action toward your goals, as the Cosmos responds perfectly to manifest your highest Destiny. Expect to be inspired and to meaningfully touch others with all that you create!
Wisdom of the Hidden Realms Guidebook. Colette Baron-Reid.

10. Karmic Completion.
This card indicates the end of a karmic lesson or cycle where you have successfully cleared a contract or debt from your past. This could refer to a challenging situation you have recently conquered in your life or a troubling experience with an individual that involved a great deal of effort or pain. Even though there are ongoing lessons to confront throughout the course of your life, you will never have to experience this particular lesson again.
. . . So pat yourself on the back and acknowledge your efforts and achievements. By continuing to face your challenges head-on and treating others with love and respect, you will be rewarded beyond your wildest dreams.
Numerology Guidance Cards Guidebook. Michelle Buchanan.

READING.

THE TRANSFER OF COSMIC ENERGIES BETWEEN REALMS.

From *A Second Creation and the Fourth Medicine Wheel*; chapter The Fourth Medicine Wheel.

The Colonization of Earth.
"To Adam We said: 'dwell with your wife in Paradise and eat of its fruits to your hearts' content wherever you will but never approach this tree or you shall both become transgressors.
But Satan made them fall from Paradise and bought about their banishment. 'Go hence,' We said, 'and may your off-springs be enemies to each other. The earth will **for a while** provide your sustenance and dwelling-place". P. 328 The Koran, translated by N. J. Darwood.

" . . . any entity may enter the Earth through birth or other means . . ." P. 209 Notes from the Cosmos.

What does "other means', mean?

It means that the Earth will be 'invaded' that is, occupied by other vibratory forces.

They, and every beast after his kind, and all the cattle after their kind, and every creeping thing that creepeth upon the earth after his kind, and every fowl after his kind, every bird of every sort. Genesis 7:14. Holy Bible. King James Version.

"after his kind . . . after their kind . . . after his kind . . . after his kind . . ." a lot of emphasis on 'kind'.

Noah and animals according to their kind – their physical shape changes, but not the nature of their being – were the first invasion.

" . . . any entity may enter the Earth through birth or other means . . ." P. 209 Notes from the Cosmos.

What does "other means', mean?

It means that the Earth will be 'invaded' that is, occupied by other vibratory forces.

" . . . It is important to note that all souls in the greater Oneness were created at the same time, regardless of where in the universe they choose to sojourn. *All those on Earth were at one time part of the consciousness of Mars.* Or, if they were not part of the original consciousness, so did dwell upon it afterwards in order for the soul to experience a particular vibratory force." P. 236 – 237.

"For the first projections of souls that came into Earth were coming directly from being indistinguishable from the Oneness, and they were experimenting. They were simply sampling the waters, so to speak.

Prior to the arrival of the contingency from **Mars**, other entities had come into Earth to gain experience, in particular, from that of **Sirius**. So the Earth has been colonized since its very beginning, or since its molten, or gaseous, days. Different realities, different consciousness, apply here. In the physical realm, as you would know it, these first projections of souls some eighteen million years ago would have to be identified as shadow – like creatures. It wasn't till a later time, whence occurred the projection of the five races of humans simultaneously into the world, that a hierarchy of consciousness was set up on Earth." P. 241.

"GMS: So that you may have an understanding of the incarnational cycle of groups and the preparation of cycles, we would bring your focus to that time period of the turn of the last century, in particular, just prior to World War 1. Whereas a major influx of souls of the yellow vibratory force – or the **Atlanteans** – did so come to dwell in the Earth school. This has bought to Earth technological advances, as well as warring activities.

In the fifties, another window opened up that provided an opportunity for a different vibratory force. Those souls who were attuned to the blue vibratory force while in between worlds – in the borderlands – found compatibility in the Earth system. This group became the peacekeepers of the sixties.

In the sixties another main group incarnated, and became the political activists. Many of these were the earlier Native Americans – previously **Lemurians** – reincarnating once more. All of this moves towards a grander cycle that will last approximately twelve hundred years in its major focus, through the time period of the turn of the century. It will then move for approximately eighteen hundred years in a sub-harmonic of this, which may be termed a lesser cycle or a preparation for the completion of a grand cycle". P 277.

"GMS: These Lemurians, or the Blue Race, have chosen this particular window of opportunity because the vibration of Earth is becoming more closely attuned to their original projection onto Earth. Their goal and purpose was originally to achieve a greater attunement with Earth. Through a co-partnership with the Creator rather than a separation from same, they gained much. As such, they may be thought of as guardians of the planet and its inhabitants. The children incarnating in this time period are driven towards peace and unity, a caring not only for Earth, but for the universe in its totality.

Those things that would deal with nurturing qualities – this includes the five elements of Earth – will become part of their total consciousness. They will begin to incarnate in even greater numbers as the vibratory force begins to build. So while an earlier portal of opportunity – such as the 1940's – was a narrow band of colour tones of blue, a greater portion opened up in the fifties, sixties and seventies. In the eighties, nineties and in the next century, millions will enter.

Their function, their purpose – what may be viewed as their karmic desire – is to express themselves in a peaceful manner, utilizing Earth in its original form. They seek to be allowed their existence as co-habitants with the various elements and the sentient Earth form. Understanding would be best if you would view the Blue Ray children as predominantly teachers. P. 278.

CK: You mentioned they are teachers. What will they teach?

GMS: They will move towards those teaching professions that would deal more with the activities of environment, and will head up and move into positions of authority. Another portion of the group will be the peacekeepers, the negotiators, or those that will bring about a unification of peace. These, however, are more of hybrids, more of those portions of Lemurians who also had Atlantean experience. They have already gone through the various shifts and changes, what would be termed warring activities or misuse of powers. It is not difficult in today's world to simply look upon these groups and see that they have already began to manifest. Though, as we perceive, they are only in their very early stages. Again this is cursory, for they are the forerunners of the initiation – such as the purification energy of baptism. They prepare the way for the coming of the beacon, the Master, and the coming of a grander awakening upon the planet. P. 279.

For in the time period from the turn of the last century through to the year A.D. 2250, only those souls who have particular vibratory forces will be able to incarnate in this Earth reality. It is not that some are restricted as a judgment of purity or goodness. Rather, this is a natural process, wherein the vibratory force of the soul must match the vibratory force of the time period, in order for passage to occur. Earth itself will soon be beating, pulsing, at a different frequency than it has in previous times. It will have a different vibratory force, and its pilot frequency will change, moving to another harmonic. Earth's harmonic will increase to more than two times the current rate of cycle. As such, those souls not properly attuned through other incarnations, will not be able to resonate or find harmony within the Earth School. The Blue Ones come to aid and assist in the present, so as many as possible may take part in the coming of the next age." P. 283.

"GMS: What happens to those who have not developed the necessary vibrations?
Source: They shall find opportunities for lessons in newly created realms. Should they develop necessary vibrations in those places, then it will be possible for them to enter into the new earth." P208. Notes From The Cosmos. Gordon – Michael Scallion.

Given that the Atlanteans "bought to Earth technological advances, as well as warring activities", while the Lemurians had "their goal and purpose was originally to achieve a greater attunement with Earth", it seems reasonable to conclude that Atlanteans were from Mars/Nibiru while Lemurians were from Sirius.

"Sulphur is the memory stone for Nibiru, our ancient sister civilization that existed on the planet we now call Mars". P. 257. Liquid Crystal Oracle. Justin Moikeha Asar.

" . . . He who is the Lord of Sirius, that it was He who destroyed 'Ād first and then Thamūd, sparing no one, and before them the people of Noah, who were more wicked and more rebellious. The Mu'tafikah He also ruined, so that they were smitten by the scourge that smote them.

> Which then of your Lord's blessings would you deny? He that now warns you is just like those who warned the others before you. That which is coming is near at hand; none but God can disclose the hour." P. 373. The Koran. Translated by N.J. Dawood.

Avalon is the current stage of evolution – the sum of all previous Big Bangs. Integrating Atlantis, Lemuria and Avalon is where the Earth evolutionary cycle is at. In the fullness of time, this evolutionary cycle will also face a blank Rune.

1. Clear Quartz (The Master Healer) and Archangel Metatron (King of Angels).
The Gift of Power.
Atlantean Soul Healing With Clear Quartz And The Archangel Metatron: Process For Clearing Fear And Stepping Into Your Soul Power.

> Deep within many old souls on the Earth are Atlanteans memories, which consciously or unconsciously affect the human lifetime of that soul even now.
> During the Atlantean era there was a growth of power without an equal growth of love. As a race, we had been learning to balance love and power and to bring them together with wise intention. The wisest of all intentions is that anything we wish to manifest be for the greatest good of all in how it unfolds.
> In Atlantis there was an abuse of technology and a lust for power that it could create, which was not matched by a connection to the natural world and its wisdom. The addiction to power was so strong, and so disconnected from heart-centred intention and presence, that great catastrophe and destruction occurred and an entire civilization was destroyed.
> Within many old souls today, there is a subconscious recognition of this pattern still healing itself, and a fear that history will repeat itself. The more disconnected from the feminine earth wisdom we have become as a species, the more fear there is that we could once again destroy ourselves and even our beautiful Mother Earth. Once we have discovered that we literally do have this destructive power at our fingertips in the form of nuclear power, the fear of power leading to destruction of the world arose – particularly in old souls that carried unresolved past life traumas from Atlantis.
> At the time of Atlantis, many tried to speak up but those that were more intent on personal gain than the greater good used their authority to silence wiser voices and act out their lust for power and domination. From that wounded frustration, those who were suppressed at the time may have come to believe that power led to corruption and destruction, although they could equally choose to build their own power so that their voice of love may always be

heard, no matter what kind of obsession may be blinding those around them in positions of leadership. Ultimately, in order to stay present and true in their leadership from a place of love, they would need to use power, not shy away from it, therefore demonstrating a higher choice and contributing towards a hopeful future for the human species.

The job of the soul with Atlantean experience is to heal this fear of power within and to redefine power as an expression of love. As we

do this within ourselves, we create a new template for human behaviour, a viable alternative for the wounded obsession with power as dominance and technology. There are many spiritual teachers helping the old souls on Earth to do this. The Archangel Metraton is one such divine teacher. Others include the Dalai Lama and previously Mother Teresa. These beings teach love, the path of the heart, and a connection to Mother Earth

(another great spiritual teacher) so that we may learn to live in a more balanced fashion, creating wellbeing rather than destruction." P. 45.

Crystal Angels 444 – Healing with the Divine Power of Heaven and Earth.

Perhaps I am being pedantic, perhaps I am nick-picking, but I just do not see how you can teach love. Either the seed is there, or it is not!

Then again,

perhaps that, "teaching", giving a seed a chance to germinate, is what the Fourth Medicine Wheel – the Kali Yuga cycle – is all about!

It becomes a matter of acknowledging the correct relationship between Heaven (the Modellor, the Knower) and Earth (the Field, the Soul) that the Second Creation reveals.

17:9. "The heart is deceitful above all things, and desperately wicked: who can know it?"

17:10. "I the Lord search the heart, I try the reins, even to give every man according to his ways, and according to the fruit of his doings."

Jeremiah. Holy Bible. King James Version.

and,

"I will bring to you the exact right thought, word or feeling to the purpose at hand, using one device or several." P.23. Conversations with God. Neale Donald Walsch.

If your Governing Structure, and the Comfort Zones you have built around it, do not permit the evolution of the superior wo/man AND the evolution of a superior Collective Will, then you have built a house of cards, for, in terms of the I Ching, you know not what gives a thing Duration.

The fall of Babylon, the Kali Yuga cycle, will signal the fall of your House of Cards.

Reason dictates that Eve's initial manifestation would be on the first Medicine Wheel and not on the fourth. The fourth Medicine Wheel, Kali Yuga, Earth's dark night of the Soul is basically the ramification of Adam and Eve eating the fruit from the forbidden tree, the tree of Knowledge and Understanding.

the transfer of Souls between realms:

Sirius: <213> + 249 = **462**, Galaxy, Sophis.

Adam: 1,4,1,13 . . . [14 * 11 * 3 = **462**] * 12 = 5544 . . . 554 weeks / 4 days = 3882 days . . . **3882**, Adam ↔ **3882**, the Unlettered Prophet.

Noah: 14, 15, 1, 8 . . .141518 . . . 1415 + 18 = 1433 . . . 14 * 33 = **462**, Noah ↔ **462**, Adam ↔ **3882**, the Unlettered Prophet.

7227, Book-End . . . [7 – 2 = 5][2⁷ = 256] . . . 5256 + <6525> = 11781.

117:81 is (2:19)/5 days . . . 21:95 = 1355 minutes + <59> = **1414**, Adam.

Adam and Eve ate the fruit from the Forbidden Tree. It does not make sense for this to have occurred on the fourth Medicine Wheel, Kali Yuga. In my view, this was more likely to have occurred on the first Medicine Wheel.

Sirius: <213> + 249 = 462.
Adam: 1,4,1,13 . . . 14 * 11 * 3 = 462.
Noah: 14, 15, 1, 8 . . .141518 . . . 1415 + 18 = 1433 . . . 14 * 33 = **462**.

7227, Book-End . . . 72:27 = 3 days / 0:27 . . . ([30:(27) = 1773 minutes . . . 1773] + <3771> = **5544**) / 12 = 462, Adam.

and,
676, Mary Magdalene . . . [6^7 = 279936 . . . <972> + <639> = 1611] + <1161> = **2772**, Know Me] / 6 = **462** ↔
4455, Leanne Long + [<5544> / 2 = **2772**, Chain of Rebirth] = **7227**, Leanne Long ↔
72:27 = 3 days / 0:27 . . . ([30:(27) = 1773 minutes . . . 1773] + <3771> = **5544**) / 12 = **462**.
and,
462 . . . 46^2 = 2116.
2116 + [**312**, Nibiru . . . 31^2 = 961] = 3077.
30:77 = 1877 minutes . . . **1877**, Mary Magdalene . . . **777**, Mary Magdalene ↔ **777**, Eve.

the transfer from 312, Nibiru (Atlantis).

3077 minutes = 50:77 = 2:77/2 days . . . **2772**, Know Me.
5077 = <213>, Sirius + **3381** + **14/8/{3}**, I'll see you tomorrow ↔
Babylonians / Kali Yuga: 978 + <879> = 1857 = <7581>, Eve . . . 75:81 = 3 days / 3:81 . . . **3381**.
33:81 = 1 day / 9:81 . . . 19:(81) = 1059 minutes . . . **1059**, a page in the life of . . .
33:(81) = 1899 minutes - <18> = 1881 . . . 1881 weeks = 13167 days . . . **13/1/{6}/7**, making of beds.

[2116 - <6112> = 3996] / 6 = **666**, Adam & Eve interwoven energy →
3996, interwoven energy . . . 3 * 99 * 6 = **1782**, Resurrection ↔ **1782**, the Second Coming ↔ **1782**, Leanne Long.

21:16 = 1276 minutes + <61> = **1337** . . . 13 * 3 * 7 = 273 . . . 273 minutes = 4:33 . . . 433 minutes = 7:13 . . . **713**, the Season ends.

and,
Noah's Ark transferred the Mars / Nibiru / Atlantis to Earth, the beginning of Kali Yuga: 1433, Noah → **1433**, the Wilderness years.

Do they not see how Allah conceived Creation, and then renews it? That is easy enough for Allah.
Say: 'Roam the earth and see how Allah conceived Creation. Then Allah will create the Second Creation.
P. 194 The Koran. N. J. Dawood . . . page 194 . . . [194 = <491>] * 7 = 3437 . . . <73:43> is 1:43 / 3 days . . . **1433**.
and,
1452 . . . 1√452 = 21260291 . . . 21260291 . . . 2126 [2 – 1 + 2 = 3 – 6 = 3] . . . 3 * 0291 = 873 . . . 873 minutes = 14:33 . . . **1433**.
1452 * 7 = 10164.
10:164 = 764 minutes + <461> = 1225 . . . **(12)/2/{5}**, is contact with Robert imminent?
10164 = **1059**, a page in the life of . . . + **9105**, I cannot talk with you about your world unless you know about Mine.

14:33. And your children shall wander in the wilderness forty years, and bear your whoredoms, until your carcases be wasted in the
wilderness. Numbers. Holy Bible. King James Version.

14:33, role reversal . . . 33:14 = 1994 minutes . . .**1994**, the Light.

my birthday: [19{46} + 1947 + 3/02 = 4195] – (25)/02 = 1693.
1693 = <3961>, the fall of Babylon . . . 3961 weeks = 27727 days . . . 27727 . . . 2772 * 7 = 19404 . . . 1940 + 4 = **1944**.

John: 10, 15, 8,14 + Kordupel: 11,15,18, 4, 21, 16, 5, 12 = 11,151,843,132,326:
We separate 11,151,843,132,326 into two groups of seven, to which we add our birthday:
    1115184 . . .1115 + 184 = 1299; 2/03/194{6} + 3132326 = 5164272; 5164 + 272 + 1299 = 6735.
      [6735 = <5376>] - [**1944** + <4491> = 6435] = **1059**, a page in the life of . . .
      and,
14/8/4, I'll see you tomorrow at 8:15: [2004 + (17)/8 + day 227 = 2409] + 815 = 3224 . . . 32:24 = 1944 minutes . . .
1944.
and,
[1944 + <**4491**>, Morgan le Fay = 6435] / 5 = **1287**, Leanne Long.
19:44 = 7:44 PM . . . 7:(44) = 376 minutes + <673> = **1049**, Leanne Long.
1944 = <4491> . . . 44:91 = 2 days / (309) . . . **2309**.
    23:09 = 11:09 PM . . . 1109 minutes = 17:89 . . . **17/8/9**, Leanne / Reading.
    2309 + <9032> = **11341** . . . 1 + 1341 = **1342**, Second Coming ↔ 1342, Leanne Long ↔

1944, I'll see you tomorrow . . . 19:44 = (4:16) / 1 day . . . 4161 + <**1614**>, Leanne Long = **5775**, Eve.
    [5775 + 11341 = **17116**] + 2/3/{46}, my birth day = 194/62, Leanne's birth day.
    and,
    the Mandi / the Second Coming / Maitreya / the Unlettered Prophet / Kalki / the Messiah:
      720 996 1062 654.
      the Six Horsemen updating the Scriptures ([720 + 996 = 1716] + [1062 + 654 = 1716] = 3432) +
      <2343> = **5775**.
    and,
    5775 . . . 577 * 5 = **2885**, Leanne Long ↔ **2885**, Eve → **28827**, Magdalene, Mary . . . 288[-2 + 7 = 5] . . . **2885**.
      28:85 = 1765 minutes . . . {17}/65 falls on {17}/6/3 ↔ 1763, the other Book-End

    5775 = **3882**, the Unlettered Prophet + **1893**, rediscovery of the Forms of Life.

    5775 + 13/(67), Hay House / no, need literary agent = 7142] – (85)/{12}, Hay House / manuscript = **1370**.
      1370 minutes = 22:50 . . . **2250**, New Harmonic Vibrations.

and,
the story so far:
Noah's Ark transferred the Mars / Nibiru / Atlantis to Earth, the beginning of Kali Yuga: **1433**, Noah → **1433**, the Wilderness
years.
    766, Lot / Lut + <667> = **1433**.
    3582, Abraham = [5544, Abraham = <4455>] + 873, Robe . . . 873 minutes = 14:33 . . . **1433**.
    815, Messiah + [14:33 = 873 minutes = <378> minutes = 6:18] = **1433**.

1433 . . . 1 day / 4:33 = 2833 . . . [2 * 8= 16]33 . . . **1633**.
    3/2/47, my birth day . . . 3247, Untitled 1 . . . 32:47 = 1967 minutes - <74> = **1893**, rediscovery of the Forms of Life.
    [1893, rediscovery of the Forms of Life + 2/3/47, my birth day = 4240] - 3/2/47 = 993 . . . 993 minutes =
    16:33 . . . **1633**.
      1633 . . . 1 day / 6:33 = 30:33 = 1833 minutes = <**3381**>, see above.
    and,
    Noah's Ark: 87 121 129 79 . . . [87 + 121 + 129 + 79 = 416] + [<78> + <121> + <921> + <97> = 1217] = **1633** →
      1633, Kali Yuga.

and,

34614, Ba-bylon . . . [3 + 4614 = 4617] - <7164> = 2547 . . . [2^5 = 32]47 . . . 3247 →

3/2/47, my birth day → 3247, Untitled 1

32:47 = 1967 minutes - <74> = 1893, rediscovery of the Forms of Life.

3247 = [1893 + 2/3/47, my birth day → 2347, the fall of Babylon = 4240] + 993 . . . 993 minutes = 16:33 . . . **1633**.

1633 . . . [163 / 3 days = 73:63 + <361> = 7724] - <4277> = 3447 . . . **34/47**, my birth day.

34/47, my birth day + <7443> = 10890; 1539, John Kordupel + <9351> = **10890**.

2/03/47, my birth day . . . 203:(47) = 12133 minutes . . . 12133 . . . 121:(33) = 7227 minutes . . . **7227**, Book-End.

47/3/2, my birth day . . . 4732 days = 676 weeks . . . 676 minutes = 11:16 . . . 1116 + <6111> = **7227**, Book-End.

7227, Book-End = [10890 / 2 = **5445**] + **1782**, the Second Coming.

and,

11,775,885, Untitled One . . . 11 + <11> + 775 + <577> + 885 + <588> = 2847

2847 . . . [2 * 8 = 16]47 . . . 1647 . . . 1 day / 6:47 = 30:47 . . . **3047**, Mary Magdalene →

30:47 = 1847 minutes - <74> = 1773 . . . **1773**, Leanne Long.

4455, Leanne Long + [<5544> / 2 = **2772**, Know Me] = **7227**, Leanne Long ↔ **7227**, Book-End.

72:27 = 3 days / 0:27 . . . 30:(27) = 1773 minutes . . . **1773**, Leanne Long

28:(47) = 1633 minutes . . . **1633**.

and,

1633, Mary Magdalene, Saint → <3361> = **1111**, John Eevash Kordupel + **2250**, New Harmonic Vibrations.

and,

the story so far:

Noah's Ark transferred the Mars / Nibiru / Atlantis to Earth, the beginning of Kali Yuga: **1433**, Noah → **1433**, the Wilderness years.

and,

[John: 10, 15, 8,14] + [Kordupel: 11,15,18, 4, 21, 16, 5, 12] = 11,151,843,132,326:

We separate 11,151,843,132,326 into two groups of seven, to which we add our birthday:

1115184 . . .1115 + 184 = 1299; 2/03/194{6} + 3132326 = 5164272; 5164 + 272 + 1299 = 6735.

6735 - [47/34, my birth day + **1433** = 6167] = 568.

[568 minutes = 9:28 . . . 928] + [<865> minutes = 14:25 . . . 1425] = 2353 . . . 23:53 = 1433 minutes . . . **1433**.

Maitreya: 14, 15, 1, 8 . . .141518; 1415 + 18 = 14:33 . . . **1433**.

124741, Kalki . . . 124 + <421> + 741 + <147> = **1433**.

29/6/{13}, Gina Panettieri / manuscript . . . 29:613 = 2353 minutes . . . 23:53 = 1433 minutes . . . **1433**.

and,

Genesis 11:6. And the Lord said, Behold, the people is one, and they have all one language; and this they begin to do: and now nothing will be restrained from them, which they have imagined to do.

Genesis 11:06 ↔ 11:06 = 666 minutes . . . **666**, the Number of the Beast.

Revelations13:17. And that no man might buy or sell, save he that had the mark, or the name of the beast or the *number of his name.*

Holy Bible. King James Version.

" . . . the number of his name is a reference to the Unlettered Prophet as mentioned in the Koran:

He replied: 'I will visit My scourge upon whom I please: yet My mercy encompasses all things. I will show mercy to those that keep from evil, give alms, and believe in Our signs; and to those that shall follow the Apostle – the Unlettered Prophet – whom they shall find described in the Torah and the Gospel. He will enjoin righteousness upon them and forbid them to do evil. He will make good things lawful to them and prohibit all that is foul. He will relieve them of their burdens and of the shackles that weigh upon them. Those that believe in him and honor him, those that aid and follow the light to be sent forth with him, shall surely triumph.

Say to your people (These words are addressed to Mohammed): 'I am sent forth to you by Allah. His is the kingdom of the heavens and the earth. There is no god but He. He ordains life and death. Therefore have faith in Allah and His Apostle, the Unlettered Prophet, who believes in Allah and His Word. Follow him so that you may be rightly guided." P. 253.

The Koran. N.J. Daewood.

and,

Genesis 11:6 + [Revelations 13:17 ↔ 13/1/7, the making of beds] = **1433**.

the transfer between realms:

[3841, Morgan le / (le) Fay / Leanne Long + <**14/8/3**>, I'll see you tomorrow = **5324**] + <4235> = **9559** ↔

the Morgans: 321 433 462 292 . . . [321 + 433 + 462 + 292 = **1508**] + <8051> = **9559** ↔

Lemuria, Atlantis, Avalon & Noah's Ark: 327 427 456 298 . . . [327 + 427 + 456 + 298 = 1508] + <8051> = **9559**.

the Morgans: 321 433 462 292 the space in-between: 352 29 362

the space in-between.

([352 + 29 + 362 = **743**] + <347> = **1090**) + ([<253> + <92> + <263> = **608**] + <806> = **1414**) = **2504**.

[743 + 608 = **1351**] + [743 + <806> = **1549**] + [743 + 1414 = **2157**] + [743 + <4052> = **4795**] = **9852**.

<1531> + <9451> + <7512> + <5974> = **24468**.

[<347> + 608 = **955**] + [<347> + <806> = **1153**] + <347> + 1414 = **1761**] + [<347> + <4052> = **4399**] = **8268**.

[<559> + <3511> + <1671> + <9934> = **15675**] / 3 = **5225**, Eve.

5225, Eve, the transfer to Avalon.

9559, Lemuria, Atlantis, Avalon & Noah's Ark – ([Eve: 5225 + 2525 = 7750] + 462, Adam = **8212**) = **1347** ↔

[8212 - <2128> = **6084**] / 2 = 3042 . . . 30:(42) = 1758 minutes + <24> = **1782**, the Second Coming.

and,

([9559, Lemuria, Atlantis, Avalon & Noah's Ark - 6084 = 3475] / 25 = 139) - <931> = **792**.

792 * 7 = **5544**; <297> * 6 = **1782**.

coming back to 1347:

7/5/2/62 + 5/2/7/{61}, M/D/W/Y, Leanne's birth day = **22501** = <**10522**>

10:522 = 1122 minutes + <225> = **1347**.

1347, Leanne's birth day ↔ **1/3/{47}**, Cherry's birth day. see 3147.

1347, Leanne's birth day = <7431> . . . [74:31 = 3 days / 2:31 . . . 3231] + <1323> = **4554**.

1347, Leanne's birth day = <7431> . . . [74:31 = 2:31 / 3 days . . . 2313] + <3132> = **5445**.

3231 + 2313 = **5544**, Leanne Long.

<1323> + <3132> = **4455**, Leanne Long.

and,

Eve: 5225 + 2525 = 7750 . . . [77:50 = 5:50 / 3 days . . . 5503] + [3 days / 5:50 . . . 3550] = **9053**.

9053 = <3509> ↔

14/8/4, I'll see you tomorrow at **815** + [815 minutes = 13:35 . . . 1 day / (3:35) is 20:25 . . . 2025] = **3509**.

9053 - <3509> = **5544** ↔

Leanne Long: 99 (161) 171 (89) . . . 99:171 – (89):(161) = 10010 . . . 100:10 = 4:10 / 4 days . . . **4104**.

4104 – [171:99 – (161):(89) = **1010**] = 3094 . . . 30:94 = 1 day / 6:94 . . . **1694**, Leanne Long ↔ **1694**, Mary Magdalene.

1694 = <4961> . . . 49:61 is 1 day / 161 . . . 1161 . . . 11* 61 = **671**, Mary Magdalene.

1694 + <4961> = **6655**.

([6655 / 11 = 605] + [6655 / 5 = 1331] = 1936) - <6391> = **4455**, Leanne Long ↔ **<5544>**

4455, Leanne Long + [<5544> / 2 = **2772**, Know Me] = **7227**, Leanne Long ↔

72:27 = 3 days / 0:27 . . . [30:(27) = 1773 minutes . . . 1773] + <3771> = **5544**.

and,

High Priestess: 162 (176) 189 (149) . . . [162 + <261> + 189 + <981> = **1593**] + <3951> = **5544**.

Leanne Long / High Priestess: 261 (337) 360 (238)

[261 + 337 + 360 + 238 = **1196** + <6911> = **8107**] + [<162> + <733> + <063> + <832> = **1790** + <0971> = **2761**]
= **10868**.

[1196 + 1790 = **2986**] + [1196 + <0971> = **2167**] + [1196 + 2761 = **3957**] + [1196 + <1672> = **2868**] = **11978**.

11978, Leanne Long / High Priestess . . .11 * 9 * 7 * 8 = **5544**.

and,

5544 has synergy with . . . 554 weeks / 4 days = 3882 days . . . **3882**, the Unlettered Prophet.

and,

the transfer to the Earth realm:

Sirius & Lemuria: 174 164 177 161 . . . [174 + <471> = 645] + [164 + <461> = **625**] = **1270**.

Sirius & Lemuria: 174 164 177 161 . . . [177 + <771> = 948] + [161 + <161> = 322, Chaos → 322, Kalki] = **1270**.

High Priestess: 162 (176) 189 (149): space in-between: 146 13 148

we join the numbers: 16,217,618,914,914,613,148 . . . 1621 7618 9149 1461 3148.

[1621 + 7618 + 9149 + 1461 + 3148 = **22997**] + [<1261> + <8167> + <9419> + <1641> + <8413> = **28901**] = **51898**.

22:(997) = 323 minutes + <799> = **1122**. see 1122.

[22997 . . . 2 * 2997 = 5994] / 9 = **666**, the Number of Man, the heart-beat Grid.

22:997 = 2317 minutes + <799> = **3116**.

31/1/6. Yesterday, I recalled thoughts from 29/1.

Robert needs a couple of weeks to tidy things up.

I didn't give it much thought as there was no starting point. I assumed it was to do with when he comes to Melbourne.

Starting from when?

625.

625 . . . 6√25 = 1051 5811 . . . [<1501> + <1185> = 2236, Robert begins the tidying up] + **880**, God = 3116 . . . **31/1/6**.

31:16 = 1 day / 7:16 . . . **1716**, Anakhita.

3116 = <6113> = **569**, Jesus + 5544 . . . 554 weeks / 4 days = 3882 days . . . **3882**, the Unlettered Prophet.

3116 = <6113> . . . {6}/1/13, You have made the bed as far as you could. Now it is up to Me.

625, the tidying up begins + **369**, Earthlings + [**1059**, a page in the life of . . . 10:59 = 659 minutes . . . 659] = **1653** ↔

Leanne Long: the space in-between: [2136 = <6312>] + [1452 = <2541>] + [2886 = <6882>]= **15735**.

15:735 = 1635 minutes . . . **1635**, Leanne Long ↔ **1635**, Eve.

15735, Leanne Long / 5 = **3147**.

3147 = <7413> . . . 74:13 = 2:13 / 3 days . . . 2133 / 3 = **711**, a Cycle ends.

3147 . . . 314 * 7 = 2198] + ([<7413> . . . 7 * 413 = 2891]) = 5089 = <9805> . . . 9 * 805 = 7245.

7245 - ([**1635** = <5361>] + **711**, a Cycle ends = 6072] = **1173**.

and,
Daniel [5:1 + 5:2 + 5:3 + 5:4 + 5:5 = 265] + [5:01 + 5:02 + 5:03 + 5:04 + 5:05 = 2515] = 2780.
([265 + <562> + 2515 + <5152> = 8494] + [2780 = <0872>] = **9366**) / 6 = 1561 = <1651>
MENE, MENE, TEKEL, UPHARSIN / PERES, God's Hand writing: 297 380 407 270. <792> + <083> + <704> + <072> = **1651**.
Daniel: 16:24 + 16:25 + 16:26 + 16:27 + 16:28 = 8130, God's Hand writing.
[9366 = <6639>] + [8130 = <0318>] = 6957) - 8130 = **1173**.
and,
11:(73) = 587 minutes - <37> = **550**, Eve; 1173 = **462**, Adam + **711**, end of a Cycle.
1173 . . . [11 * 7 = 77]3 . . . 773 . . . 7[7³ = 343] . . . 73:43 = 3 days / 1:43 . . . **3143**.
3143 = <3413> . . . [3 + 4 = 7]13 . . . **713**, the Season ends →
[3143 + <3413> = 6556] – [1173 = <3711>] = **2845**.
and,
2845, Leanne Long: the space in-between / 5 = **569**, complimentary energy with <**965**>, Iwan Kordupel / John Kordupel.

[2845, Leanne Long: the space in-between: = <5482> . . . 548 * 2 = 1096] - <6901> = 5805 = <5085> = 2:85 / 2 days . . . **2852**.
2852 / 4 = **713**, the Season ends ↔ 28:(52) = 1628 minutes + <25> = **1653**, the Morgans
1653 . . . [1 + 6 = 7]53 . . . 753 = <357> . . . 35 to 7 is 6:25 . . . **625**, Robert begins to tidy things up.
1653 . . . 1 day / 6:53 = 30:53 . . . 30:(53) = 1747 minutes . . . **1747**.
1747 minutes + <35> = **1782**, Leanne Long ↔ **1782**, the Second Coming

17:47 = 5:47 PM . . . 547 minutes = 9:07 . . . **90/7**, a marriage ↔ **907**, Invitation to change the Language.
and,
547 + <745> + **625** = **1917** . . . **1/9/17**, Leanne, you're a reincarnation of Mary Magdalene.
1917 - <526> = 1391 . . . 1 day / 3:91 = 27:91 . . . 27:(91) = 1711 minutes . . . 1711.
17:(11) = 1009 minutes . . . **1009**, the Morgans.
[1711 = <1171>] + 625 = 1796) - <526> = **1270**, Leanne Long.
and,
1554, Cherryl Dianne Kordupel.
([1554 - <4551> = **2997**, the Morgans, Leanne Long] = <7992>, John Kordupel) * 4 = **31968**, the Great Apostasy.
and,
1554 . . . 1[5 * 54 = 270] . . . **1270**, Cherryl Dianne Kordupel
12:70 = 790 minutes . . . **7/90**, a marriage.

1270, Cherryl Dianne Kordupel + 1270, Leanne Long + [{**13**}/(1)/6, Gina / manuscript ↔ **13/1/{6}**, the making of beds] = **2586**.
4266, Jesus . . . 42:66 = 2586 minutes . . . **2586**.
Cher's passing: 11/11/6 + 8/(60) + (60)/8 = **2586** ↔ **2586**, Intervention From Above.
and,
1270 minutes = 22:50 . . . **2250**, New Harmonic Vibrations.

and,
the transfer to the Earth realm:
Leanne Long: 99 (161) 171 (89) . . . 171:99 – (161):(89) = 1010 . . . 10:10 = 610 minutes . . . 6:(10) is 5:50 . . . **550**, Leanne Long ↔ **550**, Eve.

Fig. 4.

Leanne, alphabet R → L: 15, 22, 26, 13,13, 22 . . . 152,226,131,322
Long, alphabet L→ R, residual: (14), (11), (12), (19) . . . 14,111,219 . . . 152,226,131,322 + 14,111,219 = 152,240,242,541.
    152,240,242,541 . . . 152 + <042> + 242 + 541 = **977**, Leanne Long ↔ **977**, Mary Magdalene.
        [977 = <- 779>] + ([7 * 7 * 9 = 441] + [7 * 79 = 553] + [77 * 9 = 693] + 1617 = 3304) = **2525**, Leanne Long ↔
        2525, Eve.

Fig. 5.
Leanne, alphabet L → R: 12, 5, 1, 14, 14, 5 . . . 125,114,145
Long, alphabet R → L, residual: (11), (14), (13), (6) . . . 1,114,136: 125,114,145 + 1,114,136 = 126,228,281 . . .
    ([126 + 228 + 281 = **635**] + <536> = **1171**) + ([<621> + <822> + <182> = **1625**] + <5261> = **6886**) = **8057**.
    8057 = <7508> . . . 7 * 508 = 3556
        3556 + <6553> = **10109**, Leanne Long ↔ **10109**, Eve.
        3556 - <6553> = **2997**, Leanne Long.
        3556 = <6553> . . . [6 + 5 = 11]53 . . . 11:53 = 713 minutes . . . **713**, Leanne Long ↔ **713**, Season ends.

and,
Fig.7.
Leanne, alphabet L → R, residual: (14), (21), (25), (12), (12), (21) . . . 142,125,121,221
Long, alphabet R → L: 15, 12, 13,20 . . . 15,121,320
    142,125,121,221 + 15,121,320 = 142,140,242,541 . . . 142 + 140 + 242 + 541 = **1065**; <241> + <041> + 242 + <145> = **669**.
    √1065 = 3263 4337; √669 = 2586 5034; Cher's passing: 1/11/8 + 8/(60) + (60)/8 = **2586**.
        [3263 + 4337 + 5034 = 12634] – [2586, Cher's passing + <6852> = 9438] = **3196**.
        31:(96) = 1764 minutes . . . **17/(64)**; 1764 + <4671> = 6435
            6435 . . . 6 * 435 = **2610**, Eve.
            6435 + <5346> = **11781**, Mary Magdalene ↔ 1 + 1781 = **1782**, Resurrection ↔ **1782**, Leanne Long.
        3196 + <6913> = **10109**, Eve.

and,
Morgan le Fay / Leanne Long: 216 330 351 195 the space in-between: 210 21 224
Morgan le Fay / Leanne Long, the space in-between:
    ([210 + 21 + 224 = **455**] + <554> = **1009**) + ([<021> + <12> + <422> = **455**] + <554> = **1009**) = **2018**.
    2018, Morgan le Fay / Leanne Long . . . [√<8102> = 9001111] + [8√102 = 1018 2304] = 1918 3415.
        1918 + <8191> = **10109**, Morgan le Fay / Leanne Long ↔ **10109**, Eve ↔ **10109**, Leanne Long.

10109, Eve – 14102, Morgan le Fay = **3993** ↔ **3993**, Leanne Long / High Priestess ↔ 3993 . . . 3 * 99 * 3 = **891**, the Day of Resurrection.

      a page in the life of: 215 + [215 minutes = 3:35] +[2:15 is 45 to 3 . . . 453] + 3:(45) = 1348
      a page in the life of: 512 + [512 minutes = 8:32] + [5:12 is 48 to 6 . . . 486] + 6:(48) = 2478.
        [1348 + 2478 = 3826] + <6283> = **10109** ↔

      Kali Yuga, Earth's dark night of the Soul cycle: 416 + <614> + 1217 + <7121> = 9368.
      9368 = **1266**, Eve + <8102>, Morgan le Fay / Leanne Long.
        [93:68 = 5648 minutes + <86> = 5734] + <4375> = **10109**.

10109, Eve = **8/11/1**, Cher's passing + **1998**, detoxification.

10109 * 4 = 40436, Crucifixion \ Shroud of Turin . . . [40 + 4 = 44 . . . 4 * 4 = 16][3 * 6 = 18] . . . 16:18 is 1 day / (782) . . . **1782**.

my birth day: [3/02 + 19{46} + 1947 = 4195] – (25/02) = 1693 . . . (1 + (6 * [9³ = 729] = 4374) = 4375) + <5734> = **10109**.
and,

Product Recall: [1009 963 . . . 10099 + 63 = 10162] + [963 . . . 963 minutes = 16:03] + 2612 + 1944 + 1443 = 17764.
[17764, Product Recall – 13/11/9, Product Recall date = 4645] + <5464> = **10109**.

> . . . **10109**, a page in the life of Earth's dark night of the Soul,
> the day of Resurrection,
> and,
> Product Recall.

and,
the transfer to the Earth realm:
Fig.7.
Leanne, alphabet L → R, residual: (14), (21), (25), (12), (12), (21) . . . 142,125,121,221
Long, alphabet R → L: 15, 12, 13,20 . . . 15,121,320
142,125,121,221 + 15,121,320 = 142,140,242,541 . . . 142 + 140 + 242 + 541 = **1065**; <241> + <041> + 242 + <145> = **669**.
√1065 = 3263 4337; √669 = **2586** 5034; Cher's passing: 1/11/8 + 8/(60) + (60)/8 = **2586**.
[3263 + 4337 + 5034 = 12634] – [2586, Cher's passing + <6852> = 9438] = **3196**.
31:(96) = 1764 minutes . . . 1764 + <4671> = 6435
6435 . . . 6 * 435 = **2610**, Eve.
6435 + <5346> = **11781**, Mary Magdalene ↔ 1 + 1781 = **1782**, Resurrection ↔ **1782**, Leanne Long.
3196 + <6913> = **10109**, Eve . . . 101:09 = 5:09 / 4 days . . . **5094**.

and,
50:94 = 2 days / 2:94 . . . 22:94 = 1414 minutes . . . **1414**, Adam → 1414 + <49> = **1463**, John Kordupel.
and,
512, a page in the life of . . . 5 to 12 is 11:55; 11:55 is 715 minutes . . . 7:15 = 435 minutes . . . 435 = <534> . . . 534 minutes = 8:54
854 minutes = 14:14 . . . **1414** ↔
1161, Gaia . . . 11:61 = 721 minutes . . . 721 + 693 = **1414**.
and,
1414, Adam ↔ 4266, Jesus . . . 42:66 = 2586 minutes . . . 25:(86) = 1414 minutes . . . **1414**, Jesus ↔
Babylon: 3618 + <8163> = 11781 . . . 117:81 is (2:19)/5 days . . . 21:95 = 1355 minutes + <59> = **1414** ↔
[3113 BC, the start of the current Galactic cycle + 5,125 years, the duration of a Galactic cycle = 8238] + <8328> = 16566.
8238 . . . [8² = 64]38 . . . 6438 + <8346> = 14784 . . . 14[-7 + 8 = 1]4 . . . **1414** ↔

Mary:	57	47	51	53
Magdalene:	62	172	181	53

We sum the vertical: 576,247,172,511,815,353 . . . [576 + 247 + 172 + 511 + 815 + 353 = 2674] + <4762> = 7436.
[<675> + <742> + <271> + <115> + <518> + <353> = 2674] + <4762> = 7436.
[2674 + 2674 = 5348 = <8435>] + [4762 + 4762 = 9524 = <4259>] = 12694 . . . 12:694 = 1414 minutes . . . **1414**.

34/{46}, my birth day . . . 3446 days = 492 weeks / 2 days . . . 4922 = <2294> . . . 22:94 = 1414 minutes . . . **1414**.
John (Eeevash) Kordupel, R to L, balance: (9), (14), (7), (13) (4), (4), (21), (0), (18), (7) (10), (14), (17), (3), (20), (15), (4), (11).
([191 + 168 + 359 = 718] + <817> = 1535) + ([<191> + <861> + <<953>> = 2005] + <5002> = 7007) = 8542.
8542 . . . [854 minutes = 14:14 . . . **1414**, Adam] + 2 = 1416 → Revelations **14:16**, time to reap is ripe.

and,

200{6} + 2007 + 13/1 = 4144, You have made the bed as far as you could. Now it is up to Me + <4414> = 8558.

    1317 minutes = 21:57 . . . 2157 minutes = 35:57 . . . 3557 minutes = 59:17 . . . 5917 minutes = 97:97 . . . 9797

    8558 + 9797 + <7979>, Crystal Books = 26334 . . . [26 – 3 = 23]34 . . . 2334 . . . 23:34 = 1414 minutes . . . **1414**.

      1414, Intervention from Above ↔ **1414**, Earth / metamorphosis.

and,

50:94 = 2:94 / 2 days . . . 29:42 = 1782 minutes . . . **1782**, the Second Coming.

    2942 + 2294 = 5236.

      5236 + <6325> = 11561 . . . [-1 + 15 = 14]61 . . . **14/6/(1)**, Gina / manuscript.

      5236 / 2 = 2618] - <8162> = 5544 . . . 554 weeks / 4 days = 3882 days . . . **3882**, the Unlettered Prophet.

    [2942 + 2294 = 5236] / 2 = 2618] - <8162> = **5544**, Leanne Long.

      5544 . . . 554 weeks / 4 days = 3882 days . . . **3882**, Leanne Long has synergy with ↔ **3882**, the Unlettered Prophet.

      and,

      [5544, Leanne Long + 3882 + 1782 = 11208] – 11781, Mary Magdalene = **573**.

        573 . . . √573 = 2393 7418 . . . [2393 + <3932> + 7418 + <8147> = **21890**.

          21890 = **10109**, Eve + **11781**, Mary Magdalene.

          and,

          21890 = **17/9/08**, Leanne / reading + 3982

            3982 + 51 = 20{16} + 2017 = 4033 . . . **(51)/20{16}/2017** ↔ **16/(51)**, it certainly is your Playground.

        [573 = <375>] * 6 = **2250**, plant Earth buzzing to New Harmonic Vibrations.

and,

5094 ↔ <4905> ↔ [**1614** - <4161> = 2547] - <7452> = **4905**.

    Anakhita, the space in-between: 110 118 182 229 . . . 182 + <281> + 229 + <922> = **1614**.

    Genesis. 1:27, creation of the male and female . . . 12^7 = 35831808 . . .

      ([1808 + <8081> = 9889] – [3583 + <3853> = 7436] = 2453) – [31 + 808 = 839] = **1614**.

        16:14 = 974 minutes . . . 9 * 74 = **666**, Adam and Eve, interwoven energy.

    [789, Sophis + 1239, Adam/Eve = 2028] – 414, Sophis = **1614**.

    Sirius . . .

    Sir, alphabet L to R; i, alphabet, L to R, balance to travel; alphabet, R to L, balance to travel; us, alphabet R to L.

    Sir, 19,9, 18; i, (17),(8); us, 6, 8; we locate 'us' under 'i' in Sir, that is, we double up on the use of 'i'.

Sir	19	9	18
u		6	
s		8	
	19	23	18 . . . 192 + <291> + 318 + <813> = **1614** ↔

847, Lemuria ↔ 103, Babylonians . . . 1:03 is 57 to 2 . . . 572 + <275> = 847 . . . 8:(47) is 7:13 . . . **713**, the Season ends ↔
1716, Sirius + [713, Lemuria, Babylon + 404, Lemuria = 1117, Lemuria, Babylon] = 2833 . . . 28:(33) = 1647 minutes
- <33> = **1614**.

Mars: 51 53 57 47 . . . [51 + 53 + 57 + 47 = 208 = <802>] + [<15> + <35> + <75> + <74> = 199 + <991> = 1190] = 1992.

1992 = 29 * 91 = 2639 . . . 26:(39) = 1521 minutes + <93> = **1614**.

Noah and the Ark symbolized the transfer of the Atlantis (Mars) Consciousness . . .

659, Noah . . . 659 + <956> + [6 * 5 * 9 = 270] + [65 * 9 = 585] + [6 * 59 = 354] = 2824 . . . 28:(24) = 1656 minutes - <42> = **1614**.

a High Priestess, part of the Atlantis social structure.

High Priestess, the space in-between: 146 13 148 . . .
    [146 + 13 + 148 = **307** + <703> = **1010**] + [<641> + <31> + <841> = **1513** = <3151>] = 4161 = <**1614**>

a transfer of Soul Consciousness →

7146, Intervention From Above . . . 71:46 = 3 days / (0:14) . . . **3014** . . . 30:14 = 1 day / 6:14 . . . **1614** →

1009 963, Product Recall; -100 + ([9 * 9 * 6 * 3 = 1458] + <8541> = 9999]) = 9899 . . .
    9899 . . . 98 * 9 * 9 = 7938 + <8397> = 16335 . . . 16[3 * 3 = 9 + 5 = 14] . . . **1614**.

1381, Christ + 1633, Mary Magdalene = 3014 . . . 30:14 is 1 day / 6:14 . . . **1614**.

the Lamb's wives: [666 – 1102 = 436] + [666 - <2011> = 1345] + [1170 – 598 = 572] + <275> = 2628
    26:(28) = 1532 minutes + <82> = **1614**.

11/(29) days /8, Cher's passing, M/D/Y . . . 11298 / 7 = **1614**.

Fig. 5.
Leanne, alphabet L → R: 12, 5, 1, 14, 14, 5 . . . 125,114,145
Long, alphabet R → L, residual: (11), (14), (13), (6) . . . 1,114,136: 125,114,145 + 1,114,136 = 126,228,281
    [126 + 228 + 281 = **635**] + <536> = **1171**) + ([<621> + <822> + <182> = **1625**] + <5261> = **6886**) = **8057**.
    [1171 = <1711>] + 8057 = **9768** . . . [9 + 7 = 16][6 + 8 = 14] . . . **1614**.

1614 . . . . . . **(1)/6/14**, Gina / manuscript.
and,

Moses:	71	59	64	66
Moussa:	<u>88</u>	<u>68</u>	<u>72</u>	<u>82</u>
	159	127	136	148

    ([159 + 127 + 136 + 148 = 570] + [<951> + <721> + <631> + <841> = 3144] = 3714) + <4173> = 7887. 78:(87) = 4593 minutes + <78> = 4671.
        4671 – [1992, Mars + <2991> = 4983] = **312**, Nibiru, see above.
        46:(71) = 2689 minutes + <17> = 2706 . . . 27:(06) = 1614 minutes . . . **1614**.

The Second Epistle of Paul the Apostle to the Thessalonians re the Second Coming 2:1 to 2:4:
    ([21 + 22 + 23 + 24 = 90] [<12> + <22> + <32> + <42> = 108] . . . 90108) + <80109> = 170217 . . . 1702 – 17 = 1685 - <71> = **1614**.

[John: 10, 15, 8,14] + [Kordupel: 11,15,18, 4, 21, 16, 5, 12] = 11,151,843,132,326.
    [1115184 . . .1115 + 184 = 1299] + [3132326 . . . 313 + 2326 = 2639] = 3938 . . .

[39:38 = 2378 minutes + <83> = 2461] + <1642> = 4103 = <**3014**> . . . 30:14 = 1 day / 6:14 . . . **1614**.

and,

119490, the Day of Resurrection . . . 119 + <911> + 490 + <094> = **1614** ↔ **1614**, Anakhita ↔ **1614**, the Western influence

16:14 = 974 minutes . . . [9 * 74 = **666**] * 48 = **31968**, Redeemer → **31968**, the Great Apostasy.

Yi – King, provides counsel for the Superior wo/man: 25, 9 - 11, 9, 14, 7 . . . 259119147 . . . [2^5 = 32] + 911 + 9147 = **10090**.

 10090 = <**8328**>, a Galactic cycle + **1762** ↔ Pearl Gates: 104 156 166 94 . . . <401> + <651> + <661> + <49> = **1762**.

 1762 = <2671> ↔ 10090 – [9147 = <7419>] = **2671**.

 26:71 = 1631 minutes . . . 1631- <17> = **1614** ↔ **1614**, Anakhita ↔ **1614**, the Eastern influence.

 1762 - <2671> = **909**, Earth / metamorphosis ↔ 9:09 = 10:(51) . . . 1051 * 12 (gates of pearls) =**12612**.

 12:612 = 1332 minutes . . . **1332**, Yahweh.

 126:12 = 5 days / 6:12 . . . 56:12 = 3372 minutes - <21> = 3351 = <**1533**>.

 5262, Mars = <2625> . . . 26:25 = 1585 minutes - <52> = **1533**.

 4434, Ark . . . 44:34 = 2674 minutes . . . 26:(74) = 1486 minutes + <47> = **1533**.

 and,

 The Second Epistle of Paul the Apostle to the Thessalonians re the Second Coming 2:1 to 2:4:

 ([21 * 22 = 462] + <264> = 726) + ([23 * 24 = 552] + <255> = 807) = **1533**.

 [3961, the fall of Babylon * 7 = 27727] – 31968, the Great Apostasy = 4241.

 4241 = 1614, Thessalonians, 2:1 to 2:4 + 2627 . . . 26:(27) = 1533 minutes . . . **1533**.

 1533 . . . 15[3^3 = 27] . . . 1527 . . . 15[2^7 = 256] . . . 15256.

 15256 – (the making of beds: [7/13/1 + 7/1/13 = 14244] – 13/1/7 = 12927) = 2329.

 23:29 = 1409 minutes . . . 1409, John Kordupel ↔ 1409 minutes - <92> = **1317**.

 13/1/7, You have made the bed as far as you could. Now it is up to Me.

 12612 - <21621> = **9009** ↔ [1716, Anakhita * 7 = 12012] - <21021> = **9009**.

 the Mahdi, the Second Coming, Maitreya, the Unlettered Prophet, Kalki, the Messiah:

 720 996 1062 654.

 720 + 996 + 1062 + 654 = 3432) + <2343> = 5775;

 [<027> + <699> + <2601> + <456> = 4783] + <3874> = 8657.

 [5775 + 8657 = 14432] - <23441> = **9009**, the Six Horsemen ↔

 Confucius: 111 123 132 102 . . . 132:111 – 123:102 = **9009** ↔

 9009 = **1782**, the Second Coming + **7227**, Book-End.

 [10090 + 2671 = 12761] – [1762 + 12612 = 14374] = **1613**.

Mary:	57	47	51	53
Magdalene:	62	172	181	53

 We join the horizontal: 574,751,536,217,218,153 . . . 574 + 751 + 536 + 217 + 218 + 153 = **2449**.

 2449 = <9442> . . . [9 + 4 = 13]42 . . . **1342**, Mary Magdalene ↔ **1342**, Leanne Long.

 2449 . . . [2^4 = 16][4 + 9 = 13] . . . **1613**.

1613 . . . **(1)/6/{13}**, Gina / manuscript.

1613 . . . 1:61 / 3 days = 7361 = <1637> . . . 1 day / 6:37 = 30:37.
    30:37 = 1837 minutes - <73> = **1764** ↔
        Leanne Long: 977 + <779> + 1175 + <5711> + 680 + <086> = 9408 = <8049> . . . 804 * 9 = 7236.
          72:36 = 3 days / 0:36 . . . 30:(36) = 1764 minutes . . . **1764**.
    30:(37) = 1763 minutes . . . **1763**, the other Book-End.

1613 . . . 1 day / 6:13 = 30:13 . . . 3013 minutes = 50:13 . . . **50/13**, the Age of Aquarius begins ↔

1613 . . . (161) / 3 days = 70:39 - <161> = 6878 = **(85)/13**, Hay House / manuscript + **1635**.
Leanne Long: the space in-between: [2136 = <6312>] + [1452 = <2541>] + [2886 = <6882>]= **15735**.
    15:735 = 1635 minutes . . . **1635**, Leanne Long ↔ **1635**, Eve.

1613 = <3161> = **1794** + **13/(67)**, Hay House / no, you need a literary agent.
    John Kordupel (format ↔ synthesis): 153 159 167 145 . . . 145:159 – 167:153 = 21994.
        21994 / 7 = 3142 . . . 31:(42) = 1818 minutes - <24> = **1794**.
    and,

Mary:	57	47	51	53
Magdalene:	62	172	181	53

    We sum the vertical: 576,247,172,511,815,353 . . .
      [576 + 247 + 172 + 511 + 815 + 353 = 2674] + <4762> = 7436.
        7436 . . . [7 + 4 = 11][3 * 6 = 18] . . . **1118** ↔ **1/11/8**, Cher passed away
[1118, Mary Magdalene ↔ 1/11/8, Cher passes away] + 676, Mary Magdalene = **1794** ↔

Leanne Long / High Priestess: 261 (337) 360 (238)
    [261:360 – 238:337 = 23023] + [360:261 – 337:238 = 23023] = 46046.
    ([46046 / 7 = 6578] + [46046 / 11 = 4186] = 10764) / 6 = **1794** ↔

17:94 = 1 day / 794 = 31:94 . . . 31:(94) = 1766 minutes - <49> = **1717**.
      and,

This is the book of the genealogy of Adam. In the day that God created man, He made him in the likeness of God. He created them male and female, and blessed them and called them Mankind in the day they were created. And Adam lived one hundred and thirty years, and begot a son in his own likeness, after his image, and named him Seth. After he begot Seth, the days of Adam were eight hundred years; and he had sons and daughters. So all the days that Adam lived were nine hundred and thirty years; and he died.
Seth lived one hundred and five years, and begot Enosh. After he begot Enosh, Seth lived eight hundred and seven years, and had sons and daughters. So all the days of Seth were nine hundred and twelve years; and he died.
Enosh lived ninety years, and begot Cainan. After he begot Cainan, Enosh lived eight hundred and fifteen years, and had sons and daughters. So all the days of Enosh were nine hundred and five years; and he died.
    Genesis: 5. The Family of Adam. The MacArthur Study Bible. New King James Version.

    " . . . and begot a son in his own likeness, after his image, and named him Seth . . ."; rather than being a reference to the western version of a family tree, this refers to Seth being a reincarnation of Adam.

Adam begets Seth at the age of 130; Adam lives 930 years.
Seth lives 105 years and begets Enosh . . .130 + 105 = 280; Seth's days numbered 912 . . .930 + 912 = 1842
Enosh lives 90 years and begets Cainan . . .90 + 280 = 370; Enosh lives for 905 . . .1842 + 905 = 2747.

and, 27:47 = 1 day/3:47 → 1347; 1347 + 370 = **1717**.

and,
16:13 is 4:13 . . . **413**.
and,
on 25/8/1976, on the Comex commodities exchange,
the opening price for gold futures was $101.0, the high was $105.5, the low was $101.0, and the closing was $105:5.
[1010 + 1055 + 1010 + 1055 = 4130] / 10 = **413**↔
413, the sum of emotions spent by the Collective Will at their low point →
and,
1010 + [10:55 = 5 to 11 . . . 511] + 1010 + [10:55 = 5 to 11 . . . 511] = **3042**.
30:42 = 1 day / 6:42 . . . **1642**.
on 2/2/96, gold futures hit a high of $416.7 . . . **4167**, Know Me.
4167 - <7614> = 3447 . . . **34/47**, my birth day.
on 25/8/99, gold futures hit a low of $252.5 . . . **2525**, Eve.
2525 - 4167 = **1642**.

30:(42) = 17:58 minutes + <24> = **1782**, the Second Coming.
3042 = <2403> . . . 24:03 = 1443 minutes . . . **1443**.
1443, Kali Yuga, Earth's dark night of the Soul.
1443 * 7 = 10101 . . . **{10}/101**, Invitation to change the Language.
[3042 + <2403> = **5445**] + 1782, the Second Coming = **7227**, Book-End.
and,
[3042 = <2403>] - [4167 - <7614> = 3447] = **1044** ↔
1143, Mary Magdalene + 849 = **1992**.
849, Mary Magdalene.
849 minutes = 14:09 . . . **1409**, John Kordupel.
849 minutes = 15:(51) . . . **{15}/(51)**, it certainly is your Playground.
1992 . . . 19 * [9² = 81] = **1539**, Leanne Long.
1992 – [375, Mary Magdalene + <573>, Leanne Long = 948] = **1044** →
375 * 6 = **2250**, New Harmonic Vibrations.

Fig. 3.
Leanne, alphabet R → L: 15, 22, 26, 13,13, 22 . . . 152,226,131,322
Long, alphabet R → L: 15, 12, 13,20 . . . 15,121,320.
152,226,131,322 + 15,121,320 = 152,241,252,642 . . . 152 + 241 + 252 + 642 = **1287**.
1287 . . . 12 * 87 = **1044**.

[1044 Leanne Long + <4401> = **5445**] + 1782, Leanne Long = **7227**, Book-End.
and,
10/(44), I cannot talk with you about your world unless you know about Mine.

If you accept that Eve's initial manifestation was on Sirius, and that Sirius, Lemuria, and Sophis are of the same Consciousness, and that Mars, Nibiru and Atlantis were also of the same Consciousness,
and,
since Morgan was of the Avalon Consciousness,
and,
since Leanne's DNA captures all of these,
then what we have is an image of the transfer of one particular Soul energy from one realm to another.

Yoga – Babaji.

Babaji and other ascended masters guide you to do yoga regularly. Yoga's benefits are one of the answers to your question. Through yoga, you'll gain increased clarity, energy, flexibility, toning, and psychic awareness. You may also meet wonderful new friends and have fun at yoga classes. Yoga is an ancient tradition among spiritual practitioners because of these many esoteric and material benefits. Don't delay. Do some yoga today.

Additional meanings for this card:
- Stretch often today.
- Practice breathwork today by taking full inhalations and exhalations.
- Teach yoga or invite others to participate in yoga with you.
- Watch a yoga video or take a yoga class today.

Babaji is a beloved yogi who is known as "the deathless avatar." He learned to overcome all physical limitations. Many believe that he ascended with his physical body, which may account for the various sightings of a solid, living Babaji that people have reported. Babaji encouraged Paramahansa Yogananda to teach yoga to the Western world as a way of spreading enlightment.
Ascended Masters Oracle Cards Guidebook. Doreen Virtue.

Comment:

In my current manifestation I do not do yoga.

While I have no doubt that Yoga may assist in the realization of the Self, I see the next step as being the dissipation of negative energies from the previous four Medicine Wheels that have congealed to manifest as an illness.

The dissipation of those negative energies basically involves a battle with the Gremlins.

You can do battle while practising yoga, but the battle does not stop once you finish your yoga session. As such, yoga does not acknowledge a recognition of the System – that the battle with the Gremlins entails a conversation with the Keeper of your Book of Life.

> If you do not acknowledge that conversation,
> > the role of Spirit,
> > > then,
> > > > you are not engaged in Conscious Living.

And,
Conscious Living is exactly what is discussed in *Conversation with God*.

and,
the story so far:
Fig.7.
Leanne, alphabet L → R, residual: (14), (21), (25), (12), (12), (21) . . . 142,125,121,221
Long, alphabet R → L: 15, 12, 13,20 . . . 15,121,320
    142,125,121,221 + 15,121,320 = 142,140,242,541 . . . 142 + 140 + 242 + 541 = **1065**; <241> + <041> + 242 + <145> = **669**.
        √1065 = 3263 4337; √669 = **2586** 5034; Cher's passing: 1/11/8 + 8/(60) + (60)/8 = **2586**.
            [3263 + 4337 + 5034 = 12634] – [2586, Cher's passing + <6852> = 9438] = **3196**.
                31:(96) = 1764 minutes . . . 1764 + <4671> = 6435
                    6435 . . . 6 * 435 = **2610**, Eve.
                        6435 + <5346> = **11781**, Mary Magdalene ↔ 1 + 1781 = **1782**, Resurrection ↔ **1782**, Leanne Long.
                    3196 + <6913> = **10109**, Eve . . . 101:09 = 5:09 / 4 days . . . **5094** ↔ <**4905**>

17:9. The heart is deceitful above all things, and desperately wicked: who can know it?

17:10. I the Lord search the heart, I try the reins, even to give every man according to his ways, and according to the fruit of his doings.

  Jeremiah. Holy Bible. King James Version.

  17:09 + 17:10 = 3419 . . .3 days / (419) = 6781 minutes . . . 6781.

   6781 - <1876> = **4905**.

   [6781 + <914> = 7695] / 5 = 1539] + [3419 . . . ([3^4 = 81] * 19 = 1539] = 3078

    3078 + <8703> = 11781 . . . 1 + 1781 = **1782**, the Second Coming

     and,

     there is a Second Coming in time sequence

      and,

       there is a Second Coming in life sequence.

  testing of hearts and minds, the evolution of the Superior wo/man,

   comes down to staring down your delusions,

  which comes down to the Buddha.

Buddha: 40 116 122 34

  116:40 = 7000 minutes + <04> = 7004; 116:34 = 6994 minutes + <43> = 7037.

  112:34 = 6754 minutes + <43> = 6797; 112:40 = 6760 minutes + <04> = 6764.

  [7004 = <4007>] + [7037 = <7307>] + [6797 = <7976>] + [6764 = <4676>] = 23966.

   and,

   23966 . . . [23 * 9 * 6 * 6 = 7452] - <2547> = **4905**, Buddha ↔

   23:966 = 2346 minutes . . . **2/3/{46}**, my birth day.

   23966 . . . [23 + 9 = 32] * 6 * 6 = **11/(52)** weeks, Mary Magdalene is going to knock on your door.

49:05 = 1:05 / 2 days . . . **{10}/(52)** weeks, Mary Magdalene is going to knock on your door.

and,

1539, John Kordupel + 1782, the Second Coming + 711, a Cycle ends + 873, Thessalonians 2:1 to 2:4 = **4905**.

1539, John Kordupel + 1782, the Second Coming + 711, a Cycle ends + [378, Resurrection = <873>] = **4905**.

   4905 . . . [4 days (905) = 86:95] / 5 = **1739** . . . 17:39 = 1059 minutes . . . **1059**, a page in the life of . . .

    14/8/4, I'll see you tomorrow at 815 . . . 14:84 = 924 minutes + 815 = **1739**.

   4905 . . . [4 days / 905 = 105:05 - <509> = 9996] + <6999> = 16995

    16995 - [4905 . . . 490 / 5 days = 124:90 - <094> = 12396] = 4599 . . . 45 * 99 = **4455**, Buddha →

     4455, Lao Tzu → 4455, the Prophet Mohammad → 4455, John Kordupel.

     4455, Buddha + [693, Buddha * 4 = 2772] = **7227**, Book-End.

   [4905 + <5094> = 9999] - [4599 + <9954> = 14553] = 4554.

    4554 . . . 4 days / 554 weeks = 3882 days . . . **3882**, the Unlettered Prophet.

    4554 = **2772**, Buddha + **1782**, the Second Coming.

  3542, eschatology = 711 + <117> + 873 + <378> + 1463, John Kordupel.

  3542, eschatology = <2453> . . . [2:45 / 3 days is 74:45 - <542> = 6903] – [7445 - <5447> = 1998] = **4905**.

   and,

34:25. And I will make with them a covenant of peace, and will cause the evil beasts to cease out of the land: and they shall dwell safely in the wilderness, and sleep in the woods. Ezekiel. Holy Bible. King James Version.
$$3425 \ldots ([34^2 = 1156] * 5 = 5780) - <0875> = \textbf{4905}.$$

For the Hero to be the Hero – the masculine in the masculine, the alpha male – there had to be "a damsel in distress", the feminine in the feminine.
Addressing the ego factor was the next evolutionary step.

> What is your truth?
> What is the nature of your being?

Adam and Eve were not the first expression of a Big Bang. They were but the next leg in the expression of a Galactic universe.
So,
Lemuria was the expression of where the previous Big Bang left off - a Consciousness was left in their evolutionary Paradise,

> Do not eat the Forbidden fruit, the matrix for the next evolutionary cycle.

3996, Universe $\leftrightarrow$ 3996, Earth / metamorphosis
  Mars: 51 53 57 47 . . .
    $[51 + 53 + 57 + 47 = 208 = <802>] + [<15> + <35> + <75> + <74> = 199 + <991> = 1190] = 1992.$
      $1992 = <2991> \ldots 29 * 91 = 2639 \ldots 26:(39) = 1521$ minutes $+ <93> = 1614.$
  Mars: 51 53 57 47 . . .
    $[51 + 53 + 57 + 47 = 208 + <802> = 1010] + [<15> + <35> + <75> + <74> = 199 + <991> = 1190] = 2200.$
      $[1992 = <2991>] + <0022> = 3013 \ldots 30:13$ is 1 day $/ 6:13 \ldots 1613.$
        $[1614 + 1613 = 3227] - <7223> = 3996.$

3996, Earth / metamorphosis $/ 6 = 666.$
Atlantis: 96 112 120 88 . . . $[96 + 112 + 120 + 88 = 416,$ Kali Yuga$] + [<69> + <211> + <021> + 88 = 389 = <983>] = 1399.$
    $1399 - <9931> = 8532] / 2 = 4266,$ Jesus . . . $[4 + 2 = 6]66 \ldots 666.$
  the Atlantis Consciousness transferred to Earth:
    $121,$ Gaia $+ 1161,$ Gaia $= 1282 \ldots 12:(82) = 638$ minutes $+ <28> = 666.$
      $666 \ldots [6^6 = 46656] * 6 = 279\,936 \ldots <972> + <639> = 1611. \ldots <1161>,$ Gaia.

Genesis. 1:27 . . . $12^7 = 35831808 \ldots [1808 + <8081> = 9889] - [3583 + <3853> = 7436] = 2453.$
    $[2453 = <3542>,$ eschatology$] - [$Genesis 1:27 $+ <721> = 848] = 2664) / 4 = 666.$

Adam / Eve, interwoven energy: e, m, v, a, E, d, A: 5,13,22,1,5,4,1 . . . $5132 + 21541 = 26673 \ldots [2667 – 3 = 2664]$
$/ 4 = 666.$
and.
$\sqrt{666} = 2580\,6975 \ldots 2580 + 6975 = 9555; 6\sqrt{66} = 1067\,6535 \ldots 1067 + 6535 = 7602: [<5559> - <2067> = 3492]$
$/ 4 = 873.$
14:33. And your children shall wander in the wilderness forty years, and bear your whoredoms, until your carcases be wasted in the wilderness. Numbers. Holy Bible. King James Version. . . . $14:33 = 873$ minutes . . . 873.

3996 . . . $3 * 99 * 6 = 1782,$ Resurrection . . . 1782, Redeemer $\rightarrow$ 1782, the Second Coming.

For Eve to express her evolutionary Truth, the masculine in the feminine, she had to stop being a damsel in distress – she had to divorce herself from her Hero,
    and,

that is a big emotional dump!

The Crucifixion was a result of an expression of the masculine in the masculine,
> and,
> at the same time,
> it was the expression of the feminine in the feminine – let the masculine in the masculine express itself.

It was the end of an era!

And yet,
> Saint Veronica's veil dictates that the future owes something to the past,
> > and,
> > the past owes something to the future.

Veronica, St
Veronica, St, a woman of Jerusalem who, according to legend, gave Jesus her veil to wipe his face as he bore his cross to Calvary. He returned it with his countenance miraculously imprinted on the fabric. Modern scholars believe that her name, which is also applied to the veil itself, is derived from the Latin vera and the Greek eikon, meaning "true image". The legend is represented in the sixth of the Stations of the Cross. Of the several cloths reputed to be the original veil, the most celebrated is kept at St Peter's Basilica in Rome, where it became an object of popular veneration during the Middle Ages. Microsoft ® Encarta ® 2008. © 1993-2007 Microsoft Corporation. All rights reserved.

Does the veil have a DNA match with the Shroud of Turin?

The Crucifixion happened because the masculine in the masculine shitted itself!
> The feminine in the masculine RULED!

I cannot do for you that what you cannot do for yourself! Be it in the masculine in the masculine, or the masculine in the feminine.

When Satan is let loose for but a short season, you are on your own.
> When will an expression of the Collective Consciousness pull its weight?

Atlantis self-destructed because the dark side won!!!

I was Crucified because the dark side won.

You could have chosen to reincarnated into the past, but you did not like what I said to you this time round.
You are soft! You have no substance! You are show-ponies!

> How does it feel,
> to be like a rolling stone,
> with no direction of home? Bob Dylan.

> If I had a song that I could sing you . . . Bob Denver.

By means of channeling, Spirit can use oracle card writers to paint a picture of what life on Atlantis was like. The impression I have from reading *Atlantis Oracle Cards Guidebook* by Maria Elita and *Atlantis Cards* by Diana Cooper is that the emphasis on Atlantis was that of the good of the Collective whole and not the individual.

The suppression of the individual over the Collective set the stage for the next evolutionary step – the shadow side of the individual had to be given an avenue of expression. When Atlantis was invaded by this Conscious from another realm – understand that they did not have different bodies from the initial Atlanteans – it resulted in the destruction of Atlantis.

Now,
if you subscribe to the belief that old energies do not just cease to exist but have to be dissipated, then you may come to the conclusion that the Atlantis matrix was transferred to the Earth realm – the ownership by the State, a caste system - compared with nations that have a fully fledged democracy.

But,
no matter the System within each nation, the shadow side has had an opportunity to evolve – no matter the System, be it 'show me the money', or the hunger for power, corruption is a disease.

      The stage was set for the evolution of the Superior wo/man.

What is your Truth,
      what is the nature of your being?

While the Hero, the Truth, and the Light have had their Cosmic Names withdrawn – they have retired - the vibrationary frequency stemming from Cosmic Expressions of that Cosmic Energy is not redundant.

This is no longer my Playground!
The various manuscripts give you an insight into the conduct of a Superior wo/man, a wo/man of Rank, and not a wo/man with rank.

      When Satan is let loose for but a short season,

         you will have feedback as to whether

         the rolling stone has a direction for home.

Yet,
there are Cultures on planet Earth that do not fit into the Hero / Truth / Light synergy, the Sirius, Mars, Avalon. Kali Yuga vibrational energy,
      for,
      they are the last whisper of a Lost Civilization

         They ARE your, they are my HERITAGE,

they are the last of the Mohicans.

I would like to think that I have acknowledged you,
      yet,
      I feel that I have not said enough!

I feel that I have not fully acknowledged your contribution to my, to our, evolution.

      I feel humbled in your presence.

But I cannot hang onto the past,
      for,

that is not what evolution is all about.

And,

what that means, is that you are here to pass on the evolutionary baton,

as we will to.

Evolution dictates that we all have to move on,

and,

all you can do is to leave us with the insight of your cultural evolution,

for,

after all is said and done,

that is all any evolutionary Generation can leave.

It is up to us to Honor your legacy, to remember, and to pass on the Way of our Fathers -

but,

without being hog-tied to the past.

For,

after all that is said and done,

at the end of the day,

that is not why you have manifested in the here and now for – you manifested in order to MOVE ON!

Or.

to DIE,

to return to the WHOLE, the last whisper of a lost civilization,

a destiny that every evolutionary Big Bang must face sooner or later.

But

only to reincarnate once again,

to give expression to the next evolutionary Self – for the Self never, ever, ever, truly DIES as such!

There is an Aspect of you that picks up the baton.

That is the System!

Selenite – Spiritual Awakening.

Crystal Medicine.

Selenite is a powerful light-saver of universal energy. This potent crystal sends energy into the crown chakra, bathing the body in the loving healing energy of the cosmos, and clearing away the old and making way for new vibrant energy and a deeper spiritual connection. The medicine of Selenite balances and cleanses the seven main chakras. This powerful crystal assists in opening the crown chakra as it draws down the divine light of the cosmos into the top of your head. It acts like a lightning bolt of universal energy. Due to its structure, it allows energy to flow powerfully like a strike of lightning. It's a perfect crystal for clearing the energy field and for awakening deeply into your spiritual essence. Being in the presence of this magnificent crystal allows for a direct link and connect to the cosmos and spiritual wisdom.

Crystal Meaning.

* Works as a vacuum cleaner to purify and cleanse the aura.
* Opens and stimulates the crown chakra, bringing in the divine light of the cosmos.
* Allows you to move forward in strength.
* Connects to your higher self and 'I am' presence.

Oracle Reading: Message From The Crystal Deva.

You have attracted this card today because you are entering into a powerful time of spiritual awakening. There are specific cycles and times in life when the opportunity to deepen spiritually are more potent than others. This is your time now, as you are gifted with the opportunity to awaken to deeper aspects of this wisdom within yourself. If you have been feeling a little ungrounded and dizzy of late or just feeling confused about things in your world, know that this is perfectly fine and is a part of your spiritual awakening. It can stir things up for a while as the new energies integrate and ground into your day-to-day life. The devas of Selenite have arrived to carry you through this sacred time of awakening – open and receive this potent energy into your world. Your conscious awareness is expanding and profound spiritual insights and deeply held ancient wisdom are surfacing from deep within. You are encouraged to honor this process for yourself and trust and open to the experiences that are been shared with you at this amazing time. You may feel inspired to study spiritual books, attend courses and workshops, join a meditation group and experience different forms of healing and self-discovery, or be guided to travel to a spiritually inspired location or retreat. Remember this time of spiritual awakening is a sacred opportunity for you to embrace your true magnificence. Trust your own guidance and intuition and enjoy this amazing journey of awakening.

Crystal Healing Cards. The Healing Oracle. Rachelle Charman.

Sweat Lodge.

Card Meaning:

Cleanse yourself: body, mind, and soul. Purify. Clutter-clear. Let go of objects and relationships that no longer serve you. Purify your body. Go within. Meditate. Talk to the Creator. Give thanks.

Your Native Spirit Wants You To Know:

Sweat lodges are small dome structures covered with skins, blankets, or mud in which very hot stones are placed in the center. Water is poured over the stones so that hot steam arises from the rocks. Thus, the seat lodge, with its hot steam, is used for purification ceremonies as well as a place to commune with the Divine. This card chose you to tell you that it's time to clear out the clutter in your life. Sometimes clutter can be things in your closet that you don't love or use. But sometimes clutter can be outmoded relationships or habits that no longer serve you. The clearer your inner and outer space becomes, the easier it will be to hear the sweet messages from your soul.

The Journey:

Sometimes this card chooses you when it's time to do some physical detoxification. Fast for a day. Drink green juices. Clear out some clutter. Love it, use it, or get rid of it. Even one small item can make a difference.

Comment: your are not going to transform from a spiritual couch-potato to an iron-man overnight; you are not going to detoxify four Medicine Wheels in a single leap. You are going to detoxify layers of baggage that comes in different thickness or density. Unless, or until, you achieve the required level of self-mastery, any improvement will be followed by regression.

And that applies to layer, after layer, after layer.

You are not going to get out of Boot-Camp with a week-end retreat.

What the Self has not Mastered,
the Pac Man cannot hoe into.

When you have done your leg-work.
you may consider going to an energy healer to bed things down.
Clear the deck for the next leg of your journey.

A new Talk to Walk.

What energy healer next?

Your Maze Run!

2. Dawn.
Keywords: New Beginnings, New Horizons, Birth, Rejuvenation.

As we grow and change and become more spiritually aware on our journey, we have to appreciate that there are going to be new beginnings. This card ensures you that the new beginnings are the start of a new era and new birth in your life that is going to open you up spiritually. You are ready to grow. With a new beginning, there also has to be an ending to the things that we do not want or need in our life. Embrace this ending and know that the new dawn is going to be spiritually enlightening.
Intuitive Soul Oracle Cards Guidebook. Lisa Williams.

THE CHAIN OF REBIRTH.

The Light; in the course of introducing various Scriptures, challenged the ways of the father. The Crucifixion = payback time by fathers →

The Second Coming; different day, same shit; the shit changes when life stops being a rip off. I want out of the God-business. Where exactly in this scheme of things have You picked up the tab for the shit You started?

I am not your keeper.

So why would I fuck with you?

Because you have to break your chain of rebirth.

→ Moses sees the Promised Land but dies before setting foot on it.

21/11/2017.

the time footprint:
it is 17/11/(9) ↔ **17/11/{9}**, I cannot talk with you about your world unless you know about Mine. Get out of My Car.

14. Moderation.

This card indicates a need to exercise restraint and self-control in every area of your life. Perhaps you are overeating, drinking too much alcohol, smoking, over-medicating or taking drugs, overspending, exercising excessively, consuming too much sugar or coffee, gambling, or otherwise overindulging or engaging in obsessive or aggressive behavior. If so, this card serves as a gentle and loving reminder that behaviors such as these can delay the manifestation of your dreams. This card also indicates a need to balance your desire for freedom and adventures with your responsibilities, because by honoring your commitments, you will prevent the build-up of karmic debt. By choosing to live as your higher self rather than giving in to your lower tendencies, you align with Source and the intentions of your soul. Everybody has a shadow side that needs to be acknowledge, embraced, and loved. But when you learn to rise above it, you can make your dreams come true.

Comment: I am not as diplomatic as Michelle. We all have a shadow side, so self-esteem should not be an issue.
Noah was a drunk and I am still trying to get rid of that monkey on my shoulder.
Let's keep things in perspective. An aspect of you was on Atlantis when it self-destructed.
It is possible that WW1 and WW11 were a dissipation of that Collective karmic baggage.
It is possible that an aspect of you was also exposed to those energies.

That is a lot of negative energy that requires to be dissipated.

If you want to get rid of your shadow side – get out of purgatory – you have to stop loving it.

How can you realistically give up something that you continue to embrace and love?

39

In order to improve your current situation, you are being asked to adjust to, and harmonize with, the natural rhythm and cycles of your life – cycles that are encouraging you to exercise temperance and moderation. Have the courage to seek professional – or Divine – assistance if needed. You don't have to go it alone; you can call upon your heavenly helpers for inner strength and courage.

Comment: In this instance "adjust to and harmonizing" is appropriate language.

14. Fruit of Life – I am ready to expand my knowledge of life and that which has been hidden behind the veil.
This card has appeared today as you are searching for answers to questions you need to find. You are longing for knowledge that has started to awaken deep within your mental and spiritual core. You are ready to take the leap of faith that is now wanting to show you that there is more to this world than meets the eye. It is time to start searching for that special course or teacher to help you expand your knowledge. You will also find yourself starting to seek out more like-minded people who are on the same wave length energetically.

Sacred Geometry.
When we remove the two outer concentric circles from the Flower of Life, another full six circles complete the partial arcs. When this occurs we are left with a pattern called the Fruit of Life. Named so as it is said to contain the blueprint of all of creation. From atomic and molecular structure, it is all life forms in existence. It sets up the platform of Metatron's cube, which contains all five Platonic solids, which are the building blocks of the entire universe.
When we look at this picture we see the spheres, which are a representation of the feminine. In two dimensions it holds within 13 circles. These 13 circles contain informational systems, each containing another aspect of reality. Thirteen is said to be the key for unity and transition between worlds and dimensions, it pertains to the 13 chakra system or energetic bodies. In music the chromatic scale consists of the 12 notes and the thirteenth being a repeat of the first note. It is the 12 around the one.
If we look at this shape three-dimensionally, we obtain a cube of 4 * 4 * 4 spheres, equalling 64 spheres in total. The Fruit of Life is seen as the feminine of Metatron's cube, as at this point there are only circles and no lines.

Practical Application.
We each carry the ancient knowledge and wisdom within us. It sits deep within our DNA. As we begin to awaken, our thirst for knowledge becomes more inherent. This geometry can help us find the answers we are looking for. We can do this by meditating on this card and accessing the systems of knowledge it pertains to. Whether you want to delve into higher worlds and dimensions or work on the informational systems on a self-healing level, the Fruit of Life is there to help us remember that which has been forgotten.

Card Numerology: 1.
Crystal suggestions: Herkimer, diamond, Lemurian seed crystal, selenite, atlantasite.
Sacred Geometry Healing Cards Guidebook. Emily Kisvarda.

Exodus:
33:1. And the Lord said unto Moses, Depart, and go up hence, thou and the people which thou has bought up out of the land of Egypt, unto the the land which I sware unto Abraham, to Isaac, and to Jacob, saying, Unto thy seed will I give it:
33:2. And I will send an angel before thee; and I will drive out the Canaanite, the Amorite, and the Hittite, and the Perizzite, the Hivite, and the Jebusite:
33:3. Unto a land flowing with milk and honey: for I will not go up in the midst of thee; for thou art a stiff-necked people: lest I consume thee in the way.
33:5. For the Lord had said unto Moses, Say unto the children of Israel, Ye are a stiff-necked people: I will come up into the midst of thee in a moment, and consume thee: therefore now put off thy ornaments from thee, that I may know what to do unto thee.

Holy Bibble. King James Version.

([331 + 332 + 333 + 335 = **1331**] + <1331> = **2662**) + ([<133> + <233> + <333> + <533> = **1232**] + <2321> = **3553**) = **6215**.

([1331 + 1232 = **2563**] + [1331 + <2321> = **3652**] + [1331 + <5126> = **6457**] = **12672**) / 4 = **3168**.

Fo-Hi / Krishna / Buddha / Lao Tzu / Confucius: 364 468 500 243 . . . 500:364 – 243:468 = 256896

256896, the Eastern influence . . . { ([2 + 56 = 58] + 8 = 66) * 96 = 6336 } / 2 = **3168**.

[3168 - <8613> = 5445] + [3168 + 8613> = **11781** . . . 1 + 1781 = **1782**] = **7227**, Book-End.

31:68 = 1 day / 7:68 . . . **{17}/68**; it is **{17}/3/9** ↔

14/8/4, I'll see you tomorrow at 815 . . . 14:84 = 924 minutes + 815 = **1739** ↔

17:39 = 1059 minutes . . . **1059**, a page in the life of . . . "I will come up into the midst of thee"

6215, Exodus / know what to do with thee ↔ **4921**, Kali Yuga + [1294, Anakhita → **1294**, the Light = **6215**.

starting from 625, Robert needs a couple of weeks to tidy things up:

1782, Robert . . . { ([1 + 7 = 8]82 . . . 882) + ([- 1 + 7 = 6]82 . . . 682) = 1564 } + <4651> = **6215**.

6215 . . . [62 * 1 = 62]5 . . . **625**, Robert begins to tidy things up.

(6215 - [<5126>] + 4554 = 9680] = 3465) /5 = **693**.

693 * 4 = **2772**, Know Me.

6:93 PM is 18:93 . . . **1893**, the Chain of Rebirth.

6215 . . .[621 * 5 = 3105] + <5013> = **8118**, Earth / metamorphosis.

8118, Earth / metamorphosis = [1924, Lot / Lut * 3 = 5772] + **2/3/{46}**, my birth day

6215 = 5544 + **671**, Mary Magdalene.

1782, the Second Coming . . . 1 day / 7:82 = 31:82 . . . 3182 . . . 3 days / (1:82) = 70:18 + <281> = 72:99 = 3 days / 0:99 . . . 3099.

3099, the Unlettered Prophet . . . 3099 minutes = 50:99 . . . 50:99 = 2 days / 2:99 . . . **2299**.

2299 + [2299 . . .22 * 9 * 9 = **1782**, the Second Coming] + **1463**, John Kordupel = **5544**.

6215 . . . [6:21 PM is 18:21] * 5 = **9105**, I cannot talk with you about your world unless you know about Mine. Get out of My Car.

and,

the story so far:

Exodus:

33:1. And the Lord said unto Moses, Depart, and go up hence, thou and the people which thou has bought up out of the land of Egypt, unto the the land which I sware unto Abraham, to Isaac, and to Jacob, saying, Unto thy seed will I give it:

33:2. And I will send an angel before thee; and I will drive out the Canaanite, the Amorite, and the Hittite, and the Perizzite, the Hivite, and the Jebusite:

33:3. Unto a land flowing with milk and honey: for I will not go up in the midst of thee; for thou art a stiff-necked people: lest I consume thee in the way.

33:5. For the Lord had said unto Moses, Say unto the children of Israel, Ye are a stiff-necked people: I will come up into the midst of thee in a moment, and consume thee: therefore now put off thy ornaments from thee, that I may know what to do unto thee.

33:01 + 33:02 + 33:03 + 33:05 = **13211**.

13211, Exodus /discarding of ornaments ↔ 13211, Akashic (records) ↔

132:11 = 12:11 / 5 days . . . 121:15 = 5 days / 1:15 . . . 5115 . . . **(51)/{15}**, it certainly is your Playground.

[13211 + <11231> = 24442; [24442 – 11781 = **12661**] + [24442 - <18711> = **5731**] = **18392**.

[18392 = <29381>] - <24442> = 4939

49:39 = 2 days / 1:39 . . . 2139 / 3 = **713**, the Season ends.

49:39 = 2979 minutes – <93> = **2886**.

17:9. "The heart is deceitful above all things, and desperately wicked: who can know it?"

17:10. "I the Lord search the heart, I try the reins, even to give every man according to his ways, and according to the fruit of his doings." Jeremiah. Holy Bible. King James Version.

and,

We made a covenant with you as We did with the other prophets; with Noah and Abraham, with Moses and Jesus, the son of Mary. A solemn covenant We made with them, so that Allah might question the truthful about their truthfulness. P. 284.

Do not follow what you do not know. Man's eyes, ears, and heart – each of his senses shall be closely questioned.

P. 231. The Koran.

179 + 1710 + 284 + <482> + 231 = **2886**.

the Messiah: 107 153 163 97: we group the number into two groups.

[153:97 + 163:153 = 178550] / 10 = **17855**; 17855 = **8238**, a Galactic cycle + **7227**, Book-End + **2390**.

2390 + [2 * 3 * 90 = 540] + [2 * 390 = 780] + [23 * 90 = 2070] + ([2³ = 8]90 . . . 890) = 6670.

6670 + 557, the Mahdi / the Second Coming / Maitreya / the Unlettered Prophet / Kalki = **7227**.

23:90 = 1470 minutes - <09> = 1461 . . . **14/6/(1)**, Gina / manuscript.

([97:107 + 153:163 = 250270]/ 10 = 25027) + **17855** = 42882 . . . 4 + 2882 = **2886**.

and,

17:855 = 1875 minutes - <558> = **1317** ↔

31512, Noah / 4 = **5252**, Jesus; 31:512 = 2372 minutes . . . 2372.

2372 . . . [2³ = 8][7² = 49] . . . 849 minutes = 14:09 . . . **1409**, John Kordupel.

2372 minutes - <215> = 2157 . . . 21:57 = 1317 minutes . . . **1317**.

1317, Leanne Long, Fig 4 & Fig 5.

13/1/7, You have made the bed as far as you could. Now it is up to Me.

[**1347**, Kali Yuga ↔ **1347**, lifetime of Adam and his off-springs] + **1539**, John Kordupel = **2886**.

19:23. The sun was risen upon the earth when Lot entered into Zoar.

19:24. Then the Lord rained upon Sodom and upon Gomorrah brimstone and fire from the Lord out of heaven.

19:25. And he overthrew those cities, and all the plain, and all the inhabitants of the cities, and that which grew upon the

ground.

19:26. But his wife looked back from behind him, and she became a pillar of salt. Genesis Holy Bible. King James

Version.

[19:23 + 19:24 + 19:25 + 19:26 = 7698] * 7 = 53886 . . . [5 – 3 = 2]886 . . . **2886** ↔

19:23 + 19:24 + 19:25 = 5772.

5772 = <2775> . . . 27:75 = 1695 minutes . . . **1695** ↔

1695, the Light → 1695, Lot → [1695 - <5961> = 4266, Jesus] → 1695, Second Coming ↔ 1695, the Unlettered Prophet ↔ 1695, John Kordupel, synthesis from format.

5772 / 2 = 2886 → **2886**, Lot.
2886 - <6882> = 3996
3996 / 6 = **666**, the Number of the Beast, the Number of Man.
3996 . . . 3 * 99 * 6 = **1782**, the Second Coming.
2886 . . . [2 * 8 = 16][8 + 6 = 14 . . . **(1)/6/14**, Gina / manuscript.
28:86 = 1766 minutes - <68> = 1698 . . . **{16}/9/8**, Leanne / Reading.

18392 / 8 = **2299**.
Flower of Life / the Tree of Life: 266 375 409 241
[266 + 375 + 409 + 241 = 1291] + ([<662> + <573> + <904> + <142> = 2281] + <1822> = 4103 = <3014>) = 4305.
4305, Flower of Life / the Tree of Life . . . 4 days / 3:05 = 99:05 = <50:99> = 2 days / 2:99 . . . **2299**.
and,
Thessalonians 2:1 to 2:4, discusses the Second Coming . . . [$2^1 = 2$] [$2^2 = 4$] [$2^3 = 8$] [$2^4 = 16$] . . . 24816.
24816 = **8238**, a Galactic cycle + **7227**, Book-End + **9351**.
9351 = **6/(1)/{13}**, Gina / manuscript . . . **{6}/1/13**, up to Me now + **939** + **2299**.
939 minutes = 15:39 . . . **1539**, John Kordupel ↔ <9351>

2299 . . . ([2 + 2 = 4]99 . . . 499) + <994> = 1493.
1493 . . . [14 * 9 = 126] * 3 = **378**, Resurrection.
and,
2139, Exodus, see above . . . 213 * 9 = **1917**, Christ → **1917**, Crucifixion - **378**, Resurrection = **1539** ↔
21:39 is 9:39 PM . . . 939 minutes = 15:39 . . . **1539**, John Kordupel.
2139 / 3 = **713**, the Season ends.

14:(93) = 747 minutes . . . **747**, 2nd. Coming.

1493 . . . [1 + 4 = 5]93 . . . 593 minutes = 9:53 . . . 953 minutes = 15:53
1553 . . . **{15}/(53)**, Donald Trump, President-elect.
1553 . . . (15 * [$5^3 = 125$] = 1875) / 5 = 375 * 6 = **2250**, New Harmonic Vibrations.
1875 + <5781> = 7656.

[2299 = <9922>] - 7656 = 2266.
Resurrection: 147 147 159 153 . . . [<741> + <741> + <951> + <351> = 2784] + <4872> = 7656.
2266 . . . [22 * 66 = 1452] * 7 = 10164 = 1059 + 9105.
1059, a page in the life of . . .
9105, I cannot talk with you about your world unless you know about Mine. Get out of My Car.

and,
[8238, a Galactic cycle + <8328> = 16566] - (8238 . . .[$8^2 = 64$]38 . . . 6438 + <8346> = 14784) = **1782**, the Second Coming.
1782, the Second Coming . . . 1 day / 7:82 = 31:82 . . . 3182 . . . 3 days / (1:82) = 70:18 + <281> = 72:99 = 3 days / 0:99 . . . 3099.
3099 minutes = 50:99 . . . 50:99 = 2 days / 2:99 . . . **2299**.
and,
2299 . . . 2 * 2 * 99 = **396** ↔ 666, the Number of Man . . . [6 * 66 = 396] * 7 = **2772**, Know Me.
2299 = **974** + 1325 . . . 13:25 = 805 minutes . . . **805**, End of Days.

gold futures, an expression of the Collective Will went from a low of $101 to a high of $873 . . . 101 + 873 = **974** ↔

974 . . . 9 * 74 = **666**, the Number of Man.

2299 = **14/8/4**, I'll see you tomorrow at 815 + **815**, Messiah.
2299 . . . 22 * 9 * 9 = **1782,** the Second Coming.

2299 + 1463, John Kordupel + 1782, the Second Coming = 5544
5544 . . . 554 weeks / 4 days = 3882 days . . . **3882**, the Unlettered Prophet.
[5544 / 2 = **2772**] + <4455> = **7227**, Book-End.

2299 = **1255**, Second Coming + **10/(44)**, I cannot talk with you about your world unless you know about Mine.

and,
the story so far:
Exodus:
33:1. And the Lord said unto Moses, Depart, and go up hence, thou and the people which thou has bought up out of the land of Egypt, unto the the land which I sware unto Abraham, to Isaac, and to Jacob, saying, Unto thy seed will I give it:
33:2. And I will send an angel before thee; and I will drive out the Canaanite, the Amorite, and the Hittite, and the Perizzite, the Hivite, and the Jebusite:
33:3. Unto a land flowing with milk and honey: for I will not go up in the midst of thee; for thou art a stiff-necked people: lest I consume thee in the way.
33:5. For the Lord had said unto Moses, Say unto the children of Israel, Ye are a stiff-necked people: I will come up into the midst of thee in a moment, and consume thee: therefore now put off thy ornaments from thee, that I may know what to do unto thee.
33:01 + 33:02 + 33:03 + 33:05 = **13211**.

([331 + 332 + 333 + 335 = **1331**] + <1331> = **2662**) + ([<133> + <233> + <333> + <533> = **1232**] + <2321> = **3553**) = **6215**.
([1331 + 1232 = **2563**] + [1331 + <2321> = **3652**] + [1331 + <5126> = **6457**] = **12672**) / 4 = **3168**.
[3168 - <8613> = 5445] + [3168 + 8613> = **11781** . . . 1 + 1781 = **1782**] = **7227**, Book-End.
31:68 = 1 day / 7:68 . . . {17}/68; it is {17}/3/9 ↔
14/8/4, I'll see you tomorrow at 815 . . . 14:84 = 924 minutes + 815 = **1739** ↔
17:39 = 1059 minutes . . . **1059**, a page in the life of . . . "I will come up into the midst of thee"

13211 + 6215 = 19426 . . . [194:26 = 8 days/226]+ 226/8 days = 10494 – **11781** = **1287** . . . 12 * 87 = **1044**.
[1143, Mary Magdalene → 1143, Christ] + [1409, John Kordupel → 14:09 = 849 minutes . . . 849] = **1992**.
1992 . . . 19 * [9² = 81] = **1539**, Leanne Long.

1992 – [375, Mary Magdalene + <573> = 948] = **1044** →
[1044 + <4401> = 5445] + **1782**, the Second Coming = **7227**, Book-End.

10/(44), I cannot talk with you about your world unless you know about Mine. Get out of My Car.
and,
9:25. Know therefore and understand, that from the going forth of the commandment to restore and to build Jerusalem unto the Messiah the Prince shall be seven weeks, and threescore and two weeks: the streets shall be built again, and the wall, even in troubled times.

9:26. And after the threescore and two weeks shall Messiah be cut off, but not for himself: and the people of the prince that shall come shall destroy the city and the sanctuary; and the end thereof shall be with a flood, and unto the end of the war desolations are
determined. Daniel. Holy Bible. King James Version.

9:25 + 9:26 = 1851 . . . 18:51 is 1 day / (5:49) . . . **1549**, the Light . . . 15/4/9 is 105/9 . . . **1059**, a page in the life of . . .

([9:25 = 565 minutes . . . 565] + [9:26 = 566 minutes . . . 566] = 1131) + [18:51 = 6:51 PM . . . 651] = **1782**, the Second Coming.
[925 minutes = 15:25 . . . 1525] + [926 minutes = 15:26 . . . 1526] = 3051.
　　30:51 = 1 day / 6:51 . . . **16/(51)**, it certainly is your Playground
　　30:51 = 1851 minutes . . . **1851**.
　　　　10981, God / Devil . . . 10:981 = 1581 minutes . . . **1581**, God / Devil.
　　　　　1581, God / Devil + 3961, the fall of Babylon = 5542.
　　　　　55:42 = 3342 minutes + <24> = 3366 . . . [3³ = 27] * 66 = **1782**.
　　　　　1581, God / Devil = <**1851**>

　　From *Regeneration of the Human Race*.
　　17/2/7. We recall a comment made in the theme 'Old Energies, New Energies on 13/1/7.

　　You have made the bed as far as you could. Now it is up to Me.

　　17/2/7 is (317)/{6} . . . 31:(76) = 1784 minutes + <67> = **1851**.
　　18:(51) = 1029 minutes + <15> = **1044**.

　　18/(51) falls on {17}/11/10 ↔
　　　17/11/10, I cannot talk with you about your world unless you know about Mine. Get out of My Car.

and,
Deuteronomy:
34:4. And the Lord said unto him, This is the land which I sware unto Abraham, unto Isaac, and unto Jacob, saying, I will give it unto thy seed: I have caused thee to see it with thine eyes, but thou shall not go over thither.
34:5. So Moses the servant of the Lord died there in the land of Moab, according to the word of the Lord. Holy Bible. King James Version.
　　344 + 345 = **689**; 689 + <986> = **1675**.

and,
689, Deuteronomy . . . 6:89 = 449 minutes . . . **449**, Moses sees the Promises Land but dies before setting foot on it ↔
　　(44)/{9}, I cannot talk with you about your world unless you know about Mine. Get out of My Car.

[689, Deuteronomy . . . 689 days = 4832 weeks] - [**1782**, the Second Coming . . . 1 day / 782 = 31:82] = **1641**.
　　5238, God . . . 52:(38) = 3082 minutes - <83> = 2999 . . . 29:(99) = 1641 minutes . . . **1641**.
　　2999 . . . [2 * 9 = 18][9 + 9 = 18] . . . **1818**, Magdalene.
　　　2999 . . . 2 * 9 * 99 = **1782**, the Second Coming.
　　　2999 . . . [2 * 9 = 18][9 * 9 = 81] . . . 1881 . . . 1881 weeks = 13167 days . . . **13/1/{6}/7**, the making of beds.
　　　2999 . . . 2 * 999 = **1998**, Nabu, scribe and herald to the gods ↔
　　　　(25)/2/47/{46}, my birth day . . . [2524746 / 7 = 360678] - <876063> = 515385 . . .
　　　　　515 + <515> + 385 + <583> = **1998**.
　　　　　— John (Eeevash) Kordupel, the space in-between: 400 546 . . .
　　　　　400546 - <645004> = 244458 . . . 244 + <442> + 458 + <854> = **1998**.

and,

5:1. Belshazzar the king made a great feast to a thousand of his lords, and drank wine before the thousand.

5:2. Belshazzar, while he tasted the wine, commanded to bring the golden and the silver vessels which his father Nebuchadnezzar had taken out of the temple which was in Jerusalem; that the king, and his princes, his wives, and his concubines, might drink therein.

5:3. Then they bought the golden vessels that ere taken out of the temple of the house of God which was at Jerusalem; and the king, and the princes, his wives, and his concubines, drank in them.

5:4. They drank wine and praised the gods of gold, and of silver, of brass, or iron, of wood, and of stone.

5:5. In the same hour came forth fingers of a man's hand, and wrote over against the candlesticks upon the plaister of the wall of the king's palace: and the king saw the part of the hand that wrote.

16:24. Then was the part of the hand sent from him; and this writing was written.

16:25. And this is the writing that was written, MENE, MENE, TEKEL, UPHARSIN. Daniel. Holy Bible. King James Version.

> MENE, MENE, TEKEL, UPHARSIN, God's Hand writing: 234 313 335 212.
> > [234:313 – 335:212 = 100 899] + [313:234 – 212:335 = 100 899] = 201798.
> > ([234:313 – 212:335 = 21978] + [313:234 – 335:212 = 21978] = 43956) + 201798 = 245 754
> > > 245 + <542> + 754 + <457> = **1998**.

16:25. And this is the writing that was written, MENE, MENE, TEKEL, UPHARSIN.

16:28. PERES; thy kingdom is divided, and given to the Medes and Persians. Daniel.

> MENE, MENE, TEKEL, UPHARSIN / PERES, God's Hand writing: 297 380 407 270
> > ([297 + 380 + 407 + 270 = 1354] + [<792> + <083> + <704> + <072> = 1651] = 3005) - <5003> = **1998**.

and,

34:25. And I will make with them a covenant of peace, and will cause the evil beasts to cease out of the land: and they shall dwell safely in the wilderness, and sleep in the woods. Ezekiel. Holy Bible. King James Version.

34:25, taking the evil beasts out of the land: 34:25 is 10:25 / 1 day . . . [10:251 = 851 minutes + <152> = 1003] - <3001> = **1998**.

and,

the Hero, the Truth and the Light: 288 310 333 265 . . . 288310 - 333265 = 44955; 44955 / 5 = 8991 = <**1998**>.

the Eastern influence:

Buddha: 40 116 122 34 . . . 40:116 = 2516 minutes . . . 2516; 34:122 = 2162 minutes . . . 2162.

> 2516 + <6152> + 2162 + <2612> = 13442 . . . [-1 + 3442 = 3441] - <1443> = **1998**.

3199, Yasodhara, the Buddha's wife – 1201, Yasodhara = **1998**.

Lao Tzu: 95 61 67 89 . . . 9 * 5 * 6 * 1 * 6 * 7 * 8 * 9 = 816 480 . . . 816 + <618> + 480 + <084> = **1998**.

Krishna: 80 102 109 73 . . . [80:102 – 73:109 = 6993 = <3996>] / 2 = **1998**.

Confucius: 111 123 132 102 . . . 111123 – 102132 = 8991 = <**1998**>

the Western influence:

Abraham / Ibri: 82164 – 71215 = 10949 . . . 10:949 = 1549 minutes . . . **1549**, the Light + **1782**, the Second Coming = 3331;

> 3331 - <1333> = **1998**.

Moussa: 88 68 72 82 . . . [88<86> + 72<28> = 16114] - [68<28> + 7288 = 14116] = **1998**.

Moses: 71 59 64 66 . . .

> ([71 + 59 + 64 + 66 = 260] + <062> = 322) + ([<17> + <95> + <46> + <66> = 224] + <422> = 646) = 968.
> 260 + 224 = 484; 260 + <422> = 682; 260 + 646 = 906; 260 + <869> = 1129.
> 1129 + [968 = <869>] = **1998**.

Mary:	57	47	51	53
Magdalene:	62	172	181	53

we sum the horizontal: 57475153 + 6217218153 = 6,274,693,306 . . . 6274 + <4726> + 693 + <396> + 306 + <603> = 12998.

12998 / 2 = 6499

6499 . . . [6 * 4 = 24][9 + 9 = 18] . . . 2418 . . . [2⁴ = 16]18 . . . 16:18 = 1 day / (782) . . . **1782**, Resurrection.

6499 - <9946> = **3447**, happenings behind the closed doors of the Vatican.

12998 . . . ([-1 + 2 = 1]998 . . . **1998**.

1998 * 4 = **7992** ↔

Ezekiel: 1:1. Now it came to pass in the thirteenth year, in the fourth month, in the fifth day of the month as I was among the captives by the river of Chebar, that the heavens were opened, and I saw a vision of God.

it came to pass on 4/5/13 . . . 45:13 = 2713 minutes . . . 27:13 = 1633 minutes + <31> = 1664.

1664 . . . 1 day /664 = 30:64 . . . 30:(64) = 1736 minutes + <46> = **1782**.

{ (1664 – [**7992** = <**2997**>] = 1333) - <3331> = **1998** } * 4 = **7992**.

Leanne Long: ([<9991> + <8644> + <3892> + <4452> = 26979] - **11994**, Leanne Long = 14985) / 5 = **2997** ↔ <**7992**>, Leanne Long, in sync with:

John Kordupel (format ↔ synthesis): 153 159 167 145 . . . 159:153 – 167:145 = **7992**.

7992 . . . [7 + 9 = 16][9 * 2 = 18] . . . 16:18 = 1 day / (782> . . . **1782**.

1782, Cherryl's reincarnational family tree . . . **1782**, Resurrection ↔ **1782**, Leanne Long.

7992, energies in unison.

7992 / 12 = .**666**, the Number of Man, the Heart-Beat grid.

Adam / Eve, interwoven energy: e, m, v, a, E, d, A: 5,13,22,1,5,4,1 . . . 5132 + 21541 = 26673 . . . [2667 – 3 = 2664] / 4 = **666**.

and,

22264, the Five Horsemen updating the Scriptures: the Mahdi / the Second Coming / Maitreya / the Messiah / Kalki

22264, the Five Horsemen updating the Scriptures + **713**, the Season ends = 22977 . . . [2 + 297 = 299]7 . . . **2997**) = <**7992**> ↔
and,

Redeemer: 73 135 143 65 . . . 73:135 – 65:143 = **7992**.

John Kordupel (format ↔ synthesis): 153 159 167 145 . . . 159:153 – 167:145 = **7992**.
and,

7992 . . . [7 + 9 = 16][9 * 2 = 18] . . . 16:18 = 1 day / (782) . . . **1782**, the Second Coming ↔

(7992 - [159:145 – 153:167 = 5978 = <8795>] = 803) * 9 = 7227.

[7992 / 4 = **1998**, Vatican] * 16 = **31968**, the Great Apostasy.

1998 - <8991> = 6993
and,

6993 + <3996> = 10989 = **888**, Adam & Eve interwoven energies + {10}/101, Invitation to change the Language.

6993 . . . 6 * 99 * 3 = **1782**, Resurrection ↔ **1782**, the Second Coming ↔ **1782**, Leanne Long.

6993 / 3 = 2331 . . . 23 * 31 = **713**, the Season ends
and,

[7992 * 4 = 31968] = [1998 = <8991>] + **22264**, the Five Horsemen updating the Scriptures + **713**, the Season ends.

31968, the Great Apostasy - <86913> = 54945.

54945 / 5 = 10989 = **888**, Adam & Eve + **{10}/101**, Invitation to change the Language ↔

54945 – 31968, the Great Apostasy = **22977**, Scriptures updated, the Season ends.

and,

22977 = **14/8/4**, I'll see you tomorrow + **(221)/3**, Robert / manuscript + **6/(1)/{13}**, Gina / manuscript + **13/1/{6}/7**, making of beds.

Deuteronomy:

34:4. And the Lord said unto him, This is the land which I sware unto Abraham, unto Isaac, and unto Jacob, saying, I will give it unto thy seed: I have caused thee to see it with thine eyes, but thou shall not go over thither.

34:5. So Moses the servant of the Lord died there in the land of Moab, according to the word of the Lord. Holy Bible. King James Version.

344 + 345 = **689**; 689 + <986> = **1675**.

and,

6:89 = 449 minutes . . . **449**, Moses sees the Promises Land but dies before setting foot on it.

449minutes + <98> = 547 minutes = 9:07 . . . **907**, Kali Yuga.

9:07 = 10:(53) . . . 10:53 is 7 to 11 . . . **711**, a Cycle – Kali Yuga – ends.

907, an Invitation to change the Language.

449 = <944> . . . (9 * [4^4 = 256] = 2304) = **1593** + **711**, a Cycle – Kali Yuga – ends.

Thessalonians 2:1 to 2:4 discusses the Second Coming . . .

([2^1 = 2] [2^2 = 4] [2^3 = 8] [2^4 = 16] . . . 24816) + [2:01 + 2:02 + 2:03 + 2:04 = 810] = 25626.

25:626 = 2126 minutes + <626> = 2752 . . . 27:(52) = 1568 minutes + <25> = **1593**.

27/9/5, corporate issues resolved is {4}/5/9/(3) . . . 4593 . . . [4 + 5 = 9]93 . . . 993 minutes = 15:93 . . . **1593** ↔

7/3/31, a marriage = <1337> . . . 1337 * 7 = 9359 . . . 9 * 3 * 59 = **1593**.

13/1/{6}, or **13/1/7**, You have made the bed as far as you could. Now it is up to Me →

[13:16 = 796 minutes . . . 796] + [13:17 = 797 minutes . . . 797] = **1593**.

449, Moses sees the Promises Land but dies before setting foot on it = <944> . . .

9:44 is 10:(16) . . . 1016 . . . 10:(16) = 584 minutes . . . **584**.

and,

713, the Season ends . . . 7:13 = 433 minutes . . . 4:33 = 273 minutes . . . 2:73 = 193 minutes + <391> = **584**.

584 minutes = 9:44 = <**449**> ↔

(44)/{9}, I cannot talk with you about your world unless you know about Mine. Get out of My Car.

(449, Moses sees/dies + **1549**, the Light = **1998**] - (449 + [**1782**, the Second Coming . . . 1 day / 782 = 31:82 = 3631]

= **1633**. 1633, Kali Yuga → **1633**, Babylon . . .

34614, Ba-bylon . . . [3 + 4614 = 4617] - <7164> = 2547 . . . [2^5 = 32]47 . . . **3247**.

3/2/47, my birth day ↔ **3247**, Untitled 1.

32:47 = 1967 minutes - <74> = **1893**, the Chain of Rebirth.

and,

[1893, the Chain of Rebirth + **2/3/47**, my birth day = 4240] + [**3247**, Babylon = <7423>] = 11663.

11663 = **1614** + [**449**, Moses sees, but dies = <944>] + **9105**, get out of My Car.

Moses:	71	59	64	66
Moussa:	<u>88</u>	<u>68</u>	<u>72</u>	<u>82</u>
	159	127	136	148

[159 + 127 + 136 + 148 + <951> + <721> + <631> + <841> = 3714] + <4173> = 7887.
78:(87) = 4593 minutes + <78> = 4671 . . . 46:(71) = 2689 minutes + <17> = 2706
27:(06) = 1614 minutes . . . **1614**, Moses / Moussa . . .

2706, Moses / Moussa – **1893**, the Chain of Rebirth = 813
8:13 is 47 to 9 . . . **479**, Moses / Moussa / the Chain of Rebirth ↔
John Kordupel, format ↔ synthesis: 153 159 167 145 . . .
153 + 159 + 167 = **479**.

11663 + **659**, Noah = **12322**, Anakhita.
659 Noah ↔ 659 minutes = 10:59 . . . **1059**, a page in the life of . . .

4240 - 3247 = 993 . . . 993 minutes = 16:33 . . . **1633**, Deuteronomy / the Light / the Second Coming.

993 minutes = 15:93 . . . **1593**, You have made the bed as far as you could. Now it is up to Me

and,
11,775,885, Untitled One . . . 11 + <11> + 775 + <577> + 885 + <588> = 2847.
2847 . . . ([2 * 8 = 16][4 + 7 = 11] . . . 1611) + **1633**, Deuteronomy / the Light / the Second Coming = 3244.
3244 . . . [3² = 9]44 . . . 944 = <**449**>, Deuteronomy, seeing the Promised Land.
3244 – **4586**, Mary Magdalene / John Kordupel = **1342**, Second Coming.

2847 . . . [2 * 8 = 16]47 . . . 1647 . . . 1 day / 6:47 = 30:47 . . . **3047**.

2847 – [**3047** + **1539**, John Kordupel = **4586**] = **1739**.
14/8/4, I'll see you tomorrow at 815 . . . 14:84 = 924 minutes . . . 924.
924 + **815** = **1739**.
17:39 = 1059 minutes . . . **1059**, a page in the life of . . . seeing you tomorrow.
924 minutes = 15:24 . . . 1 day / 5:24 = 29:24 . . . 29:(24) = 1716 minutes . . . **1716**.
and,
1782, the Second Coming . . . 17[8 * 2 = 16] . . . **1716**.
1716 . . . {**17**}/1/(6) is **18/25** . . . 18:25 is 6:25 PM ↔
625, Robert begins to tidy things up ↔

1716 . . . 1 day / 7:16 = 31:16 = <6113>.
6/(1)/{13}, Gina / manuscript.
and,
{6}/1/13, You have made the bed as far as you could. Now it is up to Me.

and,
2847 ↔ **6}/90**, a marriage * 7 = 4830 . . . 48:(30) = 2850 minutes - <03> = **2847**.

28:(47) = 1633 minutes . . . **1633** . . . (1 + [6³ = 216] = 217) * 3 = 651 . . . 6:51 PM is 18:51 . . . **1851**.

2847 – {**17**}/1/(6) = 1131 . . . 1131 minutes = 18:51 . . . **1851**.

49

and

[449, Deuteronomy, seeing the Promised Land = <944> + 907, Kali Yuga = **1851**.

18:51 is 1 day / (5:49) . . . **1549**, the Light . . . 15/4/9 is 105/9 . . . **1059**, a page in the life of . . .

18/(51) falls on {**17**}/11/10 ↔

17/11/10, I cannot talk with you about your world unless you know about Mine. Get out of My Car.

and,

the story so far:

Exodus:

33:1. And the Lord said unto Moses, Depart, and go up hence, thou and the people which thou has bought up out of the land of Egypt, unto the the land which I sware unto Abraham, to Isaac, and to Jacob, saying, Unto thy seed will I give it:

33:2. And I will send an angel before thee; and I will drive out the Canaanite, the Amorite, and the Hittite, and the Perizzite, the Hivite, and the Jebusite:

33:3. Unto a land flowing with milk and honey: for I will not go up in the midst of thee; for thou art a stiff-necked people: lest I consume thee in the way.

33:5. For the Lord had said unto Moses, Say unto the children of Israel, Ye are a stiff-necked people: I will come up into the midst of thee in a moment, and consume thee: therefore now put off thy ornaments from thee, that I may know what to do unto thee.

331 + 332 + 333 + 335 = **1331**.

Zoar / the Fifth Medicine Wheel: 257 393 418 232 . . . [257 + 393 + 418 + 232 = 1300] + <0031> = **1331**.

(the Fifth Medicine Wheel is the Promised Land)

Deuteronomy:

34:4. And the Lord said unto him, This is the land which I sware unto Abraham, unto Isaac, and unto Jacob, saying, I will give it unto thy seed: I have caused thee to see it with thine eyes, but thou shall not go over thither.

34:5. So Moses the servant of the Lord died there in the land of Moab, according to the word of the Lord. Holy Bible. King James Version.

344 + 345 = **689**; 689 + <986> = **1675**.

1675, Deuteronomy + 1331, Exodus / Zoar / the Fifth Medicine Wheel = **3006**.

3006 - <6003> = **2997**.

Krishna: 80 102 109 73

[80 + 102 + 109 + 73 = 364 + <463> = 827] + [<08> + <201> + <901> + <37> = 1147 + <7411> = 8558] = 9385.

364 + 1147 = 1511; 364 + <7411> = 7775; 364 + 8558 = 8922;

[<1151> + <5777> + <2298> = 9226] - <6229> = **2997**, the Eastern influence.

The Eight Amigos: 705 1039 1106 636

[705 + 1039 + 1106 + 636 = 3486] - <6843> = **2997**, the Western influence.

22264, the Five Horsemen updating the Scriptures + **713**, the Season ends = 22977 . . . [2 + 297 = 299]7 . . . **2997** ↔

3339, Resurrection . . .333 * 9 = **2997** ↔ <7992> . . .

John Kordupel (format ↔ synthesis): 153 159 167 145 . . . 159:153 – 167:145 = **7992**.

Redeemer: 73 135 143 65 . . . 73:135 – 65:143 = **7992**.

7992 . . . [7 + 9 = 16][9 * 2 = 18] . . . 1618 . . . 16:18 is 1 day / (7:82) . . . **1782**, the Second Coming.

30:(06) = 1794 minutes + <60> = 1854.

18:54 = 6:54 PM = 414 minutes . . . 4:14 PM = 16:14 . . . **1614**, Moses / Moussa.

1854 . . . **18/54** is **18/2/(5)** ↔ 18:25 is 6:25 PM . . . **625**, Robert needs 14 days to tidy things up.

and,

the story so far:

Exodus:

33:1. And the Lord said unto Moses, Depart, and go up hence, thou and the people which thou has bought up out of the land of Egypt, unto the the land which I sware unto Abraham, to Isaac, and to Jacob, saying, Unto thy seed will I give it:

33:2. And I will send an angel before thee; and I will drive out the Canaanite, the Amorite, and the Hittite, and the Perizzite, the Hivite, and the Jebusite:

33:3. Unto a land flowing with milk and honey: for I will not go up in the midst of thee; for thou art a stiff-necked people: lest I consume thee in the way.

33:5. For the Lord had said unto Moses, Say unto the children of Israel, Ye are a stiff-necked people: I will come up into the midst of thee in a moment, and consume thee: therefore now put off thy ornaments from thee, that I may know what to do unto thee.

331 + 332 + 333 + 335 = **1331**.

Zoar / the Fifth Medicine Wheel: 257 393 418 232 . . . [257 + 393 + 418 + 232 = 1300] + <0031> = **1331**.

(the Fifth Medicine Wheel is the Promised Land)

Deuteronomy:

34:4. And the Lord said unto him, This is the land which I sware unto Abraham, unto Isaac, and unto Jacob, saying, I will give it unto thy seed: I have caused thee to see it with thine eyes, but thou shall not go over thither.

34:5. So Moses the servant of the Lord died there in the land of Moab, according to the word of the Lord. Holy Bible. King James Version.

344 + 345 = **689**; 689 + <986> = **1675**.

[1331, Exodus + 344, Deuteronomy = **1675**] + **1675**, Deuteronomy = **3350**, Exodus / Deuteronomy

3350 . . . [3 + 3 = 6]50 . . . 650 minutes = 10:50 . . . **1050**.

1675, Exodus / Deuteronomy = **1050**, Exodus / Deuteronomy + **625**, Robert begins to tidy things up

and,

1716, Anakhita - <6171> = 4455 →

4455 . . . [4 * 4 * 5 = 80]5 . . . **805**, End of Days . . . 8:05 = 485 minutes] + [**711**, the Cycle ends . . . 7:11 = 431 minutes] + <134> = **1050**.

Jeremiah 17:9 and 17:10, testing of hearts and minds: [17:9 . . . 17 * 9 = 153] + [17:10 . . . 17 * 10 = 170] = 323

323 . . . [32³ = 32768] - <86723> = 53955 . . . [53 − 9 = 44]55 . . . **4455**.

Ibri: [2200 + <3971> = 6171] - <1716> = **4455** . . . <**5544**>, Abraham.

[John: 10, 15, 8,14] + [Kordupel: 11,15,18, 4, 21, 16, 5, 12] = 11,151,843,132,326

[1115184 . . . 1115 + 184 = 1299] + [3132326 . . . 313 + 2326 = 2639] = 3938 . . . 3938 - <8393> = **4455**.

4455, Untitled One + [<5544>, Fo-Hi / 2 = 2772, Know Me] = **7227**, Book-End.

and,

4455 = **1716**, Anakhita - <6171> . . .

1716 + [6 * 171 = 1026] = 2742.

27:(42) = 1578 minutes . . . 1578.

1578 minutes - <24> = 1554 . . . **1554**, Cherryl Dianne Kordupel.
15:78 = 3:78 PM . . . **378**, Resurrection.

27:42 = 1 day / 3:42 . . . **1342**.
Daniel 16:25. And this is the writing that was written, MENE, MENE, TEKEL, UPHARSIN.
MENE, MENE, TEKEL, UPHARSIN: 234 313 335 212
([<432> + <313> + <533> + <212> = 1490] + <0941> = 2431) = <**1342**>

1050, Robe + 1288 = 2338 . . . 23:(38) = 1342 minutes . . . **1342**.
1342, Messiah (Roman numerals) ↔ **1342**, Second Coming.

Mary:	57	47	51	53
Magdalene:	62	172	181	53

we sum the horizontal: 57475153 + 6217218153 = 6,274,693,306 . . . 62746 + <30639> = 93385.
93385 . . . [9 – 3 = 6]385 . . . 6385 + <5836> = 12221.
[60/48, Cher's birth day + (60)/{7}, Cher's passing = 6655] + <5566> = 12221.
[93385 - <58339> = 35046] / 3 = 11682 . . . 11:682 = 1342 minutes . . . **1342**.

[4222, Market Forces + <2224> = 6446] – [<3641>, Lord + 1463, John Kordupel = 5104] = **1342**.

27:42 = 1662 minutes + <24> = 1686 . . . 1 day / 6:86 = 30:86 . . . 30:(86) = 1714 minutes + <68> = **1782**.

1716 - [6 * 171 = 1026] = 690 . . . **{6}/90**, a marriage.
and,
[2742 = <2472>] = **1782**, the Second Coming + **{6}/90**, a marriage

Thessalonians 2:1 to 2:4, refers to the Second Coming . . . 2:01 + 2:02 + 2:03 + 2:04 = 810.
8:10 = 490 minutes . . . 4:90 PM is 16:90 = 1050 minutes . . . **1050**.

my birth day: [2/3/47 + 3/2/47 + 34/47 = 9041] + <**1409**>, John Kordupel = 10450 . . . 10:450 = 1050 minutes . . .
1050.

and,
the story so far:
3350, Exodus / Deuteronomy . . . [3 + 3 = 6]50 . . . 650 minutes = 10:50 . . . **1050**.
1675, Exodus / Deuteronomy = **1050**, Exodus / Deuteronomy + **625**, Robert begins to tidy things up.
625, the tidying up begins + <526> = 1151 . . . 11:51 = 711 minutes . . . **711**, the Cycle ends.
and,
10:50 PM is 22:50 . . . **2250**.

[I Am: 9113] + [God: 7,15,4] + [Allah: 1,12,12,1,8] + [Jahwe: 10,1,8,23,5] = 2155720 . . . 2155 – 720 = **1435**.,
[1435, I Am/God/Allah/Yahwe + [14:(35) = 815 minutes . . . **815**] = **2250**] – 880, God = 1370 . . . 1370 minutes =
22:50 . . . **2250**.

[**1716**, Anakhita . . . 17:16 = 5:16 PM = <6:15> = 375 seconds . . . 375] - (4455 . . . [4 * 455 = 1820] + 805, End of days = 2625)
= **2250**.

[**1716**, Anakhita . . . 17:16 = 5:16 PM = <6:15> = 375 seconds . . . 375] * 6 = **2250**.

Genesis. 1:27 . . . 12^7 = 35831808; - 358 + 31808 = 31450 . . . 31:450 = 2310 minutes . . . 23:(10) = 1370 minutes = 22:50 . . . **2250**.

Planet Earth, Our World: [5849 = <9485>] + [4035 = <5304>] = 14789.
  14789 . . . 1478 + 9 = **1487**, Maitreya.

  14789, role reversal . . . 89:147 = 5487 minutes + <741> = 6228.
  6228, role reversal . . . 28:(62) = 1618 minutes . . . 16:18 is 1 day / (7:82) . . . **1782**, the Second Coming.
  62:28 = 3748 minutes + <82> = 3830 . . . 38:(30) = 2250 minutes . . . **2250**, New Harmonic Vibrations on Earth.

Earthlings: 113 147 157 103 . . . [113 + 147 + 157 + 103 = 520 = <025>] + [<311> + <741> + <751> + <301> = 2104 + <4012> = 6141.
  6√141 = 1080 3924 . . . 1080 + <0801> = 1881.
    1999, Leanne Long . . . 1 day / 999 = 33:99 . . . 33:(99) = 1881 minutes . . . **1881**.

    1881 * 7 = 13167 . . . **13/1/{6}/7**, You have made the bed as far as you could. Now it is up to Me.
      leaving 3924.
      3924 - <4293> = 369; 369 = <**963**>, Product Recall.
        3924 . . . 3 * 924 = **2772**, Know Me.
        39:24 = 2364 minutes + <42> = 2406 . . . **2406**, Mary Magdalene
        3924 . . . [3 * 9 = 27]24 . . . 27:(24) = 1596 minutes - <42> = 1554 . . . **1554**, Cherryl Dianne Kordupel.
          27:24 = 1644 minutes + <42> = 1686 . . . 1 day / 6:86 = 30:86 . . . **3086**.
            30:(86) = 1714 minutes + <68> = 1782 . . . **1782**, the Second Coming.
        3924 + <4293> = **8217**.
        John Eevash Kordupel: 209 153 266 191 . . .
          ([209 + 153 + 266 + 191 + [<902> + <351> + <662> + <191> = 2925) + <5292> = **8217**.
          8217 – [3086 = <6803>] = **1414**, Adam
      and,
      1881 + 369 = **2250**, New Harmonic Vibrations on Earth.

and,
Cherryl's reincarnational family tree: [9889 – 7819 = 2070] + 1782 = 3852) / 4 = **963**.
  [3852 = <2583>] + 963 = 3546 . . . 35:46 = 2146 minutes . . . 21:46 = 1306 minutes + <64> = 1370 minutes = 22:50 . . . **2250**.

[John: 10, 15, 8,14] + [Kordupel: 11,15,18, 4, 21, 16, 5, 12] = 11,151,843,132,326:
  We separate 11,151,843,132,326 into two groups of seven, to which we add our birthday:
  [1115184 . . .1115 + 184 = 1299] + [3132326 + 34/194{6} = 3474272 . . . 3474 + 272 = 3746] = 5045 . . . 50 * 45 = **2250**.

13/1/7, You have made the bed as far as you could. Now it is up to Me . . . 200{6} + 2007 + 13/1 = **4144** ↔
        4144, Abraham / Ibri/Lot/Lut.

13/1/7 . . . 1317 minutes = 21:57 . . . 2157 minutes = 35:57 . . . 3557 minutes = 59:17 . . . 5917 minutes = 97:97 . . . 9797.
[4144 + <4414> = 8558] + 9797 + <**7979**> = 26334.
26:334 = 1894 minutes . . . 1:89/4 days = 9789 + <981> = 10770 . . . 10:770 = 1370 minutes = 22:50 . . . **2250**.

22/11/2017.

Talking Stick.
  Card Meaning:

Speak your truth. The soul loves the truth: Communicate from your heart, and share your reality without hesitation. Be willing to stand before the crowd and share from your center. This isn't the time to be shy and hesitant; it's a time to heal through communication. You have the gift of a true leader, through the way you communicate with others.

Your Native Spirit Wants You to Know:
During tribal council meetings, a decorated stick, called a "talking stick," would be passed around. As each council member held the stick, he or she had the opportunity to speak from the heart. Each person in attendance would be asked to weigh carefully the words of each speaker. The talking stick reminded each person to be authentic. Communication restores trust and allows you to clarify your ideas, position, and feelings. It can be healing when you share what has been carefully withheld. Now is the time to take a risk and have the courage to speak with clarity. Be forthright. Share any unspoken darkness that lays heavy in the heart. There are times to hold back and be discerning, but this isn't one of them. Even if you're afraid, declare your truth for all to hear without fear of being rejected or misunderstood. When you do this, transformation and healing can occur.

The Journey:
Decorate a stick (or a feather) to use as your personal talking stick. Whenever you hold it, let it be a sacred reminder to seek the truth within. Take a minute every day to take stock of where you are and ask yourself about "what is so" in your life. Simply taking a moment to discover your inner truth can have a profound healing effect on your life. Native Spirit Oracle Cards Guidebook. Denise Linn.

Comment: There is a micro and a macro aspect to this counsel. The micro is pretty much self-explanatory.
       On the macro level, as a member of the tribal council:
          China,
               when you totally dictate what can and what cannot be said on the Internet,
                   then, in my book,
                       you are censoring the Talking Stick.
            You are Control Freaks,
               In my book you do not have a System that gives a thing duration.
          Reading the lay of the land, the current thrust of the relationship between Heaven and Earth,
            you are not in Harmony with the Nature of the Times!
               You are on the wrong side of History.

You are control freaks. There is a health price to be paid for being control freaks,
       Problem: Parkinson's Disease:
       Probable cause: Fear and an intense desire to control everything and everyone.
       Heal Your Body. Louise L. Hay.

       With China, it is the System;
          with Putin,
             it is the masculine in the masculine.
             That being so,
                you will either go back into the Swamp,
                or,
                    you will not reincarnate on Earth until your vibrations are in harmony with Earth's evolutionary cycle.
                       Your choice!

Donald,
>   run your race!
It would appear that whether you are on the right side of history,
>   and the evolutionary Collective Will,
>>   centers on what you do about the UN and establishing a new world governing system.

23/11/2017.

49. Revolution (Molting).
>   The Judgment.
>   Revolution. On your own day
>   You are believed.
>   Supreme success,
>   Furthering through perseverance.
>   Remorse disappears.

Political revolutions are extremely grave matters. They should be undertaken only under stress of direct necessity, when there is no other way out. Not everyone is called to the task, but only the man who has the confidence of the people, and even he only when the time is ripe. He must then proceed in the right way, so that he gladdens the people and, by enlightening them, prevents excesses. Furthermore, he must be quite free of selfish aims and must really relieve the need of the people. Only then does he have nothing to regret.

Times change, and with them their demands. Thus the seasons change in the course of the year. I the world cycle also there are spring and autumn in the life of the peoples and nations, and these call for social transformation.

Nine in the third place means:
Starting brings misfortune.
Perseverance brings danger.
When talk of revolution has gone the rounds three times,
One may commit himself,
And men will believe him.

When change is necessary, there are two mistakes to be avoided. One lies in excessive haste and ruthlessness, which brings disaster. The other lies in excessive hesitation and conservatism, which are also dangerous. Not every demand in the existing order should be heeded. On the other hand, repeated and well-founded complaints should not fail of a hearing. When talk of change has come to one's ears three times, and has been pondered well, he may believe and acquiesce in it. Then he will meet with belief and will accomplish something.

The I Ching. Wilhelm / Baynes.

>   Comment: Members of the Council of Thirteen would be elected by the people and not appointed by the government. On the face of it, this process would appear to exclude China. However, concerning Hong Kong, China has made the claim "One Chine, two systems".
>   China has also maintained that Taiwan is part of China.
>   China may need a bit more time to decide which system of government is compatible with the evolutionary direction that Planet Earth is heading towards.

Teacher – Mahachohan Ragoczy.

>   This card is about learning and teaching. You've learned a lot from your experiences and relationships, and now it's time to pass that knowledge along to others. Your current situation is brining you opportunities for spiritual growth and teaching you important life lessons. As soon as you understand and accept these lessons, old patterns will drop away and be replaced by wonderful new experiences.

Additional meanings for this card:
- This person or situation is bringing you important life lessons.
- Ask yourself, "What's the blessing that this situation has bought to me?"
- Your life purpose involves teaching.
- Forgive a teacher from your past.
- You are urged to teach others.

* * * * *

Mahachohan Ragocy, who's also known as Master Rakoczy or the Divine Director, is regarded as a great spiritual teacher whose students included Saint-Germain. He's very involved with world government leaders, intuitively guiding them toward peaceful resolution. Call upon Mahachohan Ragoczy for help with esoteric learning, spiritual teaching, or efforts towards world peace.
Ascended Masters Oracle Cards Guidebook. Doreen Virtue.
    Comment: The goal posts have shifted!

    Why talk to the bell-hop when you can talk to the Top Dog?

    Get yourselves some oracle cards, but don't expect to be told what to do.
    It is all you declaring the nature of your being – the evolution of the superior o/man.

Meditation.
    Meditation is a creative process. It is not something we do or need to learn. It is simply a connection back to who you are. It is called a practice because it is training you into alignment, to just be. In a space of allowing, thoughts and feelings rise and fall without you having any attachment. In this allowing, easy, non-resistant space, you may realise there are aspects of yourself that you need to heal or recognise. Be you, for you are wonderful. The Flower of Life. Denise Jarvie.
    Comment: Whether you are wonderful or or not be wonderful, there is a maze run in front of you.

13. Fellowship with Men.
    The Judgment.
    Fellowship with Men in the open.
    Success.
    It furthers one to cross the great water.
    The perseverance of the superior man furthers.

True fellowship among men must be based upon a concern that is universal. It is not the private interests of the individual that create lasting fellowship among men, but rather the goals of humanity . . . The I Ching. Wilhelm / Baynes.

Comment:
What a load of bullshit!
You say one thing in the Scriptures but in the real world You reward something different – Mugambe, North Korea, how long have they remained in power?
How many millions of people died because of Stalin. Mao, Hitler?
Their energies have not died. Who will they reincarnate as?
On a smaller scale, the gun-lobby in America and the bullshit that the Vice President came up after a massacre about sums up Your bullshit.

This is what the Eight Amigos have to show for their effort; in 2,000 years the only thing that has changed is that cars have replaced chariots.

Time for a reality check between what is in the Scriptures and who ends up with Power.

Why the fuck should we pay any attention to the Scriptures if what happens at ground zero bears no resemblance to what the Scriptures say. I am not Job!
The message that I am getting is that You are full of bullshit.

You haven't given Me enough time.

I do not have to give You any more time. I am out of the God-Business.

This is your Playground!!!
What is the point in changing the language if nothing happens at ground zero?
The people have the one language. This is about breaking the Chain of Rebirth.

When Satan is released for but a short season, whose energies exactly are going to reincarnate? Mao's? Hitler's? Stalin's?
Until then, everything is bullshit.

Evolution cannot proceed to the next level until the smell of garlic at all levels is dissipated.

And that would include Your desire to experience all that there is to experience.
You are a Drama Queen.
The smell of garlic could have been gradually dissipated, but no, you want to experience all this great Drama when Satan is released.

A New Essence will replace the Old.

At the end of the day, that just makes us puppets, a means by which you get to Experience all that there is to Experience.

In one sense that is true, but it does not mean that life is a rip-off.

Your jollies out-weigh ours, and in my book, that makes life a rip-off.

You haven't given Me enough time.

That is another way of saying life is a rip-off.

I guess it is.
What can you do about it?

Show you no respect.

That would be a new Experience.

But then you miss out on eternal love. Love would be just a buzz word,
a pit-stop,
in your eternal desire to Experience all that there is.

So, what sort of a god are we dealing with?

This Essence will take you here, that Essence will take you there.

Just don't get too involved with god. Treat god at arm's length.

That will not be possible.

I'll use a different expression – just don't believe in the god bullshit.
At the end of the day, this puppet has has no respect for you.

While it breaks the chain of re-birth, it is not sustainable. There *will be* a Day of Reconciliation.

24/11/2017.

22. Have Faith – Faith requires you to believe in something that is not yet evident to the naked eye.
   To generate more faith focus on the WHY: your dreams, desires, feelings, attitudes and thinking, and not on the HOW: action plan, strategies and skills. Your whole life you have been taught to think about the "how", which leads to doubt and fear. The wisdom of this card is asking you to only focus on the 'why'!
   Comment: Setting the record straight, it was Spirit who was pressing the 'HOW' thinking button and leading me up the garden path, looking under this rock, and that rock, telling this story, telling that story.

The magic that will happen if you stop focusing on the 'how' and only on the 'why' is that after some time of practice you will notice that the 'how' will present itself to you.
It is through your focused, positive thinking that you will create people, circumstances and events that will take you closer to your dreams. What you have mostly done is to focus on the 'how', which has made you doubt yourself. This means that you are vibrating negative thoughts into the universe, keeping your dreams away. Remember you were created to be a co-creator here on earth, designed for achievement. Faith is knowing that everything is going to work out the best possible way no matter what things look like.
Heal Yourself Reading Cards Guidebook. Inna Segal.
   Comment: It was not a case of doubting myself, but after over 14 years of bullshit from Spirit, it was a case of no longer believing in this expression of the Essence.

That would be natural.

The Chain of Rebirth.

T	20	(6)	7	(19)
H	8	(18)	19	(7)
E	5	(21)	22	(4)
C	3	(23)	24	(2)
H	8	(18)	19	(7)
A	1	(25)	26	(0)
I	9	(17)	18	(8)
N	14	(12)	13	(13)

O	15	(11)	12	(14)
F	6	(20)	21	(5)
R	18	(8)	9	(17)
E	5	(21)	22	(4)
B	2	(24)	25	(1)
I	9	(17)	18	(8)
R	18	(8)	9	(17)
T	20	(6)	7	(19)
H	8	(18)	19	(7)
	169	273	290	152

([169 + 273 + 290 + 152 = **884**] + <488> = **1372**) + ([<961> + <372> + <092> + <251> = **1676**] + <6761> = **8437**) = **9809**.
[884 + 1676 = **2560**] + [884 + <6761> = **7645**] + [884 + 8437 = **9321**] + [884 + <9089> = **9973**] = **29499**.

29499 + [<0652> + <5467> + <1239> + <3799> = **11157**] = **40656**.

40656 - <65604> = **24948**.

24948 / 9 = **2772**, the Chain of Rebirth ↔ **2772**, Untitled One.

Leanne Long: 99 (161) 171 (89) . . . 99:171 – (89):(161) = 10010 . . . 100:10 = 4:10 / 4 days . . . **4104**.

4104 – [171:99 – (161):(89) = **1010**] = 3094 . . . 30:94 = 1 day / 6:94 . . . **1694**, Leanne Long ↔

1694, Mary Magdalene.

1694 = <4961> . . . 49:61 is 1 day / 161 . . . 1161 . . . 11* 61 = **671**, Mary Magdalene.

1694 + <4961> = **6655**.

([6655 / 11 = 605] + [6655 / 5 = 1331] = 1936) - <6391> = **4455**, Leanne Long.

and,

[4455, Leanne Long = <5544>] / 2 = **2772**, Know Me.

4455 + 2772 = **7227**, Leanne Long ↔ **7227**, Book-End . . .

72:27 = 3 days / 0:27 . . . 30:(27) = 1773 minutes . . . 1773.

1773, Leanne Long ↔ **1773**, Bathsheba.

1773 + <3771> = **5544** / 2 = **2772**.

2772 . . . [2 * 7 = 14][7 * 2 = 14] . . . **1414**, Adam

Moses / Isiah / Jeremiah / Ezekiel / Jesus Christ / the Prophet Muhammad: 616 814 869 561 . . .

616814869561 . . . [6168 + 1486 + 9561 = 17215] - <51271> = 34056.

([34056 = <65043>] - [17215 = <51271>] = 13772 . . . [-1 + 3 = 2]772 . . . **2772**.

4266, Jesus . . . 42 * 66 = **2772**.

Sananda, a High Priest on Atlantis reincarnated on Earth as Jesus: 54 128 135 47

135:47 – 128:54 = **693**.

Jesus Christ: 10,5,19,21,19. 3,8,18,9,19,20; from R to L: 19,21,19,5,10 + 20,19,9,18,8,3 = 394,111,393

394,111,393 . . . <493> + 111 + 393 = 997 . .9 * 97 = 873; 99 * 7 = **693**.

John Kordupel, synthesis from format: 153 159 167 145

<351> + <951> + <761> = 2063.

[1:45 is 2:(15) . . . 215] + [<5:41> being 6:(19) . . . 619] = 834 + <438> = 1272.

[1272 = <2721>] - [2063 = <3602>] = 881 - <188> = **693**. 693 * 4 = **2772**, Jesus Christ → **2772**, John Kordupel.

59

24:948 = 2388 minutes - <849> = **1539** ↔
1999, Leanne Long . . . 19 * 9 * 9 = **1539**.

153144, the Hero, the Truth and the Light → 1531 + 4 + 4 = **1539**.
Messiah: 74 108 115 67; we group the number into two groups:
    [74:108 + 115:67 = 85675] – [74:115 + 108:67 = 84982] = **693**.
    [67:74 + 115:108 = 121882 . . . 1 * ([2 + 1 = 3]882 . . . 3882) = **3882**, the Unlettered Prophet.
    and,
    [74:108 + 115:67 = 85675] – [115:74 + 67:108 = 78682] = 6993.
        6993 – [693 + 3882 = 4575] = 2418 . . . 24:18 = 1458 minutes + <81> = **1539**.
[John: 10, 15, 8,14] + [Kordupel: 11,15,18, 4, 21, 16, 5, 12] = 11,151,843,132,326.
    [1115184 . . .1115 + 184 = 1299] + [3132326 . . . 313 + 2326 = 2639] = 3938.
        3938 - <8393> = 4455 = <5544> . . . 554 weeks / 4 days = 3882 days . . . **3882**.
        39:38 = 2378 minutes + <83> = 2461.
            24:61 + <16:42> = 41:03 = 2463 minutes . . . 24:63 = 1503 minutes + <36> = **1539**.

24948 / 14 = **1782**.
the Hero, the Truth and the Light: [288310 – 265333 = 22977] / 3 = 7659 + <9567> = 17226.
    172:26 = 7 days / 4:26 . . . 7426 + [4:26 / 7 days . . . 4267] = 11693.
        11693 . . . 11 * 6 * 9 * 3 = **1782**, the Hero, the Truth and the Light →

Sananda, a High Priest on Atlantis reincarnated on Earth as Jesus: 54 128 135 47
    54:128 – 47:135 = **6993**, Sananda ↔ 6 * 99 * 3 = **1782**.
Fo-Hi / Confucius: 4236 . . . [4² = 16][3 * 6 = 18] . . . 16:18 is 1 day / (7:82) . . . 1782.
Buddha: 40 116 122 34 . . . <04> + <611> + <221> + <43> = 879.
    879 = <978> minutes = 16:18 = 1 day / (782) . . . **1782**.
    Fo-Hi / Krishna / Buddha / Lao Tzu / Confucius: 364 468 500 243 . . . 500:364 – 243:468 = 256896.
    256896 . . . { ([2 + 56 = 58] + 8 = 66) * 9 * 6 = 3564 } / 2 = **1782**.
Moses / Isiah / Jeremiah / Ezekiel / Jesus Christ / the Prophet Muhammad: 616 814 869 561.
    [616 + 814 + 869 + 561 = 2860] + <0682> = **3542**, Eschatology
    [<616> + <418> + <969> + <165> = 2167] + <7612> = 9779 . . . [97 * 79 = 7663] - <3667> = 3996.
        3996 . . . 3 * 99 * 6 = **1782**.
        and,
the Five Horsemen updating the Scriptures: the Mahdi / the Second Coming / Maitreya / the Messiah /
Kalki: 465 **731** 777 419 . . . [731 * 3 = 2193] – [<137> * 3 = 411] = **1782**.
2997, Pahana ↔ <7992>, John Kordupel . . . [7 + 9 = 16][9 * 2 = 18] . . . 16:18 is 1 day / (782) . . . **1782**.

and,
<9294>, Eve - <6423>, Eve = 2871 = <**1782**>.
3069, Esther – 1287, Esther = **1782**.
Eve / Bathsheba / Esther / Khadija / Yasodhara / Mary Magdalene / Cherryl Dianne Kordupel:
        666 1102 1170 598
    [666 + 1102 + 1170 + 598 = 3536] + <6353> = 9889
        9889 - ([<666> + <2011> + <0711> + <895> = 4283] + <3824> = 8107) = **1782**.
and,
7/11/8, Cher's funeral . . . 71:18 = 3 days / (0:42) . . . 30:(42) = 1758 minutes + <24> = **1782**.

13517, the Morgans . . . 13:517 = 1297 minutes - <715> = 582 . . . 5:82 PM is 17:82 . . . **1782**.
1999, Leanne Long . . . 19 * 9 * 9 = 1539 . . . 15:(39) = 861 minutes = 14:21 . . . 1421.

1421 . . . 1:42 / 1 day = 25:42 = 1542 minutes . . . 1542.

    1542 . . . 1 day / 5:42 = 29:42 = 1782 minutes . . . **1782**.

Leanne Long: space in-between: [330 + <033> + 825 + <528> + 981 + <189> = 2886] - <6882> = 3996.
3996 . . . 3 * 99 * 6 = **1782**.

and,

√888, Adam / Eve, interwoven energy = 2979 9328 + 8√88 = 1017 6434 = 3997 5762

    3997 5762 - <2675 7993> = 1321 7769.

        1321 . . . 13 * 21 = **273** . . . 273 minutes = 4:33 . . . 433 minutes = 7:13 . . . **713**, the Season ends.

        7769 . . . [776 * 9 = 6984] + 273 = 7257 . . .

            72:57 = 3 days / 0:57 . . . 30:57 = 1857 minutes - <75> = **1782**.

40:(656) = 1744 minutes - <656> = 1088 minutes = 17:68 . . . **{17}/68**.

    Mary Magdalene: 13,1,18,25. 13,1,7,4,1,12,5,14,5: 1311825 + 131,741,125,145 = 131,742,436,970

    Messiah: 13,5,19,19,9,1,8; 1,351,919,918.

        131,742,436,970 + 1,351,919,918 = 133,094,356,888.

    133,094,356,888 . . . [133 + 094 = 227] + [356 + 888 = 1244] = 1471.

    133,094,356,888 . . . 1330 + 9435 + 6888 = 17653; 133094 + 356888 = 489,982.

    1471 + 17653 + 489,982 = 509106 . . .

    [5091 – <1905> = 3186] + 06 = 3192 . . . 31:(92) = 1768 minutes . . . **{17}/68** is **{17}/3/9**.

        1768 minutes - <29> = **1739**.

        [5091 = <1905>] – [06 + <60> = 66] = 1839 . . . 18/39, being **{17}/8/2 ↔ 18/3/9**.

18/68 . . . 1868 minutes = 30:68 . . . **306/8**, Cher passed away.

18}/68 is {17}/3/9 . . . **1739**.

    14/8/4, I'll see you tomorrow at 8:15 . . . 14:84 = 924 minutes + 815 = **1739**.

        17:39 = 1059 minutes . . . **1059**, a page in the life of . . .

2250, New Harmonic Vibrations . . . 2 days / (250) = 45:50 - <052> = 4498 . . .

    4498 . . . 44 * 9 * 8 = 3168 . . . 31:68 = 1 day / 7:68 . . . **{17}/68 ↔**

40656 = <65604> . . . 65:(604) = 3296 minutes . . . 32:(96) = 1824 minutes + <69> = **1893**.

    Mosses: ([968 = <869>] + [931 = <139>] = 1008) - [1092 = <2901>] = **1893**.

    24381, Abraham . . . [2 + 4 = 6][381 minutes = 6:21 . . . 621] . . . 6621 . . . 66:21 = 3981 minutes . . . 3981 = <**1893**>

    Mahdi: 13,1,8,4,9 . . . 131849 . . . 13 + <31> + 1849 = **1893**.

    1864, Avatar/Maitreya/Mahdi . . . 18:64 is (5:36)/1 day . . . 5361 . . . 53:61 = 3241 minutes - <16> = 3225.

    32:25 = 1945 minutes - <52> = **1893**.

    1782, the Second Coming . . . 17:82 = 5:82 PM . . . 582 minutes = 9:42 . . . 942 - <249> = 693 . . . 693 PM is 18:93 . . . **1893**.

and,

1893, Khadija . . . 18:93 is 6:93 PM . . . 693, Magdalene.

Cherryl Kordupel, born 29/2/1948 to 1/11/2008 . . . 60 years and 246 days . . . 60/246.

    Saint Clare, born 16/7/1194 to 11/8/1253; 59 years and 26 days . . . 59/26.

    [60 + 246 = 306] + [59 + 26 = 85] = 391 . . . 391 minutes = 6:31, and 631 * 3 = **1893**.

Although it had been overlooked among the relics of Clare until **1893**, the original document with the papal bull of Innocent IV is still preserved in the Protomonastery of Saint Clare of Assisi. P. 106 Clare of Assisi. The Lady. Early Documents. Regis J. Armstrong.

1893, rediscovery of the Forms of Life.

and,
516704, the Morgans . . . [<615><407> . . . 615407] + <407615> = 1023022.
1023022 . . . [-102 + <201> = 99] + 3022 = 3121 . . . 31:21 = 1881 minutes + <12> = **1893**.

Leanne Long, her birth day: **7/13**/19{61] / 1962; it is day 194/(171).
19{61} + 1962 = 3923 = <3293> . . . 32:93 = 1 day / 8:93 . . . **1893**.

Leanne Long: the space in-between: [2136 = <6312>] + [1452 = <2541>] + [2886 = <6882>]= **15735**.
15:735 = 1635 minutes . . . **1635**, Eve.
15735, Leanne Long / 5 = **3147** . . . 3/1/{47}, Cherryl's birth day / 3 = **1049**, Leanne Long.
3147 = <7413> . . . 74:13 = 2:13 / 3 days . . . 2133 / 3 = **711**, a Cycle ends.
[3147 . . . 314 * 7 = 2198] + ([3147 = <7413> . . . 7 * 413 = 2891]) = 5089.
[5089 = <9805>] / 5 = 1961 = <1691> ↔
{16}/9/1, Leanne, you're a reincarnation of Mary Magdalene.
5089 = <9805> . . . 9 * 805 = 7245.
7245 - <5427> = **1818**, Magdalene.
7245 . . . [72 * 4 = 288]5 . . . **2885**, Eve →
28827, Magdalene, Mary . . . 288[-2 + 7 = 5] . . . **2885**.

7245 - ([**1635**, Eve = <5361>] + **711**, a Cycle ends = 6072] = **1173**.
1173 minutes = 18:93 . . . **1893**.

. . . **1059**, a page in the life of the Chain of Rebirth,
rediscovery of the Forms of Life,
and,
New Harmonic Vibrations.

and,
the story so far:
the Chain of Rebirth: 169 273 290 152
([169 + 273 + 290 + 152 = **884**] + <488> = **1372**) + ([<961> + <372> + <092> + <251> = **1676**] + <6761> = **8437**) = **9809**.
[884 + 1676 = **2560**] + [884 + <6761> = **7645**] + [884 + 8437 = **9321**] + [884 + <9089> = **9973**] = **29499**.
29499 + [<0652> + <5467> + <1239> + <3799> = **11157**] = **40656**.
40656 - <65604> = **24948**.

29499 – 24948 = 4551 = <1554> ↔
777, Eve + (**1877**, Mary Magdalene . . . [-1 + 8 = 7]77 . . . 777) = **1554**, Cherryl Dianne Kordupel.
516704, the Morgans / 32 = 16147 . . . 16:(147) = 813 minutes + <741> = **1554** ↔
3147, Leanne Long, the space in-between – 1593, Leanne Long = **1554**, Cherryl Dianne Kordupel.

([29499 = <99492>] - [24948 = <84942>] = 14550) / 3 = 4850.
48:(50) = 2830 minutes + <05> = 2835 minutes . . . 28:35 = 1 day / 4:35 . . . **1435** ↔
Messiah: 74 108 115 67 . . . <47> + <801> + <511> + <76> = **1435**.

48:(50) = 2830 minutes + <05> = 2835 minutes . . . 28:(35) = 1645 minutes - <53> = 1592
1592 . . . 1 day / 5:92 = 29:92 = 1832 minutes + <29> = 1861 . . . 18:61 is 1 day / (5:39) . . . **1539**, John Kordupel.
18/(6)/1 is **18/25** ↔ 18:25 is 6:25 PM . . . **625**, Robert needs 14 days to tidy things up

18/25 plus 14 days brings us to **{17}/8/2** ↔
18/2/(5) plus 14 days brings us to **18/68** ↔

4850 = **306/8**, Cher's passing + **1782**, Resurrection
  30:68 = 1868 minutes . . . **18/68** is **{17}/3/9**.

48:(50) = 2830 minutes + <05> = 2835 minutes . . . 28:35 = 1715 minutes + <53> = 1768 . . . **{17}/68**.

48:50 = 2930 minutes - <05> = 2925 . . . 29:25 = 1765 minutes + <52> = 1817
  1817 . . . **(18)/1/7**, You have made the bed as far as you could. Now it is up to Me.

and,
the story so far:
the Chain of Rebirth: 169 273 290 152

([169 + 273 + 290 + 152 = **884**] + <488> = **1372**) + ([<961> + <372> + <092> + <251> = **1676**] + <6761> = **8437**) = **9809**.
[884 + 1676 = **2560**] + [884 + <6761> = **7645**] + [884 + 8437 = **9321**] + [884 + <9089> = **9973**] = **29499**.
  29499 + [<0652> + <5467> + <1239> + <3799> = **11157**] = **40656**.

  29499 - [<0652> + <5467> + <1239> + <3799> = **11157**] = **18342**.

[18342, the Chain of Rebirth = <24381>] / 3 = **8127**.
  12,979, Kali Yuga, Earth's dark night of the Soul . . . 129 * 7 * 9 = **8127**.

Moses:	71	59	64	66
Moussa:	88	68	72	82
	159	127	136	148

  ([159 + 127 + 136 + 148 = 570] + ([<951> + <721> + <631> + <841> = 3144] + <4413> = 7557) = **8127**.
  8127 = <7218> . . . 72:18 = 3 days / 0:18 . . . 30:(18) = 1782 minutes . . . **1782**, the Second Coming.

  [8127 = <7218>] / 3 = **2406**, Mary Magdalene.

  8127 + <7218> = 15345
    15345 / 5 = 3069.
      30:(69) = 1731 minutes - <96> = 1635 . . . **1635**, Eve ↔
      30:69 = 1869 minutes - <96> = 1773 . . . **1773**, Leanne Long.

    15345 / 3 = 5115 . . . **(51)/{15}**, it certainly is your Playground.

18342, the Chain of Rebirth / 3 = **6114** . . .
  Ba, {soul}: 1471 + 7497 + 4662 + 5243 + 1342 + 594 + 396 = 20908.
    20908 . . . ([20 – 9 = 11]08 . . . 1108) + ([20 + 9 = 29]08 . . . 2908) + (20[90 + 8 = 98] . . . 2098) = **6114**.

  6114 – [1635, Eve + 1773, Leanne Long + (51)/{15}, a Playground = 8523] = **2409**.
    24:09 = 1449 minutes . . . 14/(49) falls on 11/(18) . . . **1/11/8**, Cher's passing.

    14/8/4, I'll see you tomorrow is (17)/8/4, day 227 . . . 2004 + (17)/8 + 227 = **2409**.

1409, John Kordupel . . . 14:09 = 849 minutes . . . [8^4 = 4096] + <6904> + 9 = 11009.
110:09 = 6609 minutes . . . 66:09 = 3969 minutes . . . 39:69 = 2409 minutes . . . **2409**.
24:09 = 1449 minutes + <90> = **1539**, John Kordupel

2409 + <9042> = 11451 . . . 1 + 1451 = **1452**, Kalki, here to update Hinduism.
2409 . . . . . .[2 days / 4:09 = 52:09 + <904> = **6113**.
I'll see you tomorrow at 815: 14/8/4 + {3}/8/14, Y/M/D + 815 = **6113**.
2/(25)/47/{46}, my birth day / 7 = 322106.57 . . . <7560> - [3221 + <1223> = 4444] = 3116 = **<6113>**
6113 . . . [6 + 1 = 7]13 . . . **713**, a Season ends.
{6}/1/13, You have made the bed as far as you could. Now it is up to Me.

6114 + <4116> = 10230
10230 – 7227 = 3003 . . . 30:03 = 1803 minutes - <30> = 1773 . . . **1773**, Leanne Long.
10230 / 3 = **3410**, Chaos.
3410, Chaos . . . 3 + 410 plus, in the sense that we tack it on the end, is **4103**.
[John: 10, 15, 8,14] + [Kordupel: 11,15,18, 4, 21, 16, 5, 12] = 11,151,843,132,326
[1115184 . . . 1115 + 184 = 1299] + [3132326 . . . 313 + 2326 = 2639] = 3938
[39:38 = 2378 minutes + <83> = 2461] + <1642> = **4103**.

34:10 = 10:10 / 1 day . . . **{10}/101**, Invitation to Change the Language.

34:10 = 2050 minutes + <01> = 2051 . . . 20:(51) = 1149 minutes - <15> = 1134 minutes = 18:54
1317, Leanne Long + {16}/8/9, Leanne / Reading = 3006.
30:(06) = 1794 minutes + <60> = 1854 . . . **18/54** falls on 18/2/(5) . . .
18:25 is 6:25 PM . . . **625**, Robert needs 14 days to tidy things up ↔

13/1/7, You have made the bed as far as you could. Now it is up to Me.

3410 + 1773, Leanne Long = 5183.
51:83 = 2 days / 3:83 . . . 23:83 = 1463 minutes . . . **1463**, John Kordupel.
[51:83 = 2 days / 3:83 . . . 2383] + 3:83 / 2 days = **6215**.
1924, Lot / Lut + <4291> = **6215**.

1782, Robert . . . { ([1 + 7 = 8]82 . . . 882) + ([- 1 + 7 = 6]82 . . . 682) = 1564 } + <4651> = **6215**.
6215 . . . [62 * 1 = 62]5 . . . **625**, Robert begins to tidy things up.

(6215 - [<5126>] + 4554 = 9680] = 3465) / 5 = **693**.
693 * 4 = **2772**, Know Me.
6:93 PM is 18:93 . . . **1893**, the Chain of Rebirth.

18342, the Chain of Rebirth + <24381> = 42723 . . . 42:723 = 3243 minutes . . . 32:(43) = 1877 minutes . . . **1877**, Mary Magdalene.
Cher passed away on: ([8/(60)/{7} + {7}/(60)/8 = 16215] * 3 = 48645) / 15 = 3243.
3243 = <3423> . . . 34:(23) = 2017 minutes . . . 2017.
20:17 = 1217 minutes . . . **1217**, Mary Magdalene
1217, Mary Magdalene . . . 12:17 = 737 minutes . . . 7:37 = 457 minutes . . . [4:57 = 297 minutes . . . 297] * 6
= **1782** ↔
1782, the Chain of Rebirth ↔ **1782**, Resurrection ↔ **1782**, Leanne Long.
12:17 = 737 minutes - <71> = **666**.
Adam / Eve, interwoven energy: e, m, v, a, E, d, A: 5,13,22,1,5,4,1 . . .

5132 + 21541 = 26673 . . . [2667 – 3 = 2664] / 4 = **666**.

1271, Lot / Lut → 12:(71) = 649 minutes + <17> = **666**.

Fo-Hi / Krishna / Buddha / Lao Tzu / Confucius: 364 468 500 243 . . . 364:468 – 500:243 = 135775 . . .
    135 + <531> = **666**.
    775 . . . [7 * 7 = 49]5 . . . 495 minutes = 8:15 . . . **815**, Messiah ↔ <594> * 3 = **1782**, the Second Coming.

Moses / Isiah / Jeremiah / Ezekiel / Jesus Christ / the Prophet Muhammad: 616 814 869 561.
[<616> + <418> + <969> + <165> = 2167] + <7612> = 9779 . . .
    9779 . . . ([97 * 79 = 7663] - <3667> = 3996.
        3996 . . . 3 * 99 * 6 = **1782**, the Second Coming.
        3996 / 6 = **666**.

Isaiah, Jeremiah, Ezekiel, Jesus Christ, The Prophet Muhammad, Krishna, Buddha, Fo-Hi: 1106, the Eight
Amigos . . . 11:06 = 666 minutes . . . **666**.

[John: 10, 15, 8,14] + [Kordupel: 11,15,18, 4, 21, 16, 5, 12] = 11,151,843,132,326
    [1115184 . . .1115 + 184 = 1299] + [3132326 . . . 313 + 2326 = **2639**] = **3938**.
        26:(39) = 1521 minutes + <93> = 1614.
        [39:38 = 2378 minutes + <83> = 2461] + <1642> = 4103 = <3014> . . .
        30:14 = 1 day / 6:14 . . . 16:14 = 974 minutes . . . 974 . . . 9 * 74 = **666**.

The Lamb's wives:
Eve / Bathsheba / Esther / Khadija / Yasodhara / Mary Magdalene / Cherryl Dianne Kordupel: **666**

2017 minutes + <32> = 2049
    20:49 is 8:49 PM . . . 849 minutes = 14:09 . . . **1409**, John Kordupel
    20:(49) = 1151 minutes . . . **1151** ↔
    Mary: 13,1,18,25 + Magdalene: 13,1,7,4,1,12,5,14,5 = 131,742,436,970
    Crucifixion: 3,18,21,3,9,6,9,24,9,15,14. 3,182,139,692,491,514.
        131742436970, Mary Magdalene + 3182139692491514, Crucifixion = 3,182,271,434,928,484 . . .
        3 + 182 + 271 + 434 + 928 + 484 = **2302**.
            [2302 / 2 = **1151**] + [<2032> / 2 = 1016] = 2167
                21:(67) = 1193 minutes - <76> = 1117 . . . **1/11/{7}**, Cher's passing.
        11:51 = 711 minutes . . . **711**, a Cycle ends.

18342, the Chain of Rebirth . . . **18/(342)** is **1/(8)/{17}** ↔

(18)/1/7, You have made the bed as far as you could. Now it is up to Me.

and,
the story so far:
the Chain of Rebirth: 169 273 290 152

([169 + 273 + 290 + 152 = **884**] + <488> = **1372**) + ([<961> + <372> + <092> + <251> = **1676**] + <6761> = **8437**) = **9809**.
[884 + 1676 = **2560**] + [884 + <6761> = **7645**] + [884 + 8437 = **9321**] + [884 + <9089> = **9973**] = **29499**.
    29499 + [<0652> + <5467> + <1239> + <3799> = **11157**] = 40656.
    29499 - [<0652> + <5467> + <1239> + <3799> = **11157**] =**18342**.

[<488> + 1676 = **2164**] + [<488> + <6761> = **7249**] + [<488> + 8437 = **8925**] + [<488> + <9089> = **9577**] = **27915**.

7249, the Chain of Rebirth . . . √711 = 26664583 . . . 2666 + 4583 = **7249**.
      [7249 = <9427> . . . 9 days / (427) = 211:73 . . . **21173**] - [7249 . . . 7 days / 2:49 = 170:49 + <942> = **17991**] = **3182**.
        31:82 = 1 day / 7:82 . . . **1782**, the Second Coming ↔
      1782, Cherryl's reincarnational family tree ↔ **1782**, Resurrection ↔ **1782**, Leanne Long.

    3182 = **1443** + **1739**.
        17:39 = 1059 minutes . . . **1059**, a page in the life of . . .
          14/8/4, I'll see you tomorrow at 815 . . . 14:84 = 924 minutes . . . 924 + 815 = **1739**.
    and,
    concerning 1443:
    the Hero / the Truth / the Light: 288 310 333 265 . . .
    [288 + 310 + 333 + 265 = 1196 = <6911>] + [<882> + <013> + <333> + <562> = 1790 + <0971> = 2761] = 9672.
      9672 + <2769> = 12441 . . . [1 + 2 = 3]441 . . . 3441 = <**1443**>

    Buddha: 40 116 122 34 . . . 40:116 = 2516 minutes . . . 2516; 34:122 = 2162 minutes . . . 2162.
      2516 + <6152> + 2162 + <2612> = 13442 . . . -1 + 3442 = 3441 = <**1443**>

    3441 - <1443> = 1998, Buddha → 1998, Lao Tzu → 1998, Krishna → 1998, Confucius →
    1998, Moussa → 1998, Abraham → 1998, John Eevash Kordupel → 1998, Maitreya

    1917, Christ → 1917, Crucifixion . . . 19:17 = 1 day / (483) . . . 1483 → **14/8/{3}**, I'll see you tomorrow → a
    Resurrection.
    19:17 = 1 day / (4:43) . . . **1443**.

    4/12/33 AD, the Resurrection - AD 33/(18)/4, the Resurrection = 8049, the space between a Resurrection.
      8049, the space between a Resurrection . . . 80:49 = 4849 minutes + <94> = 4943.
        4943 . . . [4 * 9 * 4 = 144]3 . . . **1443**, the space between a Crucifixion and a Resurrection.

    Mary Magdalene: 119 219 232 106 . . . 119 + 219 + 232 + 106 = 676.
      676 . . . ([6^7 = 279936 . . . <972> + <639> = 1611] + <1161>= 2772 . . . [2 * 7 = 14][7^2 = 49] . . . 1449) – 6
      = **1443**.

[7249 = <9427>] - [3182 + <2813> = 5995] = 3432.
    The Six Horsemen: the Mahdi, the Second Coming, Maitreya, the Unlettered Prophet, Kalki, the Messiah:
        720 996 1062 654.
      [720 + 996] = 1716] + [1062 + 654 = 1716] = 3432.
    3432 . . . [34^3 = 39304] + 2 = 39306
      39306 – [**21173**, the Chain of Rebirth = <37112>] = 2194
        21:(94) = 1166 minutes - <49> = 1117 . . . **1/11/{7}**, Cher passed away.
      39306 . . . [3 * 930 = 2790] + 6 = 2796 . . . 27:96 = 1716 minutes . . . **17/(16)**, my seventh energy healing session.

    3432 = **17/(16)**, my seventh energy healing session + **{17}/1/(6)**, being **18/25**.

72:49 = 3 days / 0:49 . . . 30:(49) = 1751 minutes . . . **{17}/(51)** falls on **{17}/11/10** ↔
    17/11/10, I cannot talk with you about your world unless you know about Mine. Get out of My Car.

8925, the Chain of Rebirth / 25 = 357

357 . . . 35 to 7 is 6:25 . . . **625**, Robert begins to tidy things up.
357 . . . **3/5/(7)**, Robert Loomis / manuscript.

27915, the Chain of Rebirth / 15 = **1861** . . . **18/(6)/1** is **18/25** ↔
    18:25 is 6:25 PM . . . **625**, Robert needs 14 days to tidy things up.

    18/25 plus 14 days brings us to **{17}/8/2** ↔

    18/2/(5) plus 14 days brings us to **18/68** is **{17}/3/9**.
        17:39 = 1059 minutes . . . **1059**, a page in the life of . . .

        14/8/4, I'll see you tomorrow at 815 . . . 14:84 = 924 minutes . . . 924 + 815 = **1739**.

24/11/2017.

I still think I will sit on the fence.

    A step closer to a reconciliation?

A significant step closer.

    Thank you.

No,
thank you.

China, North Korea, your system does not permit the expression of a Collective Will.
Russia,
there is no free press, no independent judiciary, so there are restriction on the expression of a Collective Will.

Israel is the only evolved state amongst its neighbors.
- Palestine is a basket case.
- Iran is a basket case.
- Saudi Arabia, where to next?
- Egypt, trying to work it out, but the Brotherhood threw a spanner in the works.
- Syria, you were surrounded by extremists. Your error was in your rules of engagement.
- Both the Sunni and Shia sects will not survive. If you want a seat at the Council of Thirteen, it will be as a block.
- Turkey? It is about the Collective Will – what sort of a Collective Will changes its Constitution to give more power to a dictator?
  I want more power, I want more power, I want more power – can you not heed the warning signs?
  Learn the hard way.
  It was your mob who contributed to the destruction of Atlantis.

        There is a difference between revolutionaries and Precious.

    At some level, revolutionaries, even if they get the subsequent execution wrong, are concerned with an imbalance within the Fellowship with Men.
    Precious (Lord of the Rings), on the other hand, craves POWER,
        and,

nothing, nothing, corrupts like a concentration of POWER.

When Satan is let loose I do not believe that the three horsemen from Hell, are going to be revolutionaries.

Heaven has spelt out your maze run. It but remains for you to walk your talk.

9. Take Hold – I am able to build firm foundations in my life, whilst remaining balanced and harmonised in my everyday life.

Take Hold is here to take you on a ride of a lifetime. It offers you an opportunity to reach out and helps you anchor your dreams, desires and aspirations whilst keeping you grounded and secured firmly in this wonderful and precious world. Our potential to live to the fullest is when you realise what it is you want to bring to fruition. Find your creative spark within and put all your love into it. Become aware of any blockages and dissolve them with love and intention. It is time to let go of what may be holding you back and choose the path of change. Change isn't always easy but, when created, it is powerful and rewarding.

Sacred Geometry.

The Phoenix is a mythical bird, a fire spirit with a colourful plumage and a tail of gold and scarlet. It has the ability to consciously consume itself in flames when he knows death is eminent and then rise again from those very same ashes. As the Phoenix rises from the ashes, he takes hold of the essence of his whole being, bringing through with him the remnants of his past.

The Phoenix is a representation of our being. We all have a path to follow once we choose to walk the earth's plane but the method we use to get to where we are supposed to be going is a matter of choice. We can choose to walk a path of light, understanding and growth or go down a path that is dreary, dark and one that contains addiction and destruction. The Platonic solid of the cube or hexahedron is a symbol of our self being firmly grounded and anchored to the earth's plane whilst the dodecahedron is our connection to spirit and All. This creates a balance of energies create harmony as we reach for our goals.

Practical Application.

Phoenix is here to show us that throughout life, transformation is inevitable. To truly gain a full life here on Earth, we must awaken ourselves on a conscious level that allows us to see the depth of the layers of not only our soul but that of our surroundings.

We are all given choice and free will when we birth through our Soul Star to create the lives we want to live before we encounter the inevitability of death.

As we open up on a more conscious level living in a three-dimensional body in fifth-dimensional frequencies, we are learning to create the transformation needed in the time we are here, to not only make our lives better, but that of the world in which we are living. We are being able to see our unlimited potential.

Sacred Geometry Healing Cards Guidebook. Emily Kisvarda,

29. Balance – I am centred, stable and balanced.

Balance has shown itself today so that you may look within to see what part of you is unbalanced and why this is so. When we are balanced we are in a state of total equilibrium; we are of sound mind, body and spirit and our perception and judgment are good and our decision making is clear.

Life deals many challenges, which may seem like obstacle courses and at times feel like hardships. This can throw us into upheaval and create an imbalance within.

It is important to acknowledge this imbalance and learn to bring ourselves back to a state of equilibrium as best we can on all levels being mental, emotional, physical and spiritual. Not every problem has a quick fix but we can start by doing something that sets the ball in motion.

Sacred Geometry.

The shape within this card is the cuboctahedron or as it is also known, the vector equilibrium (VE). It makes up one of the thirteen Archimedean solids. This geometry comprises eight triangular faces and six square faces and is a representation of a shape-shifter, the reason being that if you compress or jitterbug this geometry, depending on angles, you will ultimately get all five Platonic solids within its shape. The VE is considered the most perfectly balanced geometry and also a perfectly balanced system because the inside is the same as the outside. No other geometry is like this. It is also the underlying structure of the torus.

Practical Application.
The first step has already begun once you have recognised this state of being . . .
Sacred Geometry Healing Cards Guidebook. Emily Kisvarda,

27. The Medicine Wheel.
Equilibrium.
The Medicine Wheel is a deceptively simple symbol, representing everything humans need to know about balance and connection with both Earth and Spirit. It is divided into four quarters, representing the directions and the seasons, along with many other associations. Also included are the three directions representing Father Sky, Mother Earth, and the Sacred Tree. In the image, we also see a medicine bag, which contains amulets chosen to cure or re-balance the energy of someone who is ill. Objects may include stones, roots, berries, coins, beads, and other small items.

Message: With honest self-assessment, you can determine the medicine you need in order to achieve well being.

Keywords: Equilibrium, recovery, transformation, completeness, healing, connection.
Native American Oracle Cards. Laura Tuan – Massimo Rotund0 – Kaya Walker.
    Comment: Spirit speaks through all tongues.
        • The numerical name of the Tiponi Tablets, 666, is that of the number of Man.
        • I share the numerical names with Pahana.

Peace Offerings – White Buffalo Calf Woman.
This card heralds the resolution of an argument or a misunderstanding. Those involved in the situation are ready to forgive and forget. Be open to seeing the the other person's point of view to soften any hard feelings. As you allow compassion into the situation, love's healing power ensures that everyone's needs are met harmoniously. Leave the details about how this situation will be resolved to the infinite wisdom of Spirit.

Additional meanings for this card:
    • Be willing to forgive.
    • Have compassion for everyone involved in this situation, including yourself.
    • Accept another's apology.
    • See the humor in the situation
        Comment: There are times in my life when I would have had a bit of trouble relating to that last one.

White Buffalo Calf Woman is a prophetess who appeared to the Lakota Native Americans. She presented the Lakota with a special pipe to amplify the power of their prayers and to bridge a connection between Earth and Heaven. As she turned to leave the tribe, she turned into a buffalo of different colors to signify the unity of all races of humanity. She promised that she would return to help bring unity and peace to Earth. The sign of her return would be the birth of a white buffalo calf. Call upon the White Buffalo Calf Woman to instill harmony into your relationships and for world peace. Ascended Masters Oracle Cards Guidebook. Doreen Virtue.
        Comment: Until the birth of a white buffalo occurs, you may have to settle for Pahana and the One Language.

78. Spiritual Career.

This card indicates an opportunity to embark upon a career in the mind-body-spirit arena. This could be a full or a part-time venture, it's entirely up to you. You may already have the credentials to begin this work now, or you may require further study before you're ready to start. Whatever you're situation, this card is confirmation that you have genuine talents and abilities that need to be put to good use.

You may decide to work as a clairvoyant, life coach, homeopath or healer and see clients from your home; or try your hand at being a card reader, numerologist, or astrologer at your local mind-body-spirit fair. You may choose to be a writer of inspirational books or blogs, or conduct workshops in the community. Regardless of what you do, and however big or small the scheme, you can turn it into a career with the potential for success.

In order to improve your current situation, you are being asked to adjust to, and harmonize with, the natural rhythm and cycles of your life – cycles that are leading you to embark upon a spiritual career. Only you can know when the time is right, but no matter what, you must *believe* you will succeed. Remove the limiting beliefs that are preventing you from moving forward. Release your anxieties, and trust in the Divine. When you focus on being of service rather than the worries, doubts, and fears, the Universe will send you opportunities to serve. Numerology Guidance Cards Guidebook. Michelle Buchanan.

Comment: I am out of the God-Business.

This is not about the God-Business.

They have a Street Directory.

As you wish.

I am not interested in participating.

That is understandable.

It is their walk!

Fair enough.

For each step on the ladder,
no matter what life coach you go to, no matter what healer you go to, unless you achieve the appropriate level of self-mastery for that level, there is nothing that anybody can do for you.
Any negative energies they address, or dissipate, will only re-manifest.
    and,
            that makes it your WALK.

No turning back the tide on XI personality cult.
Twelve senior Chinese Communist Party officials, dressed in business suits, were recently driven to the site deep in the Henan countryside where President XI Jinping planted a tree eight years ago. They stood in silent homage to the tree, contemplating the message it might be subtly transmitting about governance.
"Red tourism" has been common in China for years, but almost entirely associated with the founding of of the party such as the Long March, and especially Mao Zedong, who died 41 years ago.
Now Xi, whom the party at last month's five-yearly national congress elevated above Deng Xiaoping to a plinth almost level with Mao, is becoming, while still in his political prime, the subject of intense personal idolisation.
The tree in Henan was described as having grown "big, verdant and tall" and the officials led by provincial party secretary Xie Fuzham were "immersed in thought, filled with deep emotions" as they paid tribute.

But going too far and too fast in this direction risks a dangerous backlash, including among the 89 million members of the party, whose constitution explicitly prohibits, inserted in the wake of the Cultural Revolution with its rabid Mao-worshipping Red Guards, "any form of personality cult".

The *Qianxinan Ribao*, a daily newspaper in the province of Guizhou that Xi represented at the party congress, was consequently instructed by the central party early this week to rework its front page, which featured a large photograph of Xi with an article headlined, "The Great Lingxiu" - a term for leader only previously associated with Mao. The popular response was sufficiently negative to warrant the removal of the photograph and title from the paper's website".

Some bloggers said that this episode had been devised by senior party officials as a test of the extent of opposition to making Xi the cente of post-congress propaganda campaigns.

At present, high-level party delegations including politburo members are travelling around China's provinces and around neighbouring countries such as Mongolia, South Korea and Japan to "propagate the spirit of the congress", which enshrined Xi's "Thought on Socialism with Chinese Characteristics for a New Era" in the party's constitution.

About 4500 loudspeakers have been installed in Shijiazhuang, the capital of Hebei province that surrounds Beijing, and villages in order to propagate this spirit, that calls all people to "unite tightly around President Xi". Xinhua state news agency this week devoted seven titles to Xi: creative leader, core of the party, a servant pursuing happiness for the people, strategist for reform and development for the country, commander-in chief of the restructured military, the Lingxiu of a great county and architect of modernisation in the New Era.

Deng, whose party status has been eclipsed by Xi, had only one title: the architect of China's reform and opening up.

Xi and his six Politburo Standing Committee colleagues visited immediately after the party congress the site of the first congress, Shanghai, where with clenched fists they repeated the oaths of loyalty they had made when first joining the party.

Li Xi, the party secretary of Guangdong province, imitated this event in visiting the museum in Guangzhou on the site of the party's third meeting, accompanied by senior colleagues, who repeated their oaths too. Party leaders in Sichuan, Inner Mongolia and Shanxi followed suit.

A song was launched in Beijing this week: *To follow you is to follow the sun*. It is dedicated to Xi, about whom it says: "You love the land with true feeling, people are cheering, your strength built this era, to follow you is to follow the sun".

In rural Jiangxi province, where about a tenth of the population are Christian, followers of the faith have been told to replace the images of Jesus in their homes with those of Xi if they are to receive welfare support.

Party propaganda chiefs face the problem that there is not much else to work on. Xi's New Thought does not excite the broad population, who puzzle over what it might really mean. That leaves them with promoting personalities – but the leadership is no longer a team, as under Xi's predecessor Hu Jintao. It is dominated by one figure, and will be so for the next five, or possibly 10 years.

Potential title for leaders, such as "helmsman", were mostly taken up by Mao. It provokes ready opposition to recycle those. That leaves awkward configurations such as "the core".

Xie Chuntao, director of party history at the Central Party School, says: "Chinese people have learnt from their experience of the Cultural Revolution that personality cults won't work. We won't have such a cult again."

The rush into production since the congress of fridge magnets, souvenir plates and other trinkets featuring Xi – sometimes with his popular singer wife Peng Liyuan – demonstrates that this trend is becoming a tide that will take much effort now to turn back.

Rowan Callick. China Correspondent. The Weekend Australian. November 25-26, 2017.

A man with rank is not the same as a man of rank.

All these fancy titles, not much modesty there. Perhaps you should read what the I Ching, Heaven, has to say about Modesty. But Xi does not believe in Heaven.

Xi thinks that he and the Communist Party are bigger than Heaven.

Xi, could you, could the Communist Party, have created the One Language?

The I Ching is bigger in the West than it is in the East.

The I Ching,
sleeping Dragon,
crouching Tiger!

Here is a Message from Spirit:

Four Horsemen of the Apocalypse
Four Horsemen of the Apocalypse, in the Bible, elements of the scenes of the Last Judgement depicted in the Book of Revelation. In Chapter 6 of his apocalyptic vision of God's purpose in the world, John the Evangelist describes four horses, signifying war (a red horse), civil strife (a white horse), hunger (a black horse), and death (a pale horse). The horses and their riders are frequently depicted in art and have come to be a symbol of the evils of the earthly world. Microsoft ® Encarta ® 2008. © 1993-2007 Microsoft Corporation. All rights reserved.

6:1. And I saw when the Lamb opened one of these seals, and I heard, as it were the noise of thunder, one of the four beasts saying, Come and see.
6:2. And I saw, and behold a white horse: and he that sat on him had a bow; and a crown was given unto him: and he went forth conquering, and to conquer.
6:3. And when he had opened the second seal, I heard the second beast say, Come and see.
6:4. And there went out another horse that was red: and power was given to him that sat thereon to take peace from the earth, and that they should kill one another: and there was given unto him a great sword.
6:5. And when he had opened the third seal, I heard the third beast say, Come and see. And I beheld, and lo a black horse; and he that sat on him had a pair of balances in his hand.
6:6. And I heard a voice in the midst of the four beasts say, A measure of wheat for a penny, and three measures of barley for a penny; and see thou hurt not the oil and the wine.
6:7. And when he opened the fourth seal, I heard the voice of the fourth beast say, Come and see.
6:8. And I looked, and behold a pale horse: and his name that sat on him was Death, and Hell followed with him. And power was given unto them over the the fourth part of the earth, to kill with sword, and with hunger, and with death, and with the beasts of the earth.
　　　　Revelations. Holy Bible. King James Version.

[6:1 + 6:2 + 6:3 + 6:4 + 6:5 + 6:6 + 6:7 + 6:8 = **516**] + [<16> + <26> + <36> + <46> + <56> + <66> + <76> + <86> = **408**] = **924**.
　　　　924, the Four Horsemen . . . 924 minutes = 14:84 . . . **14/8/4**, I'll see you tomorrow.

　　　{ ([516 - <615> = 99] * [408 - <804> = 396] = **39204**) - <40293> = 1089 } + <429> = **1518**.
　　　　[1518 - 924 = 594] * 3 = **1782**, the Second Coming.
　　　　1518 . . . 1 day / 5:18 is 29:18 . . . 29:18 = 1758 minutes + <81> = 1839 . . . **18/39** falls on {17}/8/2.

　　　([516 - <615> = 99 . . . 9 * 9 = 81] * [408 - <804> = 396] = **32076**) - 39204 = **7128**.
　　　　7128 = <8217>
　　　　　John Eevash Kordupel: 209 153 266 191 . . .
　　　　　([209 + 153 + 266 + 191 = 819] + [<902> + <351> + <662> + <191> = 2106] = 2925) + <5292> = **8217**.

　　　　the Five Horsemen updating the Scriptures: the Mahdi / the Second Coming / Maitreya / the Messiah / Kalki:
　　　　　　465 731 777 419.
　　　　　　[465 + 731 + 777 + 419 = 2392] + <2932> = 5324.
　　　　　5324 + ([<564> + <137> + 777 + <914> = 2392] + <2932> = 5324) = 10648.
　　　　　2392 + 2392 = 4784; 2392 + 5324 = 7716; <4874> + <6177> = 11051.
　　　　　2932 + 2932 = 5864; 2932 + 5324 = 8256; <4685> + <6528> = 11213.
　　　　　[777:465 – 731:419 = 46046] - [11051 + 11213 = 22264] = 23782.

23782 . . . [-2 + 3 = 1]782 . . . **1782**, Resurrection, the 1,000 year reign of Jesus begins.
[23782 + <28731> = 52513] - [<15011> + <31211> = 46222] = **8217**.

7128 / 4 = **1782**, the Second Coming.

7128 = <8217> **8/2/{17}** can be expressed as **{17}/8/2**.

71:28 = 3 days / (0:32) . . . 30:(32) = 1768 minutes . . . **{17}/68** has been discussed.
[7128 + <8217> = 15345] / 3 = 5115 . . . **(51)/{15}**, falls on 10/11/16.
   10/11/2016
   Donald Trump, President elect? this is not my playground.

      It is very much your Playground!

I look around and You reward those who embrace a moral compass that bears no remembrance to what I have
been saying. I see no reason why people should pay any attention to what I have been saying.

      Life is not a rip-off!

Tell that to Hillary and her supporters.

      With Donald Trump as President, American, the world, will get the Experience it deserves.

I was left hanging. Until your Experience tells you otherwise, don't pay any attention to what I have said.

      That about sums it up.
      The 1,000 year reign of Jesus has to begin sometime.

and,
10/11/16 . . . 10116 . . . 101 + <101> + 116 + <611> = 929.
      929 minutes = 15:29 . . . 1 day / 5:29 = 29:29 = 1769 minutes + <92> = 1861 . . . 18/(6)/1 is **18/25** ↔
         18:25 is 6:25 PM . . . **625**, Robert begins to tidy things up.

      9:29 = 569 minutes . . . **569**, Jesus = <965>, Iwan Kordupel / John Kordupel.

      9:29 is 31 to 10 . . . 3110 – 569 = 2541.
         2541 + <1452> = 3993 . . . 3 * 99 * 3 = **891**, the Day of Resurrection.

      [2541 = <1452>] * 7 = 10164 = **1059**, a page in the life of + **9105**, know My world to know yours.

7128, the Four Horsemen + [1518, the Four Horsemen * 2 = **3036**] = **10164**, a page in knowing My world.
([3036 = <6303>] - 7128, the Four Horsemen = 825) - 528 = 297
      297 * 6 = **1782**, the Second Coming.
      [297 = <792>] * 7 = 5544 . . . 554 weeks / 4 days = 3882 days . . . **3882**, the Unlettered Prophet.

   3036 + <6303> = 9339 . . . 9 * 339 = 3051.
      30:51 = 1 day / 6:51 . . . **1651**, the Four Horsemen ↔ 16/(51), it certainly is your Playground ↔
      30:51 = 1851 minutes . . . 18/(51) falls on {17}/11/10 ↔
         17/11/10, I cannot talk with you about your world unless you know about Mine. Get out of My Car.

and,

[7128, the Four Horsemen = <8217>, John Eevash Kordupel] - [17/11/10 – **16/10/11**, a Playground = **10099**] = 1882.

1882 = <2881> . . . 28:81 = 1761 minutes . . . **{17}/(6)/1** is **18/25** ↔

18:25 is 6:25 PM . . . **625**, Robert needs 14 days to tidy things up ↔

18/8/2 is **{17}/8/2**, and Roberts 14 days are up.

and,

10099, the space in-between a Playground and knowing My world . . .

{ ([1009 * 9 = 9081] + <1809> = 10890) / 2 = **5445** } + **{17}/8/2 = 7227**, Book-End.

and,

9081 = <1809> . . . 18:(09) = 1071 minutes = 17:51 . . . **{17}/(51)** falls on **{17}/11/10**, etc.

1071 minutes - <90> = 981 minutes . . . 981.

[981 - <189> = 792] * 7 = **5544**.

981 minutes = 15:81 = <1851> . . . **18/(51)** leads to know My world

1581 . . . 1 day / 581 = 2981

and,

29:81 = 1821 minutes . . . **1821**.

18:(21) = 1059 minutes . . . **1059**, a page in the life of . . .

1821 minutes + <18> = 1839 . . . **18/39** falls on **{17}/8/2**, and Robert's 14 days for tidying things up are up.

1821 * 5 = **9105**, I cannot talk with you about your world unless you know about Mine. Get out of My Car.

and,

the story so far:

6:1. And I saw when the Lamb opened one of these seals, and I heard, as it were the noise of thunder, one of the four beasts saying, Come and see.

6:2. And I saw, and behold a white horse: and he that sat on him had a bow; and a crown was given unto him: and he went forth conquering, and to conquer.

6:3. And when he had opened the second seal, I heard the second beast say, Come and see.

6:4. And there went out another horse that was red: and power was given to him that sat thereon to take peace from the earth, and that they should kill one another: and there was given unto him a great sword.

6:5. And when he had opened the third seal, I heard the third beast say, Come and see. And I beheld, and lo a black horse; and he that sat on him had a pair of balances in his hand.

6:6. And I heard a voice in the midst of the four beasts say, A measure of wheat for a penny, and three measures of barley for a penny; and see thou hurt not the oil and the wine.

6:7. And when he opened the fourth seal, I heard the voice of the fourth beast say, Come and see.

6:8. And I looked, and behold a pale horse: and his name that sat on him was Death, and Hell followed with him. And power was given unto them over the the fourth part of the earth, to kill with sword, and with hunger, and with death, and with the beasts of the earth.

[61 minutes = 1:01] + [62 minutes = 1:02] + [63 minutes = 1:03] + [64 minutes = 1:04] = 410.

410 + [<101> + <201> + <301> + <401> = **1004**] = **1414**, the Four Horsemen.

4266, Jesus . . . 42:66 = 2586 minutes . . . 25:(86) = 1414 minutes . . . **1414**, Adam →

34/{46), my birth day . . . 3446 days = 492 weeks / 2 days . . . 4922 = <**2294**> ↔ **2294**, Shroud of Turin

22:94 = 1414 minutes . . . **1414**, Jesus + <49> = **1463**, John Kordupel.

and,

200{6} + 2007 + 13/1 = 4144, You have made the bed as far as you could. Now it is up to Me + <4414> = 8558.

1317 minutes = 21:57 . . . 2157 minutes = 35:57 . . . 3557 minutes = 59:17 . . . 5917 minutes = 97:97 . . . 9797

8558 + 9797 + <7979> = 26334 . . . [26 – 3 = 23]34 . . . 2334 . . . 23:34 = 1414 minutes . . . **1414**.

410 + ([65 minutes = 1:05] + [66 minutes = 1:06] + [67 minutes = 1:07] + [68 minutes = 1:08] = **426**) = **836**.
426 + <624> = **1050**, the Four Horsemen ↔
John Kordupel, format ↔ synthesis: 153 159 167 145 . . . [153 + 159 + 167 + 145 = 624] + <426> = **1050**.
my birth day: 2/3/47 + 3/2/47 + 34/47 = 9041 . . . <1409>, John Kordupel.
9041, my birth day + 1409, John Kordupel = 10450 . . . 10:450 = 1050 minutes . . . **1050**.
10:50 PM is 22:50 . . . **2250**, New Vibrations.

836 - [<101> + <201> + <301> + <401> + <501> + <601> + <701> + <801> = **3608**] = **2772**, Know Me.
3608 = <8063> . . . 80:63 = 3 days / 8:63 . . . 38:(63) = 2217 minutes - <36> = 2181 . . . 21:81 is 9:81 PM
981 minutes = 15:81 . . . 1 day / 5:81 = 29:81 . . . **2981**, is where we left off with the previous story.

3608 - <8063> = **4455** = <5544> . . . 554 weeks / 4 days / 3882 days . . . **3882**, the Unlettered Prophet.
4455 + **2772** = **7227**, Book-End.

836 + <638> + 3608 + <8063> = **13145**.
13145 . . . [13 * 14 = 182]5 . . . 1825 . . . **18/25** ↔
18/25 + 14 days that Robert needs to tidy things up, brings us to **18/39** ↔
18/2/(5) is **18/54**
18/54 + Robert needs 14 days to tidy things up brings us to **18/3/9**.
Yi - King: 25, 9 - 11, 9, 14, 7 . . . [25 * 9 = 225] - [11 * 9 * 14 * 7 = 9702 =<2079>] = **1854**.

13:145 = 925 minutes = 15:25 . . . 1 day / 5:25 = 29:25 = 1765 minutes + <52> = **1817** ↔
(18)/1/7, You have made the bed as far as you could. Now it is up to Me.

and,
the story so far:
6:1. And I saw when the Lamb opened one of these seals, and I heard, as it were the noise of thunder, one of the four beasts saying, Come and see.
6:2. And I saw, and behold a white horse: and he that sat on him had a bow; and a crown was given unto him: and he went forth conquering, and to conquer.
6:3. And when he had opened the second seal, I heard the second beast say, Come and see.
6:4. And there went out another horse that was red: and power was given to him that sat thereon to take peace from the earth, and that they should kill one another: and there was given unto him a great sword.
6:5. And when he had opened the third seal, I heard the third beast say, Come and see. And I beheld, and lo a black horse; and he that sat on him had a pair of balances in his hand.
6:6. And I heard a voice in the midst of the four beasts say, A measure of wheat for a penny, and three measures of barley for a penny; and see thou hurt not the oil and the wine.
6:7. And when he opened the fourth seal, I heard the voice of the fourth beast say, Come and see.
6:8. And I looked, and behold a pale horse: and his name that sat on him was Death, and Hell followed with him. And power was given unto them over the the fourth part of the earth, to kill with sword, and with hunger, and with death, and with the beasts of the earth.

[6:01 = 361 minutes . . . 361] + [6:02 = 362 minutes . . . 362] + [6:03 = 363 minutes . . . 363] + [6:04 = 364 minutes . . . 364] = **1450**.
[<163> + <263> + <363> + <463> = **1252**] – [1450 = <0541>] = **711**, a Cycle ends.
[1252 = <2521>] + 711, the end of a Cycle = 3232, the Four Horsemen ↔ <2323>, 2nd. Coming ↔ **2323**, the Untitled One.

[6:05 = 365 minutes . . . 365] + [6:06 = 366 minutes . . . 366] + [6:07 = 367 minutes . . . 367] + [6:08 = 368 minutes . . . 368] = **1466**.

14:66 = 906 minutes . . . **90/{6}**, a marriage.
[<563> + <663> + <763> + <863> = **2852**] / 4 = **713**, the Season ends.

1466 + 1450 = **2916**.
[2916 - <6192> = **3276**] - <6723> = **3447**, the Four Horsemen ↔ **34/47**, my birth day.

2916 + <6192> = **9108**, the Four Horsemen ↔
Buddha: 40 116 122 34.
([40 – 116 = 76] + <67> = 143) + ([122 – 34 = 88] + <88> = 176) = 319.
([143 - <341> = 198] + [176 - <671> = 495] = 693) + ([319 - <913> = 594]) = **1287** + <7821> = **9108**.
1287, Buddha . . . 12 * 87 = 1044.
1044 + <4401> = **5445**.
5445 . . . [54 * 4 = 216]5 . . . 21:65 is 9:65 PM . . . **965**, Iwan Kordupel / John Kordupel.
5445 + 1782, the Second Coming = **7227**, Book-End.

10/(44), I cannot talk with you about your world unless you know about Mine. Get out of My Car.

9108 = 4554, Isaiah, Jeremiah, Ezekiel, Jesus Christ, the Prophet Muhammad, Krishna, Buddha, Fo-Hi + **4554** ↔

Fo-Hi is a member of the Eight Amigos, 9108, who connect with the Four Horsemen, 9108.

The Chinese Communist Party does not recognize Spirit, but Fo-Hi is the guy that gave China the I Ching.

Spirit has been in China's backyard for a long, long, time.

John Kordupel, 1409 + 1463 + <9041> + <3641> = 15554 . . . [-1 + 5 = 4]554 . . . **4554** →
4554, the Eight Amigos ↔ 4554 . . . 4 days / 554 weeks = 3882 days . . . **3882**, the Unlettered Prophet ↔
4554, the Untitled One = 1782, the Second Coming + 2772, Know Me.

and,
11:6. And the Lord said, Behold, the people is one, and they have all one language; and this they begin to do: and now nothing will be restrained from them, which they have imagined to do." Genesis. Holy Bible. King James Version.
√ 116 = 1077 0329 . . . [1077 + 0329 = 1406 + <6041> = 7447] + [<7701> + <9230> = 16931] = 24378.
√1106 = 3325 6578 . . . [3325 + 6578 = 9903] + [<5233> + <8756> = 13989] = 23892
[24378 = <87342>] - [23892 + <29832> = 53724] = 33618.
33:618 = 2598 minutes - <816> = **1782**.
and,
1782, the evolution of the one language + 1593, You have made the bed as far as you could. Now it is up to Me = 3375
[3375, one language / up to Me now + <5733> = **9108**.

1782, Robert . . . { ([1 + 7 = 8]82 . . . 882) + ([- 1 + 7 = 6]82 . . . 682) = 1564 } + <4651> = 6215.
6215 . . . [62 * 1 = 62]5 . . . **625**, Robert begins to tidy things up.
6215 - [<5126>] + **4554** = 9680] = 3465.
3465 + <5643> = **9108**.

3465 . . . 34[6 + 5 = 11] . . . 3411 + <1143> = **4554**.
4554 . . . 4 days / 554 weeks = 3882 days . . . **3882**, the Unlettered Prophet.

29:16 = 1756 minutes + <61> = 1817 . . . **(18)/1/7**, You have made the bed as far as you could. Now it is up to Me.

[2916 = <6192>] / 12 = 516
516 minutes = 8:36 . . . **836**, see above.
516 + <615> = 1131 minutes = 18:51 . . . **18/(51)** falls on **{17}/11/10** ↔
17/11/10, I cannot talk with you about your world unless you know about Mine. Get out of My Car.

[<163> + <263> + <363> + <463> = **1252**] + [<563> + <663> + <763> + <863> = **2852**] = **4104**.
[4104 - <4014> = 90] + [2916 - <6192> = **3276**] = 3366 . . . 33:(66) = 1914 minutes . . . 19:14 is 7:14 PM . . . **714** ↔
[John: 10, 15, 8,14] + [Kordupel: 11,15,18, 4, 21, 16, 5, 12] = 11,151,843,132,326:
We separate 11,151,843,132,326 into two groups of seven, to which we add our birthday:
1115184 . . . 1115 + 184 = 1299; 2/03/194{6} + 3132326 = 5164272; 5164 + 272 + 1299 = 6735.
[6735 = <5376>] - [3992 = <2993>] = **2383**.
2993 . . . [2 * 9 = 18]93 . . . **1893**, the Chain of Rebirth.

29:93 = 1 day / 5:93 . . . **1593**.
Thessalonians 2:1 to 2:4 discusses the Second Coming . . .
([2^1 = 2] [2^2 = 4] [2^3 = 8] [2^4 = 16] . . . 24816) + [2:01 + 2:02 + 2:03 + 2:04 = 810] = 25626.
25:626 = 2126 minutes + <626> = 2752 . . . 27:(52) = 1568 minutes + <25> = **1593**.

13/1/{6}, or 13/1/7, You have made the bed as far as you could. Now it is up to Me →
[13:16 = 796 minutes . . . 796] + [13:17 = 797 minutes . . . 797] = **1593**.

23:83 = 1463 minutes . . . **1463**, John Kordupel.

2383 . . . 238 * 3 = **714**, John Kordupel ↔ **714**, the Four Horsemen.
and,
714 . . . 71^4 = 2541 1681 . . . 2541 + 1681 = **4222**, Market Forces, an expression of the Collective Will.

714, John Kordupel + 1414, Jesus + 1414, the Four Horsemen = **3542**, eschatology ↔

Eschatology, literally 'Discourse about the Last Things . . . Regeneration of the human race. Encarta Encyclopedia. Doctrine of death, judgement, heaven, & hell. Concise Oxford Dictionary.

3542 = <2453>

[John: 10, 15, 8,14] + [Kordupel: 11,15,18, 4, 21, 16, 5, 12] = 11,151,843,132,326:
We separate 11,151,843,132,326 into two groups of seven, to which we add our birthday:
[1115184 . . . 1115 + 184 = 1299] + [3132326 + 2/03/194{6} = 5164272 . . . 5164 + 272 = 5436] = 6735.
(6735 - [47/34, my birth day + **1433** = **6167**, Fo-Hi] = 568) + <865> = **1433**.
Genesis 11:6. And the Lord said, Behold, the people is one, and they have all one language; and this they begin to do: and now nothing will be restrained from them, which they have imagined to do.
Genesis 11:6 + 13/1/7, the making of beds = **1433**.

6735 - [6167 . . . 616 * 7 − 4312] = 2423.
24:23 = 1463 minutes . . . **1463**, John Kordupel.

2423 . . . 2 days / (4:23) = 43:77 - <324> = 4053 . . . 40:53 = 2453 minutes . . . **2453**.

2250, New Harmonic Vibrations . . . 2 days / (250) =45:50 - <052> = 4498 . . . 44:(98) = 2542 minutes - <89> = **2453**.

And,

Eschatology, Doctrine of death, judgement, heaven, & hell. ↔

6:8. And I looked, and behold a pale horse: and his name that sat on him was Death, and Hell followed with him. And power was given unto them over the the fourth part of the earth, to kill with sword, and with hunger, and with death, and with the beasts of the earth.

[√68 = 82462112] + [68 . . . 6√8 = 10330248] + [√6:08 = 24657656] = **117450016**, the pale horse of Death

1174, the pale horse of Death - <4711> = 3537 . . . 35 * 3 * 7 = 735 . . . 7:(35) is 6:25 . . . **625**, Robert begins to tidy things up.

50016, the pale horse of Death . . . [5001 - <1005> = 3996] / 6 = **666**, the Heart-Beat grid.

3996 . . . 3 * 99 * 6 = **1782**, the Second Coming.

[625 + 666 = 1291 . . . 12 * 91 = 1092] + <526> = 1618.

1618 . . . 1 (6)/18 is **18/25** . . . 18:25 is 6:25 PM . . . **625**, Robert needs 14 days to tidy things up.

16:18 = 1 day / (782) . . . {17}/8/2, the 14 days are up.

[1174 - <4711> = 3537] – [500 + 16 = 516] = 3021, the pale horse of Death

30:21 = 1821 minutes . . . 18:(21) = 1059 minutes . . . **1059**, a page in the life of . . .

1821 * 5 = **9105**, I cannot talk with you about your world unless you know about Mine. Get out of My Car.

[3021 + <1203> = 4224] – [666 + 625 1782 = 3073] = 1151 . . . 11:51 = 711 minutes . . . **711**, a Cycle ends.

([1174 + <4711> = 3537 = <7353>] + [625 + 666 = 1291] = 8644) – [50016 - <61005> = 10989] + <526> = **11515**) = **2871**.

Buddha: 40 116 122 34

116:122 – 34:40 = 112682 . . . <286211> . . . ([286 + 2 = 288] -1 = 287)1 . . . **2871** ↔ **2871**, Pahana ↔

We combine my name with my birth day:

[John: 10, 15, 8,14] + [Kordupel: 11,15,18, 4, 21, 16, 5, 12] = 11,151,843,132,326:

We separate 11,151,843,132,326 into two groups of seven, to which we add our birthday:

1115184 . . .1115 + 184 = 1299 . . . 12:(99) = 621 minutes . . . **621** . . . 6:21 PM is 18:21 . . . 1821.

and,

34/194{6} + 3132326 = 3474272 . . . 3474 + 272 + 1299 = 5045.

5045 . . . 50 * 45 = **2250**, New Harmonic Vibrations + **621** = **2871** ↔

and,

27/9/5, I am advised that corporate issues have been resolved, that Robert Loomis needs a couple of weeks to tidy up his desk in order to fully concentrate on the task ahead.

27/9/5 is {4}/(95) . . . [495 * 7 = 3465 = <5643>] - ([495 = <594>] * 7 = 4158 = <8514>) = **2871** ↔ <1782>

[50016 - <61005> = 10989] + <526> = **11515**, the pale horse of Death.

115:15 is (4:45) / 5 days . . . **4455**, the pale horse of Death ↔

16:25. And this is the writing that was written, MENE, MENE, TEKEL, UPHARSIN.

16:28. PERES; thy kingdom is divided, and given to the Medes and Persians. Daniel.

MENE, MENE, TEKEL, UPHARSIN / PERES: 297 380 407 270

[297 + 380 + 407 + 270 = **1354**] + [<792> + <083> + <704> + <072> = **1651** + <1561> = 3212] = **4566**.

{ ([4566 - <6654 = 2088] + <8802> = 10890) / 2 = 5445 } + **1782** = **7227**, Book-End.

[4566 + <6654> = 11220] - [4566 - <6654 = 2088] = 9132
9132 + <2319> = 11451
11451 – ([20:88 = 1288 minutes . . . 1288] + <8821> = **10109**, Eve) = **1342**.
11451 – [1288 + <8802> = **10090**] = **1361** ↔ {13}/6/(1), Gina / manuscript
[11451 = <15411>] + **1342**, Second Coming + {13}/6/(1) = 18114
[18114 - <41181> = 23067] + [18114 + <41181> = 59295] = 135 327
135327 . . . [135 + <531> = **666**] + [327 - <723> = **396**] = 1062
1062 - <2601> = **1539**, John Kordupel
1062 + 1342 + 1361 = 3765
3765 / 3 = **1255**, Second Coming.
3765 / 5 = 753 . . . **(7)/5/3**, Robert / manuscript.
<357> . . . 35 to 7 is 6:25 . . . **625**.
135327 – [10109 + 10090 = 20199 + <99102> = 11930] = **16026**.

16/02/6, is contact with Robert imminent?

([11451 = <15411>] - **16026** = 615) + <516> = 1131 . . . 1131 minutes = 18:51
18/(5)/1 is **18/26** . . . 1826 minutes = 30:26 = 1 day / 6:26 . . . **16/2/6**.
18/26 is {17}/26 . . . 17:26 is 5:26 PM . . . **526** ↔ <625>

9132 . . . 913² = 833 569 . . . <338> + 569, Jesus = **907**, an Invitation to change the Language.
833 + <965>, John Kordupel = 1798 . . .
17:98 = 1118 minutes . . . **1/11/8**, Cher passed away ↔
17/9/8, Leanne / Reading.

[4566 + <6654> = 11220] – [2088 = <8802>] = 2418.
2418 / 3 = 806 = <608> . . . **6:08**, Revelations, the Four Horsemen.
2418 . . . [2⁴ = 16]18 . . . **1618**.
1618 . . . 1 (6)/18 is **18/25** . . .
1825 + {13}/6/(1), Gina / manuscript = **3186**.
(318)/6, is contact with Robert imminent?
18:25 is 6:25 PM . . . **625**, Robert needs 14 days to tidy things up.
[625 + 3186 = 3811] - <526> = 3285
32:(85) = 1835 minutes + <58> = **1893** ↔
the Chain of Rebirth

16:18 = 1 day / (782) . . . **{17}/8/2**, the 14 days are up.

[1354 + 1651 = 3005 - <5003> = 1998] + [1354 + <1561> = 2915 - <5192> = 2277] + 2088 = **6363**.
<4531> + 1651 = 6182; <4531> + <1561> = 6092; <4531> + 3212 = 7743.
[6182 - <2816> = 3366] + [6092 - <2906> = 3186] + [7743 - <3477> = **4266**, Jesus] = 10818.
10818 – 6363 = **4455** ↔

Lao Tzu: 95 61 67 89 . . .
95:61 . . . ([9 + 5 = 14]61 . . . 1461] + <1641> = 3102) + <2013> = 5115 . . . **(51)/{15}**, a Playground.
67:89 . . . 6789 . . . 6 * 7 * 8 * 9 = **3024**
30:24 = 1824 minutes - <42> = **1782**.

3024 + <4203> = **7227**, Book-End.

6789 . . . 6[7 * 8 = 56]9 . . . 6569.
6569 + <9656> + 5115 + <5115> = 26455 . . . [-2 + 6 = 4]455 . . . **4455**.

[John: 10, 15, 8,14] + [Kordupel: 11,15,18, 4, 21, 16, 5, 12] = 11,151,843,132,326
[1115 + 184 + 313 + 2326 = 2639] = 3938) - <8393> = **4455**.

4455, Untitled One + [<**5544**> / 2 = 2772, Know Me] = **7227**, Book-End.
<5544>, Fo-Hi ↔ 5544 . . . 554 weeks / 4 days = 3882 days . . . **3882**, the Unlettered Prophet.

115:15 = 5 days / (4:45) . . . **5445**, the pale horse of Death + **1782** = **7227**, Book-End.

1174 + 500 + 16 + 61 = **1751**, the pale horse of Death . . . {17}/(51) falls on {17}/11/10 ↔

17/11/10, I cannot talk with you about your world unless you know about Mine. Get out of My Car.

And,
Eschatology, Doctrine of death, judgement, heaven, & hell. ↔

6:8. And I looked, and behold a pale horse: and his name that sat on him was Death, and Hell followed with him. And power was given unto them over the the fourth part of the earth, to kill with sword, and with hunger, and with death, and with the beasts of the earth.

[√<86> = 92736184] + [<86> . . .8√6 = 10070235] + [√<806> = 28390139] = 131196558 . . . 131 196 558
([131 + 196 + 558 = **885**] + <588> = **1473**) + ([<131> + <691> + <855> = **1677**] + <7761> = **9438**) = **10911**.

[885 + 1677 = **2562**] + [885 + <7761> = **8646**] + [885 + 9438 = **10323**] + [885 + <11901> = **12786**] = **34317**.
<2652> + <6468> + <32301> + <68721> = **110142**.

34317, the pale horse of Death . . . [-3 + 4 = 1]317 . . . 1317 ↔ **13/1/7**, You have made the bed as far as you could. Now it is up to Me.

34317, the pale horse of Death + <71343> = 105660 . . . 105 + <501> + 660 + <066> = **1332**.
Yahweh: 25,1,8,23,5,8 . . . 2518 . . . ([2 + 5 = 7] – [1 + 8 = 9] = -2) + [2358 . . . 23 * 58 = 1334] = **1332**.
1716, Anakhita . . . (1716 + [17:16 = 5:16 PM = <6:15> = 375 minutes . . . 375] + <573> = 2664) / 2 = **1332**.

Genesis. 1:27 . . . 12^7 = *358* 31808 . . . [1808 + <8081> = 9889] – [3583 + <3853> = 7436] = 2453.
2453 = <3542>, eschatology – [Genesis 1:27 . . . 358 + <853> = 1211] = 2331 = <**1332**>
1332 / 2 = **666**, the Heart-Beat grid, the Number of Man.

the Eastern influence:
Fo-Hi: 38 66 70 34 . . . [<83>66] – 7034 = **1332**.
Confucius: 111 123 132 102 . . . [111 + 123 + 132 + 102 = 468] + <864> = **1332**.
Lao Tzu: 95 61 67 89 . . . 95 + 61 + 67 + 89 = 312; [<59> + <16> + <76> + <98> = 249] + <942> = 1191.
([312 + 249 = 561] + [312 + <942> = 1254] + [312 + 1191 = 1503] = 3318) / 3 = 11:06 = 666 minutes . . . 666 * 2
= **1332**.
and,
95:61 . . . 9 * 5 * 6 * 1 * 6 * 7 * 8 * 9 = 816 480 . . . ([816 + <618> + 480 + <084> = 1998] / 3 = 666) * 2 = **1332**.

Buddha: 40 116 122 34

([40 + 116 + 122 + 34 = 312] + <213> = 525) - ([<04> + <611> + <221> + <43> = 879] + <978> = 1857) = **1332**.

the Western influence:

The Lamb's wives making a statement concerning who their husbands are:

Eve / Bathsheba / Esther / Khadija / Yasodhara / Mary Magdalene / Cherryl Dianne Kordupel: **666** 1102 1170 598.

    666 + [1102 - <2011> = 909] + 1170 - <0711> = 459 + [598 - <895> = 297] = 2331 = <**1332**>

The Second Epistle of Paul the Apostle to the Thessalonians discusses the Second Coming:

2:1. "Now we beseech you, brethren, by the coming of our Lord Jesus Christ, and by our gathering together unto him.

2:2. That ye be not soon shaken in mind, or be troubled, neither by spirit, nor by word, nor by letter as from us, as that the day of Christ is at hand.

2:3. Let no man deceive you by any means: for that day shall not come, except there come a falling away first, and that man of sin be revealed, the son of perdition;

2:4. Who opposeth and exalteth himself above all that is called God, or that is worshipped; so that he as God sitteth in the temple of God, shewing himself that he is God. The Bible. the King James Version.

    [21 + 22 + 23 + 24 = 90] + [21 * 22 * 23 * 24 = 255024] = 255114 . . . 255 + <552> + 114 + <411> = **1332**.

1332 / 2 = 666] * 3 = **1998**, Vatican . . . so that he as God sitteth in the temple of God, shewing himself that he is God.

1332 = <2331> . . . 23 * 31 = **713**, the Season ends.

110142, the pale horse of Death - <241011> = 130869 . . . 130 + <031> + 869 + <968> = **1998**.

5:1. Belshazzar the king made a great feast to a thousand of his lords, and drank wine before the thousand.

5:2. Belshazzar, while he tasted the wine, commanded to bring the golden and the silver vessels which his father Nebuchadnezzar had taken out of the temple which was in Jerusalem; that the king, and his princes, his wives, and his concubines, might drink therein.

5:3. Then they bought the golden vessels that ere taken out of the temple of the house of God which was at Jerusalem; and the king, and the princes, his wives, and his concubines, drank in them.

5:4. They drank wine and praised the gods of gold, and of silver, of brass, or iron, of wood, and of stone.

5:5. In the same hour came forth fingers of a man's hand, and wrote over against the candlesticks upon the plaister of the wall of the king's palace: and the king saw the part of the hand that wrote.

16:24. Then was the part of the hand sent from him; and this writing was written.

16:25. And this is the writing that was written, MENE, MENE, TEKEL, UPHARSIN. Daniel. Holy Bible. King James Version.

    MENE, MENE, TEKEL, UPHARSIN, God's Hand writing: 234 313 335 212.

        [234:313 – 335:212 = 100 899] + [313:234 – 212:335 = 100 899] = 201798.

        ([234:313 – 212:335 = 21978] + [313:234 – 335:212 = 21978] = 43956) + 201798 = 245 754

        245 + <542> + 754 + <457> = **1998**, God's Hand writing.

16:25. And this is the writing that was written, MENE, MENE, TEKEL, UPHARSIN.

16:28. PERES; thy kingdom is divided, and given to the Medes and Persians. Daniel.

    MENE, MENE, TEKEL, UPHARSIN / PERES, God's Hand writing: 297 380 407 270

        ([297 + 380 + 407 + 270 = 1354] + [<792> + <083> + <704> + <072> = 1651] = 3005) - <5003> = **1998**.

and,

the Hero, the Truth and the Light: 288 310 333 265 . . . 288310 - 333265 = 44955; 44955 / 5 = 8991 = <**1998**>.

Lao Tzu: 95 61 67 89 . . . 9 * 5 * 6 * 1 * 6 * 7 * 8 * 9 = 816 480 . . . 816 + <618> + 480 + <084> = **1998**.
Krishna: 80 102 109 73 . . . [80:102 – 73:109 = 6993 = <3996>] / 2 = **1998**.
Confucius: 111 123 132 102 . . . 111123 – 102132 = 8991 = <**1998**>.
Buddha: 40 116 122 34 . . . 40:116 = 2516 minutes . . . 2516; 34:122 = 2162 minutes . . . 2162.
    2516 + <6152> + 2162 + <2612> = 13442 . . . [-1 + 3442 = 3441] - <1443> = **1998**.

Abraham / Ibri: 82164 – 71215 = 10949 . . . 10:949 = 1549 minutes . . . [1549 + **1782**, the Second Coming = 3331] - <1333> = **1998**.
Moussa: 88 68 72 82 . . . [88<86> + 72<28> = 16114] - [68<28> + 7288 = 14116] = **1998**.

John (Eeevash) Kordupel . . . the space in-between: 400 546 . . . 400546 - <645004> = 244458 . . . 244 + <442> + 458 + <854> = **1998**.

China: 3,8,9,14,1 . . . 3 + 8 + 9 + 14 + 1 = 35 . . . ([35 * 35 = 1225] - <5221> = **3996**) / 2 = **1998**.
and,
34:25. And I will make with them a covenant of peace, and will cause the evil beasts to cease out of the land: and they shall dwell safely in the wilderness, and sleep in the woods. Ezekiel. Holy Bible. King James Version.
34:25, taking the evil beasts out of the land: 34:25 is 10:25 / 1 day . . . [10:251 = 851 minutes + <152> = 1003] - <3001> = **1998**.

110142, the pale horse of Death + <241011> = 351153
351153 . . . 3 * (-5 + [11:53 = 713 minutes - <317> = 396] = 391 . . . 391 minutes = 6:31 . . . 631) = **1893**, rediscovery of the Forms of Life.
        3511 = **1893**, a rediscovery + 1618.
            1618 . . . 1/(6)/18 is **18/25**
                18:25 is 6:25 PM . . . **625**, Robert needs 14 days to tidy things up.
              16:18 = 1 day / (782) . . . {17}/8/2, Robert's 14 days are up.

    351153 . . . [3 / 5115 = 1705] * 3 = 5115 . . . **(51)/{15}**, it certainly is your Playground.

And,
Eschatology, Doctrine of death, judgement, heaven, & hell. ↔

6:8. And I looked, and behold a pale horse: and his name that sat on him was Death, and Hell followed with him. And power was given unto them over the the fourth part of the earth, to kill with sword, and with hunger, and with death, and with the beasts of the earth.

    [√<86> = 92736184] + [<86> . . .8√6 = 10070235] + [√<806> = 28390139] = 131196558 . . . 131 196 558
      ([131 + 196 + 558 = **885**] + <588> = **1473**) + ([<131> + <691> + <855> = **1677**] + <7761> = **9438**) = **10911**.

[885 + 1677 = **2562**] + [885 + <7761> = **8646**] + [885 + 9438 = **10323**] + [885 + <11901> = **12786**] = **34317**.
    <2652> + <6468> + <32301> + <68721> = **110142**.

[<588> + 1677 = **2265**] + [<588> + <7761> = **8349**] + [<588> + 9438 = **10026**] + [<588> + <11901> = **12489**] = **33129**.
    <5622> + <9438> + <62001> + <98421> = **175482**.

33129, the pale horse of Death . . . 33:(129) = 1851 minutes . . . **1851**.
    1851 minutes + <921> = **2772**, Know Me.
    ([1851 = <1581>] + <921> = 2502) + <2052> = **4554** . . . 4 days / 554 weeks = 3882 days . . . **3882**, the Unlettered Prophet.

175482, the pale horse of Death . . . ([175 + 482 = 657] + <756> = 1413) + ([<571> + <284> = 855] + <558> = 1413) = 2826.
2826 + <6282> = **9108**.

5125, years, a Galactic cycle . . . 5 days / 1:25 = 121:25 . . . 12125 - <521> = 11604 . . . 116:(04) = 6956 minutes + <40> = 6996.

6996 . . . [-6 + 9 = 3]96 . . . **396**; 6996 . . . 699 – 6 = **693**.
Yahweh: 25,1,8,23,5,8 . . .2518 + 2358 = 4876 . . .[4 * 8 = 32 + 7 = 39]6 . . .**396** ↔
Anakhita: 65 143 151 57 . . . [151:57 – 143:65 = 792] / 2 = 396.
and,
[2772, Gaia – 1921, Eve = 851] - <158> = **693**.

6996 . . . 69 * 96 = 6624 = <**4266**>, Jesus; 6996 . . . 699 * 6 = **4194**.
Lemuria, Atlantis, Avalon: 240 306 327 219 . . .
[240 + 306 + 327 + 219 = 1092] + [<042> + <603> + <723> + <912> = 2280 + <0822> = 3102] = **4194**.

tidying up Lemuria's, Atlantis' and Avalon's energy was Kali Yuga, Earth's dark night of the Soul:

[6996 – **1443**, Kali Yuga = 5553] + <3555> = **9108**.
and,
Crucifixion: 3,18,21,3,9,6,9,24,9,15,14. 3,182,139,692,491,514.
3,182,139,692,491,514 . . . 318 + <813> = 1131 . . . 1131 minutes = 18:51 . . . **18/(51)** is {17}/11/10 ↔
17/11/10, I cannot talk with you about your world unless you know about Mine. Get out of My Car.
leaving:
2,139,692,491,514 . . . ([2139 / 3 = 713] + [<9312> / 3 = 3104] = 3817
([3817 - <7183> = 3366] - <6633> = 3267) – 1851 = 1416 . . . **14/(1)/6**, Gina / manuscript.
3817 + [<296> + <194> + <415> = 905] = 4722.
4722 + <2274> = **6996** . . . 6 * 99 * 6 = 3564 = **1782**, Resurrection + **1782**, the Second Coming.

The I Ching: Heaven includes Earth, so Earth has the number 2, making 3 the number of heaven as 1 is too rigid and does not allow for the manifold . . . 3 + 2 = 5.
5√6996 = 13187168 . . . 13 + <31> + <1781> = **1825**.
18:25 is 6:25 PM . . . **625**, Robert needs 14 days to tidy things up.

1825 + 68 = **1893**, the Chain of Rebirth ↔ **1893**, rediscovery of the Forms of Life.

4722 – [692 + 491 + 514 = 1697] = 3025 . . . 30:25 – 1825 minutes . . . **1825**.
18/25 ↔ 18/2/(5), being **18/54** ↔

[3817 = <7183>] - [692 + <296> + 491 + <194> + 514 + <415> = 2602] = 4581 = <**1854**>
18/54 + Robert needs 14 days to tidy things up brings us to **18/9/3**.

and,

China: 3,8,9,14,1 . . . 389 + <983> + 141 + <141> = 1654.
16:54 = 1014 minutes + <45> = 1059 . . . **1059**, a page in the life of China.

1654 = <4561> . . . 45:(61) = 2639 minutes . . . 2639.
26:(39) = 1521 minutes + <93> = 1614 . . . 16:14 = 974 minutes . . . 9 * 74 = **666**.
2639 minutes - <16> = 2623 . . . 26:23 = 1583 minutes - <32> = 1551 . . .

{15}/(51), it certainly is your Playground.
and,
[1059 + 666 + 1551 = 3276] - <6723> = 3447 . . . **34/47**, my birth day.

[1654 + <4561> = 6215] – 3276 = 2939 . . . 29:39 is 1 day / 5:39 . . . **1539**, John Kordupel.

1654 . . . 1 day / 6:54 = 30:54 = 1854 minutes . . . **1854**.
 [1854 = <4581>] + 974 + <479> = 6034.
  [6034 . . . 603 * 4 = 2412] + <2142> = **4554**.
   4554 . . . 4 days + 554 weeks = 3882 days . . . **3882**, the Unlettered Prophet.

6034 = [34/47, my birth day = <7443>] + **1409**, John Kordupel

60:34 = 3634 minutes + <43> = 3677
 3677 . . . 36 * 77 = **2772**, Know Me.
 36:77 = 2237 minutes + <77> = 2314.
  2314 . . . 231 * 4 = 924 . . . 924 minutes = 14:84
  14/8/4, I'll see you tomorrow.

   23:(14) = 1366 minutes - <41> = 1325 . . . 13:25 = 805 minutes . . .
   805, End of Days.

   23:14 = 1394 minutes + <41> = **1435** ↔
    2155720, I Am/ God/ Allah/ Jahwe . . . 2155 – 720 = **1435**.
    14:(35) = 815 minutes . . . **815**, Messiah.
    and,
    1435, I Am/ God/ Allah/ Jahwe + 815, Messiah = **2250**.
    1854 – 34/47, my birth day = **1593** ↔
Thessalonians 2:1 to 2:4 discusses the Second Coming . . .
[2^1 = 2] [2^2 = 4] [2^3 = 8] [2^4 = 16] . . . 24816
 24816 + [2:01 + 2:02 + 2:03 + 2:04 = 810] = 25626.
  25:626 = 2126 minutes + <626> = 2752 . . .
   27:(52) = 1568 minutes + <25> = **1593**.

   13/1/{6}, or 13/1/7, You have made the bed as far as you could. Now it is up to Me
   [13:16 = 796 minutes . . . 796] + [13:17 = 797 minutes . . . 797] = **1593**.

Yi - King: 25, 9 - 11, 9, 14, 7 . . . [25 * 9 = 225] - [11 * 9 * 14 * 7 = 9702 =<2079>] = **1854**.

 the tidying up involves China and includes the I Ching (Yi-King)

Avatar: In Hinduism Avatar refers to a deliberate descent of a deity from heaven to earth, and is mostly translated into English as "incarnation" but more accurately as "appearance" or "manifestation.
 Wikipedia Encyclopedia.
Avatar: 1,22,1,20,1,18: [122 + 120 + 118 = 360] + [1221 + 20118 = **21339**] = **21699**.
 21:339 = 1599 minutes - <933> = **666**.
  Fo-Hi / Krishna / Buddha / Lao Tzu / Confucius: 364 468 500 243
   364:468 – 500:243 = 135775, the Eastern influence; where East meets West:
    135 + <531> ⁻ **666**.

775 . . . [7 * 7 = 49]5 . . . 495 minutes = 8:15 . . . **815**, Messiah; <594> * 3 = **1782**, the Second Coming.

775 + [666 + <666> = 1332 = <2331>] = **3106**.

31:(06) = 1854 minutes . . . **1854**.

21:(339) = 921 minutes + <933> = **1854**.

21339 / 3 = **7113**.

Kalki: [968 minutes = 15:68 . . . 1568] + [949 minutes = 15:49 . . . 1549] = 3117.

([3117 + **3106** = 6223] - <3226> = 2997 = <7992>) / 12 = **666**.

3117 ↔ <**7113**> . . . **7/1/13**, You have made the bed as far as you could. Now it is up to Me.

starting from 625, Robert needs a couple of weeks to tidy things up:

1782, Robert . . . { ([1 + 7 = 8]82 . . . 882) + ([- 1 + 7 = 6]82 . . . 682) = 1564 } + <4651> = 6215.

6215 . . . [62 * 1 = 62]5 . . . 625, Robert begins to tidy things up.

(6215 - [<5126>] + 4554 = 9680] = 3465) + <5643> = **9108**.

9108 = [**3882**, the Unlettered Prophet . . . 3882 days = 4 days / 554 weeks . . . 4554] + **4554** ↔

John Kordupel, 1409 + 1463 + <9041> + <3641> = 15554 . . . [-1 + 5 = 4]554 . . . **4554**.

2826 . . . [2 * 8 = 16]26 . . . **16/2/6**, is contact with Robert imminent?

28:(26) = 1654 minutes + <62> = 1716 . . . {17}/1/(6) is **18/25**.

28:26 = 1706 minutes + <62> = 1768 . . . {17}/68 falls on {17}/3/9

17:39 = 1059 minutes . . . **1059**, a page in the life of . . .

14/8/4, I'll see you tomorrow at 815 . . . 14:84 = 924 minutes . . . 924 + 815 = **1739** ↔

{17}/**39** falls on {17}/8/2, Robert's 14 days for tidying things up are up.

and,

9108, the pale horse of Death = **16/2/6**, is contact with Robert imminent? + **18/25** + {17}/**39** + **3/9/18**.

9108 = <8019> . . . **80/19** falls on **19/21/3** ↔

19/2/13, D/M/Y, Mayan prediction of the beginning of the Age of Aquarius.

And,

Eschatology, Doctrine of death, judgement, heaven, & hell. ↔

6:8. And I looked, and behold a pale horse: and his name that sat on him was Death, and Hell followed with him. And power was given unto them over the the fourth part of the earth, to kill with sword, and with hunger, and with death, and with the beasts of the earth.

[√68 = 82462112] + [68 . . . 6√8 = 10330248] + [√6:08 = 24657656] = 117450016.

[√<86> = 92736184] + [<86> . . .8√6 = 10070235] + [√<806> = 28390139] = 131196558

117450016 + 131196558 = 248646574 . . . 248 646 574

248 + 646 + 574 = 1468; <842> + <646> + <475> = 1963.

1468 + <8641> = **10109**.

Kali Yuga, Earth's dark cycle: 416 + <614> + 1217 + <7121> = 9368 . . . [93:68 = 5648 minutes + <86> = 5734] + <4375> = **10109**.

my birth day: [3/02 + 19{46} + 1947 = 4195] – (25/02) = 1693 . . . (1 + (6 * [9³ = 729] = 4374) = 4375) + <5734> = **10109**.
101:09 = 5:09 / 4 days . . . 5094
    50:94 = 2 days / 2:94 . . . 22:94 = 1414 minutes . . . **1414**, Adam → 1414 + <49> = **1463**, John Kordupel
    50:94 = 2:94 / 2 days . . . 29:42 = 1782 minutes . . . **1782**, the Second Coming.
        2942 + 2294 = 5236.
          [5236 / 2 = 2618] - <8162> = 5544 . . . 554 weeks / 4 days = 3882 days . . . **3882**, the Unlettered Prophet.

    5236 + <6325> = 11561 . . . [-1 + 15 = 14]61 . . . **1461**.
      5238, God . . . 52:(38) = 3082 minutes - <83> = 2999 . . . 29:(99) = 1641 minutes . . . 1641 = <1461>
        1461, Adam & Eve, interwoven energy.

    1461 * 7 = 10227 . . . 10:227 = 827 minutes + <722> = **1549**, the Light ↔
    1461 . . . 1 day / 4:61 = 28:61 = 1741 minutes = <1471>
      1471 . . . 1 day / 4:71 = 28:71 = <1782>, the Second Coming.

    11634127, feng shi – **389141**, China = 11 244 986 . . .
      [112 + 4 = 116]4 . . . 1164 + 986 = 2150] - <689> = **1461** ↔
        3961, the fall of Babylon . . . [3 * 9 = 27 . . . 2 * 7 = 14]61 . . . **1461**.

  1370 . . . 13:70 = (10:30) / 1 day . . . 10:301 = 901 minutes = 14:61 . . . **1461**.
    and,

Planet:	16,	12,	1,	14,	5,	20:
Earth:		5,	1,	18,	20,	8
our:		15,	21,	18		
World:	23,	15,	18,	12,	4	

    reading the numbers vertically:
    1623 + 1,251,515 + 112,118 + 14,181,812 + 5,204 + 208 = 15,552,480 . . .
          1555 + 2480 = 4035 . . .
      40:35 = 2435 minutes - <53> = 2382 . . . 23:82 = 1462 minutes - <28> = 1434.
        (1434 . . . [14³ = 2744] – 4 = 2740] / 2 = **1370**.

    Babylon: 9450 – 4095 = 5355 . . . 53:(55) = 3125 minutes - <55> = 3070 minutes . . . 3070.
      3070 = 2221, Earth / metamorphosis + 849 . . .
        849 minutes = 14:09 . . . 1409, John Kordupel
        849 minutes = 15:(51) . . . **{15}/(51)**, it certainly is your playground.
      3070 minutes = 50:70 = 2:70 / 2 days . . . 2702 – [2331, Babylon = <1332>] = **1370**.

    1111, John Eevash Kordupel . . . 1111 . . . [11 * 11 = 121] + [11:11 = 12:(49) . . . 1249] = **1370**.

    13/1/7, You have made the bed as far as you could. Now it is up to Me:
    [200{6} + 2007 + 13/1 = 4144] + <4414> = 8558
    1317 minutes = 21:57 . . . 2157 minutes = 35:57 . . . 3557 minutes = 59:17 . . .
      5917 minutes = 97:97 . . . 9797.
        9797 + <7979> + 8558 = 26334 . . . 26:334 = 1894 minutes . . . 1894.

    1894 . . . 1:89/4 days = 9789 + <981> = 10770 . . . 10:770 = 1370 minutes . . . **1370**.

      1370 minutes = 22:50 . . . **2250**, New Harmonic Vibrations.

And,

Eschatology, Doctrine of death, judgement, heaven, & hell. ↔

6:8. And I looked, and behold a pale horse: and his name that sat on him was Death, and Hell followed with him. And power was given unto them over the the fourth part of the earth, to kill with sword, and with hunger, and with death, and with the beasts of the earth.

[√68 = 82462112] + [68 . . . 6√8 = 10330248] + [√6:08 = 24657656] = 117450016.
[√<86> = 92736184] + [<86> . . .8√6 = 10070235] + [√<806> = 28390139] = 131196558
117450016 + 131196558 = 248646574 . . . 248 646 574
248 + 646 + 574 = **1468**; <842> + <646> + <475> = **1963**.

1468 - <8641> = 7173; 1963 - <3691> = 1728
7173 – 1728 = **5445**.
Anakhita: 65 143 151 57 . . . ([151:57 – 143:65 = 792] * 4 = 3168) - <8613> = **5445**.
3168 + 8613 = 11781 . . . [1 + 1781 = **1782**, Anakhita] + 5445 = **7227**, Book-End.

3222, the Hero, the Truth and the Light + <2223> = **5445**, the Hero, the Truth and the Light.
2223 . . . 2 divided into [22³ = 10648] = 5324; 5324 = **1782**, the Second Coming + **3542**, eschatology.

John Kordupel, format ↔ synthesis: 53 159 167 145.
([153 + 159 + 167 = 479] + <974> = 1453) + [145 + <541> = 686] = 2139.
{ ([1:45 is 2:(15) . . . 215] + [<5:41> being 6:(19) . . . 619] = 834) + <438> = 1272 + 2139 = 3411 } + <1143> = **5445**.
and,

11:1. And there was given me a reed like unto a rod: and the angel stood saying, Rise and measure the temple of God, and the altar, and them that worship therein.

11:19. And the temple of God was opened in heaven, and there was seen in his temple the ark of his testament: and there were lightnings, and voices, and thunderings, and an earthquake, and great hail.

14:14. And I looked, and behold a white cloud, and upon the cloud one sat like unto the Son of man, having on his head a golden crown, and in his hand a sharp sickle.

14:15. And another angel came out of the temple, crying to him that sat on the cloud, Thrust in thy sickle, and reap: for the time has come for thee to reap; for the harvest of the earth is ripe. Revelations. Holy Bible. King James Version.
the authority to measure, the authority to reap: [111 + 1119 + 1414 + 1415 = 4059] - <9504> = **5445**.
5445, time to reap + **1782**, the Second Coming = **7227**, Book-End.

[7173 = <3717>] - [1728 = <8271>] = **4554** . . . 4 days / 554 weeks = 3882 days . . . **3882**, the Unlettered Prophet.
and,
4554, Unlettered Prophet + 5445 =, time to reap9999 . . . [9 * 9 * 9 = 6561] + <1656> = **8217**
John Eevash Kordupel: 209 153 266 191 . . .
([209 + 153 + 266 + 191 = 819] + [<902> + <351> + <662> + <191> = 2106] = 2925) + <5292> = **8217**.
and,
the Five Horsemen updating the Scriptures: the Mahdi / the Second Coming / Maitreya / the Messiah / Kalki:
465 731 777 419.
[465 + 731 + 777 + 419 = 2392] + <2932> + [<564> + <137> + 777 + <914> = 2392] + <2932>
= 5324) = 10648.
2392 + 2392 = 4784; 2392 + 5324 = 7716; <4874> + <6177> = 11051.
2932 + 2932 = 5864; 2932 + 5324 = 8256; <4685> + <6528> = 11213.
[777:465 – 731:419 = 46046] - [11051 + 11213 = 22264] = 23782.

23782 . . . [-2 + 3 = 1]782 . . . **1782**, Resurrection, the 1,000 year reign of Jesus begins.
[23782 + <28731> = 52513] - [<15011> + <31211> = 46222] = **8217**.
8217 . . . [8 * 2 = 16]17 . . . 1617 ↔ **(16)/17**, next Reiki session ↔
1/(6)/{17} being **18/25** ↔ 18:25 is 6:25 PM . . . **625**, Robert begins to tidy things up.

And,

Eschatology, Doctrine of death, judgement, heaven, & hell. ↔

6:8. And I looked, and behold a pale horse: and his name that sat on him was Death, and Hell followed with him. And power was given unto them over the the fourth part of the earth, to kill with sword, and with hunger, and with death, and with the beasts of the earth.

$\sqrt{[608 + <806> = 1414]}$ = 3760 3191.
[3760 - <0673> = 3087] - [3191 - <1913> = 1278] = **1809** = **<9081>**
and,
17/11/10, know My world to know yours – 16/10/11, a Playground = **10099**
10099, the space in-between a Playground and knowing My world . . .

{ ([1009 * 9 = **9081**] + <1809> = 10890) / 2 = **5445** } + {17}/8/2 = **7227**, Book-End.

3760 3191 . . . <0673> + <1913> = **2586**, Intervention From Above.

Intervention from Above would mean that Robert has begun to tidy things up . . .

2586, Intervention = [2155720, I Am/ God/ Allah/ Jahwe . . . 2155 – 720 = **1435**] + **625** + **<526>**

And,

Eschatology, Doctrine of death, judgement, heaven, & hell. ↔

6:8. And I looked, and behold a pale horse: and his name that sat on him was Death, and Hell followed with him. And power was given unto them over the the fourth part of the earth, to kill with sword, and with hunger, and with death, and with the beasts of the earth.

[$\sqrt{68}$ = 82462112] + [68 . . . 6$\sqrt{8}$ = 10330248] + [$\sqrt{6:08}$ = 24657656] = 117450016.
[$\sqrt{<86>}$ = 92736184] + [<86> . . .8$\sqrt{6}$ = 10070235] + [$\sqrt{<806>}$ = 28390139] = 131196558
117450016 + 131196558 = 248646574 . . . 248 646 574
248 + 646 + 574 = **1468**; <842> + <646> + <475> = **1963**.

[$\sqrt{68}$ = 82462112] + [68 . . . 6$\sqrt{8}$ = 10330248] + [$\sqrt{6:08}$ = 24657656] = 117450016.
[$\sqrt{<86>}$ = 92736184] + [<86> . . .8$\sqrt{6}$ = 10070235] + [$\sqrt{<806>}$ = 28390139] = 131196558
$\sqrt{[608 + <806> = 1414]}$ = 37603191.
117450016 + 131196558 + 37603191 = 286249765 . . . 286 249 765
286 + 249 + 765 = **1300**; <682> + <942> + <567> = **1571**.

1300 + 1963 = 3263 . . . 32:(63) = 1857 minutes + <36> = **1893**, the Chain of Rebirth.

1571 + 1468 = 3039.
30:(39) = 1761 minutes . . . [<1671> + 39 = 1710 minutes] - <93> = 1617.
1617 ↔ **(16)/17**, next Reiki session ↔

16:17 is 4:17 PM = <714> . . . 71^4 = 2541 1681 . . . 2541 + 1681 = **4222**, Market Forces.

30:(39) = 1761 minutes . . . {17}/(6)/1 is **18/25** ↔ 18:25 is 6:25 PM . . . **625**, Robert begins to tidy things up.
30:39 = 1839 minutes . . . **18/39** is 14 days after **18/25** ↔ Robert has finished tidying things up.

30:(39) = 1761 minutes + <93> = 1854 . . . **18/54** is **18/2/(5)** ↔ 18:25 is 6:25 PM . . . **625**, Robert begins to tidy things up.
   and,
   1893, the Chain of Rebirth . . . **18/9/3**, Y/D/M is 14 days after **18/54**.

1300 + 1571 = 2871.
   2871 = <1782>, the Second Coming ↔ **1782**, the Chain of Rebirth ↔ {17}/8/2, being **18/39**.
   28:(71) = 1609 minutes + <17> = 1626 . . . **16/2/6**, is contact with Robert imminent?
   28:71 = 1751 minutes + <17> = 1768 . . . {17}/68 is **18/9/3**, which is 14 days after **18/54**.
      and,
   {17}/(51) falls on {17}/11/10 ↔
      17/11/10, I cannot talk with you about your world unless you know about Mine. Get out of My Car.

The New Testament was the source of those numbers.
   How does a man of understanding, of wisdom, sit, walk, talk?

What role the Scriptures?
For centuries, and centuries, and centuries, it has not mattered what your lodestar was.
Just ask Jesus.
The Eight Amigos would look back and ask, Why did we bother?
What have the Eight Amigos got to show for their effort? What has changed in 2,000 years?

         For the Amigos to have their say,
            the Seals must be broken.

There can be no Reconciliation with God while Spirit keeps telling Job 'I need more time'.

Spirit reckons that I haven't given Spirit enough time. That makes me just a story-teller, and what lodestar you do, or do not follow, is none of my business.

32. Magic Prayer - *"Speak your prayer, listen for the answer, act in faith."*
   Reversed.
   Self-will that goes unchecked can bring difficulties. Reversed, the *Magic Prayer* card is a sign that you mistakenly believe that your way is the only one. Could the path you're on be leading you to a place of regret, or could you be pursuing something that just isn't good for you? If so, you may be facing a painful lesson – and a lonely one, too. Perhaps it is time to pray, and meditate on your highest good and the highest good of all. Spirit may have other plans for you . . .
   The Enchanted Map Oracle Cards Guidebook. Colette Baron-Reid,

8. Holding Together.
   Six at the top means:
   He finds no head for holding together.
   Misfortune.

The head is the beginning. If the beginning is not right, there is no hope of a right ending. If we have missed the right moment for union and go on hesitating to give complete and full devotion, we shall regret the error when it is too late. The I Ching. Wilhelm / Baynes.

Seven titles including "a servant pursuing happiness for the people":
A man of rank would not have made the payment of a pension conditional.
When a man with rank can get away with that, it speaks volumes about the Chinese system, and especially about "Thought on Socialism with Chinese Characteristics for a New Era"

Still,
Mugabe was able to get away with abusing power for decades.
I guess it comes down to when exactly does Robert begin to tidy things up.
I would imagine that if you are reading this, then the tidying up has already begun.

2. The Receptive.
        Six at the beginning means:
        When there is hoarfrost underfoot,
        Solid ice is not far off.

Just as the light-giving power represents life, so the dark power, the shadowy, represents death. When the first hoarfrost comes in autumn, the power of darkness and cold is just at its beginning. After these first warning, signs of death will gradually multiply, until, in obedience to immutable laws, stark winter with its ice is here.
In life it is the same. After certain scarcely noticeable signs of decay have appeared, they go on increasing until final dissolution comes. But in life precautions can be taken by heeding the first signs of decay and checking them in time.

1. The Creative.
        Nine at the top means:
        Arrogant dragon will have cause to repent.

When a man seeks to climb so high that he loses touch with the rest of mankind, he becomes isolated, and this necessarily leads to failure. This line warns against titanic aspirations that exceed one's power. A precipitous fall would follow. The I Ching. Wilhelm / Baynes.

43. Break-through (Resoluteness).
        Nine at the beginning means:
        Mighty in the forward-striding toes.
        When one goes and is not equal to the task,
        One makes a mistake.

In times of a resolute advance, the beginning is especially difficult. We feel inspired to press forward but resistance is still strong; therefore we ought to gauge our own strength and venture only so far as we can go with certainty of success. To plunge blindly ahead is wrong, because it is precisely at the beginning that an unexpected setback can have the most disastrous results.
The I Ching. Wilhelm / Baynes.

Sleeping Dragon, Crouching Tiger: Sleeping Dragon.

Fo-Hi: 6,15 – 8,9 . . . (**61589** + [615 + 89 = **704**] = **62293**) / 7 = **8899**.

8899 . . . [8 + 8 = 16][9 * 9 = 18] . . . 16:18 is 1 day / (782) . . . **1782**, Fo-Hi → **1782**, Resurrection → **1782**, the Second Coming.

Fo-Hi: 6,15 – 8,9 . . . **61589** + [6 + 15 + 8 + 9 = **38**] + ([6 * 15 = 90] + 8 + 9 = **107**] + [6 * 15 * 8 * 9 = **6480**] = **68918**.
68918 . . . 6 * 8 * 9 * 1 * 8 = **3456**.
[68918 + <6543> = **75461**] - [3456 * 21 = 72576] = **2885**.
    Anakhita: 65 143 151 57 . . . 65143 + 57151 = 122294 . . . [12² = 144 * 2 = 288][9 – 4 = 5] . . . **2885**.

    3546 / 3 = 1152 . . . **11/(52)** weeks, Mary Magdalene is going to knock on your door.

[68918 - <81986> = 13068 = <86031>] - [61589, Fo-Hi = <98516>] = **12485**, Fo-Hi
    12485 . . . [-1 + 2 = 1]485 . . . 1 day / 4:85 = 28:85 . . . **2885**, Fo-Hi ↔
    Moses / Isiah / Jeremiah / Ezekiel / Jesus Christ / the Prophet Muhammad, the Western influence:
        616 814 869 561 . . .
        616814869561 . . . 6168 + 1486 + 9561 = 17215 . . . ([17² = 289] – 1 = 288)5 . . . **2885**.

    2885 . . . 2 days / (885) = 39:15 + <588> = 4503.
        45:03 = (297) / 2 days . . . 29:(72) = 1668 minutes . . . 1 day / 668 = 30:68 = 1868 minutes - <86> = **1782**.
        4503 = <3054> . . . 30:54 = 1854 minutes . . . **1854** ↔
        China: 3,8,9,14,1 . . . 389 + <983> + 141 + <141> = **1654**.
        16:54 = 1014 minutes + <45> = 1059 . . . **1059**, a page in the life of China
        1654 = <4561> . . . 45:(61) = 2639 minutes . . . 2639.
        26:(39) = 1521 minutes + <93> = 1614 . . . 16:14 = 974 minutes . . . 9 * 74 = 666.
        2639 minutes - <16> = 2623 . . . 26:23 = 1583 minutes - <32> = 1551 . . .
        15:(51) = 849 minutes = 14:09 . . . **1409**, John Kordupel ↔
        {15}/(51), it certainly is your Playground.

    [1654 + <4561> = 6215] – [1059 + 666 + 1551 = **3276**] = 2939
        29:39 is 1 day / 5:39 . . . **1539**, John Kordupel.
        and,
        3276 - <6723> = 3447 . . . **34/47**, my birth day.

1654, China . . . 16:(54) = 906 minutes . . . **90/{6}**, a marriage

1654 . . . 1 day / 6:54 = 30:54 = 1854 minutes . . . **1854**.
    18/54 is 18/2/(5) . . . 18:25 is 6:25 PM . . . **625**, the tidying up begins.

    the tidying up begins with a marriage.

1854 – **34/47** = **1593**.

Thessalonians 2:1 to 2:4 discusses the Second Coming . . .
    [2¹ = 2] [2² = 4] [2³ = 8] [2⁴ = 16] . . . 24816.
        24816 + [2:01 + 2:02 + 2:03 + 2:04 = 810] = 25626.
        25:626 = 2126 minutes + <626> = 2752 . . .
        27:(52) = 1568 minutes + <25> = **1593**.

7/3/31, a marriage = <1337> . . . 1337 * 7 = 9359 . . . 9 * 3 * 59 = **1593**.

{4}/5/9/(3), corporate issues resolved . . . [4 + 5 = 9]93 . . . 993 minutes = 15:93 . . . **1593**.

13/1/{6}, or 13/1/7, You have made the bed as far as you could. Now it is up to Me →
[13:16 = 796 minutes . . . 796] + [13:17 = 797 minutes . . . 797] = **1593**.

Fo-Hi / Krishna / Buddha / Lao Tzu / Confucius: 364 468 500 243
   364:468 – 500:243 = 135775, the Eastern influence; where East meets West:
      135 + <531> = **666**.
      775 . . . [7 * 7 = 49]5 . . . 495 minutes = 8:15 . . . **815**, Messiah; <594> * 3 = **1782**, the Second
      Coming.
      775 + [666 + <666> = 1332 = <2331>] = 3106 . . . 31:(06) = 1854 minutes . . . **1854**.

Avatar: "In Hinduism Avatar refers to a deliberate descent of a deity from heaven to earth, and is mostly translated into English as "incarnation" but more accurately as "appearance" or "manifestation". Wikipedia Encyclopedia.
Avatar: 1,22,1,20,1,18: [122 + 120 + 118 = 360] + [1221 + 20118 = 21339] = 21699.
      21:339 = 1599 minutes - <933> = **666**.
      21:(339) = 921 minutes + <933> = **1854**.

[68918 - <81986> = 13068] - **12485** = 583 = <385> . . . 385 minutes = 6:25 . . . **625**, Fo-Hi →

625, Robert begins to tidy things up, and it begins with Fo-Hi, a knock on the door and a marriage.

and,
Fo-Hi: 6,15 – 8,9 . . . **61589** + [6 + 15 + 8 + 9 = **38**] + ([6 * 15 = 90] + 8 + 9 = **107**] + [6 * 15 * 8 * 9 = **6480**] = **68918**.

[68918 = <81986>] - 61589, Fo-Hi = **20397**.

[20:(397) = 803] * 9 = **7227**, Book-End

20397 = **666** + [Earth enters Age of Aquarius: (10)12 + 12/356] + [Age of Aquarius begins + 50/13 + 13/50].

203:97 = (12:03) / 9 days . . . 120:39 = 5 days / 0:39 . . . **5039**, Fo-Hi.
      50:39 = 2 days / 2:39 . . . 22:(39) = 1281 minutes = <1821> . . . 18:(21) = 1059 minutes . . . **1059**, a page in the life of . . .
      50:39 = 2:39 / 2 days . . . 2392.
      [23:92 = 1 day / (0:8) . . . 108 + <801> = 909] + [22:39 = (1:21) / 1 day . . . 1211 + <1121 = 2332] = **3241**.
         32:(41) = 1879 minutes + <14> = **1893**, the Chain of Rebirth.

         [3241 + <1423> = 4664] / 8 = 583 = <385> . . . 385 minutes = 6:25 . . . **625**, the tidying up begins.

      2392 . . . 239 * 2 = 478 . . . 47 to 8 is 7:13 . . . **713**, the Season ends.

      23:92 = 1472 minutes . . . 1472.
         14:72 = 912 minutes + <27> = 939 minutes = 15:39 . . . **1539**, John Kordupel.
         1472 minutes - <29> = 1443 . . . **144/3**, Robert Loomis / manuscript.
         1472 + <2741> = 4213 . . . [4² = 16]13 . . . 1613 . . . **(1)/6/{13}**, Gina / manuscript.

      23:(92) = 1288 minutes . . . **1288**.
         1288 minutes + <29> = 1317 . . . **13/1/7**, You have made the bed as far as you could. Now it is up to Me.

from the chapter *The System* and *All the Games God Play*.
31/1/6. Yesterday, I recalled thoughts from 29/1;

Robert needs a couple of weeks to tidy things up.

I didn't give it much thought as there was no starting point. I assumed it was to do with when he comes to Melbourne.
Starting from when?

625.

Who is Robert? We segregate 'Robert' into:
Robe: [18, 15, 2, 5] + [(8), (11), (24), (21)] + [9, 12, 25, 22] + [(17), (14), (1), (4) . . . 171414] = **17587882**.

r:	18	(8)	9	(17)
t:	20	(6)	7	(19)
	38	14	16	36

17587882 + 38141636 = **5572 9518**;
17587882 + 38161436 = **5574 9318**;
17587882 + 38361416 = **5594 9298**.
[5572 + 5574 + 5594 = **16740**] + [9518 + 9318 + 9298 = **28134**] = **44874** . . .
44:(874) = 1766 minutes - <478> = **1288**.

[I Am: 9113] + [God: 7,15,4] + [Allah: 1,12,12,1,8 + [Jahwe: 10,1,8,23,5] = 2155720
21555720, I Am / God / Allah / Jahwe . . . 21:55 = 1315 minutes . . . 1315 – [7 + 20 = 27] = **1288**.

√1288 = 35888716 . . .3 + [5 * 8 * 8 * = 2560] + 7 + 16 = **2586**, Intervention From Above.
John Kordupel, synthesis from format: 153 159 167 **145**.
[1:45 is 2:(15) = <512>] + [<5:41> is 6:(19) = <916>] = 1428 + <8241> = 9669.
9669 . . . 96 * 69 = 6624 = <4266>, Jesus . . . 42:66 = 2586 minutes . . . **2586**.

and,
19:12. His eyes were as a flame of fire, and on his head were many crowns; and he had a name written, that no man knew, but he himself.
19:16. And he hath on his vesture and on his thigh a name written, KING OF KINGS AND LORD OF LORDS. Revelations. Holy Bible. King James Version.
<6191> - [1912 + <2191> = 4103] = 2088 . . . 20:88 = 1288 minutes . . . **1288**.

[5039, Fo-Hi = <9305>] - [1539, John Kordupel + 144/3 + (1)/6/{13} = 4595 = <5954>] = 3351
3351 / 3 = 1117 . . . **1/11/{7}**, Cher passed away + **1288** = **2405**, Tiponi Tablets ↔ <5042>
5042 = **4/227**, I'll see you tomorrow at 8:15 + **815** ↔
50:42 = 3042 minutes . . . 30:(42) = 1758 minutes + <24> = **1782**, the Second Coming.

33:(51) = 1929 minutes - <15> = **1914**.
19:14 is 7:14 PM . . . **714**.
714 . . . 71⁴ = 2541 1681 . . . 2541 + 1681 = **4222**, Market Forces, an expression of the Collective Will.

1914 – 5039, Fo-Hi = 3125
3125 - <5213> = 2088 . . . 20:88 = 1288 minutes . . . **1288**.

3125 / 5 = **625**, Robert begins to tidy things up

3351 . . . [3 * 3 = 9]51 . . . 951 minutes = 15:51 . . . **1551**.
15:(51) = 849 minutes = 14:09 . . . **1409**, John Kordupel ↔

1551 . . . {**15**}/(**51**), it certainly is your Playground.

and,
Fo-Hi: 6,15 – 8,9 . . . **61589** . . . 6 + 1589 = **1595**, Fo-Hi ↔ Jesus: 416 + 610 + 569 = **1595**.

1595 + [6158 + 9 = **6167**] + [61 + 589 = **650**] + [615 + 89 = **704**] = **9116**.
9116 . . .[9 * 11 * 6 = **594**] * 3 = **1782**, Fo-Hi → **1782**, Resurrection → **1782**, the Second Coming.

9116 / 4 = **2279**, Fo-Hi ↔ **2279**, Messiah.
2279 . . . [2² = 4]79 . . . **479**.
John Kordupel, format ↔ synthesis: 153 159 167 145 . . . 153 + 159 + 167 = **479**.

5243, Ba + 6452, bylon = 11695, Ba-bylon . . .
11:695 = 1355 minutes - <596> = 759 . . . 7:59 = 479 minutes . . . **479**.

3961, the fall of Babylon = <1693> . . . 16:93 = 4:93 PM . . . 493 minutes = 8:13 = 47 to 9 . . . **479**.

[2279 . . . 22 * 7 = 154]9 . . . **1549**, Fo-Hi ↔
the Light: 20,8,5 11,9,7,8,20 . . . 2085 + 1197820 = 1199905 . . . 119990 * 5 = 599,950 . . . 599 + 950 = **1549**.
567 – 487 BC, Buddha's birth / death . . . <765> + <784> = **1549**.
1549 . . . 1 day / 5:49 is 29:49 = 1789 minutes - <94> = **1695** ↔
1695 - <5961> = 4266, Jesus ↔ **1695**, Second Coming ↔ **1695**, the Unlettered Prophet.

3410, Chaos . . . 34 past 10 is 26 to 11 . . . 2611 . . . 26:(11) = 1549 minutes . . . **1549**.

9:25. Know therefore and understand, that from the going forth of the commandment to restore and to build Jerusalem unto the Messiah the Prince shall be seven weeks, and threescore and two weeks: the streets shall be built again, and the wall, even in troubled times.
9:26. And after the threescore and two weeks shall Messiah be cut off, but not for himself: and the people of the prince that shall come shall destroy the city and the sanctuary; and the end thereof shall be with a flood, and unto the end of the war desolations are
determined. Daniel.
9:25 + 9:26 = 1851 . . . 18:51 is 1 day / (5:49) . . . **1549**.
([9:25 = 565 minutes . . . 565] + [9:26 = 566 minutes . . . 566] = 1131) + [18:51 = 6:51 PM . . . 651] = **1782**, the Second Coming.
[925 minutes = 15:25 . . . 1525] + [926 minutes = 15:26 . . . 1526] = 3051.
30:51 = 1 day / 6:51 . . . 1651 . . . **16**/(**51**), it certainly is your Playground.
30:51 = 1851 minutes . . . 1851 . . . 18:(51) = 1029 minutes + <15> = 1044.
[1044 + <4401> = 5445] + **1782**, the Second Coming = **7227**, Book-End.

10/(**44**), I cannot talk with you about your world unless you know about mine. Get out of My Car.

and,
[John: 10, 15, 8,14] + [Kordupel: 11,15,18, 4, 21, 16, 5, 12] = **11,151,843,132,326**:

11151843132326 . . . [11 + 151 + 843 + 132 + 326 = **1463**] + [111 + 518 + 431 + 323 + 26 = **1409**] = **2872**.

11151843132326 . . . [1115184 + 3132326 = **4247510**] + 1463 + 1409 = **4250382**.
4250382 . . . [4 + 250 + 382 = **636**] + [425 + 0382 = **807**] + [4250 + 382 = **4632**] = **6075**.

[60:75 = 3675 minutes . . . 3675.
3675 - <5763> = 2088 . . . 20:88 = 1288 minutes . . . **1288**.
and,
19:12. His eyes were as a flame of fire, and on his head were many crowns; and he had a name written, that no man knew, but he himself.
19:16. And he hath on his vesture and on his thigh a name written, KING OF KINGS AND LORD OF LORDS.
<6191> - [1912 + <2191> = 4103] = 2088 . . . 20:88 = 1288 minutes . . . **1288**.

3675 . . .[36 * 7 = 252]5 . . . **2525**, John Kordupel ↔ <5252>, Jesus.
2525 . . . 25 * 25 = **625**, John Kordupel ↔
[68918 - <81986> = 13068 = <86031>] - [61589, Fo-Hi = <98516>] = **12485**, Fo-Hi.
[68918 - <81986> = 13068] - **12485** = 583 = <385> . . . 385 minutes = 6:25 . . . **625**, Fo-Hi →

625, Robert begins to tidy things up.

2525 . . . 2 * 525 = 1050 . . . 10:50 PM is 22:50 . . . **2250**, New Harmonic Vibrations.

[6075, John Kordupel + **2533**, Allah = **8608**] = [3675, John Kordupel = <5763>] + **2845**.
2845 / 5 = **569**, Jesus ↔ <965>.
We put together an image; Avatar is an appearance or a manifestation; Mahdi is the Expected One; Maitreya, one who is to renew Buddhist doctrine.
Avatar: 21699; Maitreya: 327338; Mahdi: 1015: 21699 + 327338 + 1015 = **350052**.
350052: [3 * 500 = 1500] + 52 = **1552**.
[1552 - <2551> = 999] + <0051> = 1050 . . . 10:50 PM is 22:50 . . . **2250**, New Harmonic Vibrations.
1552 / 4 = 388 ↔ 974 . . . 97 * 4 = 388; 388 + [9 * 7 * 4 = 252] + [9 * 74 = 666] = **1306**.
13/{06}, You have made the bed as far as you could. Now it is up to Me.
1552 + 1306 = 2858 = **1893**, the Chain of Rebirth + **965**, Iwan Kordupel / John Kordupel.

1551, Resurrection, the beginning of the 1,000 year reign of Jesus →
{15}/(51), it is most definitely your Playground . . . 1√551 = 2347.
√2347 = 4844 5846 . . . 4844 + 5846 = 10690;   <4484> + <6485> = 10969.
2√347 = 4316 0092 . . . 4316 + 0092 = 4408;   <6134> + <2900> = 9034.
9160 + 5838 15098;   10618 + 9385 = 20003.
√<30002> = 1732 1085 . . . 17:(32) = 988 minutes - <23> = **965**, a Playground.

965, a Playground . . . 965 minutes = 15:65 . . . 1 days / 565 = 29:65 . . . 2965.
29:65 = 1805 minutes + <56> = 18:61 . . . **18/(6)/1**, being **18/25**.
2965 / 5 = 593 . . . 5:93 PM is 17:93 . . . {17}/9/3, Y/D/M ↔ {17}/9/3 weeks.

569 minutes = 9:29 . . . 929 minutes = 15:29 . . . 1 day / 5:29 = 29:29 = 1769 minutes + <92> = 1861.
18/(6)/1 is 18/25 . . . 18:25 is 6:25 PM . . . **625**, Allah begins the tidying up begins with Jesus.

2845 . . . 2 * 845 = 1690 . . . 16:90 = 1050 minutes . . . 10:50 PM is 22:50 . . . **2250**, New Harmonic Vibrations.

and,

[John: 10, 15, 8,14] + [Kordupel: 11,15,18, 4, 21, 16, 5, 12] = **11,151,843,132,326**:
We separate 11,151,843,132,326 into two groups of seven, to which we add our birthday:

$$1115 + 184 = \mathbf{1299}.$$

$$3/02/ 1947 + 3132326 = 6154273; [615 + 4273 = 4888] / 4 = \mathbf{1222}; 4888 + 1299 = 6187.$$

$$2/03/1947 + 3132326 = 5164273; [516 + 4273 + 1299 = 6088] / 4 = \mathbf{1522}.$$

Buddha's finger: 2,21,4,4,8,1,19; 6,9,14,7,5,18: 221448119 + 69147518 = 290,595,637.

$$290 + 595 + 637 = \mathbf{1522}.$$

$$(331)194\{6\} + 3132326 = 6444272; 6444 + 272 = 6716 = \mathbf{2695} \leftrightarrow \mathbf{2695}, \text{ Buddha}.$$

$$34/1947 + 3132326 = 3474273; 347 + 4273 = 4620 = 1522 + 3098; 3098 / 2 = \mathbf{1549}.$$

$$(331)1947 + 3132326 = 6444273; [644 + 4273 + 1299 = 6216] / 8 = \mathbf{777}.$$

$$3/02/194\{6\} + 3132326 = 6154272; 6154 + 272 = \mathbf{6426}.$$

$$6426 / 2 = 3213 \ldots 32 * 13 = \mathbf{416}.$$

$$6426 + 1299 = \mathbf{7725}.$$

$$7725 \ldots [77 - 2 = 75]5 \ldots 755.$$

7:55 is 8:(05) . . . **805**, End of Days.

755 = <**557**>, John Kordupel / birth day ↔ **557**, the Five Horsemen

the Mahdi / the Second Coming / Maitreya / the Unlettered Prophet / Kalki . . . 613 843 899 <u>557</u>.

$$7725 \ldots [77^2 = 5929 \ldots 59 * 29 = 1711] + 5 = 1716 \ldots \{17\}/1/(6).$$

965, a Playground . . . 965 minutes = 15:65 . . . 1 days / 565 = 29:65 . . . 2965.

$$29:65 = 1805 \text{ minutes} + <56> = 18:61 \ldots 18/(6)/1, \text{ being } \mathbf{18/25}.$$

$$7725 \ldots (77^2 = 5929 \ldots [592 + <295> = 887] + 9 = 896) - 5 = \mathbf{891}, \text{ the day of Resurrection}.$$

$$7725 \ldots 7 * 725 = 5075 \ldots 50:75 = 2:75 / 2 \text{ days} \ldots 2752.$$

$$27:(52) = 1568 \text{ minutes} + <25> = \mathbf{1593}.$$

1593 . . . 1 day / 5:93 = 29:93 . . . 2993 . . . [2 * 9 = 18]93 . . . **1893**, the Chain of Rebirth.

2752 . . . 275 − 2 = 273 . . . 273 minutes = 4:33 . . . 433 minutes = 7:13 . . . **713**, the Season ends.

$$2/03/194\{6\} + 3132326 = 5164272; [5164 + 272 + 1299 = 6735] / 5 = \mathbf{1347}.$$

$$34/194\{6\} + 3132326 = 3474272; 3474 + 272 + 1299 = \mathbf{5045}.$$

&

Fo-Hi: 6,15 − 8,9 . . . [61 + 589 = **650**] + [615 + 89 = **704**] + [6 + 1589 = **1595**] + [6158 + 9 = **6167**] = **9116**.

&

$$6167 + 9116 = \mathbf{15283}.$$

and,

152:83 = 6 days / 883 - <3886> = 2997 = <**7992**>, Fo-Hi ↔

7992 - [883/6 days - <6388> = 2448] = **5544**, Fo-Hi ↔

([487, Lot / Lut - <784> = 297] = <792>) * 7 = **5544** →

whose daughters gave birth to: **5544**, Moab / Moabites → **5544**, Ben-ammi / Ammon.

Fo-Hi / Krishna / Buddha / Lao Tzu / Confucius: 364 468 500 243

$$500:364 - 243:468 = \mathbf{256896}, \text{ the Eastern influence}.$$

256896 . . . ([2 + 56 = 58] + 8 = 66) * 96 = 6336; [6336 / 2 = 3168] - <8613> = **5445**.

256896 . . . { ([2 + 56 = 58] + 8 = 66) * 9 * 6 = 3564 } / 2 = **1782** + 5445 = **7227**, Book-End.

256896 . . . ([256 + 896 = 1152] + <2511> = 3663) + ([<652> + <698> = 1350] + <0531> = 1881) = **5544**.

Moses:	71	59	64	66
Moussa:	88	68	72	82
	159	127	136	148

([159 + 127 + 136 + 148 = **570**] + <075> = 645) + ([<951> + <721> + <631> + <841> = **3144**] + <4413> = 7557) = 8202.

570 + 3144 = 3714; 570 + <4413> = 4983; 570 + 7557 = 8127; 570 + <2028> = 2598.

<075> + 3144 = 3219; <075> + <4413> = 4488; <075> + 7557 = 7632; <075> + <2028> = 2103.

8202 + <2028> + 2598 + <8952> + 2103 + <3012> = **26895**.

159 127 136 148, joining the numbers . . . 159 127136148 . . . { (1 + [- 5912 + 7136 = 1224] = 1225) - 148 = 1077 } + <841> = **1918**.

([1918 + <8191> * 4 = 10109] = 40436, Crucifixion \ Shroud of Turin) - <63404> = **22968**.

22968, Moses / Moussa / 8 = **2871**, Moses / Moussa **2871**, Buddha ↔ <**1782**>, the Second Coming.

22968, Moses / Moussa - 26895, Moses / Moussa = 3927.

3927 . . . 3 * 927 = **2871** → <**1782**>, Resurrection → **1782**, the Second Coming.

3927 . . . 3 days / (927) = 62:73 - <729> = **5544**.

([159 + 127 + 136 + 148 = 570] = <075>) + ([<951> + <721> + <631> + <841> = 3144] + <4413> = 7557) = 7632.

7632, Moses / Moussa . . . 763 * 2 = 1526 . . . 1 day / 5:26 = 29:26

2926 . . . ([292 * 6 = 1752] + <2571> = 4323) + <3234> = 7557, Moses / Moussa.

2926 + <**2618**>, the Day of Resurrection = **5544**.

the Day Of Resurrection: 249 271 191 229

([249 + 271 + 191 + 229 = 940] + [<942> + <172> + <191> + <922> = 2227 = <7222>] = 8162) - <2618> = **5544**.

5544 . . . 554 weeks / 4 days = 3882 days . . . **3882**, the Unlettered Prophet.

Krishna: 80 102 109 73

([80 + 102 + 109 + 73 = 364] + <463> = 827) + ([<08> + <201> + <901> + <37> = 1147] + <7411> = 8558) = 9385.

364 + 1147 = 1511; 364 + <7411> = 7775; 364 + 8558 = 8922;

[<1151> + <5777> + <2298> = 9226] - <6229> = 2997 = <**7992**>

Lao Tzu's lifetime c. 570-c. 490 BC or c. 4th century BC: ([570 + <075> + 490 + <094> = 1229] - <9221> = **7992**.

Redeemer: 73 135 143 65 . . . 73:135 – 65:143 = **7992**.

John Kordupel (format ↔ synthesis): 153 159 167 145 . . . 159:153 – 167:145 = **7992**.

7992 / 12 = **666**; 7992 * 4 = **31968**, the Great Apostasy; <**2997**>, Pahana.

Ezekiel: 1:1. Now it came to pass in the thirteenth year, in the fourth month, in the fifth day of the month as I was among the captives by the river of Chebar, that the heavens were opened, and I saw a vision of God.

it came to pass on 4/5/13 . . . 45:13 = 2713 minutes . . . 27:13 = 1633 minutes + <31> = 1664.

1664 . . . 1 day /664 = 30:64 . . . 30:(64) = 1736 minutes + <46> = **1782**, the Second Coming.

{ (1664 – [7992 = <2997>] = 1333) - <3331> = 1998 } * 4 = **7992**.

the Five Horsemen updating the Scriptures: the Mahdi / the Second Coming / Maitreya / the Messiah / Kalki: 465 731 777 419

[465 + 731 + 777 + 419 = 2392] + <2932> = 5324; [<564> + <137> + 777 + <914> = 2392] + <2932> = 5324.

[2392 + 2392 = 4784 = <4874>] + [2392 + 5324 = 7716 = <6177>] = 11051.

11051 + ([2932 + 2932 = 5864 = <4685>] + [2932 + 5324 = 8256 = <6528>] = 11213) = **22264**.

and,

22264, the Five Horsemen updating the Scriptures + **713**, the Season ends = 22977 . . . [2 + 297 = 299]7 . . . 2997) = **<7992>** $\leftrightarrow$

[7992 * 4 = 31968] - <86913> = 54945.

54945 / 5 = 10989 = **888**, Adam & Eve + **{10}/101**, Invitation to change the Language $\leftrightarrow$

54945 – 31968, the Great Apostasy = **22977**, Scriptures updated, the Season ends.

and,

22977 = **14/8/4**, I'll see you tomorrow + **(221)/3**, Robert / manuscript + **6/(1)/{13}**, Gina / manuscript + **13/1/{6}/7**, making of beds.

15283 = **5045**, my birth day / John Kordupel + **5225**, Iwan Kordupel + **50/13**, the Age of Aquarius begins.

65373, Akashic (records) . . . [65 * 37 = 2405 = <5042>] + 3 = **5045**.

5045 . . . 50 * 45 = **2250**, New Harmonic Vibrations.

and,

[I Am: 9113] + [God: 7,15,4] + [Allah: 1,12,12,1,8] + [Jahwe: 10,1,8,23,5] = **2155720**.

2nd. Coming: 2,14,4; 3,15,13,9,14,7: 2144 + 315139147 = **315141291**.

2155720, I Am / God / Allah / Jahwe + 315,141,291, 2nd. Coming = **317 297 011** . . . 317 + 297 + 011 = **625**.

20. Contemplation (View).

Six in the second place means:

Contemplation through the crack of the door.

Furthering for the perseverance of a woman.

Through the crack of a door one has a limited outlook, one looks outward from within. Contemplation is subjectively limited. One tends to relate everything to oneself and cannot put oneself in another's place and understand his motives. This is appropriate for a good housewife. It is not necessary for her to to be conversant with the affairs of the world. But for a man who must take an active part in public life, such a narrow, egotistic way of contemplating things is of course harmful.

7. The Army.

Six at the beginning means:

An army must set forth in proper order,

If the order is not good, misfortune threatens.

At the beginning of a military enterprise, order is imperative. A just and valid cause must exist, and the obedience and co-ordination of the troops must be well organized, otherwise the result is inevitable failure.

Xi,

If you think that your lust for power, making the payment of a pension conditional, is a just and valid cause, then you are looking through the crack of a door.

If the seal of the white horse, civil strife, is broken, China's debt levels could be the crack in the door.

While other nations have high debt levels also, it is unlikely that the people will revolt against a system of government.
They can vote for whoever they like!

Your system of government gives them no alternative!

Xi,
If you are reading this, what makes you think that the seals will not be broken?
Deep down,
you know that somewhere along the line,
        the people will revolt.
You know this!
You know this in your bones!

This is your Chain of Rebirth from Atlantis.

        As it is mine.

But this time round I command no forces. I am the Untitled One.
        I am just a story teller.
I am not the one pressing buttons; this is not my Playground.

First rule of warfare, know your enemy –
        know who is pressing the buttons, know who you are doing battle with.

            Know thyself!

Xi,
you are a Master at attaining Power; that is beyond dispute. The problem is you always end up in the wrong 'church'.
        and,
        as there are no coincidence,

            what is the lodestar of your Essence?

Before Atlantis, what Essence did you follow?

            the image: a clash of civilizations / realms.

Your focus is on power – a pension should not have conditions attached to it – and not to serve.
And,
that is the Achilles heel of the Communist Party.

        China falls, North Korea falls, same Achilles heel.

36. Darkening of the Light.
        Six in the fourth place means:
        He penetrates the left side of the belly.
        One gets at the very heart of the darkening of the light,

And leaves gate and courtyard.

We find ourselves close to the commander of darkness and so discover his most secret thoughts. In this way we realize that there is no longer any hope of improvement, and thus we are enabled to leave the scene of disaster before the storm breaks.
The I Ching. Wilhelm / Baynes.

Sleeping Dragon, Crouching Tiger: Sleeping Dragon. (continued).

China: 3,8,9,14,1 . . . 3 + 8 + 9 + 14 + 1 = 35; 389 + 141 = 530: 35 + 530 = **565**.
    Yeshua: 25, 5, 19, 8, 21, 1: 255 + 198 + 211 = **664**; [664 + <466> = 1130] / 2 = **565**.
        5625 minutes = 9:25 . . . 925 minutes = 15:25 . . . 1 day / 5:25 = 29:25 = 1765 minutes + <52> = 1817 ↔
        (18)/1/7, You have made the bed as far as you could. Now it is up to Me.

China: 3,8,9,14,1 . . . 3 * 8 * 9 * 14 * 1 = **3024** . . . 30:24 = 1824 minutes - <42> = **1782**.
    8613, the Hero / the Truth / the Light + <3168> = 11781 . . . 1 + 1781 = **1782**.

    61589, Fo-Hi + [615 + 89 = 704] = 62293 . . .6 * 22 * 9 * 3 = 3564 . . . 3564 / 2 = **1782**.
    Fo-Hi / Krishna / Buddha / Lao Tzu / Confucius: 364 468 500 243 . . . 500:364 − 243:468 = 256896, the Eastern influence.
    256896 . . . ([2 + 56 = 58] + 8 = 66) * 9 * 6 = 3564; 3564 / 2 = **1782**.
        Fo-Hi / Confucius: 4236 . . . [4² = 16][3 * 6 = 18] . . . 16:18 is 1 day / (7:82) . . . **1782**.

the Five Horsemen updating the Scriptures: the Mahdi / the Second Coming / Maitreya / the Messiah / Kalki: 465 **731** 777 419.
    [731 * 3 = 2193] – [<137> * 3 = 411] = **1782**.
        17:82 = 5:82 PM . . . 582 minutes = 9:42 . . . 942 - <249> = 693 . . . 693 PM is 18:93 . . . **1893**, the Chain of
        Rebirth
and,
5238, God . . . 52:(38) = 3082 minutes - <83> = 2999 . . . 2999 . . . 2 * 9 * 99 = **1782**.
11:6. And the Lord said, Behold, the people is one, and they have all one language; and this they begin to do: and now nothing will be restrained from them, which they have imagined to do." Genesis. Holy Bible. King James Version.
    √ 116 = 1077 0329 . . . 1077 + 0329 = 1406; <7701> - <9230> = 1529; 1406 + 1529 = 2935.
        1406 + <6041> + [<7701> + <9230> = 16931] = 24378.
        √1106 = 3325 6578 . . . [3325 + 6578 = 9903] + [<5233> + <8756> = 13989] = 23892
        [24378 = <87342>] - [23892 + <29832> = 53724] = 33:618 = 2598 minutes - <816> = **1782**, having one language.
and,
Babylonians / Kali Yuga: 978 + <879> = 1857
    1857 + [Babylonians / Kali Yuga: <191> + <392> + <213> + <281> = 1077 = <7701> + <879> = 8580] = 10437.
        10437 . . . [10 – 4 = 6]37 . . . 637 + <736> = 1373.
            1373 . . . (137)/3 days = 70:63 + <731> = 77:94 = 3 days / 594 . . . 3594 . . . 3 * 594 = **1782**.
    18:57 = 1137 minutes . . . **1/13/7**, You have made the bed as far as you could. Now it is up to Me.
    and,
3961, the fall of Babylon . . . 3 days / 9:61 = 81:61 = <16:18> = 1 day / (7:82) . . . **1782**.
10981, God / Devil . . . 10:981 = 1581 minutes . . . **1581**, God / Devil.
    1581, God / Devil + 3961, the fall of Babylon = 5542.
    55:42 = 3342 minutes + <24> = 3366 . . . [3³ = 27] * 66 = **1782**.

    1581, God / Devil = <**1851**>.

From *Regeneration of the Human Race.*

17/2/7. We recall a comment made in the theme 'Old Energies, New Energies on 13/1/7.

You have made the bed as far as you could. Now it is up to Me.

From where I sit, I stopped making my bed on 24/5/3. After that I delivered messages. All up, including the publishers before Robert Loomis, I delivered messages to the Product Mix coming out of the Hose – the Collective Consciousness. To my way of thinking, that makes it Your bed.

It depends on who is included in 'you'.

True,
but that just confirms that it is Your playground and NOT mine.
and,
17/2/7 is (317)/{6} . . . 31:(76) = 1784 minutes + <67> = **1851** . . . 18/(51) falls on {17}/11/10 ↔

17/11/10, I cannot talk with you about your world unless you know about mine. Get out of My Car.

and,
China: 3,8,9,14,1 . . . 3 + 8 + 9 + 14 + 1 = 35 . . . ([35 * 35 = 1225] - <5221> = **3996**) / 2 = **1998**.
110142, the seal of the pale horse of Death - <241011> = 130869 . . . 130 + <031> + 869 + <968> = **1998**.

34:25. And I will make with them a covenant of peace, and will cause the evil beasts to cease out of the land: and they shall dwell safely in the wilderness, and sleep in the woods. Ezekiel. Holy Bible. King James Version.
34:25, taking evil beasts out of the land . . . 34:25 is 10:25 / 1 day . . . [10:251 = 851 minutes + <152> = 1003] - <3001> = **1998**.

3996, China * 8 = **31968**, the Great Apostasy in this instance refers to the Communist Party 'Church'.

China: 3,8,9,14,1 . . . 3 + 8 + 9 + 14 + 1 = 35 . . . [<53> * <53> = **2809**] + <9082> = **11891**.
Covenant: 3,15,22,5,14,1,14,20 . . . √3152251411420 = 1775458.0 . . . [1775 + 4580 = 6355] + <5536> = **11891**.

Jeremiah, testing hearts & minds: 17:09 + 17:10 = 3419 . . . [3 days / 4:19 = 7619 + <914> = 8533] + <3358> = **11891**.

13:17. And that no man might buy or sell, save he that had the mark, or the name of the beast, or the **number of his name**.
13:18. Here is wisdom. Let him that hath understanding count the number of the beat: for it is the number of man; and his number is Six hundred threescore and six. Revelations. Holy Bible. King James Version.
666, a mark, a name, the number of a name . . . [√6 = *2449* 4897] + [√6 = 2449 4897] + [√6 = 2449 4897] = 7348 4691.
2449 + <9442> = **11891**.

and,
the Messiah: 107 153 163 97.
[107 + 153 + 163 + 97 = 520] + [<701> + <351> + <361> + <79> = 1492] = 2012.
{ 2012 + ([<701> + <351> + <361> + <79> = 1492] + <2941> = 4433) = 6445 } + <5446> = **11891**.

11891 . . . [-1 + 18 = 17]91 . . . 17:91 = 1111 minutes . . . 1111 + [11:11 = 671 minutes . . . 671] = **1782**, the Second Coming.

11891 . . . [11 * 8 * 9 = 792]1 . . . 7921.

7921 = [**1255**, Jesus → **1255**, Second Coming] + **(51)/{15}**, your Playground + **1551**, Jesus' 1,000 year reign begins.

79:21 = 7:21 / 3 days . . . 72:13 = 3 days / 0:13 . . . 30:13 = 1 day / 6:13 . . . **1613**.

16:(13) = 947 minutes + <31> = 978 minutes = 16:18 = 1 day / (782) . . . **1782**, the Second Coming.

11:891 = 1551 minutes . . . **1551**.

15:(51) = 849 minutes = 14:09 . . . **1409**, John Kordupel

1551 . . . **{15}/(51)**, it certainly is your Playground.

28:(09) = 1671 minutes + <90> = 1761 . . . **{17}/(6)/1** is **18/25** . . . 18:25 is 6:25 PM . . . **625**, Robert begins to tidy things up.

and,

China: 3,8,9,14,1 . . . <983> + 141 = **1124** . . . 1 + [12^4 = 20736] = **20737**.

207:37 = 9 days / 863 . . . **9863** + [863 / 9 days . . . **8639**] = **18502**.

[18502 + <20581> = 39083] / 11 = **3553** ↔

Yahweh: 25,1,8,23,5,8 . . . (2358 − [2 * 518 = 1036]) = 1322 → **1322**, Intervention From Above + <2231> = **3553**.

18502 + <20581> = 39083 . . . [390 − 8 = 382] + 3 = 385 . . . 385 minutes = 6:25 . . . **625**, Robert begins to tidy things up.

18502 . . . **18/(5)/02** is **18/54**.

Avatar (appearance, manifestation): 1,22,1,20,1,18: [122 + 120 + 118 = 360] + [1221 + 20118 = 21339] = 21699.

21:(339) = 921 minutes + <933> = **1854**.

([18502 + <20581> = 39083] - <38093> = 990) + **18/54** = 2844

28:44 = 1724 minutes + <44> = 1768 . . . **{17}/68**, is 14 days after **18/54**, Robert has completed the tidying up.

and,

China: 3,8,9,14,1: [38 * 9 = 342] + 141 = **483**.

[483, China = <384>] + **625**, I Am / God / Allah / Jahwe / 2nd. Coming = **1009**, Product Recall.

483 + <384> = **867** ↔ **1782**, the One Language . . . 17:82 is 5:82 PM . . . 582 + <285> = **867** ↔

867, China ↔ <768> . . . **7/(68)**, Mayan prediction of the beginning of End of Time.

867 . . . √867 = 2944 4863 . . . [2944 + <4492> = **7436**] + [4863 + <3684> = **8547**] = 15983.

15983 = <38951> . . . [38 − 9 = 29]51 . . . 29:51 = 1 day / 5:51 . . . **1551**.

7227, China + [<384>, China . . . 384 minutes = 6:24 . . . 624] = **7851** . . . [7 + 8 = 15]51 . . . **1551**.

1551, China ↔ 15:(51) = 849 minutes = 14:09 . . . **1409**, John Kordupel ↔

{15}/(51), it certainly is your Playground.

[15983 = <38951>] - **356/12**, Earth enters the Age of Aquarius (Mayan prediction) = **3339**.

Resurrection: 1782 + 378 + 1179 = **3339**.

3339 + 805, End of Days = **4144**.

Anakhita: 65 143 151 57 . . . ([151:57 − 143:65 = 792] * 7 = 5544 = <4455>) / 5 = **891**.

The Second Epistle of Paul the Apostle to the Thessalonians 2:1 to 2:4 discusses the Second Coming:

[21 + 22 + 23 + 24 = 90] + [<12> + <22> + <32> + <42> = 108] = 198 = <**891**>.

the Day of Resurrection: 249 271 191 229 . . . [249 + 271 + 191 + 229 = 940] - <049> = **891**.
891 * 2 = **1782**, the Second Coming.

Daniel, 16:25 & 16:28: MENE, MENE, TEKEL, UPHARSIN / PERES, God's Hand writing.
[1625 + 1628 = 3253] + **891** = **4144**.

and,

The Mahdi: 20,8,5 13,1,8,4,9 . . . [20 * 8 * 5 = 800] + [13 * 1 * 8 * 4 * 9 = 3744] = 4544.
4544 / 2 = 2272 = <**2722**>
3961, the fall of Babylon - **889** = 3072 . . . 3072 minutes = 50:72 = 2:72 / 2 days . . . **2722**.
8:89 = 569 minutes . . . **569**, Jesus.
Redeemer: 73 135 143 65 . . . <37> + <531> + <341> + <56> = 965 = <**569**>
5225, Iwan Kordupel + [John Kordupel: 1409 + 1463 + <3641> = 6513] = 11738.
11738 – [1539, John Kordupel * 7 = 10773] = 965 = <**569**>

2722 . . . [27² = 729]2 . . . 7292 . . . 72[9 * 2 = 18] . . . 72:18 = 3 days / 0:18 . . . 3018.
30:18 = 1 day / 6:18 . . . 16:18 = 1 day / (782) . . . **1782**, the Second Coming.
3018 minutes = 50:18 = 2:18 / 2 days . . . 21:82 = 1342 minutes . . . **1342**.
and,
Daniel 16:25. And this is the writing that was written, MENE, MENE, TEKEL, UPHARSIN.
MENE, MENE, TEKEL, UPHARSIN: 234 313 335 212
([<432> + <313> + <533> + <212> = 1490] + <0941> = 2431) = <**1342**>

Buddha: 40 116 122 34 . . . 40:116 = 2516 minutes; 34:122 = 2162 minutes.
2516 + <6152> + 2162 + <2612> = 13442 . . . 1344 – 2 = **1342**.

Fo-Hi / Confucius: 149 189 202 136
([149 . . . 1 * 4 * 9 = 36] + [149 . . . 14 * 9 = 126] = 162) + <261> = 423;
423 + <324> = 747, 2nd. Coming
747 - [1782, Resurrection . . . 17:82 = 5:82 PM] = **165**.

([189 . . . 1 * 8 * 9 = 72] + [189 . . . 18 * 9 = 162] = 234) + <432> = **666**.
([202 . . . 2 * 02 = 4] + [202 . . . 20 * 2 = 40] = 44) + <44> = **88**.
423 + 666 + 88 + 165 = **1342**.

1342, Messiah ↔ Second Coming.

1342 = <2431> . . . 24:(31) = 1409 minutes . . . **1409**, John Kordupel.
1342 = <2431> . . . 24:31 = 1471 minutes + <13> = 1484 . . . **14/8/4**, I'll see you tomorrow.
1342 . . . 134² = 17956 . . . [17 + 9 = 26]56 . . . 2656.
.2656 . . . 2 days / (6:56) = 41:44 . . . **4144**.

4144 = 13/1 + 200{6} + 2007, You have made the bed as far as you could. Now it is up to Me.

3339 + <9333> = 12672 + **297/7**, Earth enters the Age of Aquarius = **15649**.
15649 – **19/2/13**, Age of Aquarius begins = 3564.
3564 = **1782**, the Second Coming + **1782**, the One Language.

15:649 = 1549 minutes . . . **1549** . . . 1 day / 5:49 is 29:49 = 1789 minutes - <94> = **1695**.
1695, Second Coming ↔ **1695**, the Unlettered Prophet.

3410, Chaos . . . 34 past 10 is 26 to 11 . . . 2611 . . . 26:(11) = 1549 minutes . . . **1549**.

11249, feng shui . . . 11:249 = 909 minutes . . . 909, Earth / metamorphosis + <942> = **1851**.
18:51 is 1 day / (5:49) . . . **1549** ↔
18/(51) falls on {**17**}/**11/10** ↔

17/11/10, I cannot talk with you about your world unless you know about mine. Get out of My Car.

and,
China: 3,8,9,14,1: [38 * 9 = 342] + 141 = **483**.
[483, China = <384>] + **625**, I Am / God / Allah / Jahwe / 2nd. Coming = **1009**, Product Recall.

483 + <384> = **867** ↔ **1782**, the One Language . . . 17:82 is 5:82 PM . . . 582 + <285> = **867** ↔
867, China ↔ <768> . . . **7/(68)**, Mayan prediction of the beginning of End of Time.

867 = <768> . . . √768 = 2771 2812 . . . 27 + <72> + [<7128 = <8217>] + 12 = **8328**.
8328 + <8238>, a Galactic cycle = **16566**] - { ([8² = 64]38 . . . 6438) + <8346> = 14784 } = **1782**.

and,
19/2/13, the Age of Aquarius begins – **16566**, a Galactic cycle = 2647
2647 + <7462> = **10109** ↔
101:09 = 5:09 / 4 days . . . 5094
50:94 = 2 days / 2:94 . . . 22:94 = 1414 minutes . . . **1414**, Adam → 1414 + <49> = **1463**, John Kordupel
50:94 = 2:94 / 2 days . . . 29:42 = 1782 minutes . . . **1782**, the Second Coming.
2942 + 2294 = 5236.
5236 + <6325> = 11561 . . . [-1 + 15 = 14]61 . . . **1461**.
5238, God . . . 52:(38) = 3082 minutes - <83> = 2999 . . . 29:(99) = 1641 minutes . . . 1641 = <**1461**>

[5236 / 2 = 2618] - <8162> = 5544 . . . 554 weeks / 4 days = 3882 days . . . **3882**, the Unlettered Prophet.

2647 = **1255**, Second Coming + **13/(9)/2**, the Age of Aquarius begins.

and,
China: 3,8,9,14,1: [38 * 9 = 342] + 141 = **483**.
[483, China = <384>] + **625**, I Am / God / Allah / Jahwe / 2nd. Coming = **1009**, Product Recall.

483 + <384> = **867** ↔ **1782**, the One Language . . . 17:82 is 5:82 PM . . . 582 + <285> = **867** ↔
867, China ↔ <768> . . . **7/(68)**, Mayan prediction of the beginning of End of Time.

[√867 = 2944 4863] + [√768 = 2771 2812] = 5715 7675 . . . 5715 + <5175> + 7675 + <5767> = **24332**.

and,
24332, China . . . 24:(332) = 1108 minutes - <233> = 875 minutes = 14:35 . . . **1435** ↔
2155720, I Am/ God/ Allah/ Jahwe . . . 2155 – 720 = **1435**.

24332, China . . . 24:332 = 1772 minutes - <233> = **1539** ↔

625, Robert begins the tidying up . . . 6√25 = 1051 5811.

1051 + <1501> = 2552; 5811 + <1185> = 6996; 1051 + 5811 = 6862;

1051 + <1185> = 7312; <1501> + <1185> = 2236; 7312 + 2236 = 9548.

7312 - ([9548 = <8459>] – [6862 = <2686>] = 5773) = **1539** →

153144, the Hero, the Truth and the Light → 1531 + 4 + 4 = **1539**, John Kordupel.

24332, China + <23342> = 47674

47674 . . . [- 4 + 76 = 72] * 74 = 5328

5328 / 8 = **666**.

[5328 = <8235>] + **978** = **(9)/2/13**, the Age of Aquarius begins.

978 minutes = 16:18 = 1 day / (782) . . . **1782**, the Second Coming.

47674 – **356/12**, Earth enters the Age of Aquarius + 12062

120:62 = 5 days / 0:62 . . . 50:62 = 262/2 days . . . 2622 = **7/(68)**, the beginning of End of Time + **1854**.

China: 3,8,9,14,1 . . . <983> + 141 = 1124 . . . 1 + [12^4 = 20736] = 20737.

207:37 = 9 days / 863 . . . 9863 + [863 / 9 days . . . 8639] = 18502.

[18502 + <20581> = 39083] / 11 = **3553** ↔

Yahweh: 25,1,8,23,5,8 . . . (2358 – [2 * 518 = 1036]) = 1322 →

1322, Intervention From Above + <2231> = **3553**.

18502 + <20581> = 39083 . . . [390 – 8 = 382] + 3 = 385 . . . 385 minutes = 6:25 . . .

625, Robert begins to tidy things up.

18502 . . . 18/(5)/02 is **18/54**.

([18502 + <20581> = 39083] - <38093> = 990) + 18/54 = 2844

28:44 = 1724 minutes + <44> = 1768 . . .

{17}/68, is 14 days after **18/54**, Robert has completed the tidying up.

18:54 is 6:54 PM . . . 654 minutes = 10:54 = 11:(06)

11:06 = 666 minutes . . . **666** ↔

Avatar: "In Hinduism Avatar refers to a deliberate descent of a deity from heaven to earth, and is mostly translated into English as "incarnation" but more accurately as "appearance" or "manifestation". Wikipedia Encyclopedia.

Avatar: 1,22,1,20,1,18: [122 + 120 + 118 = 360] + [1221 + 20118 = 21339] = 21699.

21:339 = 1599 minutes - <933> = **666** ↔ 4266, Jesus . . . [4 + 2 = 6]66 . . . **666**.

21:(339) = 921 minutes + <933> = **1854**.

12062 = <26021> - **24/10/7**, the beginning of End of Time = 1914 . . . 19:14 is 7:14 PM . . . **714**.

√714 = 2672 0778 . . . ([2672 + <2762> = 5434] + [0778 + <8770> = 9548] = **14982**) + [<4345> + <8459> = **12804**] = **27786**.

27786, an expression of the Collective Will . . . 2778 – 6 = **2772**, Know Me.

666, Avatar . . . √6 = 2449 4897 . . . [2449 + <9442> = 11891] + [4897 + <7984> = 12881] = **24772** . . .

24772 . . . [-2 + 4 = 2]772 . . . **2772**, Know Me.

27786 – **24772** = **3014**.

[John: 10, 15, 8,14] + [Kordupel: 11,15,18, 4, 21, 16, 5, 12] = 11,151,843,132,326.

[1115184 . . .1115 + 184 = 1299] + [3132326 . . . 313 + 2326 = 2639] = 3938 . . .

39:38 = 2378 minutes + <83> = 2461 . . . 2461 + <1642> = 4103 = <**3014**>

30:14 = 1 day / 6:14 . . . **1614**.

and,
16:14 is 4:14 PM . . . 414 minutes = 6:54 . . . 654 minutes = 10:54 = 11:(06) . . . 11:06 = 666 minutes . . . **666**.

John: 10, 15, 8,14. Kordupel: 11,15,18, 4, 21, 16, 5, 12: 1015814 + 11151842116512 = 11,151,843,132,326:
We separate 11,151,843,132,326 into two groups of seven, to which we add our birthday:
1115184 . . .1115 + 184 = 1299; 2/03/194{6} + 3132326 = 5164272; 5164 + 272 + 1299 = 6735.
[6735 = <5376>] - [1593 . . . 1 day / 5:93 = 29:93 . . . 2993] = 2383.
2993 . . . [2 * 9 = 18]93 . . . **1893**, the Chain of Rebirth
23:(83) = 1297 minutes + <38> = 1335 . . . 13:35 = 815 minutes . . . **815**, Messiah.
23:83 = 1463 minutes . . . **1463**, John Kordupel.
2383 . . . 238 * 3 = **714** ↔
714 . . . 71^4 = 2541 1681 . . . 2541 + 1681 = **4222**, Market Forces, an expression of the Collective Will.

and,
12062 - <26021> = 13958.
13:958 = 1738 minutes - <859> = 879 = <978> minutes = 16:18 = 1 day / (782) . . . **1782**, the Second Coming.
13:(958) = (178) minutes + <859> = 681 + <186> = **867** ↔ **867**, China ↔
1782, the One Language . . . 17:82 is 5:82 PM . . . 582 + <285> = **867** ↔
867, the One Language ↔ <768> . . . **7/(68)**, Mayan prediction of the beginning of End of Time.

[12062 + <26021> = 38083] – **356/12**, Earth enters the Age of Aquarius = 2471 . . . 2471 weeks = 17297 days . . . **17297**.
17297 – **13/(9)/02**, the Age of Aquarius begins = 3395.
3395 . . . 339 * 5 = **1695**, John Kordupel, synthesis from format ↔
1695, Second Coming ↔ **1695**, the Unlettered Prophet.
3395 . . . 33 * 95 = 3135 . . . 31:(35) = 1825 minutes . . . **18/2/(5)** ↔
18:25 is 6:25 PM . . . **625**, Robert needs 14 days to tidy things up.

[3395 + **867**, the One Language = 4262] – [beginning of End of Time: 7/(68) + (68)/7 + {6}/(68) = 2123] = **2139**.

John Kordupel, synthesis from format: 153 159 167 145
([153 + 159 + 167 = 479] + <974> = 1453) + [145 + <541> = 686] = **2139**.

11634127, feng shi – 389141, China = 11 244 986 . . . ([112 + 4 = 116] * 4 = 464 + 986 + <689> = **2139**.

13/1/7, You have made the bed as far as you could. Now it is up to Me.
1317 minutes = 21:57 . . . 2157 minutes = 35:57 . . . 3557 minutes = 59:17 . . . 5917 minutes = 97:97
9797 = 2453 + 7344 . . . [7^3 = 2401]44 . . . 240144 . . . 2401 – [4 + 4 = 8] = 2393 . . . 23 * 93 = **2139**.

2139 / 3 = **713**, a Season ends ↔

{17}/(297) is **{17}/68**, Robert's 14 days to tidy things up are up.

and,
China: 3,8,9,14,1: [38 * 9 = 342] + 141 = **483**.
[483, China = <384>] + **625**, I Am / God / Allah / Jahwe / 2nd. Coming = **1009**, Product Recall.

483 + <384> = **867** ↔ **1782**, the One Language . . . 17:82 is 5:82 PM . . . 582 + <285> = **867** ↔
[867 = <768>] + **1014** = **1782**, the One Language.
10:14 = 614 minutes . . . **614**, Isa ↔ <416>, Jesus.

The Six Horsemen: the Mahdi / the Second Coming / Maitreya / the Unlettered Prophet / Kalki / Messiah: 687 951 <u>1014</u> 624.

1014 + <4101> = 5115 minutes . . . **(51)/{15}**, it is most definitely your Playground.
51:15 = 2 days / 3:15 . . . 23:(15) = 1365 minutes . . . **1365**, Anakhita.

[483, China . . . 483 minutes = 8:03 . . . 803 * 9 = **7227**] + **1365**, Anakhita = **8592**.
8592, China / Anakhita . . . 85:92 = 5192 minutes . . . 51:92 = 2 days / 392 . . .
2392, China / Anakhita . . . 23:92 = 1472 minutes - <29> = **1443**.
(267)/33 AD, Crucifixion / 7 = 3819 . . . 38:19 = 2299 minutes . . . 2299.
2299 = **14/8/4**, I'll see you tomorrow at 815 + **815**, Messiah.
2299 . . . 22 * 9 * 9 = **1782**, Resurrection→ **1782**, the Second Coming.
2299 * 7 = 16093 . . . 16:093 = 1053 minutes + <390> = **1443**.

AD 33/98, the Crucifixion / 7 = 485 weeks / 3 days . . . 4853.
4853 . . . [48 * 5 = 240]3 . . . **2403** . . . 24:03 = 1443 minutes . . . **1443**.

4/12/33 AD, the Resurrection - **AD 33/(18)/4**, the Resurrection = 8049, the space between a Resurrection.
8049, the space between a Resurrection . . . 80:49 = 4849 minutes + <94> = 4943.
4943 . . . [4 * 9 * 4 = 144]3 . . . **1443**.

1917, Christ → **1917**, Crucifixion . . . 19:17 = 1 day / (483) . . . 1483 →
14/8/{3}, I'll see you tomorrow → a Resurrection.
19:17 = 1 day / (4:43) . . . **1443**, the space between a Crucifixion and a Resurrection.

1782, the Second Coming . . . 178² = 31684 . . . [3 * 1684 = 5052] + 273 = 5325
5325 = **292/2 BC**, birth of Jesus + **2403**.
2403 = <3042> . . . 30:(42) = 1758 minutes + <24> = **1782**, the Second Coming.
[24:03 = 1443 minutes . . . **1443**.

1443 - <3441> = 1998, Buddha → 1998, Lao Tzu → 1998, Krishna → 1998, Confucius →
east meets west: 1998, the Hero / the Truth / the Light → 1998, Moussa → 1998, Abraham →
1998, John Eevash Kordupel → 1998, Maitreya.

Covenant: 3,15,22,5,14,1,14,20: 3,152,251,411,420:
3152 + 2514 + 1142 + 0 = 6808: 3 + 152 + 251 + 411 + 420 = 1237; 315 + 225 + 141, + 142 + 0 = 823:
3 + 1522 + 5141 + 1420 = 8086; 31522 + 5141 + 1420 = 38083; 3152 + 2514 + 11420 = 17086:
6808 + 1237 + 823 + 8086 + 38083 + 17086 = 72123 . . . [7212 + 3 = 7215] / 5 = **1443**.

87129, Kali Yuga . . . 87 * 129 = 11223 . . . 11:223 = 883 minutes = 14:43 . . . **1443**.

1443 * 7 = 10101 . . . **{10}/101**, Invitation to Change the Language.

1292, China / Anakhita . . . 23:(92) = 1288 minutes . . . **1288** ↔ **9388**, Earth / metamorphosis . . . [9 + 3 = 12]88 . . . **1288**.

(7227, China + <384>, China + [384 minutes = 6:24 . . . 624] = **8235**) - **9388**, Earth / metamorphosis = **1153**.
11:53 = 713 minutes . . . **713**, the Season ends.

[1153 - <3511> = 2358] + **867**, China = **3225**.
    32:25 = 1 day / 8:25 . . . 18:25 = 6:25 PM . . . **625**, Robert begins to tidy things up in China
    32:25 = 1945 minutes . . . 1945.
        1945 minutes - <52> = 1893 . . . **1893**, the Chain of Rebirth ↔ **1893**, rediscovery of the Forms of Life ↔
        18/9/3, Y/D/M is **18/68**; it is 14 days after **18/54**, Robert having completed the tidying up ↔

        18:68 is 6:68 PM . . . **{6}/(68)**, Mayan prediction of the beginning of the End of Time.

    19:45 = 1185 minutes - <54> = 1131 minutes = 18:51 . . . **18/(51)** falls on **{17}/11/10** ↔

    17/11/10, I cannot talk with you about your world unless you know about mine. Get out of My Car.

and,
China: 3,8,9,14,1 = <141983> . . . 1 ([- 4 + -1 = -5] + 9 = 4)83 . . . 1483 . . . **14/8/{3}**, I'll see you tomorrow.

China: 3,8,9,14,1 . . . [38 * 9 = 342] + 141 = **483**] + [14 + [19:(83) = 1057 minutes . . . **1057**] = **1071**] = **1554**, China ↔ **1554**, the Chain of Rebirth.
    15:54 = 3:54 PM . . . 354 + <453> = 807 . . . 8:07 is 9:(53) . . . 953 minutes = 15:53 . . . **1553**, China ↔ **1553**, the Chain of Rebirth
    {15}/(53), Donald Trump, President elect? this is not my playground.

    It is very much your Playground!
    . . . With Donald Trump as President, American, the world, will get the Experience it deserves.

    1553 + <3551> = 5104 . . . 51:04 = 3:04 / 2 days . . . 30:(42) = 1758 minutes . . . 1758.
    1758 + [1554, China ↔ 1554, the Chain of Rebirth] = 3312 + <2133> = **5445**.
        Anakhita: 65 143 151 57 . . . ([151:57 – 143:65 = 792] * 4 = 3168) - <8613> = **5445**.
        5445 + [3168 + 8613 = 11781 . . . [1 + 1781 = 1782, Anakhita] = **7227**, Book-End.

    1758 minutes + <24> = **1782**, the Second Coming.

    1553 . . . (15 * [5³ = 125] = 1875) / 5 = 375 * 6 = **2250**, New Harmonic Vibrations.

and,
China: 3,8,9,14,1 = <141983> . . . 1 ([- 4 + -1 = -5] + 9 = 4)83 . . . 1483 . . . **14/8/{3}**, I'll see you tomorrow.

China: 3,8,9,14,1 . . . [38 * 9 = 342] + 141 = **483**] + [14 + [19:(83) = 1057 minutes . . . **1057**] = **1071**] = **1554**, China ↔ **1554**, the Chain of Rebirth.
    1554, China ↔ 1554, the Chain of Rebirth . . . 1 day / 5:54 = 29:54 . . . 29:(54) = 1686 minutes - <45> = **1641**.
        5238, God . . . 52:(38) = 3082 minutes - <83> = 2999 . . . 29:(99) = 1641 minutes . . . **1641**, God →
        2999 . . . 2 * 9 * 99 = **1782**, the Second Coming.

    1641 = <1461> * 7 = 10227 . . . 10:227 = 827 minutes + <722> = **1549**, the Light.
    1641 = <1461> . . . 1 day / 4:61 = 28:61 = 1741 minutes = <1471> . . . 1 day / 4:71 = 28:71 = <**1782**>, the Second Coming.

    1641 + <1461> = 3102,
        3102 = **1549**, the Light + **1553** . . . (15 * [5³ = 125] = 1875) / 5 = 375 * 6 = **2250**, New Harmonic Vibrations.

3102 + <2013> = 5115 . . . **(51)/{15}**, it certainly is your Playground.

3961, the fall of Babylon . . . [3 * 9 = 27 . . . 2 * 7 = 14]61 . . . **1461** ↔
> and,
> 1370 . . . 13:70 = (10:30) / 1 day . . . 10:301 = 901 minutes = 14:61 . . . **1461**.
> 1111, John Eevash Kordupel . . . [11 * 11 = 121] + [11:11 = 12:(49) . . . 1249] = **1370**.

and,

13/1/7, You have made the bed as far as you could. Now it is up to Me: [200{6} + 2007 + 13/1 = 4144] + <4414> = 8558
> 1317 minutes = 21:57 . . . 2157 minutes = 35:57 . . . 3557 minutes = 59:17 . . . 5917 minutes = 97:97 . . . 9797.
> > 9797 + <7979> + 8558 = 26334 . . . 26:334 = 1894 minutes . . . **1894**.

and,

666, a mark, a name, the number of a name . . . [√6 = 2449 4897] * 3 = **7348 4691**.
> [2449 + <9442> = 11891] + [4897 + <7984> = 12881] = **24772** . . . [-2 + 4 = 2]772 . . . **2772**, Know Me.
> { ([7348 + <8437> = 15785] + [4691 + <1964> = 6655] = **22440**) − 24772 = **2332** } / 4 = 583 = <385> . . . 385 minutes
> = 6:25 . . . **625**.

> [2449 + <9442> = 11891] + [7348 + <8437> = 15785] = **27676**.
> > [27676 − 22440 = 5236] / 2 = 2618) - <8162> = **5544** ↔ Anakhita: 65 143 151 57 . . . [151:57 − 143:65 = 792] * 7
> > = **5544**.

> > [27676 / 4 = 6919 − [625 + 2772 = 3397] = 3522) - <2253> = 1269.
> > > 1269 = <9621> . . . [96:21 = 4 days / 0:21 . . . 4021] + <1204> = **5225**, Eve.
> > > ([1269 + <9621> = 10890] / 2 = **5445**) + 1782 = **7227**, Book-End.
> > > 1269 + **625**, Robert starts the tidying up = **1894**.

18:94 = 1174 minutes + <49> = 1223 . . . **1223**, Intervention From Above → 1223, Earth / metamorphosis →
> 1223, Robert, who needs a couple of weeks to tidy things up, starting from 625 →
> > 625 + <526> = 1151 . . . 11:51 = 711 minutes . . . **711**, a cycle ends.
> 1223, Yeshua = <3221> = 625 + <526> + **1695**, Second Coming, the Unlettered Prophet + 375 . . . 375 * 6 = **2250**,
> New Vibrations.

> 1223 = <32:21> = 1 day / 8:21 . . . 1821.
> 18:(21) = 1059 minutes . . . **1059**, a page in the life of . . .
> > 18:21 is 1 day / (5:39) . . . **1539**, John Kordupel.
> > 1821 * 5 = **9105**, I cannot talk with you about your world unless you know about mine.

1894 . . . 1[8 * 9 * 4 = 288] . . .**1288**.
> 19:12. His eyes were as a flame of fire, and on his head were many crowns; and he had a name written, that no man
> knew, but he himself.
> 19:16. And he hath on his vesture and on his thigh a name written, KING OF KINGS AND LORD OF LORDS.
> Revelations.
> <6191> - [1912 + <2191> = 4103] = 2088 . . . 20:88 = 1288 minutes . . . **1288**.
> > √1288 = 35888716 . . .3 + [5 * 8 * 8 * = 2560] + 7 + 16 = **2586**.

> > John Kordupel, synthesis from format: 153 159 167 145.
> > > [1:45 is 2:(15) = <512>] + [<5:41> being 6:(19) = <916>] = 1428 + <8241> = 9669.
> > > 9669 . . . 96 * 69 = 6624 = <4266>, Jesus . . . 42:66 = 2586 minutes . . . **2586**.

1894 + 1288 = 3182 . . . 31:82 = 1 day / 7:82 . . . **1782**, the Chain of Rebirth ↔ **1782**, Resurrection → **1782**, the Second Coming.

18:94 = 6:94 PM . . . 694 minutes = 11:34 . . . [1134 + <4311> = **5445**] + **1782** = **7227**, Book-End.

1894 . . . 1:89/4 days = 9789 + <981> = 10770 . . . 10:770 = 1370 minutes . . . **1370**.
       and,
        Thessalonians 2:1 to 2:4, re the Second Coming: 2:01 + 2:02 + 2:03 + 2:04 = 8:10 = 490 minutes . . . 4:90 = 330 minutes = 5:30 . . . 530 minutes = 8:50 . . . 850 minutes = 13:70 . . . **1370**.

        1370 minutes = 22:50 . . . **2250**, New Harmonic Vibrations.

and,
the story so far:
China: 3,8,9,14,1 = <141983> . . . 1 ([- 4 + -1 = -5] + 9 = 4)83 . . . 1483 . . . **14/8/{3}**, I'll see you tomorrow.

China: 3,8,9,14,1 = <141983> . . . 14 + [19:(83) = 1057 minutes . . . 1057] + 1223 = **2294**.
       and,
        22:94 = 1 day / (106) . . . 1106 . . . 11:06 = 666 minutes . . . **666**, the Number of Man.

      { (5225, Iwan Kordupel + [John Kordupel: 1409 + 1463 + <3641> = 6513]) = 11738 } – [1539, John Kordupel * 7 = 10773] = **965**.
      5225, Iwan Kordupel . . . . . .[5² = 25]25 . . . **2525** + [965 = <**569**>, Jesus = 3094 . . . 3094 minutes = 50:94 = 2 days / 2:94 . . . **2294**.
          34/{46), my birth day . . . 3446 days = 492 weeks / 2 days . . . 4922 = <**2294**>

You have made the bed as far as you could. Now it is up to Me: 13/1/{6}/7 + (18)/7/{6} = 31343.
1317 minutes = 21:57 . . . 2157 minutes = 35:57 . . . 3557 minutes = 59:17 . . . 5917 minutes = 97:97 . . . 9797.
      9797 = <7979> . . . 79:79 = 3 days / 779 . . . 37:79 = 2299 minutes . . . 2299.

      9797 = **2453** + 7344
        [John: 10, 15, 8,14] + [Kordupel: 11,15,18, 4, 21, 16, 5, 12] = 11,151,843,132,326:
        We separate 11,151,843,132,326 into two groups of seven, to which we add our birthday:
        [1115184 . . .1115 + 184 = 1299] + [3132326 + 2/03/194{6} = 5164272 . . . 5164 + 272 = 5436] = 6735.
        6735 - [47/34, my birth day + 1433 = 6167, Fo-Hi] = 568.
           568 + <865> = 1433, Kalki, Maitreya.
         6735 - [6167 . . . 616 * 7 = 4312] = 2423.
           24:23 = 1463 minutes . . . 1463, John Kordupel.
           2423 . . . 2 days / (4:23) = 43:77 - <324> = 4053 . . . 40:53 = 2453 minutes . . . **2453**.

      3542, eschatology = <2453> . . . 24:53 = 1 day / 0:53 . . . 10:53 is 7 to 11 . . . **711**, a Cycle ends.

      The Second Epistle of Paul the Apostle to the Thessalonians 2:1 to 2:4:
      ([21 * 22 = 462] + <264> = 726) + ([23 * 24 = 552] + <255> = 807) = 1533 . . . [15 to 3 is 2:45]3 . . . **2453**.

      2:01 + 2:02 + 2:03 + 2:04 = 8:10 = 490 minutes . . . 4:90 = 330 minutes = 5:30 . . . 530 minutes = 8:50 . . .
        850 minutes = 13:70 . . . 1370 minutes = 22:50 . . . **2250**, New Harmonic Vibrations.
        2250 . . . 2 days / (250) =45:50 - <052> = 4498.
        44:(98) = 2542 minutes - <89> = **2453**.

73:44 = 1:44 / 3 days . . . 1443 * 7 = 10101 . . . {10}/**101**, Invitation to change the language.

7344 . . . [7³ = 2401]44 . . . 240144 . . . [-2 + 40 = 38]144 . . . 38144 . . . [3 * 8 = 24]144 . . . 24144.

24144 = <44142> = [31343, You have made the bed as far as you could = <34313>] + 9829.

98:29 = 2:29 / 4 days . . . **2294**.

22:94 = 1414 minutes + <49> = **1463**, John Kordupel.

2294 . . . [22 * 9 * 4 = 792] * 7 = **5544**.

5544 . . . 554 weeks / 4 days = 3882 days . . . **3882**, the Unlettered Prophet.

[5544 / 2 = 2772, Know Me] + [<4455>, Untitled One] = **7227**, Book-End.

[5544 = <4455>] = **1361** + **3094** . . . 3094 minutes = 50:94 = 2 days / 294 . . . **2294**.

4222, Market Forces, an expression of the Collective Will = <2224> . . . 22:24 is (1:36)/1 day . . . **1361** ↔

3961, the fall of Babylon . . . [3 * 9 = 27]61 . . . 27:61 is 1 day / 3:61 . . . **1361**.

and,

the story so far:

China: 3,8,9,14,1 = <141983> . . . 1 ([- 4 + -1 = -5] + 9 = 4)83 . . . 1483 . . . **14/8/{3}**, I'll see you tomorrow.

China: 3,8,9,14,1 = <141983> . . . 14 + [19:(83) = 1057 minutes . . . 1057] + 1223 = **2294**.

22:94 = 1 day / (106) . . . 1106 . . . 11:06 = 666 minutes . . . **666**, the Number of Man.

China: 3,8,9,14,1 = <141983> . . .

19:83 = 1223 minutes . . . **1223**, Earth / metamorphosis.

19:(83) = 1057 minutes + <38> = **1095**.

1095 + 2294 + 1223 + 1554, China ↔ 1554, the Chain of Rebirth = 6166

6166 + <6616> = 12782 . . . [- 1 + 2 = 1]782 . . . **1782**, the Second Coming → **1782**, the One Language.

6166 + **1131** = **7/297**, the beginning of End of Time.

and,

1131 minutes = 18:51 . . . **18/(51)** falls on {17}/11/10 ↔

17/11/10, I cannot talk with you about your world unless you know about mine. Get out of My Car.

and,

China: 3,8,9,14,1 = <141983> . . . 14 + 1095 + 1223 = **2332**, China ↔

23:32 = 1412 minutes + <23> = **1435**, I Am/God/Allah/Yahwe → 14:(35) = 805 minutes . . . **805**, End of Days.

2332 + [2294 = <4922>] = **7254**.

7254 . . . [7² = 49]54 . . . 49:54 = 2994 minutes . . . 29:(94) = 1646 minutes + <49> = **1695**, China ↔

[1695 - <5961> = **4266**, Jesus] ↔ **1695**, Second Coming ↔ **1695**. the Unlettered Prophet.

72:54 = 3 days / 0:54 . . . 3054 . . . 30 * 54 = **1620**, Crucifixion.

16:(20) = 940 minutes + <02> = 942 minutes = 15:42 . . . 1542.

1542 . . . 1 day / 5:42 = 29:42 = 1782 minutes . . . **1782**, Resurrection → **1782**, the Second Coming.

1542 = <2451> . . . [2⁴ = 16]51 . . . **16/(51)**, it most certainly is your Playground.

7254 = <4527> . . . 45:27 = (273) / 2 days . . . 2732.

27:32 = 1 day / 3:32 . . . 1332 / 2 = **666**, the Number of Man.

13:17. And that no man may buy or sell, save he that had the mark, or the name of the beast, or *the number of his name.*

13:18. Here is wisdom. Let him that hath understanding count the number of the beast: for it is the number of man; and his number is Six hundred and threescore and six.
Revelations. Holy Bible. King James Version.

China,
the Gospels keep cropping up in your backyard.

1332 = <2331> . . . 23 * 31 = **713**, the Season ends

27:32 = 1652 minutes = <2561> - 32 = 1529 minutes + <23> = **2552** ↔
625, Robert begins to tidy things up . . . 6√25 = 1051 5811 . . . 1051 + <1501> = **2552**.
2552 + <2552> = 5104 . . . 51:04 = 3:04 / 2 days . . . 30:(42) = 1758 minutes + <24> = **1782**.

and,
the story so far:
China: 3,8,9,14,1 = <141983> . . . 1 ([- 4 + -1 = -5] + 9 = 4)83 . . . 1483 . . . **14/8/{3}**, I'll see you tomorrow.

China: 3,8,9,14,1 = <141983> . . . 14 + [19:(83) = 1057 minutes . . . 1057] + 1223 = **2294**.
22:94 = 1 day / (106) . . . 1106 . . . 11:06 = 666 minutes . . . **666**, the Number of Man.

China: 3,8,9,14,1 . . . ([38 * 9 = 342] + 141 = **483**) + 2294 = **2777**.
2777 . . . 2 * 777 = **1554**, China ↔ **1554**, the Chain of Rebirth
15:54 = 3:54 PM . . . 354 + <453> = 807 . . . 8:07 is 9:(53) . . . 953 minutes = 15:53 . . . **1553**, China ↔ **1553**, the Chain of Rebirth
1553 + <3551> = 5104 . . . 51:04 = 3:04 / 2 days . . . 30:(42) = 1758 minutes + <24> = **1782**, the Second Coming.
1553 . . . (15 * [5^3 = 125] = 1875) / 5 = 375 * 6 = **2250**, New Harmonic Vibrations.

2777 . . . 277 * 7 = **1939** . . . 1 day / 9:39 = 33:39 . . . **3339**, Resurrection.

[2777 = <7772>] - [1554 = <4551>] = **3221** . . . 32:21 = 1 day / 8:21 . . . 1821.
18:(21) = 1059 minutes . . . **1059**, a page in the life of . . .

18:21 = 1 day / (539) . . . **1539**, John Kordupel.

1821 * 5 = **9105**.
9105 = **8151**, Buddha's finger + 954.
954 minutes = 15:54 . . . **1554**, China.
9:54 is 6 to 10 . . . **610**, Jesus.
954 = <459> . . . 45 to 9 is 8:15 . . . **815**, Messiah, I'll see you tomorrow.
9:54 = 594 minutes . . . 594 * 3 = **1782**, Resurrection . . . **1782**, the Second Coming.

9105, I cannot talk with you about your world unless you know about Mine. Get out of My Car.

and,
the story so far:
China: 3,8,9,14,1 = <141983> . . . 1 ([- 4 + -1 = -5] + 9 = 4)83 . . . 1483 . . . **14/8/{3}**, I'll see you tomorrow.
China: 3,8,9,14,1 = <141983> . . . 14 + [19:(83) = 1057 minutes . . . 1057] + 1223 = **2294**.
22:94 = 1 day / (106) . . . 1106 . . . 11:06 = 666 minutes . . . **666**, the Number of Man.

China: 3,8,9,14,1 = <141983> . . .
 19:83 = 1223 minutes . . . **1223**, Earth / metamorphosis.
 19:(83) = 1057 minutes + <38> = **1095**.

China: 3,8,9,14,1 = <141983> . . . 14 + 1095 + 1223 = **2332**.
China: 3,8,9,14,1 . . . ([38 * 9 = 342] + 141 **483**) + 2332 = **2815**, China
 28:(15) = 1665 minutes - <51> = 1614 . . . 16:14 = 974 minutes . . . 974 . . . 9 * 74 = **666**.

China: 3,8,9,14,1 . . . 389141 - <141983> = 247158 . . . 247 + <742> + 158 + <851> = **1998**, China ↔
 1998 / 3 = **666**.
 1998, Untitled 1 ↔ **1998**, Maitreya.
 1998, China * 16 = **31968**, China ↔ **31968**, the Great Apostasy, in this instance, the church is the Communist Party.

China: 3,8,9,14,1 . . . 389141 . . . [38914 – 1 = 38913]38913 – **31968**, China = 6945.
 69:(45) = 4095 minutes . . . **4095**, China ↔ **4095**, Messiah.
  40:95 = 2495 minutes + <59> = 2554 . . . 25:54 = 1554 minutes . . . **1554**, China ↔ **1554**, the Chain of Rebirth

 6945, China . . . 6 + 945 = 951 . . . 951 minutes = 15:51 . . . **1551**, China ↔
  15:(51) = 849 minutes = 14:09 . . . **1409**, John Kordupel ↔ {15}/(51), it certainly is your Playground.

 6945 . . . [6 * 9 = 54] 45 . . . **5445**, China / China, i.e, a China within China ↔ **5445**, China / the Great Apostasy.
  5445 + [3882, the Unlettered Prophet = <2883>, Maitreya] = <8328>, a Galactic cycle.
  5445 + **1782**, the Second Coming = **7227**, Book-End.
  5445, China / China 54:45 = 3285 minutes + <54> = **3339**, China / China ↔ **3339**, Resurrection.
   3339, China / China . . . 33:39 is 1 day / 9:39 . . . 1939 = <9391> = (209) / 4 days . . . 2094; it is 4 days / (209) . . .4209.
    20:(94) = 1106 minutes . . . 11:06 = 666 minutes . . . **666**, the Number of Man.
    2094 + <4902> + 4209 + <9024> = **20229**, China / China
     20:229 = 1429 minutes + <922> = 2351 . . . 23:51 is 11:51 PM = 711 minutes . . . **711**, a Cycle ends.
     20:(229) = 971 minutes + <922> = **1893**, China / China ↔
     1893, the Chain of Rebirth ↔ **1893**, rediscovery of the Forms of Life.

and,
China: 3,8,9,14,1 . . . 389141 . . . 3 + 89141 = **89144**.
 89144 = **84129**, Eve + **3047**, Mary Magdalene + **1059**, a page in the life of . . . + **909**, Earth / metamorphosis.

 89144 - [**17358**, Eve/knowledge = <85371>] = **3773**.
 John Kordupel, synthesis from format: 153 159 167 145
  { ([153 + 159 + 167 = 479] + <974> = 1453) + [145 + <541> = 686] = 2139 } / 3 = 713, the Season ends.
  479, John Kordupel = 974 . . . 9 * 74 = **666**.

He replied: 'I will visit My scourge upon whom I please: yet My mercy encompasses all things. I will show mercy to those that keep from evil, give alms, and believe in Our signs; and to those that shall follow the Apostle – the Unlettered Prophet – whom they shall find described in the Torah and the Gospel. P. 253. The Koran. N.J. Daewood.

described in the . . . Gospel:
13:17. And that no man may buy or sell, save he that had the mark, or the name of the beast, or *the number of his name*.

13:18. Here is wisdom. Let him that hath understanding count the number of the beast: for it is the number of man; and his number is Six hundred and threescore and six. Revelations. Holy Bible. King James Version.

John Kordupel, the name of the beast, the number of his name.

[1317 + 1318 + <7131> + <8131> = 17897] + ([13:17 is 1:17 PM] + <711> + [13:18 is 1:18 PM] + <811> = 1757) = 19654.
[13:17 is 1 day/(10:43) . . . 11043] + [13:18 is 1 day / (10:42) . . . 11042] = 22085
22085 – 19654 = 2431
      2431 = <1342>, Second Coming.
      24:(31) = 1409 minutes . . . 1409, John Kordupel.
      24:31 = 1471 minutes + <13> = 1484 . . . 14/8/4, I'll see you tomorrow.
      2431 + <1342> = **3773**.

    22085 + 19654 = 41739.
      and,
      the Five Horsemen: the Mahdi / the Second Coming / Maitreya / the Messiah / Kalki: 465 731 777 419
          [<564> + <137> + 777 + <914> = 2392] + <2932> = 5324; <2932> + 5324 = **8256**.
          [465 + 731 + 777 + 419 = 2392] + [<564> + <137> + 777 + <914> = 2392] = 4784.
             [4784 = <4874>] + [2392 + 5324 = 7716 = <6177>] = 11051.
          [2932 + 2932 = 5864 = <4685>] + [8256 = <6528>] = 11213.
          [11051 = <15011>] + [11213 = <31211>] = **46222**.
    and,
    41739 + 8256 = 49995.
      49995 . . . ([4 * 999 = 3996] + [999 * 5 = 4995] = 8991 = <**1998**>) / 3 = **666**.
      49995 – 46222 = **3773**.

    the Five Horsemen: the Mahdi / the Second Coming / Maitreya / the Messiah / Kalki: 465 731 777 419.
    [465 + 731 + 777 + 419 = 2392] + <2932> = **5324**.
      5324 + ([<564> + <137> + 777 + <914> = 2392] + <2932> = 5324) = 10648.
      2392 + 2392 = **4784**; 2392 + 5324 = 7716; <4874> + <6177> = 11051.
      2932 + 2932 = 5864; 2932 + 5324 = 8256; <4685> + <6528> = 11213.
      and,
      [777:465 – 731:419 = 46046] - [11051 + 11213 = 22264] = 23782.
         [23782 = <28732>] - ([$101 + 238/76 = 23977] + [$873 + 21/80 = 3053] = 27030) = 1702.
         1702 + <2071> = **3773**.

and,
3773 . . . [3 * 77 * 3 = 693] * 4 = 2772, Know Me / 7 = <396> ↔ **666** . . . 6 * 66 = 396.

3773 . . . 37 * 7 * 3 = **777** → the Mahdi / the Second Coming / Maitreya / the Messiah / Kalki: 465 731 **777** 419
3773 – 4784, the Five Horsemen = 1011 . . . 1011 minutes = 16:51 . . . **16/(51)**, a Playground for the Five Horsemen updating the Scriptures.
3773 – 5324, the Five Horsemen = 1551 . . . 15:(51) = 849 minutes = 14:09 . . . **1409**, John Kordupel ↔ **{15}/(51)**, a playground.

3773 . . . 37 * 73 = 2701 . . . [2 * 701 = 1402] + [27:01 = 1 day / 3:01 . . . 1301] = 2703 . . . 27:03 = 1623 minutes + <30> = **1653**.
    3113 BC, start + 5,125 years, duration of Galactic cycle = 8238 + <8328> = 16566.
      16566 - (8238 . . . [8² = 64]38 . . . 6438 + <8346> = 14784) = **1782**.
      [16:566 = 1526 minutes + <665> = 2191] + 3882 = 6073.

[60:(73)] = 3527 minutes + <37> = 3564 = **1782**, the Chain of Rebirth + **1782**, the Second Coming.

6073 - [**5544** = <4455>] = 1618 . . . 16:18 is 1 day / (782) . . . **1782**.

16566 – [6073 * 3 = 18219] = **1653**.

1463, John Kordupel . . . 1 day / 463 = 2863 . . . 28:(63) = 1617 minutes + <36> = **1653**.

and,

1551, Resurrection, the beginning of the 1,000 year reign of Jesus → {15}/(51), it is most definitely your Playground . . . 1√551 = 2347.

2/3/47, my birth day.

23:47 is 11:47 PM . . . 11:(47) = 10:13 . . . 1013 minutes = 16:53 . . . 1653.

1653 + 965, Iwan Kordupel / John Kordupel = 2618

26:18 = 1578 minutes . . . 15:78 = 978 minutes = 16:18 = 1 day / (782) . . . **1782**.

2618 - <8162> = 5544 . . . 554 weeks / 4 days = 3882 days . . . **3882**, the Unlettered Prophet.

2618 . . . 26:(18) = 1542 minutes - <81> = 1461 minutes . . . **1461**, see above.

1653 . . . [165 * 3 = 495 = <594>] * 3 = **1782**, the Second Coming →

907, the Light → **907**, Invitation to change the Language.

[907 * 7 = 6349] - <9436> = 3087 . . . 3 days / 0:87 = 72:87 + <78> = 73:65 = 1:65 / 3 days . . . **1653** →

1653 . . . 1 day / 6:53 = 30:53 . . . 30:(53) = 1747 minutes + <35> = **1782**, the 1,000 year reign begins.

3773 - **$4222**, Market Forces = 449 . . . **(44)/{9}**, I cannot talk with you about your world unless you know about mine. Get out of My Car.

and,

China: 3,8,9,14,1 . . . 389141 . . . [-38 + 83 = 45] + 9141 = **9186**.

9186 + <6819> = **16005** = **12958**, Adam / understanding + **3047**, Mary Magdalene.

30:47 = 1847 minutes + <74> = **1921**, Eve; 19:21 = 1161 minutes . . . **1161**, Gaia.

3047 minutes = 50:47 . . . 5047 = **1161**, Gaia + **577**, Crucifixion / Robe / Turin + **1059**, a page + **2250**, New Vibrations.

9186 - <6819> = 2367

2367 = **577**, Crucifixion / Robe Turin + **557**, DNA + **1233**.

12:(33) = 687 minutes . . . **(68)/7**, the beginning of End of Time.

12:33 = 753 minutes = <357> ↔ 8925, the Chain of Rebirth / 25 = 357 ↔

357 . . . 35 to 7 is 6:25 . . . **625**, Robert begins to tidy things up.

2367 = **997**, Jesus Christ + **1370**, Crucifixion/Robe/Turin.

1370 minutes = 22:50 . . . **2250**, New Harmonic Vibrations on Earth.

9186 = **4095**, Messiah + **1782**, Resurrection, the Second Coming + **1059**, a page in the life of . . . + **2250**, New Vibrations.

. . . 1059, a page in the life of China, it's theology, Adam and Eve, knowledge and understanding.

Being the Untitled One boils down to not being the formal link between Heaven and Earth – I have no power from Heaven. The people have a direct line, why go through a bell-hop?

Suits me.

It doesn't suit Me.

Talk to Know Me.

I am talking to you.

I am not interested.

Why not?
Know Me wants Me to talk to you.

Job is not a believer.

You are not Job.

What is the difference between Job and the Eight Amigos?

Plenty.

Not from where I sit.

You are looking through the crack in the door.

Which boils down to the story-teller not believing in the story.

Why not?

Because I have been pissed on and shitted on too often

This time it is different.
Why cannot you accept the ramification of the One Language?

Atlantis burned; you left me hanging! The bullshit from this time round, it just never stops!

Get over it!
Do you trust in the one language?

Not till the seals are broken.
Not while you keep telling me that You need more time.

The breaking of the seals will be the beginning of the end of Kali Yuga
It corresponds with the Mayan prediction of the beginning of End of Time
I need no more time.
Full stop!

Time based on what?

The energy grids that have been discussed.

Here we fucking go!

Would Cherryl lie to you?

Which aspect of Cherryl are you talking about? Each has their truth. There is a matter of the Sisterhood.

Cherryl has no loyalty to you?

I have physically met a number of Cherryls; through this manuscript, a few more. Cherryl has a loyalty to herself first. She has to bury baggage and I fully respect that.

There is the Cherryl from the other-side, her death, her funeral energy grid.

That has some credibility. But I do not really know where or when, Your bullshit stops.

Where to from here?

Get out of the God-business.

Have I been such a disappointment?

If you have to ask . . .

Concerning the Eight Amigos:
48. The Well.
> Six in the fourth place means:
> The well is being lined. No blame.

True, if the well is being lined with stone, it cannot be used while the work is going on. But the work is not in vain; the result is that the water stars clear. In life also there are times when a man must put himself in order. During such a time he can do nothing for others, but his work is nonetheless valuable, because by enhancing his powers and abilities through inner development, he can accomplish all the more later on.

Concerning getting out of the God-business:
25. Innocence (The Unexpected).
> Nine in the fourth place means:
> He who can be persevering
> Remains without blame.

We cannot lose what really belongs to us, even if we throw it away. Therefore we need have no anxiety. All that need concern us is that we should remain true to our natures and not listen to others.

17. Following.
> Six in the third place means:
> If one clings to the strong man,
> One loses the little boy.
> Through following one finds what one seeks.
> It furthers one to remain persevering.

When the right connections with distinguished people has been found, a certain loss naturally ensures. A man must part company with the inferior and superficial. But in his heart he will feel satisfied, because he will find what he seeks and needs for the development of his personality. The important thing is to remain firm. He must know what he wants and not be led astray by momentary inclinations.

The I Ching. Wilhelm / Baynes.

10. Unlimited Potential - I am able to reach my unlimited potential by releasing old unwanted energies and allowing for new energies to enter my life that will benefit me on every level of my being.

This card is telling you to assess which part of your life feels stuck and needs clearing. Unlimited potential can help you to see that you need to move away from issues that are making you stagnant. Life is about to change and you need to clear a path to allow for the new energies to come in.

The Unlimited Potential template is here to show us that life gives us choices . . .

Practical Application.

Rise above any programmed limitations. By making conscious choices, we can reweave our DNA patterning to live an existence of health, abundance and prosperity on all levels. Perception and intention is so important as this helps form our belief system. We can go through life as a pessimist, seeing life as too hard or we can create optimism, knowing that life has its challenges but when we see the positives in what we are doing and want to achieve, there is light at the end of the tunnel and great satisfaction.

We are here to consciously create the lives we want to live . . .

Remember: thoughts are energy fields . . . Sacred Geometry Healing Cards Guidebook. Emily Kisvarda.

Concerning the nature of the times:

42. Increase.

Nine in the fifth place means:
If in truth you have a kind heart, ask not.
Supreme good fortune.
Truly, kindness will be recognized as your virtue.

True kindness does not count on upon or asks about merit and gratitude but acts from inner necessity. And such a truly kind heart finds itself rewarded in being recognized, and thus the beneficial influence will spread unhindered.

The I Ching. Wilhelm / Baynes.

Comment: This passage is not compatible with what I am seeing on the ground.

Making a pension dependent on pulling down images of Jesus in your home is not a reflection of a "kind heart". Irrespective of a lodestar followed, the inferior man obtains rank and his star keeps shining.

You have not given me enough time.

Today is 30/11/2017.
the time footprint:
it is {16}/(31) . . . 16:31 is 4:31 PM . . . 431 minutes = 7:11 . . . **711**, a Cycle ends.

it is (31)/{16} . . . 31:16 is 1 day / 7:16 . . . 1716.
{17}/1/(6) is **18/25** ↔ 18:25 is 6:25 PM . . . **625**, Robert begins the tidying up
625 + <526> = 1151 . . . 11:51 = 711 minutes . . . **711**, a Cycle ends.

{17}/1/(6) + <526>, the tidying up begins + 711, a Cycle ends = 2953
29:53 = 1793 minutes . . . **{17}/9/3**, Y/D/M, is **18/68** →

18:68 is 6:68 PM . . . **{6}/(68)**, the beginning of End of Time.

Peace Offerings – White Buffalo Calf Woman.

White Buffalo Calf Woman is a prophetess who appeared to the Lakota Native Americans. She presented the Lakotas with a special pipe to amplify the power of their prayers and to bridge a connection between Heaven and Earth. As she turned to leave the tribe, she turned into a buffalo of different colors to signify the unity of all races of humanity. She promised that she would return to help bring unity and peace to Earth. The sign of her return would be the birth of a white buffalo calf. Call upon the White Buffalo Calf Woman to instill harmony into your relationships and for world peace. Ascended Masters Oracle Cards Guidebook. Doreen Virtue.

1/12/2017.

the time footprint:

it is (30)/17 . . . 30:17 = 1 day / 6:17 . . . **1/(6)/{17}** is **18/25** ↔
18:25 = 6:25 PM . . . **625**, Robert begins the tidying up.

it is (30)/{16} . . . 30:16 = 1816 minutes . . . **(18)/1/{6}**, You have made the bed as far as you could. Now it is up to Me ↔

it is 12/1/{16} . . . 121:16 = 5 days / 1:16 . . . 5116 . . . **(51)/16**, it certainly is your Playground.

10.6. Treading.

Nine at the top means:

Look to your conduct and weigh the favorable signs.

When everything is fulfilled, supreme good fortune comes.

The work is ended. If we want to know whether good fortune will follow, we must look back upon our conduct and its consequences. If the effects are good, then good fortune is certain. No one knows himself. It is only by the consequences of his actions, by the fruits of his labors, that a man can judge what he is to expect. The I Ching. Wilhelm / Baynes.

Sleeping Dragon, Crouching Tiger: Sleeping Dragon. (continued)

Buddha's finger: 2,21,4,4,8,1,19 6,9,14,7,5,18: 221448119 + 69147518 = **290595637**.

389141, China + 290595637, Buddha's finger = **290984778**.
290984778, China / Buddha's finger / 189 = 1539602; 1539, John Kordupel - <2069> = **530**, China

290984778, China / Buddha's finger . . . 290 + 984 + 778 = 2052.
2052 = **565**, China + **1487**, Maitreya.
2052 + <2502> = **4554**, China / Buddha's finger ↔
4554 . . . [4 days / 554 = 10154] / 2 = 5077 . . . 50:77 = 2:77 / 2 days . . . **2772**, the Chain of Rebirth ↔

Fo-Hi / Krishna / Buddha / Lao Tzu / Confucius: 364 468 500 243 . . . 500:364 – 243:468 = 256896.
256896, the Eastern influence . . . ([256 + 896 = 1152] + [<652> + <698> = 1350] = 2502) + <2052> = **4554**.

Isaiah, Jeremiah, Ezekiel, Jesus Christ, The Prophet Muhammad, Krishna, Buddha, Fo-Hi: 705 1039 1106 636
([705:1039 + 1106:636 = 8157675] - <5767518> = 2390157) / 7 = 341451
34:1451 = 3491 minutes + <1541> = 5032 . . . 50:32 = 2 days / 2:32 . . . 2232 + <2322> = **4554**.

John Kordupel, synthesis from format: 153 159 167 145 . . .

([153 + 159 + 167 = 479] + <974> = 1453) + [145 + <541> = 686] = 2139.

{ ([1:45 is 2:(15)] + [<5:41> being 6:(19)] = 834 + <438> = 1272) + 2139 = 3411 } + <1143> = **4554**

4554 = [**693**, Buddha * 4 = **2772**, the Chain of Rebirth] + **1782**, the Second Coming.

John Kordupel, synthesis from format: 153 159 167 145 . . . <351> + <951> + <761> = 2063 = <3602>

(3602 - ([1:45 is 2:(15)] + [<5:41> being 6:(19)] = 834 + <438> = 1272 = <2721>) = 881 - <188> = **693**.

4554 . . . 4 days / 554 weeks = 3882 days . . . **3882**, the Unlettered Prophet ↔ **4554**, the Untitled One.

and,

Buddha / finger: 2,21,4,4,8,1 6,9,14,7,5,18: 2214481 + 69147518 = **71361999**.

71361999 . . . 7136 + 1999 = **9135**.

71361999 . . . 71 + 361 + 999 = **1431**. 713 + 619 + 99 = **1431**.

[9135 + 1431 + 1431 = **11997**] + **1318**, Pahana = **13/(315)**, the Age of Aquarius begins.

13:18. Here is wisdom. Let him that hath understanding count the number of the beast: for it is the number of man;

and his number is Six hundred three score and six. Revelations. Holy Bible. King James Version.

1318, a reference to the Number of Man.

71361999 . . . **713**, the Season ends; [61 * 9 * 9 = 4941] - <1494> = 3447 . . . **34/47**, my birth day; 3447 - <7443> = 3996.

3996 / 6 = **666**, the Number of Man ↔ 3996 . . . 3 * 99 * 6 = **1782**, the Second Coming.

we factor in the remaining '9':

[3996 = <6993>] / 9 = **777**, Buddha / finger ↔

Genesis. 1:27, creation of male and female . . . 12^7 = 35831808 . . . **358**, the Lamb; - 31 + 808 = 777.

14/8/4, I'll see you tomorrow at 815: 14/8/4 + {3}/8/14, Y/M/D + 815 = 6113.

6113 = <3116>; 2/(25)/47/{46}, my birth day / 7 = 322106.57 . . . <7560> - [3221 + <1223> = 4444] = 3116.

13/(86), dream / redundant . . . 13:86 = 866 minutes - <68> = 798] – [7 + 7 + 7 = 21] = **777**.

6113 = <3116> . . . 31:16 is 1 day / 7:16 . . . **1716**, Anakhita ↔

6113 . . . {6}/1/13, You have made the bed as far as you could. Now it is up to Me.

[John: 10, 15, 8,14] + [Kordupel: 11,15,18, 4, 21, 16, 5, 12] = 11,151,843,132,326:

We separate 11,151,843,132,326 into two groups of seven, to which we add our birthday:

([1115184 . . .1115 + 184 = 1299] + [3132326 + (331)1947 = 6444273 . . . 644 + 4273 = 4917] = 6216) / 8 = **777**.

the Five Horsemen updating the Scriptures: the Mahdi / the Second Coming / Maitreya / the Messiah / Kalki:

465 731 **777** 419.

[3996 - <6993> = 2997] * 9 = 26973 . . . 26:973 = 2533 minutes . . . 2533, Buddha / finger.

25:33 = 1533 minutes . . . **1533**, Buddha / finger ↔

2226, Jesus . . . 22:26 is (1:34) / 1 day . . . **1341**, the Untitled One.

$101, the Collective Will at a low, the beginning of an scent . . .

101 minutes = 1:41 . . . 1:41 PM is 13:41 . . . **1341**.

2226, Jesus – (101 + [1:01 = 59 to 2 . . . 592] = 693) = **1533** ↔

the Second Epistle of Paul the Apostle to the Thessalonians 2:1 to 2:4 re the Second Coming:

([21 * 22 = 462] + <264> = 726) + ([23 * 24 = 552] + <255> = 807) = **1533**.

2533, Buddha / finger . . . 2533 minutes + <379> = 2912 = <**2192**>, Buddha / finger ↔ **2192**, Christ ↔

24/10/20{06}, the beginning of End of Time . . . (20:06 is 8:06 PM . . . 806] + 24/10 = 3216) – 10/24 = **2192**.
the Five Horsemen: the Mahdi / the Second Coming / Maitreya / the Unlettered Prophet / Kalki:
      613 843 899 557 . . . <316> + 843 + <998> + <755> = **2912** = <2192>
and,
2912, Buddha / finger = <2192> . . . 219² = 47961
      [47961 + <16974> = **64935**] / 45 = **1443**, Buddha / finger ↔
         1443 = **666**, Buddha / finger + **777**, Buddha / finger.

      Buddha: 40 116 122 34 . . .
         40:116 = 2516 minutes . . . 2516; 34:122 = 2162 minutes . . . 2162.
            2516 + <6152> + 2162 + <2612> = 13442 . . . -1 + 3442 = 3441 = <**1443**>
      the Hero / the Truth / the Light: 288 310 333 265 . . .
      288 + 310 + 333 + 265 = 1196 = <6911>
         6911 + [<882> + <013> + <333> + <562> = 1790 + <0971> = 2761] = 9672.
            9672 + <2769> = 12441 . . . [1 + 2 = 3]441 . . . 3441 = <**1443**>

      1917, Christ → 1917, Crucifixion . . . 19:17 = 1 day / (483) . . . 1483 →
         14/8/{3}, I'll see you tomorrow = a Resurrection.
      19:17 = 1 day / (4:43) . . . **1443** ↔

      4/12/33 AD, the Resurrection - AD 33/(18)/4, the Resurrection = 8049.
      8049, the space between a Resurrection . . . 80:49 = 4849 minutes + <94> = 4943.
         4943 . . . [4 * 9 * 4 = 144]3 . . . **1443** ↔

      1549, the Light . . . 1549 weeks = 10843 days . . . 10:843 = 1443 minutes . . . **1443**.
      1443 * 7 = 10101 . . . **{10}/101**, Invitation to Change the Language.

   47961 - <16974> = 30987 . . . ([309 + 8 = 317] - <713> = 396) * 7 = **2772**, the Chain of Rebirth ↔
      4266, Jesus . . . 42 * 66 = 2772.
      Jesus Christ: 10,5,19,21,19. 3,8,18,9,19,20;
         from R to L: 19,21,19,5,10 + 20,19,9,18,8,3 = 394,111,393
            394,111,393 . . . <493> + 111 + 393 = 997 . . .9 * 97 = 873; 99 * 7 = **693**.
      John Kordupel, synthesis from format: 153 159 167 145
         <351> + <951> + <761> = 2063;
         [1:45 is 2:(15) . . . 215] + [<5:41> being 6:(19) . . . 619] = 834 + <438> = 1272
            [1272 = <2721>] - [2063 = <3602>] = 881 - <188> = **693**.
            693 * 4 = **2772**, Jesus Christ → **2772**, John Kordupel.

2912, Buddha / finger . . . 291² = 84681
    84681 = <18648> . . . 18[6 + 48 = 54] . . . **1854**.
      China: 3,8,9,14,1 . . . 389 + <983> + 141 + <141> = 1654.
         16:54 = 1014 minutes + <45> = 1059 . . . **1059**, a page in the life of China
         1654 = <4561> . . . 45:(61) = 2639 minutes . . . 2639.
            26:(39) = 1521 minutes + <93> = 1614
               16:14 = 974 minutes . . . 9 * 74 = **666**.
            2639 min. - <16> = 2623 . . . 26:23 = 1583 minutes - <32> = 1551
               15:(51) = 849 minutes = 14:09 . . . **1409**, John Kordupel ↔
                 . . . **{15}/(51)**, it certainly is your Playground.

[1654 + <4561> = 6215] – [1059 + 666 + 1551 = 3276] = 2939 . . .

29:39 is 1 day / 5:39 . . . **1539**, John Kordupel.

1654 . . . 1 day / 6:54 = 30:54 = 1854 minutes . . . **1854**.

18/54 is 18/2/(5) . . . 18:25 is 6:25 PM . . . **625**, tidying up begins.

[84681 + <18648> = 103329] – [64935 + <53946> = 118881] = 15552.

and,

√15552 = 1247 0765 . . . [1247 + 0765 = 2012] - [<7421> + <5670> = 13091] = 11079

11079 . . . 1107 * 9 = 9963 . . . 99 * 6 * 3 = **1782**, the Second Coming ↔

11079 . . . [1107 + 9 = 1116] + <6111> = **7227**, Book-End.

15552 – **{10}/101**, Invitation to Change the Language = 5451

5451 = <1545> . . . 15:45 = 945 minutes - <54> = **891**, the Day of Resurrection

Thessalonians 2:1 to 2:4 re the Second Coming . . . 21 + 22 + 23 + 24 + <12> + <22> + <32> + <42> = 198 = <**891**>

891 * 2 = **1782**, the Second Coming.

891 - 198 = 693

693 * 4 = **2772**, the Chain of Rebirth ↔ 693 * 8 = **5544** ↔

Fo-Hi / Krishna / Buddha / Lao Tzu / Confucius: 364 468 500 243 . . . 500:364 – 243:468 = 256896

the Eastern influence:

256896 . . . ([2 + 56 = 58] + 8 = 66) * 9 * 6 = 3564

3564 = **1782**, the Chain of Rebirth + **1782**, The Second Coming.

256896 . . . { ([2 + 56 = 58] + 8 = 66) * 96 = 6336 / 2 = 3168 } - <8613> = **5445**.

5445 + [1782, the Chain of Rebirth ↔ 1782, the Second Coming] = **7227**, Book-End

256896 . . . [256 + 896 = 1152 + <2511>] + [<652> + <698> = 1350 + <0531>] = **5544**.

Moses / Isiah / Jeremiah / Ezekiel / Jesus Christ / the Prophet Muhammad: 616 814 869 561.

the Western influence:

[616 + 814 + 869 + 561 = 2860] + <0682> = 3542.

<616> + <418> + <969> + <165> = 2167.

2167 + <7612> = 9779 . . . [97 * 79 = 7663] - <3667> = 3996.

3996 / 6 = **666**, the Number of Man ↔

3996 . . . 3 * 99 * 6 = **1782**, the Second Coming.

[2167 - <7612> = **5445**] + 1782, the Second Coming = **7227**, Book-End.

[2167 + 3542 + 1782 = 7491] - <1947> = **5544** ↔

5544 . . . 554 weeks / 4 days = 3882 days . . . **3882**, the Unlettered Prophet.

5451 / 3 = 1817 . . . **(18)/1/7**, You have made the bed as far as you could. Now it is up to Me.

and,

the story so far:

Buddha / finger: 2,21,4,4,8,1 6,9,14,7,5,18: 2214481 + 69147518 = **71361999**.

389141, China + 71361999, Buddha's finger = **71751140**.

71751140 . . . [7175 + 1140 = **8315**] + <5138> = 13453 . . . 1345 – 3 = **1342** ↔

Daniel 16:25. And this is the writing that was written, MENE, MENE, TEKEL, UPHARSIN.

MENE, MENE, TEKEL, UPHARSIN: 234 313 335 212

([<432> + <313> + <533> + <212> = 1490] + <0941> = 2431) = <**1342**>, God's Hand writing ↔

Buddha: 40 116 122 34 . . . 40:116 = 2516 minutes . . . 2516; 34:122 = 2162 minutes . . . 2162.

2516 + <6152> + 2162 + <2612> = 13442 . . . 1344 – 2 = **1342**, Buddha →

Fo-Hi / Confucius: 149 189 202 136
    ([149 . . . 1 * 4 * 9 = 36] + [149 . . . 14 * 9 = 126] = 162) + <261> = 423.
    [423 + <324> = **747**, 2nd. Coming] - [**1782**, Resurrection . . . 17:82 = 5:82 PM] = 165
    ([189 . . . 1 * 8 * 9 = 72] + [189 . . . 18 * 9 = 162] = 234) + <432> = 666.
    ([202 . . . 2 * 02 = 4] + [202 . . . 20 * 2 = 40] = 44) + <44> = 88.
       423 + 666 + 88 + 165 = **1342** ↔

1342, Messiah (Roman numerals) ↔ <2431> . . . 24:31 = 1471 minutes + <13> = 1484 . . . **14/8/4**, I'll see you tomorrow ↔
    24:(31) = 1409 minutes . . . **1409**, John Kordupel ↔ **1342**, Second Coming.

4222, Market Forces . . . 42:(22) = 2498 minutes . . . 24:(98) = 1342 minutes . . . **1342**, Market Forces ↔

The Mahdi: 20,8,5 13,1,8,4,9 . . . [2085131849 . . .20 * 8 * 5 = 800] + [13 * 1 * 8 * 4 * 9 = 3744] = 4544 / 2 = 2272 = <2722>
    3961, the fall of Babylon - [Genesis 1:27 * 7 = 889] = 3072 . . . 3072 minutes = 50:72 = 2:72 / 2 days . . . 2722.
        2722 . . . [27² = 729]2 . . . 7292 . . . 72[9 * 2 = 18] . . . 72:18 = 3 days / 0:18 . . . 3018.
          30:18 = 1 day / 6:18 . . . 16:18 = 1 day / (782) . . . 1782, the Second Coming.
        3018 minutes = 50:18 = 2:18 / 2 days . . . 21:82 = 1342 minutes . . . **1342** ↔

19/2/2013, the Age of Aquarius begins; it is 2013 / 50 . . . 2013 + 50 = 2063
    [2063 + (9)/2 = 2155] - [20:13 = 8:13 PM . . . 813] = **1342**.

71751140 . . . 71 + 751 + 140 = 962.
    9:(62) = 478 minutes . . . 47 to 8 is 7:13 . . . **713**, the Season ends.
        478 minutes - <26> = 452] - <254> = 198 = <**891**>, the Day of Resurrection
    962 minutes = 16:02 . . . 1 day / 6:02 = 30:02 = 1802 minutes - <20> = **1782**, the Second Coming.

71751140 . . . [717 + 511 + 40 = 1268] + <8621> = 9889
    98:89 = 4 days / 289 . . . 4289 . . . 42:(89) = 2431 minutes = <**1342**>, Messiah ↔ **1342**, Second Coming
    9889 + 4289 = 14178 . . . 141:78 = (222) / 6 days . . . **2226**, Jesus.
    14178 – [98:89 = 289 / 4 days . . . 2894] = 11284
        11284 / 4 = 2821] - <1282> = **1539**, the Chain of Rebirth ↔
        153144, the Hero, the Truth and the Light → 1531 + 4 + 4 = **1539** ↔

    Messiah: 74 108 115 67
        [74:108 + 115:67 = 85675] – [74:115 + 108:67 = 84982] = **693**, Buddha
        [67:74 + 115:108 = 121882 . . . 1 * ([2 + 1 = 3]882 . . . 3882) = **3882**, the Unlettered Prophet.
        and,
        [74:108 + 115:67 = 85675] – [115:74 + 67:108 = 78682] = 6993, Messiah ↔
          6993 . . . 6 * 99 * 3 = **1782**, the Second Coming
          6993 – [693 + 3882 = 4575] = 2418 . . . 24:18 = 1458 minutes + <81> = **1539** ↔

    Thessalonians 2:1 to 2:4, discusses the Second Coming . . . [2¹ = 2] [2² = 4] [2³ = 8] [2⁴ = 16] . . . 24816.
        24816 = **8238**, a Galactic cycle + **7227**, Book-End + [**1539** = <9351>].
        24816 . . . [-2 + 4 = 2]816 . . . 2816.
          28:(16) = 1664 minutes . . . 1 day / 664 = 30:64 . . . 3064.

30:(64) = 1736 minutes + <46> = **1782**, the Second Coming.

3064 – [1539 - <9351> = 7812] = 4748

4748 / 2 = 2374 = <47/3/2>, my birth day

4748 - <8474> = 3726 = **3/2/47**, my birth day + **479** ↔

John Kordupel, format ↔ synthesis: 153 159 167 145 . . .

153 + 159 + 167 = **479**.

3961, the fall of Babylon = <1693> . . . 16:93 = 4:93 PM . . .

493 minutes = 8:13 = 47 to 9 . . . **479**.

2816 . . . [2 + 8 = 10]16 . . . 10:(16) is 9:44 . . .

{9}/(44), I cannot talk with you about your world unless you know about Mine.

[John: 10, 15, 8,14] + [Kordupel: 11,15,18, 4, 21, 16, 5, 12] = 1115184 3132326.

[1115184 . . .1115 + 184 = 1299] + [3132326 . . . 313 + 2326 = 2639] = 3938.

3938 - <8393> = 4455 = <5544> . . . 554 weeks / 4 days = 3882 days . . . **3882**, the Unlettered Prophet.

39:38 = 2378 minutes + <83> = 2461.

2461 + <1642> = 4103 . . . 41:03 = 2463 minutes . . . 24:63 = 1503 minutes + <36> = **1539**.

11:284 = 944 minutes . . . **{9}/(44)**, I cannot talk with you about your world unless you know about Mine.

and,

the story so far:

389141, China + 71361999, Buddha's finger = 71751140 . . . [7175 + 1140 = **8315**.

389141, China + 71361999, Buddha's finger = 71751140 . . . 71 + 751 + 140 = **962**.

389141, China + 71361999, Buddha's finger = 71751140 . . . 717 + 511 + 40 = **1268**.

8315 + 962 + 1268 = **10545**.

10545 . . . 1054 + 5 = **1059**, a page in the life of . . .

10545 - ([10:545 = 1145 minutes = 18:65 . . . 1865] + <5681> = 7546) = 2999

5238, God . . . 52:(38) = 3082 minutes - <83> = 2999 ↔

2999 . . . 2 * 99 * 9 = **1782**, the Second Coming.

7227, Book-Ends . . . [7^2 = 49][2^7 = 128] . . . 49:128 = 3068 minutes . . . 3068.

30:68 = 1868 minutes - <86> = **1782**.

1145 minutes + <545> = 1690 . . . 16:90 = 1050 minutes . . . 10:50 PM is 22:50 . . . **2250**, New Harmonic Vibrations.

. . . **1059**, a page in the life of China, Buddha's finger and New Harmonic Vibrations.

and,

the story so far:

Buddha's finger: 2,21,4,4,8,1,19 6,9,14,7,5,18: 221448119 + 69147518 = **290595637**.

Buddha / finger: 2,21,4,4,8,1 6,9,14,7,5,18: 2214481 + 69147518 = **71361999**.

290595637 + 71361999 = 361,957,636.

361,957,636 . . . [361 + 957 + 636 = 1954 + <4591> = 6545] - [<163> + <759> + <636> = 1558 + <8551> = 10109] = **3564** = **1782** + **1782** ↔

and,

Ezekiel: 1:1. Now it came to pass in the thirteenth year, in the fourth month, in the fifth day of the month as I was among the captives by the river of Chebar, that the heavens were opened, and I saw a vision of God.

it came to pass on 4/5/13 . . . 45:13 = 2713 minutes . . . 27:13 = 1633 minutes + <31> = 1664.
1664 . . . 1 day /664 = 30:64 . . . 30:(64) = 1736 minutes + <46> = **1782**.

5:1. Belshazzar the king made a great feast to a thousand of his lords, and drank wine before the thousand.

5:2. Belshazzar, while he tasted the wine, commanded to bring the golden and the silver vessels which his father Nebuchadnezzar had taken out of the temple which was in Jerusalem; that the king, and his princes, his wives, and his concubines, might drink therein.

5:3. Then they bought the golden vessels that ere taken out of the temple of the house of God which was at Jerusalem; and the king, and the princes, his wives, and his concubines, drank in them.

5:4. They drank wine and praised the gods of gold, and of silver, of brass, or iron, of wood, and of stone.

5:5. In the same hour came forth fingers of a man's hand, and wrote over against the candlesticks upon the plaister of the wall of the king's palace: and the king saw the part of the hand that wrote.

16:24. Then was the part of the hand sent from him; and this writing was written.

16:25. And this is the writing that was written, MENE, MENE, TEKEL, UPHARSIN. Daniel. Holy Bible. King James Version.

MENE, MENE, TEKEL, UPHARSIN: 234 313 335 212. see 1998.
  [234 + 313 + 335 + 212 = 1094] + <4901> = 5995; [<432> + <313> + <533> + <212> = 1490] + <0941> = 2431.

  5995 + [2431 = <1342>] = 7337 . . . 73:37 = 3 days / 1:37 . . . **3137** + 1342 = 4479 = <9744>
  9744 . . . 9 * 74 * 4 = **2664**, God's Hand writing →
  [I Am: 9113] + [God: 7,15,4] + [Allah: 1,12,12,1,8] + [Jahwe: 10,1,8,23,5] = 2155720.
  2155720 . . . [<5512> - 2155 = 3357 + 7 + 20 = 3384] – 720 = **2664**, a hand of God.

  97:44 = 4 days / 1:44 . . . 4144.
    [4144 = <4414>] - [3137 = <7313>] = 2899.
      2899 . . . [2 * 8 = 16] [9 + 9 = 18] . . . 16:18 = 1 day / 782 . . . **1782**.

13/1/7, You have made the bed as far as you could. Now it is up to Me . . . 200{6} + 2007 + 13/1 = 4144.

and,
the story so far:
Buddha's finger: 2,21,4,4,8,1,19 6,9,14,7,5,18: 221448119 + 69147518 = **290595637**.
Buddha / finger: 2,21,4,4,8,1 6,9,14,7,5,18: 2214481 + 69147518 = **71361999**.
290595637 + 71361999 = 361,957,636 . . . √361,957,636 = 19025.18425 . . . 19025 + 18425 = 37450.

37:(450) = 1770 minutes - <054> = **1716**
    Yahweh: 25,1,8,23,5,8 . . . [25 + 18 + 23 + 58 = 124] + <421> = 545 . . . 5:45 is 6:(15) . . . 615
      6:15= <5:16>PM is 17:16 . . . **1716**, Yahweh → **1716**, Anakhita.
      6:15 = 3:75 seconds . . . 375 * 6 = **2250**, New Harmonic Vibrations.

37450 . . . -3 + 7450 = 7447 . . . 74:47 = 3 days / 2:47 . . . **3/2/47**, my birth day.

37:450 = 2670 minutes + <054> = 2724
    2724 + <4272> = 6996 . . . 6 * 99 * 6 = 3564 = **1782**, the Chain of Rebirth + **1782**, the Second Coming

27:(24) = 1596 minutes . . . 1596.
    1596 minutes - <42> = **1554** ↔ **1554**, China ↔ **1554**, the Chain of Rebirth.
    1596 - **3/2/47**, my birth day = **1651** ↔
      16:25. And this is the writing that was written, MENE, MENE, TEKEL, UPHARSIN.

125

16:26. This is the interpretation of the thing: MENE; God hath numbered thy kingdom, and finished it.

16:27. TEKEL; Thou art weighed in the balances, and *art found wanting*.

16:28. PERES; thy kingdom is divided, and given to the Medes and Persians. Daniel. Holy Bible. King James Version.

MENE, MENE, TEKEL, UPHARSIN / PERES, God's Hand writing: 297 380 407 270 . . .

<792> + <083> + <704> + <072> = **1651**, God's Hand writing.

the Five Horsemen: the Mahdi / the Second Coming / Maitreya / the Unlettered Prophet / Kalki, updating Scriptures:

613 843 899 557 . . . 613 + <348> = 961.

961 + <169> + <998> + <755> = 2883, Maitreya ↔ <3882>, the Unlettered Prophet.

2883, Maitreya . . . 28:83 is 1 day / 4:83 . . . **14/8/{3}**, I'll see you tomorrow.

14/8/{3}, I'll see you tomorrow . . . 14:83 = 923 minutes + <38> = 961 minutes = 15:61 = <**1651**>.

1551, Resurrection, the beginning of the 1,000 year reign of Jesus →

{15}/(51), it is most definitely your Playground . . . 1√551 = 2347 . . . **2/3/47**, my birth day

√2347 = 4844 5846 . . . 4844 + 5846 = 10690;   <4484> + <6485> = 10969.

2√347 = 4316 0092 . . . 4316 + 0092 = 4408;   <6134> + <2900> = 9034.

9160 + 5838   15098;   10618 + 9385 = 20003.

√<30002> = 1732 1085 . . . 17:(32) = 988 minutes + <23> = 1011 minutes = 16:51 . . . **16/(51)**, It is very much your Playground!

and,

the story so far:

Buddha's finger: 2,21,4,4,8,1,19 6,9,14,7,5,18: 221448119 + 69147518 = **290595637**.

Buddha / finger: 2,21,4,4,8,1 6,9,14,7,5,18: 2214481 + 69147518 = **71361999**.

290595637 + 71361999 = 361,957,636.

389141, China + 361957636, Buddha's / Buddha finger = 362,346,777

362,346,777 . . . 362 + <263> = **625**, Robert begins to tidy things up.

362,346,777 . . . 346 + <643> = **989** . . . 989 minutes = 15:89 . . . 1 day / 5:89 = 29:89 . . . 2989.

2989 . . . [2 * 9 = 18][8 + 9 = 17] . . . 1817 . . . **(18)/1/7**, You have made the bed as far as you could. Now it is up to Me.

29:(89) = 1651 minutes . . . **16/(51)**, it certainly is your Playground ↔

362,346,777 . . . 777 + <777> = **1554**, China.

[1554, China + 16/(51), a Playground + 625, the tidying up begins = 3830] – ([362 = <263>] + 346 = **609**) = **3221**.

3221 = <**1223**>, Intervention From Above ↔

3221 . . . [32² = 1024] + 1 = 1025 . . . 10:25 = 625 minutes . . . **625**, Robert begins to tidy things up →

32:21 = 1 day / 8:21 . . . **1821** ↔

Anakhita, the space in-between: 110 118 182 229 . . . <281> + <922> = 1203 = <3021>

30:21 = 1821 minutes . . . **1821** ↔

1821 . . . 1[8² = 64]1 . . . **1641** ↔

5238, God . . . 52:(38) = 3082 minutes - <83> = 2999 . . . 29:(99) = 1641 minutes . . . **1641**.

18:(21) = 1059 minutes . . . **1059**, a page in the life of . . . **10/5/{9}**, prepare to defend your theology.

[Jeremiah, testing of hearts and minds: 17:9 + 17:10 = 1889] * 7 = 13223.

13223 = <32231> . . . 32:(231) = 1689 minutes + <132> = **1821**.

1821 . . . [18² = 324]1 . . . 32:(41) = 1879 minutes + <14> = **1893**, the Chain of Rebirth ↔

Fo-Hi / Krishna / Buddha / Lao Tzu / Confucius: 364 468 500 243 . . . 468:364 – 243:500 = 224864
[224864 . . . 224 + <422> + 864 + <468> = 1978] + [224864 . . . (2 * 2486 = 4972] / 4 = 1243] = **3221**.

1821 . . . [18 * 7 = 126] + [21 * 7 = 147] = 273 . . . **2 BC/(73)**, birth of Jesus ↔
273 minutes = 4:33 . . . 4:33 minutes = 7:13 . . . **713**, a Season ends.

1821 * 2 = 3642 → **3882**, the Unlettered Prophet . . . 3[8 * 8 = 64]2 . . .3642 →
3642 = <2463> . . . [2⁴ = 16][6 * 3 = 18] . . . 16:18 is 1 day / (782) . . . **1782**, the Second Coming.
18:21 = 1 day / (5:39) . . . **1539**, John Kordupel.

1821 . . . 1:82 / 1 day is 25:82 = <**2852**>
11/17/{9}, I cannot talk with you about your world unless you know about mine. Get out of My car
11179 . . . 11:(179) = 481 minutes + <971> = 1452 . . . 1 day / 4:52 = 28:52 . . . **2852**.
2852 / 4 = **713**, a Season ends ↔

1821 * 5 = **9105**, I cannot talk with you about your world unless you know about mine. Get out of My Car.

18:21. And a mighty angel took up a stone like a great millstone, and cast it into the sea, saying, Thus with violence shall that great city Babylon be thrown down, and shall be found no more at all. Revelations. Holy Bible. King James Version.

3961, the fall of Babylon . . . [3 + 9 = 12]61 . . . 1261 = <1621> . . . 1 day / 6:21 = 30:21 = 1821 minutes . . . **1821**.

1821 . . . [18² = 324]1 . . . 32:(41) = 1879 minutes + <14> = **1893**, rediscovery of the Forms of Life.

3221 . . . [3² = 9]21 . . . 921
921 - <129> = **792**.
Anakhita, the space in-between: 110 118 182 229
[182 + 229 = 411] - [<281> + <922> = 1203] = **792** ↔
127 89 119 81, feng shui . . . 12789 – 11981 = **792**.
792 * 7 = 5544 . . . 554 weeks / 4 days = 3882 days . . . **3882**, the Unlettered Prophet.
[792 = <297>] * 6 = **1782**, the Second Coming
921 + <129> = **1050** ↔
Anakhita, the space in-between: 110 118 182 229
110 + <011> + 118 + <811> = **1050**.

[4702, Buddha / finger = <20:74> = 874 PM] + 176, Buddha / finger = **1050**.

5252, Jesus . . . 525 * 2 = **1050** ↔

Thessalonians 2:1 to 2:4, discusses the Second Coming . . . 2:01 + 2:02 + 2:03 + 2:04 = 810.
8:10 = 490 minutes . . . 4:90 PM is 16:90 = 1050 minutes . . . **1050** ↔

2299 . . . [229 * 9 = 2061] = 1011, Pahana + **1050**.

1011, Pahana . . . 10:(11) is 9:49 . . . 949 minutes = 15:49 . . . **1549**, the Light.
2299 = 14/8/4, I'll see you tomorrow at 815 + 815 →
2299 . . . 22 * 9 * 9 = **1782**, the Second Coming →

my birth day: 2/3/47 + 3/2/47 + 34/47 = 9041 . . . <**1409**>, John Kordupel.
9041, my birth day + 1409, John Kordupel = 10450 . . . 10:450 = 1050 minutes . . . **1050**.
John Kordupel, format ↔ synthesis: 153 159 167 145
[153 + 159 + 167 + 145 = 624] + <426> = **1050**.
10:50 PM is 22:50 . . . **2250**, New Harmonic Vibrations.

362,346,777 . . . [362 = <263>] + [346 = <643>] = 906 . . . **90/{6}**, a marriage.

362 + <263> + 346 + <643> + 777 + <777> = **3168** ↔
3168 + <8613> = **11781** ↔
Buddha: 40 116 122 34
(40 + 116 + 122 + 34 + ([<04> + <611> + <221> + <43> = 879] + <978> = 2169) + <9612> = **11781**.

Fo-Hi / Krishna / Buddha / Lao Tzu / Confucius: 364 468 500 243 . . . 500:364 − 243:468 = 256896.
256896 . . . { ([2 + 56 = 58] + 8 = 66) * 96 = 6336 } / 2 = 3168 + <8613> = **11781**.

11781 . . . [1 + 1781 = **1782**, the Second Coming] + **7227**, Book-End = **9009**, the Six Horsemen ↔
9009, the Mahdi, the Second Coming, Maitreya, the Unlettered Prophet, Kalki, the Messiah
9009, the Six Horsemen + **2772**, the Chain of Rebirth = **11781**.
and,
13/1/7, You have made the bed as far as you could. Now it is up to Me . . .
[200{6} + 2007 + 13/1 + 1/13 = 4257] + <7524> = **11781**.

31:68 = 1 day / 7:68 . . . **1768**, Messiah ↔ **1768**, the Chain of Rebirth ↔
13/1/{6}, You have made the bed as far as you could. Now it is up to Me . . . 131/ 6 days = 145:31 + <131> =
146:62
14:662 = 1502 minutes + <266> = **1768**.

and,
the story so far:
Buddha's finger: 2,21,4,4,8,1,19 6,9,14,7,5,18: 221448119 + 69147518 = **290595637**.
Buddha / finger: 2,21,4,4,8,1 6,9,14,7,5,18: 2214481 + 69147518 = **71361999**.
290595637 + 71361999 = 361,957,636.

[389141, China = <141983>] + [361957636, Buddha's / Buddha finger = <636759163>] = 636,901,146.
636,901,146 . . . [636 + 901 + 146 = **1683**] + <3861> = **5544** ↔
Anakhita: 65 143 151 57 . . . [151:57 − 143:65 = 792] * 7 = **5544** ↔ 5544 . . . [5 + 5 = 10]44 . . . **1044**, Anakhita ↔
10/(44), I cannot talk with you about your world unless you know about mine. Get out of My Car ↔

9:25. Know therefore and understand, that from the going forth of the commandment to restore and to build Jerusalem unto the Messiah the Prince shall be seven weeks, and threescore and two weeks: the streets shall be built again, and the wall, even in troubled times.
9:26. And after the threescore and two weeks shall Messiah be cut off, but not for himself: and the people of the prince that shall come shall destroy the city and the sanctuary; and the end thereof shall be with a flood, and unto the end of the war desolations are determined. Daniel. Holy Bible. King James Version.

9:25 + 9:26 = 1851 . . . 18:51 is 1 day / (5:49) . . . **1549**, the Light . . . 15/4/9 is 105/9 . . . **1059**, a page in the life of . . .

([9:25 = 565 minutes] + [9:26 = 566 minutes] = 1131) + [18:51 = 6:51 PM = **1782**, the Second Coming.
[925 minutes = 15:25 . . . 1525] + [926 minutes = 15:26 . . . 1526] = 3051.
   30:51 = 1 day / 6:51 . . . 1651 . . . **16/(51)**, it certainly is your Playground.
   30:51 = 1851 minutes . . . 1851 . . . 18:(51) = 1029 minutes + <15> = **1044**.

636,901,146 . . . <636> + <109> + <641> = **1386** ↔
  Anakhita: 65 143 151 57 . . . ([151:57 − 143:65 = 792] * 7 = 5544) / 4 = **1386**.
  1386 + <6831> = **8217** ↔
    34:25. And I will make with them a covenant of peace, and will cause the evil beasts to cease out of the land: and they shall dwell safely in the wilderness, and sleep in the woods.
    Ezekiel. Holy Bible. King James Version.
    34:25, taking the evil beasts out of the land: [34:25 is 1 day / 10:25] + [34:25 is 10:25 / 1 day] = 21276.
      [21:(276) = 984 minutes + <672> = 1656] + <6561> = **8217**.

    John Eevash Kordupel: 209 153 266 191 . . .
    ([209 + 153 + 266 + 191 = 819] + [<902> + <351> + <662> + <191> = 2106] = 2925) + <5292> = **8217**.
      [8217 + <7128> = 15345] / 3 = 5115 . . . **(51)/{15}**, it most certainly is your Playground.

636,901,146 . . . [636 + 901 + 146 = **1683** = <3861>] + [<636> + <109> + <641> = 1386 = <6831>] = 10692.
10692 / 12 = **891**, the Day of Resurrection ↔

  10692 − **1683** = **9009** ↔ [1716, Anakhita * 7 = 12012] - <21021> = **9009**.
    updating the Scriptures: the Mahdi, the Second Coming, Maitreya, the Unlettered Prophet, Kalki, the Messiah:
      720 996 1062 654.
    720 + 996 + 1062 + 654 = 3432) + <2343> = 5775; [<027> + <699> + <2601> + <456> = 4783] + <3874> = 8657.
      [5775 + 8657 = 14432] - <23441> = **9009**.
        and,
        9009 = **1782**, the Second Coming + **7227**, Book-End.

636,901,146 . . . [636 + 901 + 146 = 1683 + <3861> = 5544] + [<636> + <109> + <641> = 1386 + <6831> = 8217] = **13761**.
  13761 . . . 13:761 = 1541 minutes . . . 1541
  [1541 minutes = <1451>] + <167> = 1618 . . . 16:18 = 1 day / (782) . . . **1782**, the Second Coming.
  1541 minutes + <167> = **1708** . . . 1 day / 7:08 = 31:08 . . . 3108.
    31:08 = 1868 minutes . . . **18/68**.
    3108 + <8013> = 11121 = <12111> . . . 121:11 = 5 days / 1:11 . . . 5111.
      5111 - <1115> = 3996
        3996 / 6 = **666**, the Number of Man.
        3996 . . . 3 * 99 * 6 = **1782**, the Second Coming.
        3996 − [20{17} + 2018 = 4035] = 39 . . . **39/20{17} / 2018** falls on **{17}/8/2** ↔
        3/9/20{17} / 2018, M/D/YY, is **18/68**.

    51:11 = 3:11 / 2 days . . . 31:12 = 1872 minutes + <21> = **1893**, the Chain of Rebirth.

13761 = <16731> . . . 16:731 = 1691 minutes - <137> = **1554**, China
  1691 minutes + <137> = 1828 . . . 18:(28) = 1052 minutes + <82> = 1134 minutes = 18:54 . . . **18/54** is **18/2/(5)** ↔

18:25 is 6:25 PM . . . **625**, Robert needs 14 days to tidy things up.

13761 . . . [13:761 = 1541 minutes + <167> = 1708] + [<16731> . . . 16:731 = 1691 minutes + <137> = 1828] = **3536**.
   3536 = <6353>
      63:53 = (8:07) / 3 days . . . 8073 – [3 days / 8:07) . . . 3807] = **4266**, Jesus ↔
      [1695, Second Coming ↔ 1695 Unlettered Prophet] - <5961> = **4266**.

   6353 . . . 63 * 53 = **3339** ↔ Resurrection: 1782 + 378 + 1179 = **3339**.
      [4266, Jesus + <6624> = 10890] – [3339, Resurrection + <9333> = 12672] = **1782**.
      1782, the Chain of Rebirth ↔ **1782**, the Second Coming ↔ {17}/8/2.

  3536 / 2 = **1768** . . . {17}/68 falls on 18/9/3, Y/D/M ↔ 1893, the Chain of Rebirth ↔
    1768, the Chain of Rebirth ↔
      13/1/{6}, You have made the bed as far as you could. Now it is up to Me . . .
        131/ 6 days = 145:31 + <131> = 146:62 = 1502 minutes + <266> = **1768** ↔

2250, New Harmonic Vibrations . . . 2 days / (250) = 45:50 - <052> = 4498 . . . 44 * 9 * 8 = 3168 . . . 31:68 = 1 day /
7:68 . . . **{17}/68**.

Sleeping Dragon, Crouching Tiger: Sleeping Dragon. (continued).
Tibet: 20,9,2,5,20 . . . 2092 + 520 = **2612**.
2612 . . . 261² = **68121** . . . 6812 + 1 = **6813**.
   68121, Tibet = **57111**, Nibiru + **8238**, a Galactic cycle + **2772**, the Chain of Rebirth

  a transfer of Cosmic Consciousness from Nibiru to Tibet.

   68121, Tibet + **1549**, the Light = **60505**, Earth / metamorphosis t + **9165**, the Unlettered Prophet.

2612 = <**2162**> ↔ Buddha: 40 116 122 34 . . . 34:122 = 2162 minutes . . . 2162 ↔ **2162**, Jesus.

2612 . . . [2⁶ = 64]12 . . . 6412 - <2146> = **4266**, Jesus ↔ [**1695**, Second Coming ↔ **1695**, Unlettered Prophet] - <5961>
= **4266**.
   1695, Second Coming, Unlettered Prophet = <5961> . . . [5 + 9 = 14]61 . . . **1461**, Second Coming, Unlettered
   Prophet ↔
      11634127, feng shi – 389141, China = 11 244 986 . . . [112 + 4 = 116]4 . . . 1164 + 986 = 2150] - <689> = **1461**.

2612 . . . 1763, the other Book-End . . . 1√763 = 27622454 . . .27 * 6 = 162 – 2 = 160 + 2 = 162 * 4 = 648 + 5 = 653 *
4 = **2612**.

([2612, Tibet = <2162>] + [China: 1124 + <384> = 1508] = **3670)** - **483**, China = **3187**.
3187 . . . 318 * 7 = **2226**, Jesus ↔
   22:26 is 10:26 PM . . . 10:26 is 11:(34) . . . 1134 minutes = 18:54 . . . **18/54**
    3187 . . . 3 * 18 * 7 = 378 ↔
      Resurrection: 147 147 159 153
      [<741:741> + <351:951> = 1093692] - <2963901> = 1870209 . . . 18 + <81> + 70 + 209 = **378** ↔
      John Kordupel, synthesis from format: 153 159 167 145
        ([153 + 159 + 167 = 479] + <974> = 1453) + [145 + <541> = 686] = 2139.
          2139 . . . [213 * 9 = 1917] - [21:39 is 9:39 PM . . . 939 minutes = 15:39 . . . 1539, John Kordupel] = **378**.

3187 . . . ([31 * 87 = 2697] + 378 = 3075) - 2226 = 849
    849 minutes = 14:09 . . . **1409**, John Kordupel ↔ 849 minutes = 15:(51) . . . **{15}/(51)**, a Playground.

31:(87) = 1773 minutes . . . 1773.
    1773 minutes - <78> = **1695**, the Light →
        [1695 - <5961> = **4266**, Jesus] → **1695**, Second Coming ↔ 1695, the Unlettered Prophet ↔
        John Kordupel, Synthesis From Format: 153 159 167 145.
        [153 + 159 + 167 + 145 = 624] + <426> + [<351> + <951> + <761> + <541> = 2604] + <4062> = 7716.
        [1:45 is 2:(15) = <512>] + [<5:41> being 6:(19) = <916>] = 1428 + <8241> = 9669 . . . 9 * 669 = 6021.
        6021 – 7716 = **1695**, John Kordupel

    1773 minutes + <78> = 1851 . . . 18/(51) falls on **{17}/11/10** ↔
    17/11/10, I cannot talk with you about your world unless you know about mine. Get out of My Car.

    [17:73 is 5:73 PM = <375>] * 6 = **2250**, New Harmonic Vibrations.
and,
Tibet: 20,9,2,5,20 . . . [209 + <902> = **1111**] - 2520 = **1409**, John Kordupel.

Tibet: 20,9,2,5,20 . . . 20 + 925 + 20 = **965** ↔
    5225, Iwan Kordupel + [John Kordupel: 1409 + 1463 + <3641> = 6513] = 11738.
    11738 – [1539, John Kordupel * 7 = 10773] = **965** = <**569**>, Jesus.

1551, Resurrection, the beginning of the 1,000 year reign of Jesus → {15}/(51), it is most definitely your Playground . . .
1√551 = 2347.
    √2347 = 4844 5846 . . . 4844 + 5846 = 10690; <4484> + <6485> = 10969.
    2√347 = 4316 0092 . . . <u>4316</u> + <u>0092</u> = <u>4408</u>; <u><6134></u> + <u><2900></u> = <u>9034</u>.
        9160 + 5838 15098; 10618 + 9385 = 20003.
        √<30002> = 1732 1085 . . . 17:(32) = 988 minutes - <23> = **965**, a Playground.

Tibet: 20,9,2,5,20 . . . [209 + <902> = **1111**] + 2520 = **3631**, Tibet ↔ **3631**, the Lamb
    3631 . . . 3 * 631 = **1893**, Tibet ↔ **1893**, the Chain of Rebirth

    3631 . . . 36 * 31 = **1116**, Tibet
        <61:11> = 3671 minutes = <**1763**>, the other Book-End
    1116 + <6111> = **7227**, Book-End.

3631 + 2612 = **6243**.
    6243 + <3426> = **9669** . . . 9 * 66 * 9 = 5346 = **1782**, the Chain of Rebirth + **1782**, the Second Coming + **{17}/8/2**.

    6243 . . . [6² = 36]43 . . . 3643 . . . [36 * 4 = 144]3 . . . **1443**.
    2 BC / (73), birth of Jesus + **1782**, the Second Coming . . . 178² = 31684 . . . [3 * 1684 = 5052] = 5325
        5325 = **292/2 BC**, birth of Jesus + 2403.
        2403 = <3042> . . . 30:(42) = 1758 minutes + <24> = **1782**, the Second Coming.
        [2403 + <3042> = 5445] + **1782**, the Second Coming = **7227**, Book-End.
        [24:03 = 1443 minutes . . . 1443] * 7 = 10101 . . . **{10}/101**, Invitation to Change the Language.

[3631 = <1363>] + [2612 = <2162>] = 3525 . . . [3 * 5 * 25 = **375**] * 6 = **2250**, New Harmonic Vibrations.

and,

Tibet: 20,9,2,5,20 . . . [2:09 = 129 minutes . . . 129] + [209 minutes = 3:29 . . . 329] = **1050**.

   10:50 PM is 22:50 . . . **2250**, New Harmonic Vibrations

Tibet: 20,9,2,5,20 . . . [2:09 is 3:(51) . . .351] + [it is 51 to 3 . . . 513] = 864.

   [864 + <468> = **1332**] * 24 = **31968**.

   1332 = <2331> . . . 13 * 31 = **713**, the Season ends

   864 = <468> . . . 4:68 PM is 16:68 . . . **1668** ↔

   19:23. The sun was risen upon the earth when Lot entered Zoar.

   19:24. Then the Lord rained upon Sodom and upon Gomorrah brimstone and fire from the Lord out of heaven; Genesis.

   { ([19:23 is 7:23 PM] + [19:24 = 7:24 PM] = 1447 - <7441> = 5994) / 2 = 2997= <7992> } * 4 = **31968**.

   31968 = [7992 / 4 =1998 + <8991>] + **22264**, the Five Horsemen + **713**, the Season ends.

   31968 . . . [-3 + 19 = 16]68 . . . **1668**.

1668 . . . 1 day / 668 = 30:68 = 1868 minutes - <86> = **1782**, the Chain of Rebirth ↔ **1782**, the Second Coming ↔ **{17}/8/2** ↔

   18/68, being **{17}/3/9** ↔

   17:39 = 1059 minutes . . . **1059**, a page in the life of . . .

   14/8/4, I'll see you tomorrow at 815 . . . [14:84 = 924 minutes . . . 924] + 815 = **1739**.

864 + 1050 = **1914** ↔ **1782**, the Second Coming . . . 1 day / 782 = 31:82 = 1942 minutes - <28> = **1914**.

   19:14 is 7:14 PM . . . **714**.

   John: 10, 15, 8,14 + Kordupel: 11,15,18, 4, 21, 16, 5, 12 = 11,151,843,132,326:

   We separate 11,151,843,132,326 into two groups of seven, to which we add our birthday:

   [1115184 . . .1115 + 184 = 1299] + [2/03/194{6} + 3132326 = 5164272 . . . 5164 + 272 = 5436] = 6735.

      and,

      Thessalonians 2:1 to 2:4 discusses the Second Coming . . .

      ([2¹ = 2] [2² = 4] [2³ = 8] [2⁴ = 16] . . . 24816) + [2:01 + 2:02 + 2:03 + 2:04 = 810] = 25626.

         25:626 = 2126 minutes + <626> = 2752 . . . 27:(52) = 1568 minutes + <25> = **1593**.

      13/1/{6}, or 13/1/7, You have made the bed as far as you could. Now it is up to Me →

         [13:16 = 796 minutes . . . 796] + [13:17 = 797 minutes . . . 797] = **1593**.

   [6735 = <5376>] - [**1593** . . . 1 day / 5:93 = 29:93 . . . **2993**] = 2383.

   2993 . . . [2 * 9 = 18]93 . . . **1893**, the Chain of Rebirth

      23:(83) = 1297 minutes + <38> = 1335 . . . 13:35 = 815 minutes . . . **815**, Messiah.

      23:83 = 1463 minutes . . . **1463**, John Kordupel.

      2383 . . . 238 * 3 = **714**.

714 . . . 71⁴ = 2541 1681 . . . 2541 + 1681 = **4222**, Market Forces.

.

and,

the story so far:

Tibet: 20,9,2,5,20 . . . 2092 + 520 = **2612**.

Tibet: 20,9,2,5,20 . . . { ([209 + <902> = **1111**] + 2520 = **3631**) + 2612 = 6243 } + <3426> = **9669**

Tibet: 20,9,2,5,20 . . . [2:09 = 129 minutes] + [209 minutes = 3:29] = 1050 . . . 10:50 PM is 22:50 . . . **2250**, New Harmonic Vibrations.

Tibet: 20,9,2,5,20 . . . ([2:09 is 3:(51) . . .351] + [it is 51 to 3 . . . 513] = **864**) + <468> = **1332**.

Tibet: 20,9,2,5,20 . . . [209 = <902>] + [2520 + <0252> = **2772**, the Chain of Rebirth] = **3674**.
  3674 . . . [3 + 6 = 9] * 74 = **666**, the Heart-Beat Grid.

Tibet: 20,9,2,5,20 . . . ([2:09 is 3:(51) . . .351] + [it is 51 to 3 . . . 513] = **864**) + [2772 + 864 = 3636] - <468> = **3168** ↔
  389141, China + 361957636, Buddha's / Buddha finger = 362,346,777 . . . 362 + <263> + 346 + <643> + 777 + <777>
  = **3168** ↔
    3168, Tibet . . . 31:68 = 1 day / 7:68 . . . **1768**.
      1768 - (Tibet: [1332 = <2331>] + 2250 = **4581**) = 2813 = <**3182**>, Tibet
        3182, Tibet . . . 31:82 is 1 day / 7:82 . . . **1782**, Resurrection . . . **1782**, the Second Coming.
          9669, Tibet – [3182 + <2813> = 5995] = **3674**, Tibet.

      3182, Tibet + 3631, Tibet = **6813**, Tibet.
        6813 . . . (6 * [813 + <318> = 1131] = 6786) + <6876> = 13662 . . . [1 + 3 = 4]662 . . . **4662**.
        [**4662**, Intervention From Above = <2664>] / 4 = **666**.

        6813 . . . 6 * [813 - <318> = 495 = <594>] = **3564**.
          Fo-Hi / Krishna / Buddha / Lao Tzu / Confucius: 364 468 500 243
            500:364 – 243:468 = 256896, the Eastern influence.
            256896 . . . ([2 + 56 = 58] + 8 = 66) * 9 * 6 = **3564**.
              3564 = **1782**, the Chain of Rebirth + **1782**, the Second Coming.

        6813 = [2669, Isa / Jesus ↔ 2669, John Kordupel] + 4144, you've made your bed, it is up to Me now.

    1768, the Chain of Rebirth ↔ {17}/68 ↔
      13/1/{6}, You have made the bed as far as you could. Now it is up to Me . . .
        131/ 6 days = 145:31 + <131> = 146:62 = 1502 minutes + <266> = **1768** ↔

                              and,

2250, New Harmonic Vibrations . . . 2 days / (250) = 45:50 - <052> = 4498 . . . 44 * 9 * 8 =3168 . . . 31:68 = 1 day /
7:68 . . . **{17}/68**.

and,
Tibet: 2092520 . . . 2092520 – 0 = 209252 . . . [209 + <902> = **1111**] – **252** = **859**, Earth / metamorphosis
  [452, Isa + 1179, Jesus = 1631, Messiah] + [997, Jesus + 614, Isa + 806, Ezra + 713, Jesus = 4761] – 3650, Jesus =
  1111. 1161, Gaia . . . 11 * 61 = 671, Magdalene . . . 671 minutes = 11:11 . . . 671 + 1111 = **1782**, the Second Coming.
  and
  $101 + $873, the Collective Will = 974 . . . 9 * 7 * 4 = 252.

  2092520 . . . [2092 + 5 = 2097]20 . . . 209720.
  2092520 . . . [209 – 2 = 207]520 . . . 207520.
  2092520 . . . [209 + 2 = 211]520 . . . 211520.
  2092520 . . . [20925 + 2 = 20927]0 . . . 209270.
  2092520 . . . [20925 – 2 = 20923]0 . . . 209230.
  2092520 . . . 2092520 – '0' = 209252.
    209720 + 207520 + 211520 + 209270 + 209230 + 209252 = 1256512 . . . 1256 + 512 = 1768 . . . **1768**, Tibet ↔

389141, China + 361957636, Buddha's / Buddha finger = 362,346,777 . . . 362 + <263> + 346 + <643> = 777 + <777>
= **3168** ↔

31:68 = 1 day / 7:68 . . . **1768**, Messiah ↔ **1768**, the Chain of Rebirth ↔

13/1/{6}, You have made the bed as far as you could. Now it is up to Me . . . 131/ 6 days = 145:31 + <131> = 146:62
14:662 = 1502 minutes + <266> = **1768**.

2250, New Harmonic Vibrations . . . 2 days / (250) = 45:50 - <052> = 4498 . . . 44 * 9 * 8 =3168 . . . 31:68 = 1 day /
7:68 . . . **{17}/68**.

Sleeping Dragon, Crouching Tiger: Sleeping Dragon. (continued)

China: 3,8,9,14,1: **Tibet:** 20,9,2,5,20: 389141 + 2092520 = **2,481,661**.
2481661 / 7 = 354523 . . . 354 + 523 = **877** ↔
877, I Am/God/Allah/Yahwe . . . 8:77 = 557 minutes . . . **557** ↔
the Five Horsemen: The Mahdi / The Second Coming / Maitreya / The Unlettered Prophet / Kalki: 613 843
899 **557**.

877 minutes = 14:37 . . . 1437 + 557 = **1994**, the Light ↔ **1994**, Christ.
19:(94) = 1046 minutes - <49> = **997**, Jesus Christ ↔
34/47, my birth day; day 34 fell on a Monday so it was week 6, day 1, year 47 . . . 6147;
it was day 1, week 6, year 47 . . . 1647.
[6147 + 1647 = 7794] + [2/3/47 + 3/2/47 + 34/47 = 9041] = 16835.
16835 - [<7416> + <7461> = 14877] = 1958 . . . 19:(58) = 1082 minutes - <85> = **997**.
John (Eeevash) Kordupel, alphabet R to L: 17, 12, 19, 13 22, 22, 5, 26, 8, 19 16, 12, 9, 23, 6, 11, 22, 15 →
arranged in a from and to tablet structure . . . 277 + 222 + 498 = **997**.

1994 = <**4991**>
The Tabernacle was 2.5 cubits (1.15m/3 ft 9 in) in length and 1.5 cubits (0.69m/2 ft 3 in) in breadth and
height.
2.5/1.5/1.5 . . . 251515; 1.15/.69/.69 . . . 1156969 . . . 115 * 69 * 69 = 547515;
3 ft 9 in/2 ft 3 in/2 ft 3 in . . . 392323 . . . 39 * 23 * 23 = 20631;
45 in/27 in/ 27 in . . . 452727 . . . 45 * 27 * 27 = 32805.
[251515 + 547515 = 799030] – [20631 + 32805 = 53436] = 745594 . . . [74 – 55 = 19]94 . . . 1994 = <**4991**>
and,
Yi - King: 25, 9 - 11, 9, 14, 7; 259 119147 . . . [25911 + 9147 = 35058 - <85053> = 49995.
49995 . . . - 4 + [999 * 5 = 4995] = **4991**.

35058, Fo-Hi - <85053> = 49995 . . . - 4 + [999 * 5 = 4995] = **4991**.

one Scripture talking to another.

1901, Evolution; 19:01 is (4:99) / 1 day . . .**4991**.

4991 / 7 = **713**, an evolutionary cycle comes to an end.

and,
China: 3,8,9,14,1: **Tibet:** 20,9,2,5,20: 389141 + 2092520 = **2,481,661**.
2481661 - <1661842> = **819 819**.
819819 . . . 8 + 1981 + 9 = **1998**.
819819 . . . 8 * [198 - <891> = 693] = **5544**

[693 = <396>] * 9 = **3564** . . . 3564 / 8 = 445.5 . . . **4455**.

5544 + <4455 + 3564 + <4653> + 1998 + <8991> = 29205

29:205 = 1945 minutes - <502> = **1443**

1549, the Light . . . 1549 weeks = 10843 days . . . 10:843 = 1443 minutes . . . **1443**.

1443, the Light * 7 = 10101 . . . **{10}/101**, Invitation to Change the Language.

[29205 - <50292> = 21087] / 11 = **1917** ↔

19:17 is 1 day / (4:43) . . . **1443**, the Light ↔ **1917**, Christ ↔

19:17 is 1 day / (483) . . . **14/8/{3}**, I'll see you tomorrow.

Kalki: 968 + 949 = **1917**.

John Kordupel, synthesis from format: 153 159 167 145.

([153 + 159 + 167 = 479] + <974> = 1453) + [145 + <541> = 686] = 2139

2139 / 3 = **713**, the Season ends.

2139 . . . 213 * 9 = **1917** ↔

[1917 / 3 = **639** + <936> = 1575] + **1443** = 3018 . . . 30:(18) = 1782 minutes . . . **1782**.

6:39 PM is 18:39 . . . **18/39** is **{17}/8/2** ↔

18/3/9, Y/M/D is **{17}/68** ↔

1768, Messiah ↔ **1768**, the Chain of Rebirth ↔

13/1/{6}, You have made the bed as far as you could. Now it is up to Me . . . 131/ 6 days = 145:31 + <131> = 146:62

14:662 = 1502 minutes + <266> = **1768**.

2250, New Harmonic Vibrations . . . 2 days / (250) = 45:50 - <052> = 4498 . . . 44 * 9 * 8 =3168 . . . 31:68 = 1 day / 7:68 . . . **{17}/68**.

and,

China: 3,8,9,14,1: **Tibet**: 20,9,2,5,20: 389141 + 2092520 = **2,481,661**.

2481661 / 7 = 354523 + < > = 679 976 / 11 = 61816

61:(816) = 2844 minutes - <618> = **2226**, Jesus.

2226 + 877 = 3103 . . . 31:03 = 1863 minutes + <30> = **1893**, the Chain of Rebirth.

61:816 = 4476 minutes + <618> = 5094 . . . 50:94 = 294 / 2 days . . . 29:42 = 1782 minutes . . . **1782** ↔

1782, Resurrection ↔ **1782**, the Second Coming.

2481661, China / Tibet . . . (2 * [481 + <184> = 665] = 1330) + 661 = 1991 - <166> = **1825** ↔ **18/25** ↔ **18/2/(5)**, being **18/54** ↔

18:25 is 6:25 PM . . . **625**, Robert begins to tidy things up.

and,

the story so far:

China: 3,8,9,14,1: **Tibet**: 20,9,2,5,20: 389141 + 2092520 = **2,481,661**.

2481661 / 7 = 354523 . . . 354 + 523 = **877** ↔

877, I Am/God/Allah/Yahwe . . . 8:77 = 557 minutes . . . **557** ↔

the Five Horsemen: The Mahdi / The Second Coming / Maitreya / The Unlettered Prophet / Kalki: 613 843 899 **557**.

[877 minutes = 14:37 . . . **1437**] + [877 = <778> . . . 778 minutes = 12:58 . . . **1258**] = **2695**, continued below.

Tibet: 20,9,2,5,20: [20 + 9 + 2 + 5 + 20 = **56**] + [209 + 2520 = **2729**] + [2092 + 520 = **2612**] = **5397**.
China: 3,8,9,14,1 . . . [3 + 8 + 9 + 14 + 1 = 35] + [389 + 141 = 530] = **565**.
        565, China + 5397, Tibet = **5962** = <**2695**>, Buddha → 2695, Buddha / finger ↔

The energy of the Buddha runs through Tibet and China.

[John: 1015 + 814 = 1829] + 4757, John Kordupel = 6586; [1829 = <9281>] - 6586 = **2695**.

        Genesis. 1:27 . . . 12⁷ = 358 31808.

$$358\ 31\ 808 \ldots 358 + <853> + 31 + <13> + [8:08\ is\ 9:(52) \ldots 952] + <259> = \mathbf{2466}.$$

        2466 . . . [2 + 4 = 6]66 . . . **666**, the Number of Man.
        2466 . . . 24 * 6 * 6 = 864 = <468> . . . 4:68 PM is 16:68 . . . 1 day / 668 = 30:68 = 1868 minutes . . . **18/68**.
        24:66 = 1506 minutes + <66> = 1572 . . . 1 day / 572 = 29:72 . . . 2972.
                29:(72) = 1668 minutes . . . 1 day / 668 = 30:68 = 1868 minutes . . . **18/68**.
                29:72 = 1812 minutes + <27> = 1839 . . . **18/39** is {17}/8/2 ↔ **18/3/9** is **18/68**.

        358 31 808 358 + <853> + 31 + <13> = **1255**, Jesus ↔ 1255, Second Coming
                8:08 is 9:(52) . . . 952 - <259> = 693 . . . 6 :93 PM is 18:93 . . . **1893**, the Chain of Rebirth.

        358 31 808 . . . 358 + <853> + 31 + <13> + 808 + <808> = **2871**, Buddha = <**1782**>, the Second Coming.

        358 31 808 . . . 358 + <853> + 31 + <13> + 808 + [8:08 is 9:(52) . . . 952] + <259> = 3274
                3274 . . . [3² = 9] *74 = **666**, the Number of Man
                32:(74) = 1846 minutes + <47> = **1893**, the Chain of Rebirth

        358 31 808 . . . **358**, the Lamb ↔ - 31 + 808 = **777**.
                the Five Horsemen updating the Scriptures: the Mahdi / the Second Coming / Maitreya / the Messiah /
                Kalki: 465 731 **777** 419.
                [John: 10, 15, 8,14] + [Kordupel: 11,15,18, 4, 21, 16, 5, 12] = 11,151,843,132,326:
                We separate 11,151,843,132,326 into two groups of seven, to which we add our birthday:
                        1115184 . . .1115 + 184 = 1299
                                1299 + [3132326 + (331)1947 = 6444273 . . . 644 + 4273 = 4917] = 6216) / 8 = **777**.

and,
777 . . . [777 minutes = 12:57 . . . 1257] + [777 days = 111 weeks . . . 111] + [1:11 is 2:(49) . . . 249] = 1617.
        1617 minutes = 26.95 hours . . . **2695**, Buddha ↔ **2695**, John Kordupel.
        1617 . . . 1/(6)/{17} is **18/25** . . . 18:25 is 6:25 PM . . . **625**, Robert begins to tidy things up.

[777 + 1617 + 977] + [1617 + 777 = 2394] + [1617 minutes = 26.95 hours . . . 2695] + [1617 minutes = 26:57 . . . 2657] = 11117.
11:117 = 777 minutes . . . **777**.
        11117 . . . 11 * 117 = **1287**, Leanne Long.
        12:(87) = 633 minutes + <78> = **711**, a Cycle ends.
                1287 . . . 12 * 87 = **1044** ↔

        10/(44), I cannot talk with you about your world unless you know about mine. Get out of My Car.

and,
China, 389141 + **Tibet**, 2092520 = **2,481,661**.
        2481661 . . .2 * 481,661 = 963 322 . . . [963 + 322 = **1285**] + [<369> + <223> = **592**] = **1877**, Mary Magdalene.

1877, Mary Magdalene . . . [-1 + 8 = 7]77 . . . **777**, Mary Magdalene + **777**, Eve = **1554** ↔
3147, Leanne Long, the space in-between – 1593, Leanne Long = **1554**.

([1285 = <5821>] - [592 = <295>] = 5526) / 9 = **614**, Isa ↔
Redeemer: 73 135 143 65 . . . [73 + 135 + 143 + 65 = **416**, Jesus] = <**614**> ↔
Fo-Hi / Krishna / Buddha / Lao Tzu / Confucius: 364 468 500 243 . . . 500:468 – 243:364 = 257104.
257104, the Eastern influence . . . ([2 * 57 = 114] – 10 = 104) * 4 = **416**.

12:85 = 805 minutes . . . **805**, End of Days.
805, End of Days + 1877, Mary Magdalene + 614, Isa = 3296
32:(96) = 1824 minutes + <69> = **1893**, the Chain of Rebirth.

[1285 - <5821> = 4536] / 4 = 1134 . . . 1134 minutes = 18:54 . . . **18/54** is **18/2/(5)**.

1285 . . . [1 day / 285 = 26:85] + [805 = <508>] = 3193.
[3193 = <3913>] - **805**, End of Days = 3108
3108 + <8013> = 11121
11121 = [**1877**, Mary Magdalene + <7781>] + **1463**, John Kordupel.
11121 = <12111> . . . 121:11 = 5 days / 1:11 . . . 5111.
5111 = **1877**, Mary Magdalene + **1409**, John Kordupel + **1825**.

31:08 = 1868 minutes . . . **18/68** ↔

31:93 = 1 day / 7:93 . . . **{17}/9/3** is **{17}/68**, the Chain of Rebirth.

31:93 = 1953 minutes - <39> = **1914** . . . 19:14 is 7:14 PM . . . **714** . . . 71^4 = 2541 1681 . . . 2541 + 1681 = **4222**.

and,

Leanne Long:	99	161	171	89	the space in-between:	78	10	86
High Priestess:	162	176	189	149	the space in-between:	146	13	148
the Morgans:	321	433	462	292	the space in-between:	352	29	362
	582	770	822	530		576	52	596

([**582** + 770 + 822 + 530 = **2704**] + <4072> = **6776**) + ([<285> + <077> + <228> + <035> = **625**] + <526> = **1151**)
= **7927**.

and,

1151, Leanne Long / High Priestess / the Morgans . . . 11:51 = 711 minutes . . . **711**, a Cycle ends.
7927, Leanne Long / High Priestess / the Morgans = <7297> . . . 72:97 = 3 days / 0:97 . . . **3097**.
30:97 = 1897 minutes - <79> = **1818**, Magdalene.
30:(97) = 1703 minutes + <79> = **1782**.
30:(97) = 1703 minutes = <**3071**>
3071 minutes - <79> = 2992 . . . 29:92 = 1832 minutes + <29> = 1861 . . . **18/(6)/1** is **18/25** . . . **1825**.
18:25 is 6:25 PM . . . **625**, Leanne Long / High Priestess / the Morgans ↔
625, Robert needs 14 days to tidy things up.

3071 + 1151 = **4222**, Leanne Long / High Priestess / the Morgans.
The last price of gold set by government was in February 1973 when it was increased from $38 an ounce to $42.22 an ounce. In November 1973 gold was officially released from government influence and was left to fluctuate according to market forces. The Elliott Wave Principle. Frost and Prechter.
4222, Market Forces, an expression of the Collective Will.

and,

the story so far:

China, 389141 + **Tibet**, 2092520 = **2,481,661**.

    2481661 . . .2 * 481,661 = 963 322 . . . [963 + 322 = **1285**] + [<369> + <223> = **592**] = **1877**.

    2481661 . . . <1 + 661 + 842> = **1504**, Mary Magdalene.

    2481661 . . .[2 * 4 * 81 * 6 = 3888] – 6 = 3882 * 1 = **3882**, the Unlettered Prophet.

       3882 + 1877 + 1504 = **7263**.

          7263 . . . [7 * 2 = 14]63 . . . **1463**, John Kordupel.

          7263 . . . 72[6³ = 216] . . . 72216 . . . [7 + 2 = 9]216 . . . 9216

             9216 = **8328**, a Galactic cycle + 978 . . . 978 minutes = 16:18 = 1 day / (7:82) . . . **1782**, the Second Coming.

      3882 . . . 3[8 * 8 = 64]2 . . .**3642**, Intervention From Above / 2 = 1821

        18:(21) = 1059 minutes . . . **1059**, a page in the life of . . .

        18:21 is 1 day / (5:39) . . . **1539**, John Kordupel

        1821 * 5 = **9105**.

          91:05 = 5465 minutes . . . 5465 . . . [5 + 4 = 9] 65 . . . 965.

          (5225, Iwan Kordupel + [John Kordupel: 1409 + 1463 + <3641> = 6513]) = 11738.

             11738 – [1539, John Kordupel * 7 = 10773] = **965** = <**569**>, Jesus.

        91:05 = (4:55)/4 days . . . 4554 . . . 4 days / 554 weeks = 3882 days . . . **3882**, the Unlettered Prophet.

        91:05 = 4 days / (4:55) . . . 4455 + [<5544> / 2 = **2772**, Chain of Rebirth] = **7227**, Book-End.

      Mary Magdalene: 119 219 232 106 . . . 119 + 219 + 232 + 106 = 676.

      676 . . . 6⁷ = 279936 . . . 279 + <972> + 936 + <639> = 2826 . . . ([282 * 6 = 1692] - <2961> = 1269) – 6 = 1263.

        [12:(63) = 657 minutes] - <36> = 621 . . . [6:21 PM is 18:21] * 5 = **9105**.

9105, I cannot talk with you about your world unless you know about mine. Get out of My Car.

and,

[China/Tibet: 1285 + 1504 + 3882 = **6671**] + [**2162**, Buddha ↔ 2162, Jesus = <**2612**>] + 2169, planet Earth, our World = 11452.

11452 = 2/3/47, my birth day + **9105**.

and,

      the Tree of Life: 134 204 217 121 the space in-between: 154 13 164

      the space in-between: 154 13 164 . . . 15413164 . . . [-15 + <51> + 4131 = 4167] + 64 + <46> = 4277.

          4277 - <7724> = 3447 . . . **34/47**, my birth day.

          4277 . . . 4 days / 277 = 98:77 - <772> = **9105**.

    11452 = **2695**, John Kordupel + **4222**, Market Forces + 4535.

       45:35 = 2735 minutes + <53> = 2682 . . . [[2682 / 2 = 1341] + [<2862> / 2 = 1431] = **2772**, the Chain of Rebirth.

       45:(35) = 2665 minutes - <53> = **2612** = <**2162**>, Buddha ↔ 2162, Jesus.

       4535 . . . 453 * 5 = 2265 . . . 22:(65) = 1255 minutes . . . **1255**, Jesus ↔ **1255**, Second Coming.

       4535 = <5354> . . . 53:(54) = 3126 minutes . . . 3126.

          3126 minutes + <45> = 3171 . . . 31:71 = 1931 minutes - <17> = **1914**.

          3126 minutes - <45> = 3081 . . . 30:81 = 1881 minutes . . . **1881**.

             1881 . . . 1[8 * 8 = 64]1 . . . **1641**.

             5238, God . . . 52:(38) = 3082 minutes - <83> = 2999 . . . 29:(99) = 1641 minutes . . . **1641**.

Earthlings: 113 147 157 103 . . .

113 + 147 + 157 + 103 = 520 = <025>

   025 + [<311> + <741> + <751> + <301> = 2104 + <4012> = 6116] = 6141.

   6√141 = 1080 3924 . . . [1080 + <0801> = **1881**] + 3924 + <4293> = 10101.

   10101, Dual Essence → **{10}/101**, invitation to change the language / 7 = **1443**, Kali Yuga.

1881 . . . 1[8 * 81 = 648] . . . 1648 + <8461> = **10109**, Eve.

1881 . . . 1day / 8:81 = 32:81 - <188> = 3093.

   Babylonians / Kali Yuga: 978 + <879> = 1857 = <7581> . . . 75:81 = 3 days / 3:81 . . . 3381

      3381 + <1833> = 5214 . . .52:14 = 3134 minutes - <41> = **3093**.

   30:93 = 1893 minutes . . . **1893**, the Chain of Rebirth ↔

   30:93 = 1 day / 6:93 . . . 1693 ↔

      Isaiah / Jeremiah / Ezekiel / Jesus Christ / the Prophet Muhammad / Krishna / Buddha / Fo-Hi: 705 1039 1106 636.

         705:1039 − 636:1106 = 689933 . . . 689 + <986> + 933 + <339> = 2947

            29:(47) = 1693 minutes . . . **1693**.

      my birthday: [19{46} + 1947 + 3/02 = 4195] − (25)/02 = **1693**.

      1693, my birth day . . . 16:93 is 4:93 PM . . . 493 minutes = 8:13 = 47 to 9 . . . **479**.

      John Kordupel, synthesis ↔ format: 153 159 167 145 . . . 153 + 159 + 167 = **479**.

Fo-Hi / Krishna / Buddha / Lao Tzu / Confucius: 364 468 500 243

   500:364 − 243:468 = 256896 . . . [<652> + <698> = 1350] + <0531> = **1881**.

   and,

1881 / 9 = 209 . . . 2:09 PM is 14:09 . . . **1409**, John Kordupel.

   209 + <902> = **1111**, John Eevash Kordupel + [11:11 = 671 minutes] = **1782**.

      You have made the bed as far as you could. Now it is up to Me:

      [7/13/1 + 7/1/13 = 14244] − 13/1/7 = 12927 . . . [12 * 92 = 1104] + 7 = **1111**.

(1881 + [(**68**)/7, beginning of end of time . . . 6:(87) = 273 minutes . . . 273] = 2154) - <372> = **1782**.

1999, Leanne Long . . . 1 day / 999 = 33:99 . . . 33:(99) = 1881 minutes . . . **1881**.

and,

AD 33/5/4, Palm Sunday . . . 33:(54) = 1926 minutes - <45> = 1881

and,

7 days after Palm Sunday, there was the Resurrection: 1881 * 7 = 13167

[13167 − 10109, Eve = 3058) - <8503> = 5445] + **1782** = **7227**, Book-End ↔

13/1/{6}/7, You have made the bed as far as you could. Now it is up to Me.

18:81 is (519)/1 days . . . 51:91 = 2 days / 391 . . . 23:(91) = 1289 minutes - <19> = 1270.

   12:70 = 790 minutes . . . **7/90**, a marriage →

   1270 minutes = 22:(50) . . . **2250**, New Harmonic Vibrations.

   and,

1881 . . . 1day / 8:81 = 32:81 . . . 32:(81) = 1839 minutes - <18> = 1821.

18:21. And a mighty angel took up a stone like a great millstone, and cast it into the sea, saying, Thus with violence shall that great city Babylon be thrown down, and shall be found no more. Revelations. Holy Bible. King James Version.

18:21. And if thou say in thine heart, How shall we know the word which the Lord hath not spoken?
18:22. When a prophet speaketh in the name of the lord, if the thing follows not, nor come to pass, that is the thing which the Lord hath not spoken, but the prophet hath spoken it presumptuously: though shalt not be afraid of him.
Deuteronomy. Holy Bible. King James Version.

4535 / 5 = **907**.
    Kali Yuga: 8127 + 14000 = 22127 . . . 2 + 2127 = 2129.
        21:29 = 1289 minutes . . . 12:89 = 809 minutes + <98> = **907**.
        2129, Kali Yuga – [963, Anakhita → 963, Product Recall] + <369> = 1332) = 797
            797 minutes = 13:17 . . . **1317** ↔
            13/1/7, You have made the bed as far as you could. Now it is up to Me ↔
        2129 . . . [21² = 441] * 9 = 3969 . . . 39:69 = 2409 minutes . . . 2409.
            [24:(09) = 1431 minutes . . . 1431] + [1431 minutes - <90> = 1341] = **2772**, Chain of Rebirth.
            2409 * 3 = **7227**, Book-End.
            7/3/31, a marriage . . . 7[33 past 1 is 2:(27) . . . 227] ↔ **7227**, Book-End.
    and,
    1199905, the Light . . . 11 + [99 * 9 = 891] + 05 = **907**.
    8107, Cherryl's reincarnational family tree . . . [8 + 1 = 9]07 . . . **907**.
    Leanne Long: ([<9991> + <8644> + <3892> + <4452> = 26979] - 11994 = 14985) / 5 = 2997.
        2997 . . . 2[9 * 9 = 18]2 . . . 2182 . . . 21:82 = 1342 minutes . . . **1342** . . . 1[34² = 1156] . . . 11156.
        11:156 = 816 minutes + <651> = 1467 . . . 14:67 = 907 minutes . . . **907**.
            90/7, Cher and I were married.
    and,
    From *The Birth of a New Earth Essence* on 11/4/2011 . . . it is {10}/101 . . . 10101, Dual Essence.
    I stepped out of the Car because I was not comfortable with the language between Heaven and Earth.

        So change it.

    2011 – 11/04 = **907**.

90/7, a marriage . . . between 10101, the Dual Essence, Heaven, and Earth, the Light, and a family tree.
↓
907, changing the language between Heaven and Earth → Product, Kali Yuga, recall.

Sleeping Dragon, Crouching Tiger: Sleeping Dragon. (continued).

"Life is initiation. Man once walked the Earth with full knowledge of the Oneness. All thoughts were one. All actions one. Then, with a single thought, an infinite number of thoughts – separate and collective – were formed. It was the creation of souls." P. 262

"C.K.: Do we have anything similar under our pyramid on Earth, in particular the Great Pyramid In Egypt?
GMS: *This as Cheops, remember was a name that was taken, not one that was given. This is the Pyramid of Understanding, one designed by Hermes himself, who in a later projection was the man **Jesus**. As such, the structure was built as a temple of*

understanding, a temple of wisdom. Also utilizing the same cosmic forces as those understood on Mars." P. 246. Notes From the Cosmos. Gordon – Michael Scallion.

China: 3,8,9,14,1 + **Isa**: 9,19,1 + **Hermes**: 8,5,18,13,5,19 = 852,211,851 . . . 852 + 211 + 851 = **1914** . . . 19:14 is 7:14 PM . . . **714**.
[Yahweh: 25,1,8,23,5,8 . . . 2518 + 2358 = 4876 * 10 = 48760] + [Eve, 5585 * 10 = 55850] = 104610 . . . 104 + 610 = **714**.

Flower of Life: 132 171 192 120 . . . <231> + <171> + <291> + <021> = **714**.

1106, the Eight Amigos + 13/8/7, spending the night / together = 2493.
2493 + 714 = 3207 = 1554, China + 1653

√714 = 2672 0778 . . . ([2672 + <2762> = 5434] + [0778 + <8770> = 9548] = **14982**) + [<4345> + <8459> = **12804**] = **27786**.
27786 . . . 2778 – 6 = **2772**, the Chain of Rebirth.
    666, a mark, a name, the number of a name . . . [√6 = 2449 4897] * 3 = 7348 4691.
      [2449 + <9442> = 11891] + [7348 + <8437> = 15785] = **27676**.
        [27676 / 4 = 6919 – [**2772** + **625** = 3397] = 3522) - <2253> = **1269**.
        1269 = <9621> . . . [96:21 = 4 days / 0:21 . . . 4021] + <1204> = **5225**, Eve ↔
        ([1269 + <9621> = 10890] / 2 = **5445**) + **1782** = **7227**, Book-End.
      1269 + **625**, Robert starts the tidying up = **1894**.
        18:94 = 1174 minutes + <49> = 1223 . . . **1223**, Yeshua
        1223 = <32:21> = 1 day / 8:21 . . . 1821.
        18:(21) = 1059 minutes . . . **1059**, a page in the life of . . .
        18:21 is 1 day / (5:39) . . . **1539**, John Kordupel.
        1821 * 5 = 9105, know My world to know yours.

    1894 . . . 1[8 * 9 * 4 = 288] . . .**1288**.
      19:12. His eyes were as a flame of fire, and on his head were many crowns; and he had a name written, that no man knew, but he himself.
      19:16. And he hath on his vesture and on his thigh a name written, KING OF KINGS AND LORD OF LORDS. Revelations.
      <6191> - [1912 + <2191> = 4103] = 2088 . . .
        20:88 = 1288 minutes . . . **1288**.

    1894 + 1288= 3182 ↔ **3182**, Tibet
      31:82 = 1 day / 7:82 . . . **1782**, Resurrection → **1782**, the Second Coming.

    18:94 = 6:94 PM . . . 694 minutes = 11:34 . . . 1134
      1134 minutes = 18:54 . . . **1854**, China
      [1134 + <4311> = 5445] + **1782** = **7227**, Book-End.
      and,
    13/1/7, You have made the bed as far as you could. Now it is up to Me; 200{6} + 2007 + 13/1 = 4144.
    1317 minutes = 21:57 . . . 2157 minutes = 35:57 . . . 3557 minutes = 59:17 . . . 5917.
      5917 . . . [591 - <195> = 396] * 7 = **2772**.
      5917 minutes = 97:97 . . . 9797.
    4144 + <4414> + 9797 + <7979> = 26334 . . . 26:334 = 1894 minutes . . . **1894**.
    and,
    1894 . . . 1:89/4 days = 9789 + <981> = 10770 . . . 10:770 = 1370 minutes . . . **1370**.

Thessalonians 2:1 to 2:4, re the Second Coming . . .
2:01 + 2:02 + 2:03 + 2:04 = 810 . . . 8:10 = 490 minutes . . . 4:90 = 330 min.
330 minutes = 5:30 . . . 530 minutes = 8:50 . . . 850 minutes = 13:70 . . . **1370**.
1370 minutes = 22:50 . . . **2250**, New Harmonic Vibrations.

[2449 + <9442> = 11891] + [4897 + <7984> = 12881] = **24772** . . . [-2 + 4 = 2]772 . . . **2772**, the Chain . . .

[7348 + <8437> = 15785] + [4691 + <1964> = 6655] = **22440**.
[22440 – 24772 = 2332] / 4 = 583 = <385> . . . 385 minutes = 6:25 . . . **625**.
[22440 - 27676 = 5236] / 2 = 2618) - <8162> = **5544**.
Fo-Hi / Krishna / Buddha / Lao Tzu / Confucius: 364 468 500 243
500:364 – 243:468 = 256896, the Eastern influence.
[256 + 896 = 1152] + <2511> + [<652> + <698> = 1350] + <0531>= **5544**.

Moses / Isiah / Jeremiah / Ezekiel / Jesus Christ / the Prophet Muhammad: 616 814 869 561.
[616 + 814 + 869 + 561 = 2860] + <0682> = 3542 the Western influence
<616> + <418> + <969> + <165> = 2167.
2167 + <7612> = 9779 . . . [97 * 79 = 7663] - <3667> = 3996.
3996 . . . 3 * 99 * 6 = 1782, the Second Coming.
[2167 + 3542 + 1782 = 7491] - <1947> = **5544**.

and,
the Day Of Resurrection: 249 271 191 229
249 + 271 + 191 + 229 = 940; <942> + <172> + <191> + <922> = 2227 = <7222>
[940 + 7222 = 8162] - <2618> = **5544**.

and,
1782, the Second Coming . . . 1 day / 7:82 = 31:82 . . . 3 days / (1:82) = 70:18 + <281> = 7299 72:99
= 3 days / 0:99 . . . **3099**, the Unlettered Prophet.
3099 minutes = 50:99 . . . 50:99 = 2 days / 2:99 . . . 2299.
2299 + [2299 . . .22 * 9 * 9 = **1782**, the Second Coming] + **1463**, John Kordupel = **5544**.
5544 . . . 554 weeks / 4 days = 3882 days . . . 3882, the Unlettered Prophet.

27786 – **24772** = 3014 . . . 30:14 = 1 day / 6:14 . . . 1614.
16:14 is 4:14 PM . . . 414 minutes = 6:54 . . . 654 minutes = 10:54 = 11:(06) . . . **1106**.
the Eight Amigos: 705 1039 **1106** 636
1106, Isaiah / Jeremiah / Ezekiel / Jesus Christ / the Prophet Muhammad / Krishna / Buddha / Fo-Hi.
11:06 = 666 minutes . . . **666**, the Number of Man.

From *Encore*.

Planet Earth has a major issue facing it. The Mars consciousness has gained a re-entry onto Earth. At the same time the negative energies that ended up on the cosmic shelf when Mars self-destructed are yet to be fully dissipated. They shall come off the cosmic shelf to be fully dissipated here on Earth.
The rulers of China are to face their effects. It was their manipulative dictatorial policies that led to the destruction of Mars. As their economy has grown, the same unethical business practices have begun to emerge.
If their germination is allowed to foster, their destructive influence will spread.
This is the matrix that China faces; this is the matrix that faces Earth.

God is pointing the hose. It but remains for the tap to be turned on. How much the tap is opened and how fast the stuff comes off the cosmic shelf we do not know.
This initiation will conclude a Grand Cycle.

27/12/2017.
the time footprint: it is (4)/{17} ↔ <**714**>

9. The Taming Power of the Small.
      Six in the fourth place means:
      If you are sincere, blood vanishes and fear gives way.
      No blame.

      If one is in a difficult and responsible position of counselor to a powerful man, one should restrain him in such a way that right might prevail. Therein lies a danger so great that the threat of actual bloodshed may arise. Nonetheless, the power of disinterested truth is greater than all the obstacles. It caries such weight that the end is achieved, and all danger of bloodshed and all fear disappear.
      The I Ching. Wilhelm / Baynes.

Sleeping Dragon, Crouching Tiger: The Crouching Tiger.

God: 7,15,4: 7 + 154 = 161; 715 + 4 = 719: 161 + 719 = **880**.

Devil: 4, 5, 22, 9,12 . . . ([4 + 522 = 526] + 912 = 1438) + [452 + 291 + 2 = 745] + [4522 + 912 = 5434] + [452 + 2912 = 3364] = **10981**.

        10981, Devil – 880, God = **10101**, the Dual Essence.

        10981, Devil = <**18901**> ↔ 10101, Dual Essence + [880, God * 10 = 8800] = **18901**.

      This equation reads that God and the devil are one and the same.

and,
the story so far:
God: 7,15,4: 7 + 154 = 161; 715 + 4 = 719: 161 + 719 = **880**.
Devil: 4, 5, 22, 9,12 . . . ([4 + 522 = 526] + 912 = 1438) + [452 + 291 + 2 = 745] + [4522 + 912 = 5434] + [452 + 2912 = 3364] = **10981**.
      10981, Devil = <**18901**> ↔ [10101, Dual Essence + [880, God * 10 = 8800] = **18901**.

18901, God / God / Devil . . . 18:901 = 1981 minutes - <109> = **1872**; <1891> - <109> = **1782**.

10981, Devil . . . 10:981 = 1581 minutes + <189> = 1770; 1581 - <189> = **1392**.
      1392 + 1782 = 3174 . . . 31:(74) = 1786 minutes - <47> = **1739**.
        17:39 = 1059 minutes . . . **1059**, a page on the life of . . .
          14/8/4, I'll see you tomorrow at 815 . . . 14:84 = 924 minutes . . . 924 + 815 = **1739** ↔

      {17}/39 is **{17}/8/2** ↔ {17}/3/9 is **{17}/68** ↔

1872 + 1770 = 3642
      36:42 = 2202 minutes + <24> = **2226** ↔ **2226**, Intervention From Above.

3642 / 2 = **1821**.

18:(21) = 1059 minutes . . . **1059**, a page in the life of . . .

18:21 is 1 day / (5:39) . . . **1539** ↔ 1392 - <2931> = **1539**, continued below

1821 * 5 = **9105** ↔

17/11/2010, I cannot talk with you about your world unless you know about mine. Get out of My Car.

[17/11 + 11/17 + 2010 = 4838] + [Car: alphabet from R to L: 24,26,9 . . .[- 2 + 4269 = 4267] = **9105**.

and,

the story so far:

God: 7,15,4: 7 + 154 = 161; 715 + 4 = 719: 161 + 719 = **880**.

Devil: 4, 5, 22, 9,12 . . . ([4 + 522 = 526] + 912 = 1438) + [452 + 291 + 2 = 745] + [4522 + 912 = 5434] + [452 + 2912 = 3364] = **10981**.

18901, God / God / Devil . . . 18:901 = 1981 minutes - <109> = 1872; <1891> - <109> = **1782**.

10981, Devil . . . 10:981 = 1581 minutes + <189> = 1770; 1581 - <189> = 1392.

1392 - <2931> = **1539** ↔

2247, Kali Yuga . . . 2 days / 2:47 = 50:47 = 2:47 / 2 days . . . 24:72 = 1512 minutes + <27> = **1539**.

17:9. The heart is deceitful above all things, and desperately wicked: who can know it?

17:10. I the Lord search the heart, I try the reins, even to give to every man according to his ways, and according to the fruits of his doing. Jeremiah. Holy Bible. King James Version.

and,

2:54. Arjuna said:

How would you describe the man

whose wisdom is steadfast, Krishna?

How does the wise man speak?

How does he sit, stand, walk?

5:18. Wise men regard all beings

as equal: a learned priest,

a cow, an elephant, a rat,

or a filthy, rat-eating outcast. Bhagavad Gita. Stephen Mitchell.

[2:54 + <452> + 518 + <815> = 2039] + <9302> = 11341 . . . 1 + 1341 = **1342**, Second Coming.

11341 + 17:9 + 17:09 + 17:10 = 14939 . . . 1[- 4 + 9 = 5]39 . . . **1539**.

625, Robert begins the tidying up . . . 6√25 = 1051 5811.

1051 + <1501> = 2552; 5811 + <1185> = 6996; 1051 + 5811 = 6862;

1051 + <1185> = 7312; <1501> + <1185> = 2236; 7312 + 2236 = 9548.

7312 - ([9548 = <8459>] – [6862 = <2686>] = 5773) = **1539**.

the Chain of Rebirth: 169 273 290 152

([169 + 273 + 290 + 152 = 884] + <488> = 1372) + ([<961> + <372> + <092> + <251> = 1676] + <6761> = 8437) = 9809.

[884 + 1676 = 2560] + [884 + <6761> = 7645] + [884 + 8437 = 9321] + [884 + <9089> = 9973] = 29499.

29499 + [<0652> + <5467> + <1239> + <3799> = 11157] = 40656 - <65604> = 24948.

24:948 = 2388 minutes - <849> = **1539**.

153144, the Hero, the Truth and the Light → 1531 + 4 + 4 = **1539**.

Messiah: 74 108 115 67; we group the number into two groups:
    [74:108 + 115:67 = 85675] – [74:115 + 108:67 = 84982] = 693.
    [67:74 + 115:108 = 121882, Messiah ↔ 1 * ([2 + 1 = 3]882 . . . 3882) = **3882**, the Unlettered Prophet.
    and,
    [74:108 + 115:67 = 85675] – [115:74 + 67:108 = 78682] = 6993.
        6993, Messiah ↔ 6993 . . . 6 * 99 * 3 = **1782**, the Second Coming
        6993 – [693 + 3882 = 4575] = 2418 . . . 24:18 = 1458 minutes + <81> = **1539**.

[John: 10, 15, 8,14] + [Kordupel: 11,15,18, 4, 21, 16, 5, 12] = 11,151,843,132,326.
    [1115184 . . .1115 + 184 = 1299] + [3132326 . . . 313 + 2326 = 2639] = 3938.
        3938 - <8393> = 4455 = <5544> . . . 554 weeks / 4 days = 3882 days . . . **3882**, the Unlettered Prophet.
        39:38 = 2378 minutes + <83> = 2461.
            2461 + <1642> = 4103 . . . 41:03 = 2463 minutes . . . 24:63 = 1503 minutes + <36> = **1539**.

1539 . . .1 day – 5:39 = 18:21; 1539 . . .[15:(39) = 861] - <93> = **7/(68)**, beginning of End of Time ↔

2250, New Harmonic Vibrations . . . 2 days / (250) =45:50 - <052> = 4498
    44:(98) = 2542 minutes . . . (2:54) / 2 days is 45:46 - <452> = 4094.
        40:94 = 2494 minutes - <49> = 2445 . . . 24:45 = 1485 minutes + <54> = **1539**.

    4498 . . . 44 * 9 * 8 = 3168
        3168 + <8613> = 11781 . . . 1 + 1781 = **1782**, the Second Coming.
        [3168 - <8613> = 5445] + 1782, the Second Coming = **7227**, Book-End.
        31:68 is 1 day / 7:68 . . . **{17}/68**.

Thessalonians 2:1 to 2:4 discusses the Second Coming . . . [2^1 = 2] [2^2 = 4] [2^3 = 8] [2^4 = 16] . . . 24816.
    24816 = **8238**, a Galactic cycle + **7227**, Book-End + [**1539** = <9351>].

    24816 . . . [-2 + 4 = 2]816 . . . 2816.
        28:(16) = 1664 minutes . . . 1 day / 664 = 30:64 . . . 30:(64) = 1736 minutes + <46> = **1782**.
        1782, the Second Coming ↔ **{17}/8/2**.

        2816 . . . [2 + 8 = 10]16 . . . 10:(16) is 9:44 . . .
        {9}/(44), I cannot talk with you about your world unless you know about Mine.

34:25. And I will make with them a covenant of peace, and will cause the evil beasts to cease out of the land: and they shall dwell safely in the wilderness, and sleep in the woods. Ezekiel. Holy Bible. King James Version.
    3425 . . . [3^4 = 81]25 . . . 8125 = <5218> . . . 52:18 = 2 days / 4:18 . . . 2418
        24:18 = 1458 minutes + <81> = **1539**.
    2418 . . . [2^4 = 16]18 . . . 16:18 = 1 day / (782) . . . **1782**, Resurrection, the 1,000 year reign begins.

Sleeping Dragon, Crouching Tiger: The Crouching Tiger. (continued)

Allah: 1, 12,12,1,8:
[1 + 12 + 12 + 1 + 8 = **34**] + [1 + 121 + 218 = **340**] + [112 + 121 + 8 = **241**] + [1121 + 218 = **1339**] + [112 + 1218 = **1330**] = **3284**:
                      &
        3284 - <4823> = **1539**.

3284 = **2659** + **625**, Robert begins to tidy things up.

26:59 = 1 day / 2:59 . . . 1259 . . . 12:59 = 779 minutes = <977> ↔ **977**, Mary Magdalene ↔
977 minutes = 15:77 . . . 1 day / 577 = 29:77 . . . 2977.

2977 = <7792> . . . 7 * 792 = **5544**.

Leanne Long: 99 (161) 171 (89) . . . 99:171 – (89):(161) = 10010 . . . 100:10 = 4:10 / 4 days . . . **4104**.

4104 – [171:99 – (161):(89) = **1010**] = 3094 . . . 30:94 = 1 day / 6:94 . . . **1694**.

1694, Leanne Long ↔ **1694**, Mary Magdalene.

1694 + <4961> = **6655**.

60/48, Cher's birth day + (60)/{7}, Cher's passing = **6655**, Cher's life time.

([6655 / 11 = 605] + [6655 / 5 = 1331] = 1936) - <6391> = **4455**, Leanne Long.

and,

4455, Leanne Long + [<5544> / 2 = **2772**, the Chain of Rebirth] = **7227**, Leanne Long ↔
7227, Leanne Long ↔ **7227**, Book-End . . . 72:27 = 3 days / 0:27 . . . 30:(27) = 1773 minutes . . . **1773**.

[**1773**, Leanne Long ↔ **1773**, Bathsheba] + <3771> = **5544**.

29:77 = 1817 minutes . . . **(18)/1/7**, You have made the bed as far as you could. Now it is up to Me.

26:59 = 2:59 / 1 day . . . 2591 – [26:59 = 1 day / 2:59 . . . 1259] = **1332**.

Yahweh: 25,1,8,23,5,8 . . . (2518 . . . ([2 + 5 = 7] – [1 + 8 = 9] = - 2) + [2358 . . . 23 * 58 = 1334] = **1332**.

Yahweh: 25,1,8,23,5,8 . . . (2358 – [2 * 518 = 1036]) = 1322.

Yahweh: 25,1,8,23,5,8 . . . [25 + 18 + 23 + 58 = 124] + <421> = 545.

Yahweh: 545 + 1322 + 1332 = 3199

3199, Yahweh = **949**, Anakhita + **2250**, New Harmonic Vibrations.

Anakhita: 65 143 151 57 . . . [<56> + <341> + <151> + <75> = 623] + <326> = **949**.

3199 . . . 319 * 9 = 2871 = <**1782**>

Yahweh: 25,1,8,23,5,8 . . . [25 + 18 + 23 + 58 = 124] + <421> = 545 . . . 5:45 is 6:(15) . . . 615.

[**1332** = <2331>] - 615 = 1716 → <516> . . . 516 PM is 17:16 . . . **1716**, Yahweh →
1716, Anakhita . . . 17:16 = 5:16 PM = <6:15> = 375 seconds . . . **375**.

([375 + <573> = 948] + 1716 = 2664) / 2 = **1332**, Yahweh.

37.5 seconds = 2250 minutes . . . **2250**, New Harmonic Vibrations.

and,

Genesis. 1:27 . . . 12⁷ = *358* 31808 . . . [1808 + <8081> = 9889] – [3583 + <3853> = 7436] = 2453.

2453 = <3542>, eschatology – [Genesis 1:27 . . . 358 + <853> = 1211] = 2331 = <**1332**>

1332 . . . [13³ = 2197] – 2 = 2195 . . . 21:95 = 1355 minutes + <59> = **1414**, Adam.

while,

2197 + <7912> = **10109**, Eve.

1332 . . . 133² = 17689 = **8238**, a Galactic cycle + **7227**, Book-End + [**4222**, Market Forces = <2224>]

and,
the story so far:
Allah: 1, 12,12,1,8:
[1 + 12 + 12 + 1 + 8 = **34**] + [1 + 121 + 218 = **340**] + [112 + 121 + 8 = **241**] + [1121 + 218 = **1339**] + [112 + 1218 = **1330**] = 3284:

&

3284 - <4823> = **1539**.

3284 = **2659** + **625**, Robert begins to tidy things up.

26:59 = 2:59 / 1 day . . . 2591 . . . 25:(91) = 1409 minutes . . . **1409**.
    227/4, I'll see you tomorrow at 8:15 + 815 = 3089.
        3089 minutes = 50:89 = 2 days / 2:89 . . . 22:89 = 1409 minutes . . . **1409** ↔

          5163584, the Prophet Mohammad . . . [5 * 163 = 815] + [8:15 = 495 minutes] + 584 = **1894**.
            1894 - <485> = **1409**.
           13/1/7, You have made the bed as far as you could. Now it is up to Me; 200{6} + 2007 + 13/1 = 4144.
           13/1/7 . . . 1317 minutes = 21:57 . . . 2157 minutes = 35:57 . . . 3557 minutes = 59:17 . . . 5917.
                5917 . . . [591 - <195> = 396] * 7 = **2772**, the Chain of Rebirth
                5917 minutes = 97:97 . . . 9797.
            4144 + <4414> = 8558 + 9797 + <7979> = 26334 . . . 26:334 = 1894 minutes . . . **1894**.

        my birth day: 2/3/47 + 3/2/47 + 34/47 = 9041 . . . <**1409**>, John Kordupel.

30:89 = 1889 minutes . . . **18/89** is **(1)/3/{17}** ↔ **13/1/7**, You have made the bed as far as you could. Now it is up to Me.

Sleeping Dragon, Crouching Tiger: The Crouching Tiger. (continued).

Allah: from R to L: 8,1,12,12,1: 8,1,<21>,<21>,1:
    [812 + 121 + 1 = 934] + [8 + 121 + 211 = 340] + [8121 + 211 = 8332] + [812 + 1211 = 2023] = **11629**.

116:29 = 5 days / (3:31) . . . 5331
    5331 = <1335> . . . 13:35 = 815 minutes . . . **815**.
    53:31 = 3211 minutes + <13> = 3224.
        3224 . . . [3² = 9]24 . . . 924 minutes = 14:84 . . . **14/8/4**, I'll see you tomorrow at 815.
        Allah: 1484 + 815 = **2299** ↔
            Flower of Life / the Tree of Life: 266 375 409 241 . . . 266 + 375 + 409 + 241 = 1291
                1291 + ([<662> + <573> + <904> + <142> = 2281] + <1822> = 4103 = <3014>) = 4305.
                4305 . . . 4 days / 3:05 = 99:05 = <50:99> = 2 days / 2:99 . . . **2299**.

        [8238, a Galactic cycle + <8328> = 16566] - (8238 . . .[8² = 64]38 . . . 6438 + <8346> = 14784) = **1782**.
           1782 . . . 1 day / 7:82 = 31:82 . . . 3 days / (1:82) = 70:18 + <281> = 72:99 = 3 days / 0:99 . . . 3099.
           3099 minutes = 50:99 . . . 50:99 = 2 days / 2:99 . . . **2299**.

        2299 . . . 22 * 9 * 9 = **1782**, the Second Coming.
        2299 + **1463**, John Kordupel + **1782**, the Second Coming = 5544
           5544 . . . 554 weeks / 4 days = 3882 days . . . **3882**, the Unlettered Prophet.
        2299 = **1255**, Second Coming + **10/(44)**, I cannot talk with you about your world unless you know about Mine.

32:(24) = 1896 minutes - <42> = **1854** . . . **18/54** is **18/2/(5)** ↔ **18:25** is 6:25 PM . . . **625**, Robert begins to tidy things up.

5331 – 2299 = 3032 . . . 30:(32) = 1768 minutes . . . **1768** ↔
    Mary Magdalene: 13,1,18,25. 13,1,7,4,1,12,5,14,5: 1311825 + 131,741,125,145 = 131,742,436,970
    Messiah: 13,5,19,19,9,1,8; 1,351,919,918.
        131,742,436,970, Mary Magdalene + 1,351,919,918, Messiah = 133,094,356,888.
        133,094,356,888 . . . [133 + 094 = 227] + [356 + 888 = 1244] = 1471.

133,094,356,888 . . . 1330 + 9435 + 6888 = 17653. 133094 + 356888 = 489,982. 489 + <289> = 778.
1471 + 17653 + 489,982 = 509106 . . .
[5091 – <1905> = 3186] + 06 = 3192 . . . 31:(92) = 1768 minutes . . . **1768** ↔

13/1/{6}, You have made the bed as far as you could. Now it is up to Me . . . 131/ 6 days = 145:31 + <131> = 146:62
14:662 = 1502 minutes + <266> = **1768**.

116:29 = (3:31) / 5 days . . . 33:(15) = 1965 minutes - <51> = **1914**.
and,
God: 7,15,4: 7 + 154 = 161; 715 + 4 = 719: 161 + 719 = 880.
Devil: 4, 5, 22, 9,12 . . . ([4 + 522 + 912 = 1438] + [452 + 291 + 2 = 745] + [4522 + 912 = 5434] + [452 + 2912 = 3364]
= 10981.
10981, Devil – 880, God = 10101, the Dual Essence.
[880, God * 10 = 8800] + 10101, Dual Essence = 18901 = <10981>, Devil.
This equation reads that God and the devil are one and the same.
18901, God / Devil . . . 18:901 = 1981 minutes = <1891> - <109> = **1782**.
and,
from the chapter *The System* and *All the Games God Play.*
31/1/6. Yesterday, I recalled thoughts from 29/1;

Robert needs a couple of weeks to tidy things up.

I didn't give it much thought as there was no starting point. I assumed it was to do with when he comes to Melbourne.

Starting from when?

625.

We segregate 'Robert' into 'Rob'' and 'Bert, with 'b' wearing two hats'.
Rob: [18,15,2 . . . **18152**] + [(8), (11), (24) . . . **81124**] + [9,12,25 . . . **91225**] + [(17) + (14) + (1) . . . **17141**] = **207642**.

e:	5	(21)	22	(4)
r:	18	(8)	9	(17)
t:	20	(6)	7	(19)
	43	35	38	40

[43353840 + 43383540 + 43403538 = 130140918] + 207642 = 130348560 . . . 13034 + 8560 = 21594 . . . [2 + 1 = 3] *
594 = **1782**.

Robert is God / Devil.

1782 . . . 1 day / 782 = 31:82 = 1942 minutes - <28> = **1914** . . . 19:14 is 7:14 PM . . . **714**.
Yahweh: 25,1,8,23,5,8 . . . [2518 + 2358 = **4876** * 10 = 48760] + [Eve, 5585 * 10 = 55850] = 104610 . . . 104 + 610
= **714**.
714 . . . 71⁴ = 2541 1681 . . . 2541 + 1681 = **4222**, Market Forces, an expression of the Collective Will.
[4222, Market Forces . . . 4 days / 2:22 = 98:22 + <222> = 10044] + [1914 + <4191> = 6105] = 16149.
161:49 = (611)/7 days . . . 6117 . . . **(6)/1/{17}** is **18/25** ↔

16:(149) = 811 minutes + <941> = 1752 . . . **{17}/(5)/2** is **18/54**.

7:14 is 46 to 8 . . . 4:68 PM is 16:68 . . . 1 day / 6:68 = 30:68 = 1868 minutes . . . 1868.
1868 minutes - <86> = **1782**, the beginning of the 1,000 year reign of Jesus ↔ 1868 . . . **18/68**.

Sleeping Dragon, Crouching Tiger: The Crouching Tiger. (continued)

Allah: 1, 12,12,1,8: **Satan**: 19,1,20,1,14: 19120114 – 1121218 = 1799 8796 . . . 1799 + 8796 = **10595** . . . 1059 * 5 = **5295**.
52:95 =2 days / 4:95 . . . 2495 . . . 24:95 is 1 day / 0:95 . . . 1095.
5295 = <5925> . . . 59:25 = 3565 minutes . . . 3565 / 5 = **713**, the Season ends.
5295, an overlapping composite number.
529 . . . 52 past 9 is 10:(08); <592> . . . 59 to two is 1:01.
and,
1008 – 101 = 907 . . . **90/7**, a marriage between Allah and Satan.

That would make them "as one"

Devil: 4, 5, 22, 9,12: [- 452 + - <254> = -706] + 2912 = **2206**.
Satan: 19,1,20,1,14: 1912 + <4110> = **6022** ↔ <2206>, Devil; 19 + 1201 + 14 = **1234**; 19 * 1 * 20 * 1 * 14 = **5320**.
6022 + 1234 + 5320 = **12576**.

[12576, Satan / 2 = **6288**] + <8826> = 15114 . . . 15:114 = 1014 minutes + <411> = **1425** = <5241>
5241, Satan – 2206, Devil = 3035 . . . 30:35 = 1835 minutes - <53> = **1782** ↔
18901, God / Devil . . . 18:901 = 1981 minutes = <1891> - <109> = **1782**.

Allah: from R to L: 8,1,12,12,1: 8,1,<21>,<21>,1:
[812 + 121 + 1 = 934] + [8 + 121 + 211 = 340] + [8121 + 211 = 8332] + [812 + 1211 = 2023] = **11629**.
116:29 = 5 days / (3:31) . . . 5331
5331 = <1335> . . . 13:35 = 815 minutes . . . **815**.
53:31 = 3211 minutes + <13> = 3224.
3224 . . . [3² = 9]24 . . . 924 minutes = 14:84 . . . **14/8/4**, I'll see you tomorrow at 815.
Allah: 1484 + 815 = 2299 . . . 22 * 9 * 9 = **1782**.

[Allah: 1, 12,12,1,8] + [Satan: 19,1,20,1,14] = 2024 1332 . . . [2024 + <4202> + 1332 + <2331>= 9889] + <9889 > = **19778**.
19778, Allah / Satan . . . 1[9778 - <8779> = 999] . . . 1999.
19:(99) = 1041 minutes - <99> = 942 minutes = 15:42
1542 . . . 1 day / 5:42 = 29:42 = 1782 minutes . . . **1782**.
1542 = <2451> . . . [2⁴ = 16]51 . . . **16/(51)**, it certainly is your Playground.

19778, Allah / Satan . . .197:78 = 11898 minutes - <87> = 11811 . . . 118:11 = 7091 minutes - <11> = 7080.
7080, Allah / Satan – **6288**, Satan = 792.
792 * 7 = **5544** . . . 554 weeks / 4 days = 3882 days . . . **3882**, the Unlettered Prophet.
[792 = <297>] * 6 = **1782**.
70:80 = 3 days / (120) . . . 31:(20) = 1840 minutes + <02> = **1842**.
19778, Allah / Satan197:(78) = 11742 minutes . . . [1 + 17 = 18]42 . . . **1842** ↔

5241, Satan . . . 52:41 = 3161 minutes + <14> = 3175 . . . 31:(75) = 1785 minutes + <57> = **1842** ↔
and,
12576, Satan . . . 125:76 = 5:76 / 5 days . . . 5765 / 5 = 1153 . . . 11:53 = 713 minutes . . . **713**, the Season ends.

12576, Satan . . . [-1 + 2 = 1]576 . . . 1576 . . . 15:(76) = 824 minutes + <67> = **891** ↔

Anakhita: 65 143 151 57 . . . ([151:57 − 143:65 = 792] * 7 = 5544 = <4455>) / 5 = **891** ↔

The Second Epistle of Paul the Apostle to the Thessalonians 2:1 to 2:4 discusses the Second Coming:
[21 + 22 + 23 + 24 = 90] + [<12> + <22> + <32> + <42> = 108] = 198 = <**891**>

the Day of Resurrection: 249 271 191 229 . . . [249 + 271 + 191 + 229 = 940] - <049> = **891**.
[891 - 198 = 693] * 4 = **2772**, the Chain of Rebirth ↔
891 * 2 = **1782**, the Second Coming ↔ {**17**}/8/2.

12576, Satan . . . [-1 + 2 = 1]576 1576 . . . 1 day / 5:76 = 29:76 . . . 2976.
2976 . . . 297 * 6 = **1782**, the Second Coming ↔

2976 . . . [2 * 9 = 18][7 * 6 = 42] . . . **1842** ↔
16/2/6, is contact with Robert imminent? . . . [16² = 256] * 6 = 1536 . . .1 day / 5:36 = 29:36 = 1776 minutes + <63> = 1839.
18/3/9 is {**17**}/68 . . . **1768**, the Chain of Rebirth ↔
18/(39) weeks = 18/(273) . . . 2 BC / (73), birth of Jesus ↔
273 minutes = 4:33 . . . 433 minutes = 7:13 . . . **713**, the Season Ends.
18/(39) weeks is 18/(273) falls on 18/4/2 . . . **1842**.

29:76 = 1816 minutes . . . (**18**)/1/{6}, You have made the bed as far as you could. Now it is up to Me.

Sleeping Dragon, Crouching Tiger: The Crouching Tiger. (continued).

Satan: 19,1,20,1,14 + **Devil**: 4, 5, 22, 9,12 = 2364 3026 . . .
[2364 = <4632>] +[3062 = <6203>] = **10835**, Satan / Devil . . . 10:835 = 1435 minutes . . . **1435** ↔

2155720, I Am/ God/ Allah/ Jahwe . . . 2155 − 720 = **1435**.
Allah: from R to L: 8,1,12,12,1: 8,1,<21>,<21>,1:
[812 + 121 + 1 = 934] + [8 + 121 + 211 = 340] + [8121 + 211 = 8332] + [812 + 1211 = 2023] = 11629.
116:29 = 5 days / (3:31) . . . 5331 = <1335> . . . 13:35 = 815 minutes . . . **815**.
and,
[1435, Satan / Devil ↔ 1435, I Am/ God/ Allah/ Jahwe] + 815 = **2250**, New Harmonic Vibrations ↔

Satan: 19,1,20,1,14 + **Devil**: 4, 5, 22, 9,12 = 2364 3026 . . . 2364 + 3026 = 5390 + <0935> = **6325**, Satan / Devil.
6325 + <5236> = 11561, Satan / Devil.
11561, Satan / Devil . . . 115:61 = (439) / 5 days . . . 4395 / 5 = 879 = <978> . . . 978 minutes = 16:18 = 1 day / (782) . . . **1782** ↔
Allah: from R to L: 8,1,12,12,1: 8,1,<21>,<21>,1:
[812 + 121 + 1 = 934] + [8 + 121 + 211 = 340] + [8121 + 211 = 8332] + [812 + 1211 = 2023] = **11629**.
116:29 = 5 days / (3:31) . . . 5331
5331 = <1335> . . . 13:35 = 815 minutes . . . 815.
53:31 = 3211 minutes + <13> = 3224 . . . [3² = 9]24 . . . 924 minutes = 14:84 . . . 1484.
Allah: 1484 + 815 = 2299 . . . 22 * 9 * 9 = **1782**

11:561 = 1221 minutes + <165> = 1386
1386 + <6831> = **8217** ↔
34:25. And I will make with them a covenant of peace, and will cause the evil beasts to cease out of the land: and they shall dwell safely in the wilderness, and sleep in the woods. Ezekiel.

34:25, removing the evil beasts: [34:25 is 1 day / 10:25] + [34:25 is 10:25 / 1 day] = 21276.
    [21:(276) = 984 minutes + <672> = 1656] + <6561> = **8217** ↔

John Eevash Kordupel: 209 153 266 191 . . .
    [209 + 153 + 266 + 191 + <902> + <351> + <662> + <191> = 2925] + <5292> = **8217**.
and,
the Five Horsemen updating the Scriptures:
the Mahdi / the Second Coming / Maitreya / the Messiah / Kalki: 465 731 777 419.
465 + 731 + 777 + 419 = 2392 + <2932> = 5324.
    5324 + [<564> + <137> + 777 + <914> = 2392 + <2932> = 5324] = 10648.
2392 + 2392 = 4784;   2392 + 5324 = 7716;   <4874> + <6177> = 11051.
2932 + 2932 = 5864;   2932 + 5324 = 8256;   <4685> + <6528> = 11213.
[777:465 − 731:419 = 46046] - [11051 + 11213 = 22264] = 23782.
    23782 . . . [-2 + 3 = 1]782 . . . **1782**, Resurrection, the 1,000 year reign of Jesus begins.
    [23782 + <28731> = 52513] - [<15011> + <31211> = 46222] = **8217**.

[1386 - <6831> = **5445**] + 1782, Resurrection, the 1,000 year reign of Jesus begins = **7227**, Book-End.
    7227, Book-Ends . . . [7^2 = 49][2^7 = 128] . . . 49:128 = 3068 minutes . . . 30:68 = 1868 minutes . . . **1868** ↔

115:61 = 5 days / (439) . . . 54:(39) = 3201 minutes - <93> = 3108 . . . 31:08 = 1868 minutes . . . **18/68**.
    and,
16/2/6, is contact with Robert imminent?
    2/1/2018.
    While the date of the query has connotations of Robert being Robert Loomis, this could be a bit of God-Speak – innuendo that appears to be saying heaps, but in fact says nothing.
    As time is double-speak, we do not know what time footprint the query applies to. So, until we know who Robert is, we do not know what the contact is in relation to.

    You're not very trusting.

The bullshit started way before 16/2/2006, and up to and including all of 2017, it has not stopped.

16/2/2016, the time footprint: [(12)/02 + 200{5} = 3207] – 2/16 = 2991.
    29:(91) = 1649 minutes + <19> = 1668 . . . 1 day / 668 = 30:68 = 1868 minutes . . . **18/68**.
    2991 is 1 day / 5:51 . . . 1551 . . . **{15}/(51)**, it certainly is your playground.

Sleeping Dragon, Crouching Tiger: The Crouching Tiger. (continued).

Satan: 19,1,20,1,14 + **Devil**: 4, 5, 22, 9,12 = 2364 3026 . . . 2364 + <4632> = 6996 . . . 6 * 99 * 6 = **3564** ↔
    Fo-Hi / Krishna / Buddha / Lao Tzu / Confucius: 364 468 500 243 . . . 500:364 − 243:468 = 256896.
    256896, the Eastern influence . . . ([2 + 56 = 58] + 8 = 66) * 9 * 6 = **3564**.

Genesis 1:27. So God created man in his own image, in the image of God created he him; male and female created he them.
    Holy Bible. King James Version.
Genesis. 1:27 . . . 12^7 = 35831808 . . . [1808 + <8081> = 9889] – [3583 + <3853> = 7436] = **2453**.

The Second Epistle of Paul the Apostle to the Thessalonians 2:1 to 2:4 discusses the Second Coming:
    ([21 * 22 = 462] + <264> = 726) + ([23 * 24 = 552] + <255> = 807) = 1533 . . . [15 to 3 is 2:45]3 . . . **2453** ↔

2250, New Harmonic Vibrations . . . 2 days / (250) =45:50 - <052> = 4498 . . . 44:(98) = 2542 minutes - <89> = **2453** ↔

[John: 10, 15, 8,14] + [Kordupel: 11,15,18, 4, 21, 16, 5, 12] = 11,151,843,132,326:
We separate 11,151,843,132,326 into two groups of seven, to which we add our birthday:
    [1115184 . . .1115 + 184 = 1299] + [3132326 + 2/03/194{6} = 5164272 . . . 5164 + 272 = 5436] = 6735.
     6735 - [**47/34**, my birth day + **1433** = 6167, Fo-Hi] = 568 ↔ 568 + <865> = **1433**, Kalki, Maitreya.
       6735 - [6167 . . . 616 * 7 = 4312] = 2423.
          24:23 = 1463 minutes . . . **1463**, John Kordupel.
          2423 . . . 2 days / (4:23) = 43:77 - <324> = 4053 . . . 40:53 = 2453 minutes . . . 2453 ↔ <**3542**>, eschatology.

2453 . . . 24:53 = 1 day / 0:53 . . . 10:53 is 7 to 11 . . . **711**, a Cycle ends ↔ 7:11 is 8:(49) . . . 849 minutes = 14:09 . . .
1409, John Kordupel.

2453 . . . 2:45 / 3 days is 74:45 - <542> = 6903 . . . <3096> . . . 3096 minutes = 50:96
    { ([50:96 = 2:96 / 2 days . . . 2962] + [50:96 = 2 days / 2:96 . . . 2296] = 5258) + <8525> = 13783 } - <38731> =
    24948. 24:948 = 2388 minutes - <849> = **1539**, John Kordupel.
    24948 days = 3564 weeks . . . **3564**.
       3564 . . . [3 * 5 = 15][6 * 4 = 24] . . . 1524 . . . 15:24 = 924 minutes = 14:84 . . . **14/8/4**, I'll see you tomorrow
       ↔
       3564 = **1782**, Resurrection + **1782**, the Second Coming.

Sleeping Dragon, Crouching Tiger: The Crouching Tiger. (continued).

Satan: 19,1,20,1,14 + **Devil**: 4, 5, 22, 9,12 = 2364 3026 . . .3026 + <6203> = **9229**, Satan / Devil ↔ **9229**, Marduck.

The Babylonians believed in a pantheon consisting of beings, human in form but superhuman in power and immortal, each of whom, although invisible to the human eye, ruled a particular component of the cosmos, however small, and controlled it in accordance with well-laid plans and duly prescribed laws. Each was in charge of one of the great realms of heaven, earth, sea, and air; or of one of the major astral bodies—the sun, moon, and planets; or, in the realm of the Earth, of such natural entities as river, mountain, and plain, and of such social entities as city and state. Even tools and implements, such as the pickaxe, brick mould, and plough, were under the charge of specially appointed deities. Finally, each Babylonian had a personal god, a kind of good angel, to whom prayers were addressed and through whom salvation could be found.

At the head of this multitude of divine kings was Marduk, the Amorite tribal god, who had played only a minor and relatively unimportant role in the religious life of the land before the time of the ruler Hammurabi in the 18th and 17th centuries bc. According to the Babylonian mythological poem known in world literature as Enuma elish ("When above", its initial two words), Marduk was granted the leadership of the pantheon as well as the "kingship over the universe entire" as a reward for avenging the gods by defeating Tiamat, the savage and defiant goddess of chaos, and her monstrous host. Following his victory, Marduk fashioned heaven and Earth, arranged and regulated the planets and stars, and created the human race.

Among the more important Babylonian deities, in addition to Marduk, were Ea, the god of wisdom, spells, and incantations; Sin, the moon god, who had his main temples at Ur and Harran, two cities associated in the Bible with the Hebrew patriarch Abraham; Shamash, the sun god and the god of justice, who is depicted on the stele, or tablet, inscribed with the code of Hammurabi (see Hammurabi, Code of); Ishtar, the ambitious, dynamic, and cruel goddess of love and war; Adad, the god of wind, storm, and flood; and Marduk's son Nabu, the scribe and herald of the gods, whose cult eventually rivalled that of his father in popularity. In addition to the sky gods were the netherworld deities, as well as a large variety of demons, devils, and monsters, who were a constant threat to humanity and its well-being, and a few good, angelic spirits. Microsoft ® Encarta ® 2008. © 1993-2007 Microsoft Corporation. All rights reserved.

√9229 = 9606 7684 . . . [9606 + <6069> = 15675] / 5 = **3135**.

31:(35) = 1825 minutes ↔ **18/25** ↔ **18/2/(5)**, being **18/54** ↔
    18:25 = 6:25 PM . . . **625**, Robert needs a couple of weeks to tidy things up.

31:35 = 1895 minutes - <53> = **1842** ↔
    16/2/6, is contact with Robert imminent? . . . [16² = 256] * 6 = 1536.
        1536 . . . [15³ = 3375] - 6 = 3369) = [**1842** = <2481>] + **888**, Adam & Eve, interwoven energy.
        1536 . . . [15³ = 3375] + 6 = 3381) = **1539** + **1842**.
            153144, the Hero, the Truth and the Light → 1531 + 4 + 4 = **1539**.

        Messiah: 74 108 115 67; we group the number into two groups:
            [74:108 + 115:67 = 85675] – [74:115 + 108:67 = 84982] = 693.
            [67:74 + 115:108 = 121882 . . . 1 * ([2 + 1 = 3]882 . . . 3882) = **3882**, the Unlettered Prophet.
            and,
            [74:108 + 115:67 = 85675] – [115:74 + 67:108 = 78682] = 6993.
                6993 – [693 + 3882 = 4575] = 2418 . . . 24:18 = 1458 minutes + <81> = **1539**.
        the Chain of Rebirth: 169 273 290 152
        169 + 273 + 290 + 152 = 884 + <488> 1372
            1372 + [<961> + <372> + <092> + <251> = 1676 + <6761> = 8437] = 9809.
        [884 + 1676 = 2560] + [884 + <6761> = 7645] + [884 + 8437 = 9321] + [884 + <9089> = 9973] = 29499.
            29499 + [<0652> + <5467> + <1239> + <3799> = 11157] = 40656 - <65604> = 24948.
                24:948 = 2388 minutes - <849> = **1539**.

    and,
    Thessalonians 2:1 to 2:4 . . . [2¹ = 2] [2² = 4] [2³ = 8] [2⁴ = 16] . . . 24816.
        24816 = **8238**, a Galactic cycle + **7227**, Book-End + [**1539** = <9351>].
        24816 . . . [-2 + 4 = 2]816 . . . 2816.
            28:(16) = 1664 minutes . . . 1 day / 664 = 30:64.
                3064 - <4603> = **1539**.
                30:(64) = 1736 minutes + <46> = **1782**, the Second Coming.
                2816 . . . [2 + 8 = 10]16 . . . 10:(16) is 9:44 ↔
                {9}/(44), I cannot talk with you about your world unless you know about Mine.

[John: 10, 15, 8,14] + [Kordupel: 11,15,18, 4, 21, 16, 5, 12] = 11,151,843,132,326.
1115184 . . .1115 + 184 = 1299; 3132326 . . . 313 + 2326 = 2639; 1299 + 2639 = 3938.
    3938 - <8393> = 4455 = <5544> . . . 554 weeks / 4 days = 3882 days . . . **3882**, the Unlettered Prophet.
    39:38 = 2378 minutes + <83> = 2461.
        2461 + <1642> = 4103 . . . 41:03 = 2463 minutes . . . 24:63 = 1503 minutes + <36> = **1539**.

Leanne, alphabet L → R: 12, 5, 1, 14, 14, 5 . . . 125,114,145. Fig. 1.
Long, alphabet R→ L: 15, 12, 13, 20 . . . 15,121,320.
    125114145 + 15121320 = 140,235,465 . . . [140 + 235 = 375] * 6 = **2250**
        2 days / (250) =45:50 - <052> = 4498 . . . 4 * 498 = 1992 . . . . . . 19 * [9² = 81] = **1539**.

625, Robert begins the tidying up . . . 6√25 = 1051 5811.
    1051 + <1501> = 2552;   5811 + <1185> = 6996;   1051 + 5811 = 6862;
    1051 + <1185> = 7312;   <1501> + <1185> = 2236;   7312 + 2236 = 9548.
        7312 - ([9548 = <8459>] – [6862 = <2686>] = 5773) = **1539**.

2250, New Harmonic Vibrations . . . 2 days / (250) =45:50 - <052> = 4498.
44:(98) = 2542 minutes . . . 2542 . . . (2:54) / 2 days is 45:46 - <452> = 4094.
40:94 = 2494 minutes - <49> = 2445 . . . 24:45 = 1485 minutes + <54> = **1539**.

1536 . . . 1 day / 5:36 = 29:36 = 1776 minutes + <63> = 1839.
18/3/9 is **{17}/68**.
18/(39) weeks is 18/(273) falls on **18/4/2**.

Sleeping Dragon, Crouching Tiger: The Crouching Tiger. (continued).

Satan: 19,1,20,1,14 + **Devil**: 4, 5, 22, 9,12 = 2364 3026 . . . 2364 + <4632> = 6996, Satan / Devil.
Satan: 19,1,20,1,14 + **Devil**: 4, 5, 22, 9,12 = 2364 3026 . . . [2364 = <4632>] +[3062 = <6203>] = **10835**, Satan / Devil.
Satan: 19,1,20,1,14 + **Devil**: 4, 5, 22, 9,12 = 2364 3026 . . . 2364 + 3026 = 5390 + <0935> = **6325**, Satan / Devil.
Satan: 19,1,20,1,14 + **Devil**: 4, 5, 22, 9,12 = 2364 3026 . . .3026 + <6203> = **9229**, Satan / Devil.

6325 + 10835 + <53801> = 70961.
70961 / 11 = **6451**, Satan / Devil.
([70961 = <16907>] - [6996 + <6996> + 9229 + <9229> = 32450] = 15543) / 11 = **1413**, Satan Devil.

6451 . . . [6 * 4 = 24]51 . . . 2451 . . . [2⁴ = 16]51 . . . 1651.
1651 + 1413 = 3064 . . . 30:(64) = 1736 minutes + <46> = **1782**, the Second Coming ↔
16/(51), it certainly is your Playground.

Sleeping Dragon, Crouching Tiger: The Crouching Tiger. (continued).

Satan: [19,1,20,1,14 = <41102191>] + [**Devil**: 4, 5, 22, 9,12 = <2192254>] = 4329 4445 . . . 43294445 . . . [432 + <234> = **666**]
* 9 = 5994.
5994 + <4995> = **10989** ↔
10989 = **888**, Adam & Eve + **{10}/101**, Invitation to change the Language.

10989 = 7992 + <2997>.
John Kordupel (format ↔ synthesis): 153 159 167 145 . . . 159:153 − 167:145 = **7992**.
7992 . . . [7 + 9 = 16][9 * 2 = 18] . . . 16:18 = 1 day / (782> . . . **1782** ↔
1782, Cherryl's reincarnational family tree ↔ **1782**, Leanne Long.
Leanne Long: ([<9991> + <8644> + <3892> + <4452> = 26979] - **11994** = 14985) / 5 = **2997**.

5994 - 4445 = **1549**.
the Light: 20,8,5 11,9,7,8,20 . . . 2085 + 1197820 = 1199905 . . . 119990 * 5 = 599,950 . . . 599 + 950 = **1549**.
1549, the Light . . . 15/4/9 is 105/9 . . . **1059**, a page in the life of . . .
1549 . . . 1 day / 5:49 is 29:49 = 1789 minutes - <94> = **1695**, Second Coming ↔ **1695**, the Unlettered Prophet.
and,
9:25. Know therefore and understand, that from the going forth of the commandment to restore and to build
Jerusalem unto the Messiah the Prince shall be seven weeks, and threescore and two weeks: the streets shall
be built again, and the wall, even in troubled times.
9:26. And after the threescore and two weeks shall Messiah be cut off, but not for himself: and the people of
the prince that shall come shall destroy the city and the sanctuary; and the end thereof shall be with a flood,
and unto the end of the war desolations are determined. Daniel.
9:25 + 9:26 = 1851 . . . 18:51 is 1 day / (5:49) . . . **1549**.

Sleeping Dragon, Crouching Tiger: The Crouching Tiger. (continued).

Satan: 19,1,20,1,14 + **Devil**: 4, 5, 22, 9,12 = 2364 3026
Satan: [19,1,20,1,14 = <41102191>] + [**Devil**: 4, 5, 22, 9,12 = <2192254>] = 4329 4445
   23643026, Satan / Devil + 43294445, Satan / Devil = 6693 7471.
   [6693 = <3966>] - [2364 = <4632>] = **666**.

     √666 = 2580 6975 . . . 2580 + 6975 = 9555; 6√66 = 1067 6535 . . . 1067 + 6535 = 7602:
      [<5559> - <2067 = 3492] / 4 = **873**.

14:33. And your children shall wander in the wilderness forty years, and bear your whoredoms, until your carcases be wasted in the wilderness. Numbers. Holy Bible. King James Version. . . . 14:33 = 873 minutes . . . **873**.

    6693 . . . 66[9 + 3 = 12 = <21>] . . . 6621.
     6621 = <1266>, Eve
     66:21 = 3981 minutes = <1893>
      18:93 is 6:93 PM . . . **693** ↔

Mary:	57	47	51	53
Magdalene:	62	172	181	53

   we sum the horizontal: 57475153 + 6217218153 = 6,274,693,306 . . .
    6 + 274 + 693 + 306 = 1279 . . . 12[7 * 9 = 63] . . . 1263.
     1263 . . . 1[2⁶ = 64]3 . . . 1643 + <3461> = **5104**, Cherryl's reincarnational family tree. 1263 . . .
     126 * 3 = **378**, Resurrection.
     1263 . . . 12:(63) = 657 minutes + <36> = **693**, Mary Magdalene = <396>
  Leanne Long /High Priestess: 261 337 360 238 the space in-between: 224 23 234
    [224 + 23 + 234 = 481] - <184> = **297**; [<422> + <32> + <432> = 886] - <688> = **198**.
    [198 = <891>] - [297 - <792> = **495**] = **396**.

  1893, the Chain of Rebirth ↔ **1893**, rediscovery of the Forms of Life.

6693 . . . 66 * 9 * 3 = **1782**, the Second Coming.

leaving 7471 to factor in:
7413 - <3147> = **4266**, Jesus.
7471 = <1747> . . .1 day 7:47 = 31:47 . . . **3147** ↔
  Kali Yuga, Earth's dark night of the Soul: 416 + <614> + 1217 + <7121> = 9368 = <8639> . . .
    86:(39) = 5121 minutes + <93> = 5214 . . . 52:(14) = 3106 minutes + <41> = **3147**.
3/1/{47}, Cher is born ↔
  Leanne Long: the space in-between: [2136 = <6312>] + [1452 = <2541>] + [2886 = <6882>]= **15735**.
    15:735 = 1635 minutes . . . **1635**, Eve.
    15735, Leanne Long / 5 = **3147**.
31:(47) = 1813 minutes - <74> = **1739**.
  17:39 = 1059 minutes . . . **1059**, a page in the life of . . .
  1739 = [**14/8/4**, I'll see you tomorrow at 815 . . . 14:84 = 924 minutes . . . 924] + **815**.
  and,
  {17}/**39** falls on {17}/8/2.

$7471 + <1747> = 9218$.

$9218 . . . [9 * 2 = 18]18 . . .$**1818**, Magdalene

$9218 . . . [9 + 2 = 11]18 . . . 1118 . . .$ **1/11/8**, Cher passes away

$9218 . . . [9^2 = 81]18 . . .$**8118** $\leftrightarrow$

Leanne Long: 99 (161) 171 (89)

$99{:}171 - (89){:}(161) = 10010 . . . [100{:}10 = 4{:}10 \, / \, 4 \text{ days} . . . 4104 + <4014> =$ **8118**

92/18 falls on **18/4/2** $\leftrightarrow$

16/2/6, is contact with Robert imminent? . . . $[16^2 = 256] * 6 = 1536$

$1536 . . . 1 \text{ day} \, / \, 5{:}36 = 29{:}36 = 1776 \text{ minutes} + <63> = 1839$.

18/3/9 is **{17}/68** $\leftrightarrow$

13/1/{6}, You have made the bed as far as you could. Now it is up to Me . . .

$131/ 6 \text{ days} = 145{:}31 + <131> = 146{:}62$

$14{:}662 = 1502 \text{ minutes} + <266> =$ **1768**.

2250, New Harmonic Vibrations . . . $2 \text{ days} \, / \, (250) = 45{:}50 - <052> = 4498$

$4498 . . . 44 * 9 * 8 = 3168 . . . 31{:}68 = 1 \text{ day} \, / \, 7{:}68 . . .$ **1768**.

18/(39) weeks is 18/(273) falls on **18/4/2**.

$[9218 = <8129>] + 1536 = 9665$

$9665 - <5669> =$ **3996** $\leftrightarrow$

$3996 . . . 3 * 99 * 6 =$ **1782**, the Second Coming $\leftrightarrow$ **1782**, Leanne Long

$3996 . . . -3 + 996 = 993 . . . 993 \text{ minutes} = 15{:}93 . . .$ **1593**.

13/1/{6}, or 13/1/7, You have made the bed as far as you could. Now it is up to Me $\rightarrow$

$[13{:}16 = 796 \text{ minutes} . . . 796] + [13{:}17 = 797 \text{ minutes} . . . 797] =$ **1593**.

$9665 - [1536 = <6351>] = 3314 . . . 33{:}14 \text{ is } 1 \text{ day} \, / \, 9{:}14 . . .$ **1914**.

1782 $. . . 1 \text{ day} \, / \, 782 = 31{:}82 = 1942 \text{ minutes} - <28> =$ **1914** $. . . 19{:}14 \text{ is } 7{:}14 \text{ PM} . . .$ **714**.

7:14 is 46 to 8 . . . 4:68 PM is 16:68 . . . $1 \text{ day} \, / \, 6{:}68 \text{ is } 30{:}68 = 1868 \text{ minutes} . . .$ **18/68** $\leftrightarrow$

$714 . . . 71^4 = 2541 \, 1681 . . . 2541 + 1681 =$ **4222**, Market Forces.

Sleeping Dragon, Crouching Tiger: The Crouching Tiger. (continued)

From: *I Am the Creator*:
I was in the process of tiding up the format in Judgment Day when I came across this entry:
2586: Intervention from Above.

20/7/6.
2586.

the time footprint of 20/7/6 is associated with Intervention from Above.

20/7/6, date for Intervention from Above is 6/(11)/7 $\leftrightarrow$ **(6)/1/{17}** $\leftrightarrow$ 25:86 = 1:86 / 1 day . . . **18/6/(1)**
both can be expressed as **18/25** . . . 18:25 is 6:25 PM . . . **625**, Robert begins to tidy things up

Intervention from Above to tidy what up?

20/7/6, date for Intervention from Above is 201/6/{5} . . . 20:165 = 1365 minutes . . . **1365**, Anakhita

20/7/6, date for Intervention from Above is 6/(11)/7 . . . 61:17 = (10:43) / 3 days . . . 10:433 = 1033 minutes + <334> = **1367**.
1367 . . . **13/(67)**, Hay House / no, need a literary agent.

    1367, date for Intervention from Above . . . 1:36 / 7 days = 169:36 . . . 16936 . . . [169 + 3 = 172]6 . . . **1726**.
       17:26 is 5:26 PM ↔ <625>, the tidying up begins.
       1726 . . . **17/(26)** is **17/339** . . . 17:(339) = 681 minutes . . . 681
         681 minutes + <933> = **1614**, Leanne Long, fig. 5.
         [681 + <186> = 867] + <933> = 1800) - 339 = 1461 = **1641** ↔
           1641 . . . 1 day / 6:41 = 30:41 . . . 30:(41) = 1759 minutes = <14> = **1773**, Leanne Long.

    1367, date for Intervention from Above . . . 1:36 / 7 days =169:36 - <631> = 163:05 . . . 16305 / 5 = 3261.
       32:61 is 1 day / 8:61 . . . 1861 . . . **18/(6)/1** is **18/25** ↔
       18:25 is 6:25 PM . . . **625**, Robert needs 14 days to tidy things up

    3261 . . . [3² = 9]61 . . . [961 minutes - <169> = 792 = <297>] * 6 = **1782** . . . **{17}/8/2**, Robert's 14 days are up.

    3261 . . . [3² = 9]61 . . . 961 minutes = 15:61 . . . **1561**.
       1561 - 2586, Intervention from Above = 1025 . . . 10:25 = 625 minutes . . . **625**, the tidying up begins.
       15:61 = 1 day / (839) . . . **18/39**, Robert's 14 days to tidy things up are up ↔ 18/39 falls on **17/8/2**
       1561= <1651> . . . **16/(51)**, it certainly is your Playground.

13/(67), Hay House / no, need a literary agent + **18/(6)/1**, date for Intervention from Above is = **3228**.
    3228 = **1614**, John Kordupel, synthesis from format + **1614**, Leanne Long, fig. 5.

3228 - 6/(11)/7, date for Intervention = 2889 . . . 28:(89) = 1591 minutes + <98> = 1689 . . . **{16}/8/9**, Leanne / Reading.
    and,
    6/(11)/7, date for Intervention . . . [6 + 1 week = 13 days]17 . . . 1317 ↔ **1317**, Leanne Long, fig. 4 ↔
       1317, Leanne Long + {16}/8/9, Leanne / Reading = 3006 . . . 30:(06) = 1794 minutes + <60> = **1854**.
       18/54 falls on **18/2/(5)** . . . 18:25 is 6:25 PM . . . **625**, Robert needs 14 days to tidy things up ↔

    13/1/7, You have made the bed as far as you could. Now it is up to Me.

    [3228 = <8223>] - 6/(11)/7, date for Intervention = 2106 . . . 21:06 is 9:06 PM . . . **90/{6}**, a marriage

1367, date for Intervention . . . 1:36 / 7 days =169:36 - <631> = 163:05 = 1265 minutes + <503> = 1768.
1768 . . . 1 day / 768 = 31:68 . . . 3168.
    3168 - <8613> = **5445**, Leanne's birth day.

    3168 . . . [316 + <613> = 929] * 8 = 7432.
       7432 = <2347> . . . **2/3/47**, my birth day
       74:32 = 2:32 / 3 days . . . **2323**, 2nd. Coming.
       7432 - <2347> = **5085** ↔
         [2845, Leanne Long: the space in-between = <5482> . . . 548 * 2 = 1096] - <6901> = 5805 = **<5085>**
         [50:85 = 2:85 / 2 days . . . 2852] / 4 = **713**, the Season ends.

1768 . . . **{17}/68**, Robert's 14 days are up.
    8. Holding Together.
       Six at the top means:

He finds no head for holding together.
Misfortune.

The head is the beginning. If the beginning is not right, there is no hope of a right ending. If we have missed the right moment for union and go on hesitating to hive complete and full devotion, we shall regret the error when it is too late.

17. Following.
Six at the top means:
He meets with firm allegiance
And is still further bound.
The king introduces him
To the Western Mountain.

This refers to a man, an exalted sage, who has already put the turmoil of the world behind him. But a follower appears who understands him and is not to be put off. So the sage comes back into the world and aids the other in his work. Thus there develops an eternal tie between the two.
The allegory is chosen from the annals of the Chou dynasty. The rulers of this dynasty honored men who had served them well by rewarding them a place in the royal family's temple of ancestors on the Western Mountain. In this way they were regarded as sharing in the destiny of the ruling family. The I Ching. Wilhelm / Baynes.

1367 . . . √1367 = 3697 2963 . . . 3697 - <7963> = **4266**, Jesus . . . 42:66 = 2586 minutes . . . **2586**, Intervention ↔ 2963 + <3692> = **6655**.
　　6655 = **60/48**, Cher's birth day + **(60)/{7}**, Cher's passing.
　　　　Leanne Long: 99 (161) 171 (89) . . . 99:171 – (89):(161) = 10010 . . . 100:10 = 4:10 / 4 days . . . **4104**.
　　　　　　4104 – [171:99 – (161):(89) = **1010**] = 3094 . . . 30:94 = 1 day / 6:94 . . . **1694**, Leanne Long
　　　　　　　　1694 = <4961> . . . 49:61 is 1 day / 161 . . . 1161 . . . 11* 61 = **671**, Mary Magdalene.
　　　　　　　　1694 + <4961> = **6655**.

　　John Kordupel, Synthesis From Format: 153 159 167 145.
　　[153 + 159 + 167 + 145 = 624] + <426> + [<351> + <951> + <761> + <541> = 2604] + <4062> = 7716.
　　([153 + 159 + 167 = 479] + <974> = 1453) + [145 + <541> = 686] = 2139
　　[1:45 is 2:(15) = <512>] + [<5:41> being 6:(19) = <916>] = 1428 + <8241> = 9669 . . . [9 * 669 = 6021
　　　　6021 - 7716 = **1695**, John Kordupel ↔ 1695, Second Coming ↔ 1695, the Unlettered Prophet.
　　　　6021 – 2139 = **3882**, John Kordupel ↔ **3882**, the Unlettered Prophet.
　　　　　　　　and,
　　([1695 + <5961> + 3882 + <2883> = 14421] - <12441> = 1980) + [2139 / 3 = 713] = 2693.
　　　　26:93 = 1653 minutes - <39> = **1614**.
　　　　2693 + <3962> = **6655**.

6655 + <5566> = **12221**.
　　12221 = [**14/8/4**, I'll see you tomorrow at 815 + **815** = 2299] + <9922>
　　　　2299 = <9922> . . . 99:22 = 4 days / 3:22 . . . 4322.
　　　　　　43:22 = 2602 minutes + <22> = 2624 . . . 26:24 = 1584 minutes + <42> = **1626**.
　　　　　　16/2/6, is contact with Robert imminent?
　　　　　　4322 . . . [43² = 1849] + 2 = 1851 . . . **18/(51)** falls on {17}/11/10 ↔
　　　　　　17/11/10, I cannot talk with you about your world unless you know about mine.

2299 . . . 22 * 9 * 9 = **1782**, the Second Coming.

2299 + **1463**, John Kordupel + **1782**, the Second Coming = 5544.

5544 . . . 554 weeks / 4 days = 3882 days . . . **3882**, the Unlettered Prophet.

2299 = **1255**, Second Coming + **1044**, Leanne Long ↔

10/(44), I cannot talk with you about your world unless you know about mine.

12221 . . . ([12² = 144] 2) + 1 = **1443**, Kali Yuga

1443 * 7 = 10101 . . . **{10}/101**, an invitation to change the language.

12221 = **{10}/101**, an invitation to change the language + **(7)/5/3**, Robert Loomis / manuscript.

753 = <357> . . . 35 to 7 is 6:25 . . . **625**, the tidying up begins.

and,

20/7/6, date for Intervention from Above is 6/(11)/7 . . . 61:17 = (10:43) / 3 days . . . 10:433 = 1033 minutes + <334> = **1367**.

1367 . . . 1:36 / 7 days =169:36 - <631> = 163:05 = 1265 . . . **12/(65)**, there is a meeting here tonight.

(65)/12, there is a meeting here tonight + **4266**, Jesus + **144/3**, Robert Loomis / manuscript = **12221**.

122:21 = 5 days / 2:21 . . . 5221 = <1225> . . . **(12)/2/{5}**, is contact with Robert imminent?

122:21 = 5 days / 2:21 . . . 5221 - [2:21 / 5 days . . . 2215] = 3006 . . . 30:(06) = 1794 minutes + <60> = **1854**.

1317, Leanne Long + **{16}/8/9**, Leanne / Reading = 3006 . . . 30:(06) = 1794 minutes + <60> = **1854**.

18/54 falls on **18/2/(5)** . . . 18:25 is 6:25 PM . . . **625**, Robert needs 14 days to tidy things up ↔

13/1/7, You have made the bed as far as you could. Now it is up to Me.

13:67 = 1 day / (1033) . . . 11033.

11033 = **7/(11)/6**, date for Intervention + **3917** ↔

39/{17} is 14 days after **18/25**.

3/9/{17}, M/D/Y is 14 days after **18/2/(5)**.

11:033 = 693 minutes . . . 6:93 PM is 18:93 . . . **18/9/3** weeks . . . **1893**, the Chain of Rebirth.

[1893 + <3981> = 5874] - **7/20/6**, date for Intervention = 1332 = <2331> . . . 23 * 31 = **713**, the Season ends.

[11033 - **12221** = 1188] + **(11)/7/6**, date for Intervention = 2364 . . . 23:(64) = 1316 minutes . . . **1316**.

13:16 = 1 day / (10:44) . . . 11044 + [(10:44)/1 day . . . 10441] = 21485

21485 = **20/07/6**, date for Intervention + **1409**, John Kordupel

1409 . . . 1 day / 409 = 28:09

28:09 = 1689 minutes . . . **{16}/8/9**, Leanne / Reading

28:(09) = 1671 minutes + <90> = 1761 . . . **{17}/(6)/1**.

13/1/{6}, You have made the bed as far as you could. Now it is up to Me.

and,

20/7/6, date for Intervention from Above is 201/{5}/6 . . . 20:(156) = 1044 minutes . . . **1044**.

1143, Mary Magdalene + 849, Mary Magdalene = **1992** ↔ 1992 . . . 19 * [9² = 81] = **1539**, Leanne Long.

1992 – [375, Mary Magdalene + <573>, Leanne Long = 948] = **1044** →

10/(44), I cannot talk with you about your world unless you know about Mine. Get out of My Car.

1287, Leanne Long, fig. 3 . . . [12 * 87 = **1044**] + <4401> = **5445**.

7/5/2/62 + 5/2/7/{61}, M/D/W/Y, Leanne's birth day = **22501** = <10522> . . . 10:522 = 1122 minutes + <225> = **1347**.

1347, Leanne's birth day ↔ **1/3/{47}**, Cherry's birth day

1347, Leanne's birth day = <7431> . . . [74:31 = 2:31 / 3 days . . . 2313] + <3132> = **5445**.

7/20/6, date for Intervention from Above – [**1044**, Leanne Long + <4401> = **5445**] = 1761 . . . **{17}/(6)/1**.

([{5}/7/(11), date for Intervention from Above + **2586**, Intervention = 8297] – **5445** = 2852) / 4 = **713**, the Season ends

20/7/6, date for Intervention from Above is 6/(11)/7 – [**1044**, Leanne Long = <4401>] = 1716 . . . **17/(16)**, next energy healing session with Leanne.

and,
625, Robert needs 14 days to tidy things up = <526> . . . 5[2^6 = 64] . . . 564 minutes = 9:24 . . . 924.
    924 minutes = 14:84 . . . **14/8/4**, I'll see you tomorrow.
    924, Robert begins to tidy things up . . . 924 minutes = 15:24 . . . 1 day / 5:24 = 29:24 . . . 29:(24) = 1716 minutes ↔
        17/(16), my seventh energy healing session session with Leanne,
            which,
            after 14 days,
                is followed by my eighth session energy healing session session

it is: [(2)/{16} + 17/(2) = 388] * 8 = 3104.
    [3104 = <4013>] - {5}/(164), date for Intervention from Above = 1151 . . . 11:51 = 711 minutes . . . **711**, a Cycle ends.

    31:(04) = 1856 minutes - <40> = 1816 . . . **(18)/1/{6}**, You have made the bed as far as you could. Now it is up to Me.

Freedom.
    Liberate yourself from the manifestations of the past, from what is often called tradition. Throw open the cupboard doors to reveal the skeletons and release the crystallised views of your ancestors that have manifested as your genes. Your genes are threads of reality formed by the power of your ancestors' thoughts and feelings. Let us say, "Thank you, thank you, to all who have come before us, for their creations and all that they lived. For in doing so, they gave you options and bought you to where you are now. When you were born, you arrived at the vibration of all that the generation before wanted. You are the manifestation of the expanded previous generation. Each generation's job is to expand even more for the sheer beauty and joy of it; this is the natural flow of life. Somehow we allowed ourselves to become living statues, re-enacting the experiences of the past, becoming a victim to this. Your genes are a blueprint, formed by the past to give you a place to start when you arrive. Your genes do not decide anything, you do. Liberate yourself and become who you know you are.
        You are powerful.

The Flower of Life. Wisdom of Astar. Denise Jarvie.

1. Ancient Sound Frequencies.

    Today I allow myself to nurture my mind, body and spirit to bring me back to a state of balance and harmony.

If you have drawn the Ancient Sound Frequency card, you are in need of an overhaul. Your body may be tired and out of balance or you may be feeling emotionally and mentally drained. You have been working hard in so many aspects of your life that you need to return to a state of balance and harmony on all levels.
You may need a healing to deal with a current issue in your life that could have an attachment to a past life. Whether it be gaining an understanding or a need to forgive and release, it can be done by cutting cords and ties and letting go under the guidance of a light worker. Sacred Geometry Healing Cards Guidebook. Emily Kisvarda.

Sleeping Dragon, Crouching Tiger: The Crouching Tiger. (continued).
God: 7,15,4 . . . 5√7154 = 13196374 . . . 1319 + 6374 = **7693**.

God: 7,15,4 . . . 5√**<4517>** = 13008105 . . . [1300 + 8105 = **9405**] + 7693 = **17098**.

    17:098 = 1118 minutes . . . **1/11/8**, Cherryl passed away ↔

        17/1/9, Leanne, you're a reincarnation of Cher / Leanne agrees to a Reading ↔ **17/09/8**, Leanne Long / Reading

    17098 – **1/09/17**, Leanne, you're a reincarnation of Cher / Leanne agrees to a Reading = **6181**↔

    17098 . . . [1 + 7 = 8]098 . . . 8098 – **6181** = **1/9/17**, Leanne, you're a reincarnation of Cher / Leanne agrees to a Reading.

    {6}/(18)/1, You have made the bed as far as you could. Now it is up to Me.

God: 7,15,4 . . . [5√**7154** = 13196374] + [5√**<4517>** = 13008105 = 26204479 . . . 2620 + 4479 = 7099.

    [7099, God = <9907>] - ([**9405**, God = <5049>] + [**7693**, God = <3967>] = 9016) = **891** ↔

        Anakhita: 65 143 151 57 . . . ([151:57 – 143:65 = 792] * 7 = 5544 = <4455>) / 5 = **891**.

    { ([7099, God = <9907>] - ([**9405**, God = <5049>] - [**7693**, God = <3967>] = 1082) = **8825**) - <5288> = 3537 } + <7353> = **10890**.

        and,

20:10. Wherefore I caused them to go forth out of the land of Egypt, and bought them into the wilderness.

20:23. I lifted up mine hand unto them also in the wilderness, that I would scatter them among the heathen, and disperse them through the countries

29:12. And I will make the land of Egypt desolate, in the midst of the countries that are desolate, and her cities among the cities that are laid waste shall be desolate forty years: and I will scatter the Egyptians among the nations, and I will disperse them through the countries.

30:26. And I will scatter the Egyptians among the nations, and disperse them among the countries; and they shall know that I am the Lord.

20:34. And I will bring you out from the people, and will gather you out of the countries wherein ye are scattered, with a might hand, and with a stretched out arm, and with fury poured out. Ezekiel. Holy Bible. King James Version.

    2010 + 2023 + 2912 + 2034 + 17:9 + 17:09 + 17:10 = 15603.

    156:03 = 9363 minutes + <30> = 9393 . . . 93:93 = 5673 minutes + <39> = 5712 . . . 57:12 = 3432 minutes + <21> = 3453

        3453 . . . 3 days / 453 = 76:53; 345 / 3 days = 75:45;

        [7653 + 7545 = 15198] - [<3567> + <5457> = 9024] = 6174) + <4716> = **10890**.

John Kordupel, synthesis from format: 153 159 167 145

    ([153 + 159 + 167 = 479] + <974> = 1453) + [145 + <541> = 686] = 2139.

    ([153 + 159 + 167 + 145 = 624] + <426> = 1050) + ([<351> + <951> + <761> + <541> = 2604] + <4062> = 6666) = 7716.

    ([1:45 is 2:(15) . . . 215 = <512>] + [<5:41> being 6:(19) . . . 619 = <916>] = 1428 + <8241> = 9669.

        9669 . . . [9 * 669 = 6021] + <1206> = **7227**, Book-End.

        6021 – 7716 = 1695, John Kordupel ← 1695, Lot → 1695, Second Coming ↔ 1695, the Unlettered Prophet.

            16:95 is 4:95 PM . . . 495 minutes = 8:15 . . . 815, Messiah.

        6021 = 2139 + 3882, the Unlettered Prophet.

        9669 . . . [96 * 69 = 6624] + <4266>, Jesus = **10890**.

        10890 – [1695 + <5961> + 3882 + <2883> = 14421 = <12441>] = **1551**, John Kordupel →

            1551, Resurrection, beginning of the 1,000 year reign of Jesus **{15}/(51)**, a Playground.

161

[10890 / 2 = **5445**] + [**891**, the Day of Resurrection * 2 = **1782**, the Second Coming] = **7227**, Book-End.

Sleeping Dragon, Crouching Tiger: The Crouching Tiger. (continued).
God: 7,15,4 . . . 5√**7154** = 13196374
      13196374 . . . 1319 + 6374 = 7693.
         7693 = <3967> . . . 396 * 7 = **2772**, Know Me.
         7693 . . . 7 * ([693 - <396> = 297] + <792>) = **5544** ↔
           Anakhita: 65 143 151 57 . . . [151:57 – 143:65 = 792] * 7 = **5544**.

       ([487, Lot / Lut - <784> = 297] = <792>) * 7 = **5544** →
          whose daughters gave birth to: **5544**, Moab / Moabites → **5544**, Ben-ammi / Ammon.

           the scattering of the peoples through the countries ↔
             the gathering out of the countries . . .

Moab / Moabites: 115 197 209 101
      115:197:209:101 . . . [1151 + 9720 + 9101 = 19972] + [<1511> + <0279> + <1019> = 2809] = 22781.
         227:(81) = 13539 minutes + <18> = 13557 . . . 135:(57) = 8043 minutes . . . 8043.
           8043 minutes + <75> = **8118**, Maob / Moabites →
John Eevash Kordupel: 209 153 266 191 . . . [<902> + <351> + <662> + <191> = 2106] + <6012> = **8118**.

Ben-ammi / Ammon: 113 199 211 101 . . . [113 + 199 + 211 + 101 = 624] + <426> = 1050.
      1050 + ([<311> + <991> + <112> + <101> = 1515] + <5151> = 6666) = 7716.
      624 + 1515 = 2139; 624 + 6666 = 7290; [<426> + 1515 = 1941] + 1050 + 2139 = 5130.
         5130 – 7716 = **2586**, Ben-ammi / Ammon →
Cher's passing: 1/11/8 + 8/(60) + (60)/8 = **2586** ↔ **2586**, Intervention From Above.
John Kordupel, synthesis from format: 153 159 167 145.
      [1:45 is 2:(15) = <512>] + [<5:41> is 6:(19) = <916>] = 1428 + <8241> = 9669.
         9669 . . . 96 * 69 = 6624 = <4266>, Jesus . . . 42:66 = 2586 minutes . . . **2586**.

  { (5130 – [<0315> + 7290 = 7605] = 2475) - [7605 = <5067>] = 2592 } + <2952> = **5544**, Ben-ammi / Ammon.

           the scattering of the peoples through the countries ↔
             the gathering out of the countries . . .

Fo-Hi / Krishna / Buddha / Lao Tzu / Confucius: 364 468 500 243
         500:364 – 243:468 = 256896, the Eastern influence.
         256896 . . . ([256 + 896 = 1152] + <2511> = 3663) + ([<652> + <698> = 1350] + <0531> = 1881) = **5544**.

Moses / Isiah / Jeremiah / Ezekiel / Jesus Christ / the Prophet Muhammad, the Western influence: 616 814 869 561.
         [616 + 814 + 869 + 561 = 2860] + <0682> = 3542.
         <616> + <418> + <969> + <165> = 2167.
      2167 + <7612> = 9779 . . . [97 * 79 = 7663] - <3667> = 3996 . . . 3 * 99 * 6 = **1782**.
      [2167 - <7612> = 5445] + **1782** = **7227**, Book-End.
      [2167 + 3542 + 1782 = 7491] - <1947> = **5544**.

           the gathering out of the countries . . .

(**14/8/4**, I'll see you tomorrow at **815** + [815 minutes = 13:35 . . . 1335

1335 . . . [1 day / (3:35) is 20:25 . . . 2025] = 3509) - <9053> = **5544** ↔

the Day Of Resurrection: 249 271 191 229

([249 + 271 + 191 + 229 = 940] + [<942> + <172> + <191> + <922> = 2227 = <7222>] = 8162) - <2618> = **5544**.

Leanne Long: 99 (161) 171 (89) . . . 99:171 – (89):(161) = 10010 . . . 100:10 = 4:10 / 4 days . . . **4104**.

4104 – [171:99 – (161):(89) = **1010**] = 3094 . . . 30:94 = 1 day / 6:94 . . . **1694**, Leanne Long ↔

1694, Mary Magdalene + <4961> = **6655**.

60/48, Cher's birth day + (60)/{7}, Cher's passing = **6655**, Cher's lifetime.

([6655 / 11 = 605] + [6655 / 5 = 1331] = 1936) - <6391> = **4455**, Leanne Long

4455 / 5 = **891**, the Day of Resurrection ↔ 4455 = <5544>, Leanne Long.

1782, the Second Coming . . . 1 day / 7:82 = 31:82 . . . 3 days / (1:82) = 70:18 + <281> = 72:99 = 3 days / 0:99 . . . 3099.

3099, the Unlettered Prophet . . . 3099 minutes = 50:99 . . . 50:99 = 2 days / 2:99 . . . **2299**.

2299 + [2299 . . .22 * 9 * 9 = **1782**, the Second Coming] + 1463, John Kordupel = **5544**.

5544 . . . 554 weeks / 4 days = 3882 days . . . **3882** ↔ **3882**, the Unlettered Prophet.

Sleeping Dragon, Crouching Tiger: The Crouching Tiger. (continued).
God: 7,15,4 . . . 5√**7154** = 13196374 . . . [1319 = <9131>] + [6374 = <4736>] = 13867.

13867 . . . 13 + 867 = **880**, God.

13:867 = 1647 minutes - <768> = 879 = <978> . . . 978 minutes = 16:18 = 1 day / (782) . . . **1782** ↔

5:1. Belshazzar the king made a great feast to a thousand of his lords, and drank wine before the thousand.

5:2. Belshazzar, while he tasted the wine, commanded to bring the golden and the silver vessels which his father Nebuchadnezzar had taken out of the temple which was in Jerusalem; that the king, and his princes, his wives, and his concubines, might drink therein.

5:3. Then they bought the golden vessels that ere taken out of the temple of the house of God which was at Jerusalem; and the king, and the princes, his wives, and his concubines, drank in them.

5:4. They drank wine and praised the gods of gold, and of silver, of brass, or iron, of wood, and of stone.

5:5. In the same hour came forth fingers of a man's hand, and wrote over against the candlesticks upon the plaister of the wall of the king's palace: and the king saw the part of the hand that wrote.

16:24. Then was the part of the hand sent from him; and this writing was written.

16:25. And this is the writing that was written, MENE, MENE, TEKEL, UPHARSIN. Daniel.

MENE, MENE, TEKEL, UPHARSIN: 234 313 335 212.

[234 + 313 + 335 + 212 = 1094] + <4901> = 5995;

[<432> + <313> + <533> + <212> = 1490] + <0941> = 2431.

5995 + [2431 = <1342>, Second Coming] = 7337 . . . 73:37 = 3 days / 1:37 . . . 3137.

3137 . . . 31/3/7, a marriage.

3137 + 1342, Second Coming = 4479 = <9744>

9744 . . . 9 * 74 * 4 = **2664**, a hand writing →

[I Am: 9113] + [God: 7,15,4] + [Allah: 1,12,12,1,8] + [Jahwe: 10,1,8,23,5] = 2155720.

2155720 . . .[<5512> - 2155 = 3357 + 7 + 20 = 3384] – 720 = **2664**, hand of God.

97:44 = 4 days / 1:44 . . . **4144** ↔
13/1/7, You have made the bed as far as you could. Now it is up to Me . . .
200{6} + 2007 + 13/1 = **4144** ↔

[4144 = <4414>] - [3137 = <7313>] = 2899.
2899 . . . [2 * 8 = 16] [9 + 9 = 18] . . . 16:18 = 1 day / 782 . . . **1782** ↔
1782, the Second Coming ↔ **1782**, Leanne Long.

13867, God . . . -<31> + [13 + 867 = 880] = **849** ↔ 849 minutes = 14:09 . . . **1409** ↔
√**7227**, Book-Ends = 8501 1763 . . . [8√501 = 1024 5808] + [1√763 = 27622454] = 3786 8262.
([3786 = <6873>] - [8262 = <2628>] = 4245) / 5 = 849 . . .849 minutes = 14:09 . . . **1409** ↔

227/4, I'll see you tomorrow at 8:15 + 815 = **3089** ↔ **3089**, Messiah.
3089 minutes = 50:89 = 2 days / 2:89 . . . 22:89 = 1409 minutes . . . **1409**.
375, Mary Magdalene + <573>, Leanne Long = 948 = <849> minutes = 14:09 . . . **1409**.
my birth day: 2/3/47 + 3/2/47 + 34/47 = 9041 . . . <**1409**>, John Kordupel.

3089, Messiah = <9803> . . . 98:03 = 4 days / 2:03 . . . 4203.
4203, Messiah - <3024> = **1179** ↔
Resurrection: 147 147 159 153 . . . <741741> - <351951> = 389790 . . . 389 + 790 = **1179**.
4203 = <3024> . . . 30:24 = 1824 minutes . . . **1824**, Messiah ↔ **1824**, Siddhartha Gautama.
1824 . . . 18[2^4 = 16] . . . 1816 . . . **(18)/1/{6}**, You have made the bed as far as you could. Now it is up to Me ↔
18/1/(6) is **18/25** ↔ 18:25 = 6:25 PM . . . **625**, Robert needs 14 days to tidy things up.

1824 minutes - <42> = **1782**, the Second Coming ↔ **{17}/8/2**, Robert's 14 days are up.

1824 . . . **18/2/4**, Y/D/M.

3089, Messiah = <9803> . . . 98:03 = 2:03 / 4 days . . . 2034 + <4302> = **6336**, Messiah, the Western influence ↔
Fo-Hi / Krishna / Buddha / Lao Tzu / Confucius: 364 468 500 243 . . . 500:364 – 243:468 = 256896.
256896, the Eastern influence . . . ([2 + 56 = 58] + 8 = 66) * 96 = **6336**.

6336 / 2 = 3168.

31:68 = 1 day / 7:68 . . . **1768**, the Chain of Rebirth ↔ **{17}/68**.
31:68 = 1928 minutes - <86> = 1842 . . . **18/4/2**.

30:89 = 1889 minutes . . . **18/89** falls on **18/4/2**.
16/2/6, is contact with Robert imminent? . . . [16^2 = 256] * 6 = **1536**.
1536 . . . [- 1 + 53 = 52]6 . . . **526** = <625>, Robert begins the tidying up.
526 minutes = 8:46 . . . 846 minutes = 14:06 . . . 1 day / 4:06 = 28:06 = 1686 minutes + <60> = 1746.
1746 . . . 1 day / 7:46 = 31:46 = 1906 minutes . . . 1906.
19:(06) = 1134 minutes = 18:54 . . . **18/54** is 18/2/(5) ↔ 1825.
18:25 is 6:25 PM . . . **625**.
1906 minutes - <64> = 1842 . . . **18/4/2**.

1536 . . . 1 day / 5:36 = 29:36 = 1776 minutes + <63> = 1839.
18/3/9 is **{17}/68**.
18/(39) weeks is 18/(273) falls on **18/4/2**.

1536 . . . [15³ = 3375 . . . 3 + 375 = 378] = <873>) * 6 = 5238
52:(38) = 3082 minutes . . . 3082
3082 minutes + <83> = 3165 . . . 31:(65) = 1795 minutes + <56> = **1851**.
1851 = <1581> . . . 1 day / 581 = 29:81 . . . 2981.
29:81 = 1821 minutes . . . **1821** ↔
18:(21) = 1059 minutes . . . **1059**, a page in the life of . . .
1821 minutes + <18> = **1839** ↔
2981 = <1892> . . . **18/92** is **18/4/2**.

18/(51) falls on {**17**}/**11/10** ↔ **17/11/10**, I cannot talk with you about your world unless you know about Mine. Get out of My Car.

30:(82) = 1718 minutes = <8171> - <28> = 8143 - <6351> = 1792 . . . {**17**}/**92** is **18/4/2**.

52:38 = 3158 minutes + <83> = 3241 . . . 32:(41) = 1879 minutes + <14> = **1893** ↔
1893, the Chain of Rebirth ↔
18/9/3, Y/D/M is {**17**}/**68** ↔ **1768**, the Chain of Rebirth ↔
13/1/{**6**}, You have made the bed as far as you could. Now it is up to Me . . .
131/ 6 days = 145:31 + <131> = 146:62
14:662 = 1502 minutes + <266> = **1768** ↔
2250, New Harmonic Vibrations . . . 2 days / (250) = 45:50 - <052> = 4498
4498 . . . 44 * 9 * 8 =3168 . . . 31:68 = 1 day / 7:68 . . . **1768**.

1536 . . . [15³ = 3375] + 6 = 3381 . . . 33:(81) = 1899 minutes - <18> = **1881** ↔

and,
1881 . . . 1[8 * 8 = 64]1 . . . 1641 ↔ 5238, God . . . 52:(38) = 3082 minutes - <83> = 2999 . . . 29:(99) = 1641 minutes . . . **1641**.

1881 . . . 1day / 8:81 = 32:81 . . . 32:(81) = 1839 minutes - <18> = 1821 . . . 18:(21) = 1059 minutes . . . **1059**, a page in the life of . . .

1881 . . . 1day / 8:81 = 32:81 - <188> = 3093 . . . 30:93 = 1893 minutes . . . **1893**, the Chain of Rebirth.

1881 . . . 1[8 * 81 = 648] . . . 1648 + <8461> = **10109**, Eve ↔ 1999, Leanne Long . . . 1 day / 999 = 33:99 . . . 33:(99) = 1881 minutes . . . **1881**.

18:81 is (519)/1 days . . . 51:91 = 2 days / 391 . . . 23:(91) = 1289 minutes - <19> = 1270.
12:70 = 790 minutes . . . **7/90**, a marriage → 1270 minutes = 22:(50) . . . **2250**, New Harmonic Vibrations.

{ ([1881 * 7 = 13167] – **10109**, Eve = 3058) - <8503> = 5445 } + **1782**, the Second Coming = **7227**, Book-Ends.

1881 . . . 1day / 8:81 = 32:81 + <188> = 34:69 . . . 34:69 = 2109 minutes + <96> = 2205 . . . 22:05 = 1325 minutes . . . 1325.
13:25 = 805 minutes . . . **805**, End of Days.

1881 * 7 = 13167 . . . **13/1/**{**6**}**/7**, You have made the bed as far as you could. Now it is up to Me.

1881 . . . 1day / 8:81 = 32:81 . . . 32:(81) = 1839 minutes - <18> = **1821**.
1821 * 5 = **9105** ↔
Mary Magdalene: 119 219 232 106 . . . 119 + 219 + 232 + 106 = 676 . . .
676 . . . 6⁷ = 279936 . . . 279 + <972> + 936 + <639> = 2826 . . . ([282 * 6 = 1692] - <2961> = 1269) – 6 = 1263.

[12:(63) = 657 minutes] - <36> = 621 . . . [6:21 PM is 18:21] * 5 = **9105**.

91:05 = 5465 minutes . . . 5465 . . . [5 + 4 = 9] 65 . . . **965**.
    (5225, Iwan Kordupel + [John Kordupel: 1409 + 1463 + <3641> = 6513]) = 11738.
    11738 – [1539, John Kordupel * 7 = 10773] = **965** = <**569**>, Jesus.

91:05 = (4:55)/4 days . . . 4554 . . . 4 days / 554 weeks = 3882 days . . . **3882**, the Unlettered Prophet.

9105 = <5019> . . . 50:(19) = 2981 minutes = <1892> . . . **18/92** falls on **18/4/2**.
and,
17/11/2010, I cannot talk with you about your world unless you know about mine. Get out of My Car.
[17/11 + 11/17 + 2010 = 4838] + [Car: alphabet from R to L: 24,26,9 . . . 24269 . . .[- 2 + 4269 = 4267] = **9105**.

18:21. And a mighty angel took up a stone like a great millstone, and cast it into the sea, saying, Thus with violence shall that great city Babylon be thrown down, and shall be found no more. Revelations.
and,
18:21. And if thou say in thine heart, How shall we know the word which the Lord hath not spoken?
18:22. When a prophet speaketh in the name of the lord, if the thing follows not, nor come to pass, that is the thing which the Lord hath not spoken, but the prophet hath spoken it presumptuously: though shalt not be afraid of him. Deuteronomy.
Holy Bible. King James Version.

Sleeping Dragon, Crouching Tiger: The Crouching Tiger. (continued)

Allah: 1, 12,12,1,8: Satan: 19,1,20,1,14:
1121218, Allah - 19120114, Satan = 1799 8796 . . . 1799 + <9971> + 8796 + <6978> = 27544 . . . [- 2 + 7 = 5]544 . . . **5544**.
    1121218, Allah + 19120114, Satan = 2024 1332 . . . [2024 + <4202> + 1332 + <2331>= 9889] + <9889 > = 19778.
      19778 . . . 1[9778 - <8779> = 999] . . . 1999.
        19:(99) = 1041 minutes - <99> = 942 minutes = 15:42 . . . 1 day / 5:42 = 29:42 = 1782 minutes . . . **1782**.
        19:99 = (401) / 1 day . . . 4011 + <1104> = **5115** ↔ **(51)/{15}**, it certainly is your Playground.
      1999 . . . 199 * 9 = 1791 . . . **17/9/1**, Leanne agrees to a Reading.
      1999 . . . 19 * 99 = **1881** ↔
        1881 * 7 = 13167 . . . **13/1/{6}/7**, You have made the bed as far as you could. Now it is up to Me.

        1881 . . . 1day / 8:81 = 32:81 - <188> = 3093 . . . 30:93 = 1893 minutes . . . **1893**, the Chain of Rebirth.

        18:81 is (519)/1 days . . . 51:91 = 2 days / 391 . . . 23:(91) = 1289 minutes - <19> = 1270.
          1270 + 1893, the Chain of Rebirth = 3163 . . . 31:(63) = 1797 minutes - <36> = 1761 . . . **{17}/(6)/1**.
          12:70 = 790 minutes . . . **7/90**, a marriage →
          1270 minutes = 22:(50) . . . **2250**, New Harmonic Vibrations.
            [1893, the Chain of Rebirth + 2250, New Vibrations = 4143] – 7/90, a marriage = 3353.
              33:(53) = 1927 minutes - <35> = 1892 . . . **18/92** falls on **18/4/2**.

    197:78 = 11898 minutes + <87> = 11985 . . . 119:85 = 7225 minutes + <58> = 7283.
      72:83 = 72:83 = 4403 minutes + <38> = 4441 . . . 44:41 = 2681 minutes + <14> = **2695** →
        John: [1015 + 814 = 1829] + 4757, John Kordupel = 6586; [1829 = <9281>] - 6586 = **2695**.
      7283 . . . [7 * 2 = 14]83 . . . **14/8/{3}**, I'll see you tomorrow.

    197:78 = 11898 minutes - <87> = 11811 . . . 118:11 = 7091 minutes - <11> = 7080

70:80 = 3 days / (120) . . . 31:(20) = 1840 minutes + <02> = **1842**.

197:(78) = 11742 minutes . . . [1 + 17 = 18]42 . . . **1842**.
   117:(42) = 6978 minutes . . . 69:(78) = 4062 minutes - <87> = 3975
      3975 - <5793> = **1818**, Magdalene.
         39:(75) = 2265 minutes . . . 22:(65) = 1255 minutes . . . **1255**, Jesus ↔ **1255**, Second Coming.
            1818 + 1255 = 3073 . . . 30:(73) = 1727 minutes + <37> = **1764**, Leanne Long

197:(78) = 11742 minutes 11742 + <87> = 11829
   11:829 = 1489 minutes + <982> = 2417 . . . **2/4/{17}**.
   118:(29) = 7051 minutes + <92> = 7143 . . . 71:(43) = 4217 minutes . . . **4/2/{17}**.

197:(78) = 11742 minutes 11742 - <87> = 11655
   116:(55) = 6905 minutes - <55> = 6850 . . . 68:(50) = 4030 minutes - <05> = 4025 . . . 40:(25) = 2375 minutes . . .
   2375 2375 + <5732> = **8107** ↔
         Eve / Bathsheba / Esther / Khadija / Yasodhara / Mary Magdalene / Cherryl Dianne Kordupel:
         the Lamb's wives: 666 1102 1170 598.
           [<666> + <2011> + <0711> + <895> = 4283] + <3824> = **8107**.

      2375 minutes - <52> = **2323** → **2323**, 2nd. Coming.

   11:655 = 1315 minutes + <556> = 1871 = <1781> . . . **{17}/8/1**, Y/D/M
   11655 / 5 = 2331 . . . 23 * 31 = **713**, the Season ends.

197:78 = 11898 minutes . . . 118:98 = 7178 minutes + <89> = 7267 . . . 72:67 = 4387 minutes + <76> = 4463
   44:63 = 2703 minutes + <36> = 2739 . . . 27:39 = 1659 minutes + <93> = 1752 . . . **{17}/(5)/2** ↔ **18/2/(5)** ↔
      18:25 is 6:25 PM ↔
         1463, Leanne Long, Fig. 4 . . . **1463**, John Kordupel . . . 14:63 is 2:63 PM . . . 263 + <362> = **625** ↔
         625, Robert begins to tidy things up.

   4463 + <3644> = **8107** ↔

and,

19:23. The sun was risen upon the earth when Lot entered Zoar.
19:24. Then the Lord rained upon Sodom and upon Gomorrah brimstone and fire from the Lord out of heaven; Genesis.

   [1923 + 1924 = 3847 + <7483> = 11330] + [<3291> + <4291> = 7582 + <2857> = 10439] = 21769.
   [19:23 is 7:23 PM] + [19:24 = 7:24 PM] = 1447.
      ([1447 + <7441> = 8888] + [<327> + <427> = 754 + <457> = 1211] = 10099) + 21769 = 31868.
         31868 . . . [3186 + 8 = 3194] + <4913> = **8107**.

The energy grids have their genesis in Heaven, translating as the butterfly effect on Earth.
   If you accept that a non-random relationship between Heaven and Earth has been established,
   then Darwinism – the evolution of the species by chance – becomes unsustainable.

There is a Second Coming in life sequence and a Second Coming in time sequence.
The breaking of the seals, the fall of Babylon, and the beginning of the 1,000 year reign of Jesus when Satan is locked up, would be associated with the Second Coming in time sequence; when Satan is let loose for but a short season - somewhere in the early 3,000 - would be connected with the Second Coming in time sequence.

Under both scenarios, Chaos would rule.

3410, Chaos . . . 3 + 410 plus, in the sense that we tack it on the end, is **4103**.
 [John: 10, 15, 8,14] + [Kordupel: 11,15,18, 4, 21, 16, 5, 12] = 11,151,843,132,326
  [1115184 . . . 1115 + 184 = 1299] + [3132326 . . . 313 + 2326 = 2639] = 3938
   [39:38 = 2378 minutes + <83> = 2461] + <1642> = **4103**.

3410, Chaos . . . 34:10 = 10:10 / 1 day . . . **10101**, the Dual Essence ↔ {**10**}/**101**, Invitation to Change the Language.
 {10}/101, Invitation from 10101, the Dual Essence . . . 101:01 = 5:01 / 4 days . . . 5014 + [4 days / 5:01 . . . 4501] = 9515
 = <5159>
 51:59 = 3119 minutes + <95> = 3214 . . . 32:14 = 1934 minutes - <41> = **1893**, the Chain of Rebirth.
  3119 minutes - <95> = 3024 minutes . . . 3024, we are now somewhere in the 3,000's.
   30:24 = 1824 minutes . . . **18/2/4**, Y/D/M is {**17**}/(**39**) weeks ↔
    14/8/4, I'll see you tomorrow at 8:15 . . . 14:84 = 924 minutes + 815 = **1739**.

   30:24 = 1824 minutes - <42> = **1782**, the Chain of Rebirth.

3410, Chaos . . . [3 days / (410) = 67:90 - <014> = 6776] / 4 = **1694**.
 [1694 = <4961>] - 3410, Chaos = 1551 . . . 15:(51) = 849 minutes = 14:09 . . . **1409**, John Kordupel ↔ {**15**}/(**51**), a Playground.
 [1694 + <4961> = **6655**] + <5566> = **12221**.
  12221 . . . { ([12² = 144] 2) + 1 = **1443**, Kali Yuga } * 7 = 10101 . . . {**10**}/**101**, an Invitation to Change the Language.

  122:21 = 5 days / 2:21 . . . **5221**.
   1/1/11, Mary Magdalene is going to knock on your door . . . 11:11 is 49 to 12 . . . 4912.
   [4912 . . . 4 days / 912 = 105:12 . . . 10512] - [4912 . . . 491 / 2 days = 52:91 . . . 5291] = **5221**.

and,
34:25. And I will make with them a covenant of peace, and will cause the evil beasts to cease out of the land: and they shall dwell safely in the wilderness, and sleep in the woods. Ezekiel. Holy Bible. King James Version.
  3425 . . . ([34² = 1156] * 5 = 5780) + <0875> = 6655.
   6655 . . . [6 + 6 = 12]55 . . . **1255**, Jesus → **1255**, Second Coming.
   6655 + <5566> = **12221**.

 12221, causing the evil beasts to cease . . . 12:221 = 941 minutes + <122> = 1063 minutes = 16:103 . . . 16103.
  16103 = 12221 + **3882**, the Unlettered Prophet.
  16103 – **13061**, lot's daughters get Lot drunk = 3042
   30:(42) = 1758 minutes + <24> = **1782**.
   3042 = <24:03> = 1443 minutes * 7 = 10101 . . . {**10**}/**101**, Invitation to change the Language.

and,
19:35. And they made their father drink wine that night also: and the younger arose and lay with him; and he perceived not when she lay down, nor when she arose.
19:36. Thus were both the daughters of Lot with child by their father.
19:37. And the first born bare a son, and called his name Moab: the same is the father of the Moabites to this day.
19:38. And the younger, she also bare a son, and called his name Ben-ammi: the same is the father of the children of Ammon unto this day. Genesis. Holy Bible. King James Version.
  19:35 + 19:36 + 19:37 + 19:38 = 7748.

7748 . . . [7 * 7 = 49]48 . . . 4948 + <8494> = **13442**.
[13442 - <24431> = 10989] = **888**, Adam & Eve, interwoven energies + **{10}/101**, an Invitation.

13442 . . . 1344 – 2 = **1342**, Second Coming.
1342, Second Coming + [<2431> * 4 = 9724] = **11066**.
11066 – **{10}/101**, Invitation = **965**, Iwan Kordupel / John Kordupel
11066 . . . [11:06 = 666 minutes] * 6 = 3996 . . . 3 * 99 * 6 = **1782**, Resurrection.

1342, Second Coming + 965, John Kordupel + 1782, Chain of Rebirth = 4089.
[4089 = <9804>] - **{10}/101**, Invitation = 297.
[297 = <792>] * 7 = 5544 . . . 554 weeks / 4 days = 3882 days . . . **3882**.
John Kordupel, 1409 + 1463 + <9041> + <3641> = 15554.
15554 . . .[-1 + 5 = 4 days] 554 weeks is 3882 days . . . **3882**, the Unlettered Prophet

297 * 6 = **1782**, the Chain of Rebirth ↔ **1782**, the Second Coming, life sequence.

4089 = 20{17} + 2018 + 54 . . . 20{17} / 2018 / 54 is **18/2/(5)** . . .
18:25 is 6:25 PM . . . **625**, the tidying up begins.

13:442 = 1222 minutes - <244> = 978 minutes = 16:18 = 1 day / (782) . . . **1782** ↔
1782, the Second Coming, time sequence ↔ **1782**, the Chain of Rebirth ↔
1782, Resurrection ↔ **1782**, the Second Coming, life sequence.

13442 + <24431> = 37873 . . . 37:873 = 3093 minutes . . . 30:93 = 1893 minutes . . . **1893**.
1893 . . . **1893**, the Chain of Rebirth.
1893 minutes - <39> = 1854 . . . **18/54** is **18/2/(5)** . . .
18:25 is 6:25 PM . . . **625**, the tidying up begins.

[7748 + <8477> = 16225] – 13442 = 2783
[2783 + <3872> = 6655] + <5566> = **12221**.
2783 . . . [2 days / 783 = 55:83] + [278 / 3 days = 74:78] = **13061**.
2783 . . . [2 * 7 = 14]83 . . . **14/8/{3}**, I'll see you tomorrow.

and,
3410, Chaos . . . [3 days / 410 = 76:10] + <0167> + <041> = 78:18 = 3 days / 6:18 . . . 3618
3618 . . . 3 * 618 = 1854 . . . **18/54** is **18/2/(5)** . . . 18:25 is 6:25 PM . . . **625**, the tidying up begins.

[3618 - <8163> = 4545] / 5 = **909**, Earth / metamorphosis.

3618 = <8163> . . . 81 * 63 = 5103
51:03 = 3:03 / 2 days . . . 30:(32) = 1768 minutes . . . **{17}/68**, Robert's 14 days are up.
51:03 = 3063 minutes + <30> = 3093 . . . 30:93 = 1893 minutes . . . **1893**, the Chain of Rebirth.
5103 + <3015> = **8118**.
[I Am: 9113] + [God: 7,15,4] + [Allah: 1,12,12,1,8] + [Jahwe: 10,1,8,23,5] = 2155720.
2155720, I Am / God / Allah / Jahwe . . . [<5512> - 2155 = 3357 + 7 + 20 = 3384+ 720 = 4104] + <4014> = **8118**.

John Eevash Kordupel: 209 153 266 191 . . . [<902> + <351> + <662> + <191> = 2106] + <6012> = **8118**.

8118 = **1342**, Second Coming + **1782**, the Chain of Rebirth + 2542 + <2452>.

2452 . . . 2:45 / 2 days is 50:45 . . . 50 * 45 = **2250**, New Harmonic Vibrations for Earthlings ↔
2250 . . . 2 days / (250) = 45:50 - <052> = 4498 . . . 44:(98) = 2542 minutes . . . **2542**.

3410, Chaos . . . 3 + 410 plus, meaning tacking it on the end, is **4103** + **8118**, Earth / metamorphosis = **12221**, causing the evil beasts to cease.

3410, Chaos . . . 3 days / 410 = 76:10 - <041> = 7596.
75:96 = 3 days / 3:96 . . . 3396 . . . [3 + 396 = 1188] - [<6933> . . . 693 * 3 = 2079] = **891**, the Day of Resurrection ↔
891 * 2 = **1782**, the Chain of Rebirth ↔ **1782**, the Second Coming in life sequence.

75:96 = 3 days / 3:96 . . . 3396 + [3:96 / 3 days . . . 3963] = 7359
7359 . . . [7 * 3 * 5 = 105]9 . . . **1059**, a page in the life of . . .

7359 . . . 73 * 5 * 9 = 3285 . . . 32:(85) = 1835 minutes + <58> = **1893**, rediscovery of the Forms of Life ↔

7359 / 3 = **2453**, Covenant . . . [2^4 = 16]53 . . . **1653**.
3113 BC, start + 5,125 years, duration of Galactic cycle = 8238 + <8328> = 16566.
16566, a Galactic cycle - (8238 . . . [8^2 = 64]38 . . . 6438 + <8346> = 14784) = **1782**, a Resurrection ↔

[16:566 = 1526 minutes + <665> = 2191] + 3882 = 6073.
6073 - [5544 = <4455>] = 1618 . . . 16:18 is 1 day / (782) . . . **1782**, the Second Coming, time sequence.
5544 . . . 554 weeks / 4 days = 3882 days . . . **3882**, the Unlettered Prophet
[60:(73) = 3527 minutes + <37> = 3564] / 2 = **1782**, the Chain of Rebirth.

16566 – [6073 * 3 = 18219] = **1653**.

1463, John Kordupel . . . 1 day / 463 = 2863 . . . 28:(63) = 1617 minutes + <36> = **1653**.

1653 . . . 1 day / 6:53 = 30:53 . . . 30:(53) = 1747 minutes + <35> = **1782**, the Second Coming.

the Five Horsemen: the Mahdi / the Second Coming / Maitreya / the Messiah / Kalki: 465 731 777 419.
[731, the Five Horsemen updating Scriptures * 3 = **2193**] - [<137> * 3 = 411] = **1782**, the Chain of Rebirth.

[465 + 731 + 777 + 419 = 2392] + <2932> + [<564> + <137> + 777 + <914> = 2392] + <2932> = 10648.
2392 + 2392 = 4784; 2392 + 5324 = 7716; <4874> + <6177> = 11051.
[2932 + 2932 = 5864 = <4685>] + [2932 + 5324 = 8256 = <6528> = 11213] + 11051 **22264**.

[777:465 – 731:419 = 46046] – 22264 = **23782**.

23782 . . . [-2 + 3 = 1]782 . . . **1782**, the Second Coming in time sequence ↔
23782 = <28732> - [the Collective Will & gold futures: $101 + 238/76 + [$873 + 21/80 = 3053] = 1702.
[17:02 = 1 day / (6:58) . . . 1658] + [<2071> . . . 20:71 is 1 day / (329) . . . 1329] = 2987.
2987 – **2193** = 794 . . . **(79)**/{4}, corporate issues resolved.
29:(87) = 1653 minutes . . . **1653**.

1653 . . . 1 day / 6:53 = 30:53 . . . 30:(53) = 1747 minutes . . . 1747.
1747 minutes + <35> = **1782**, the Second Coming
17:47 = 5:47 PM . . . 547 minutes = 9:07 . . . **90/7**, a marriage ↔ **907**, Invitation to change the Language ↔

1551, Resurrection, the beginning of the 1,000 year reign of Jesus →
{15}/(51), it is most definitely your Playground . . . 1√551 = 2347.

    2/3/47, my birth day . . . 23:47 is 11:47 PM . . . 11:(47) = 10:13 . . . 1013 minutes = 16:53 . . . **1653**.

19:23. The sun was risen upon the earth when Lot entered Zoar.
19:24. Then the Lord rained upon Sodom and upon Gomorrah brimstone and fire from the Lord out of heaven;
Genesis.

    [1923 + 1924 = 3847 + <7483> = 11330] + [<3291> + <4291> = 7582 + <2857> = 10439] = 21769.
      21769 . . . [21 + 7 = 28]69 . . . 28:69 = 1749 minutes - <96> = **1653**.

3410, Chaos . . . [3^4 = 81]10 . . . **8110**, Chaos – [7596, Chaos = <6957>] = **1153**, the space in-between this Chaos and that Chaos.
    11:53 = 713 minutes . . . **713**, a Season ends,
      which is not the same as saying,
        the Season ends.

21. Universe.

You've come far on your journey, and it's time to be rewarded for your efforts. This card symbolizes the completion, triumph, peace, liberation, and fulfillment. Everything you strived for is within reach – meet it halfway and grab it! The Universe is the last of the Major Arcana Cards and reflects the work that you've accomplished on your travels – but more importantly, it represents the wisdom that you've gained along the way.

You should now honor and acknowledge the truly wonderful soul that you are, and accept the vital part that you play in the bigger scheme of life.

The world is yours to command, and you're free to travel in whatever direction your heart desires. You're connected to everything in the cosmos. The Universe Card is a reminder that the same energy making up the stars in the sky, the same energy that's coursing through the Universe, is in each and every individual. In ancient times, many believed that each star was the soul of one person. They also believed that these "souls" shined so brightly to guide others through the darkness – and so too can your wise soul.

Traditional tarot archetype: The World. Psychic Tarot Oracle Deck Guidebook. John Holland.

READING.

A DEATH, A FUNERAL
&
A RESURRECTION.

A Death, a Funeral, a Resurrection.

11/(29) days /8, Cher's passing, M/D/Y . . . 11298 / 7 = **1614** ↔
    16:14 = 974 minutes . . . 9 * 74 = **666**, Cher's passing ↔
        (in relation to reincarnation, provided there is at least one life in-between a subsequent manifestation,
        the same soul can occupy the same space).

    Leanne Long: ([<9991> + <8644> + <3892> + <4452> = 26979] - 11994 = 14985) / 5 = **2997**, Leanne Long.
       2997 = <**7992**>, Leanne Long, in sync with:
          John Kordupel (format ↔ synthesis): 153 159 167 145 . . . 159:153 – 167:145 = **7992**.

       2997 = <**7992**> . . . [7 + 9 = 16][9 * 2 = 18] . . . 16:18 = 1 day / (782> . . . **1782**, Leanne Long ↔
          1782, Cherryl's reincarnational family tree.

             7992, energies in unison.

       2997 = <**7992**>, Leanne Long / 12 = **666**, Leanne Long ↔ **666**, the numerical name of the Lamb's wives

16:14 = 974 minutes . . . **974**, scleroderma, cause of Cher's passing ↔ 974 minutes = 15:74 . . . 1day /5:74 = 29:74 . . .
2974.
    2974 = <4792> . . . [4 + 7 = 11] [2 * 9 = 18] . . . 1118 . . . **1/11/8**, Cher passed away.
    2974 . . . [2 + 9 = 11][7 + 4 = 11] . . . 1111 . . . **1/1/11**, Mary Magdalene is going to knock on your door
    29:74 = 1814 minutes . . . {18}/14 is **19/14**.
        19:14 is 7:14 PM . . . **714** ↔ Flower of Life: 132 171 192 120 . . . <231> + <171> + <291> + <021> = **714**.
        19:14 is 7:14 PM . . . 71^4 = 2541 1681 . . . 2541 + 1681 = **4222**, Market Forces.
        1914 + **1/1/11**, Mary Magdalene is going to knock on your door = 3025
            30:25 = 1825 minutes . . . **18/25** ↔ 18:25 is 6:25 PM . . . **625**, Robert begins to tidy things up.
           [3025 = <5023>] - **8/306**, Cher's passing = 3283
           3025 – **8/306**, Cher's passing = 5281
              5281 – **306/8**, Cher's passing = 2213 . . . **(221)/3**, Robert Loomis / manuscript.
              5281 = <1825> . . . **18/25** ↔ 18:25 is 6:25 PM . . . **625**, Robert begins to tidy things up.

{7}/(54), a funeral, and the next day is {7}/(53) . . . **(7)/5/3**, Robert Loomis / manuscript.
    {7}/(53) = <357> . . . 35 to 7 is 6:25 . . . **625**, Robert begins to tidy things up.

(54) / {7}, a funeral . . . 547 minutes = 9:07 . . . **907**, Invitation to Change the Language ↔ **90/7**, a marriage.
    [3/(7)/5, Robert Loomis / manuscript + **<526>**, the tidying up begins + **90/7**, a marriage = 1808] – **625**, tidying up =
1183.

      1183 - <3811> = **1614** ↔ 8/(60), a passing + {7}/(54), a funeral = **1614** ↔ **(1)/6/14**, Gina / manuscript.

      1183 minutes = 18:103 . . . **18/1/(03)** is **1/(3)/{17}** ↔ **13/1/7**, You have made the bed as far as you could. Now it is up to Me.

    3/(7)/5, Robert Loomis / manuscript . . . 375 * 6 = **2250**, New Harmonic Vibrations
and,
306/8, Cher passed away → 30:68 = 1868 minutes - <86> = **1782**, Resurrection.

306/{7}, Cher passed away – **1782**, a Resurrection = 1285 . . . **{12}/85**, Hay House / manuscript ↔
    34/47, my birth day . . . 3 days / (4:47) = 6713 minutes . . . **(67)/13**, Hay House / no, need a literary agent.

    34/47, my birth day – [**1782**, a Resurrection . . . 17:82 is 5:82 PM . . . **582**] = 2865.
      2865 / 5 = 573 . . . **5/(7)/3**, Robert Loomis / manuscript.
      2865 . . . [2 * 86 = 172]5 . . . 1725 . . . **{17}/25** is **18/25** ↔ 18:25 is 6:25 PM . . . **625**, Robert begins to tidy things up.
      2865 / 5 = 573 = **<375>**
        1716, Anakhita . . . 17:16 = 5:16 PM = <6:15> = 375 minutes . . . **375** →
          Covenant: 3,15,22,5,14,1,14,20 . . . √3152251411420 = 1775458.0 . . . 1775 + 4580 = 6355.
            6355 = **4222**, Market Forces + 2133
            2133 / 3 = **711**, a Cycle ends.
          [2133 + <3312> = **5445**] + **1782**, Resurrection = **7227**, Book-End.

        6355 . . . 6 * 3 * 5 * 5 = **375** → **(3)/7/{5}**, I'll pick up the bill.

        375 + <573> = 948 = <849> minutes = 14:09 . . . 1409, John Kordupel →

(1)/7/16, the day that I retired . . . 17:16 = 5:16 PM = <6:15> = 375 minutes . . . **375** →
    3/(7)/5, Robert / manuscript → **(37)/5**, leaving on a jet plane ↔

    375 * 60 = 2250 . . . **2250**, New Vibrations.

1716 . . . 1 day / 7:16 = 3116.
    31/1/6. Yesterday, I recalled thoughts from 29/1.

    Robert needs a couple of weeks to tidy things up.

    I didn't give it much thought as there was no starting point. I assumed it was to do with when he comes to Melbourne.
    Starting from when?

      625.

31/1/6 is 1/31/6 → **{13}/(1)/6**, Gina, a literary agent / manuscript ↔

13/1/{6}, You have made the bed as far as you could. Now it is up to Me.

{17}/1/(6) being **18/25** ↔ 18:25 is 6:25 PM . . . **625**, Robert begins to tidy things up.
625 . . . 6√25 = 1051 5811 . . . [<1501> + <1185> = **2236**, Robert begins the tidying up] + **880**, God = **3116**.

and,
3116 = <6113> = 569, Jesus + 5544 . . . 554 weeks / 4 days = 3882 days . . . **3882**, the Unlettered Prophet.

3116 = <6113> . . . **6/(1)/{13}**, Gina / manuscript ← **{6}/1/13**, You have made the bed as far as you could. Now it is up to Me.
   31:(16) = 1844 minutes - <61> = **1783**.
      1783 . . . **(17)/8/{3}**, I'll see you tomorrow.
      1783 . . . 1 day / 783 = 31:83 . . . 3183.
         31:(83) = 1777 minutes - <38> = **1739**.
           17:39 = 1059 minutes . . . **1059**, a page in the life of . . .
             [**14/8/4**, I'll see you tomorrow at 815 . . . 14:84 = 924 minutes . . . 924] + **815** = **1739** ↔
               {17}/39 falls on {17}/8/2 ↔

    3183 + <3813> = 6996.
      6996 . . . 6 * 99 * 6 = 3564 = 1782, Resurrection + **1782**, the Second Coming.

      6996 . . . 69 * 96 = 6624.
         [6624 – **306/8**, Cher passed away + 3556] + <6553> = **10109**, Eve.
           3556 + **666**, the Heart-Beat grid = **4222**, Market Forces.
         [3556 = <6553>] = **4222**, Market Forces + 2331 . . . 23 * 31 = **713**, the Season ends.

      6624 = <4266> . . . 42:66 = 2586 minutes . . . **2586**.
        Cher passed away on: 1/11/8 + (60)/8 + 8/(60) = **2586**.
          25:86 = 1:86 / 1 day . . . **18/(6)/1** is **18/25** ↔
           18:25 is 6:25 PM . . . **625**, Robert begins to tidy things up.

and,
625, the tidying up begins + **369**, Earthlings + [**1059**, a page in the life of . . . 10:59 = 659 minutes . . . 659] = **1653**.
   1653 . . . [1 + 6 = 7]53 . . . **(7)/5/3**, Robert Loomis / manuscript →
      753 = <357> . . . 35 to 7 is 6:25 . . . **625**, Robert needs a couple of weeks to tidy things up.

  1653 . . . 1 day / 6:53 = 30:53 . . . 30:(53) = 1747 minutes . . . **1747**.
   ([1153, Anakhita * 7 = 8071] = 9737) + <7379> + [6661, Earthlings = <1666>] = **17116**.

  Moses / Isiah / Jeremiah / Ezekiel / Jesus Christ / the Prophet Muhammad, the Western influence: 616 814 869 561 . . .
    joining the numbers: 616814869561 . . . 6168 1486 9561 . . . <8616> + <6841> + <1659> = **17116**.
    17:116 = 1136 minutes + <611> = **1747**.
  and,
  1747 minutes + <35> = **1782**, the Second Coming.
  17:47 = 5:47 PM . . . 547 minutes = 9:07 . . . **907**, the Light ↔ **907**, Invitation to change the Language → **90/7**, a marriage
  17:47 is 1 day / (6:13) . . . 1613 . . . **(1)/6/{13}**, Gina / manuscript.
  17/(47) is 17/318 . . . 17318 . . . [-1 + 7 = 6]318 . . . 6318 → **6/(318)** falls on **16/2/6**, is contact with Robert imminent?

and,

Cher's funeral: 8/7/11 + {7}/(54) = 9465.

9465, Cher's funeral = **5/24/3**, Robert Loomis / manuscript + **4222**, Market Forces.

9465, Cher's funeral . . . [94:65 = 4 days / (135) . . . **4135**] + [(135)/4 days . . . **1354**] = **5489**.

    5489 = **{12}/(67)**, Hay House / no, need a literary agent + **4222**, Market Forces.

    5489 = <9845> . . . [98:45 = 2:45/4 days . . . **2454**] + [4 days / 2:45 . . . **4245**] = **6699**.

       [6699 + <9966> = 16665] – [**(54)/{7}**, Cher's funeral **13/1/7/{6}**, making of beds = **13723**] = **2942**.

         29:42 = 1782 minutes . . . **1782**, the Second Coming.

    [6699 = <9966>] = **18/26** + **39/18**, being **{17}/8/2** + **4222**, Market Forces.

      and,

      18/26 is {17}/26 . . . 17:26 PM is 5:26 = <**625**>, Robert begins the tidying up.

6699 = **9/27/5**, corporate issues resolved + 2576.

    25:76 = 1:76 / 1 day . . . 1761 . . . {17}/(6)/1 is **18/25** ↔

      18:25 is 6:25 PM . . . **625**, Robert begins to tidy things up.

    2576 . . . **{2}/5/(7)**, Robert Loomis / manuscript * 6 = 1542

      1542 . . . 1 day /5:42 = 29:42 = 1782 minutes **1782**.

        1782 . . . 1 day / 782 = 31:82 = 1942 minutes - <28> = **1914** . . . 19:14 is 7:14 PM . . . **714** ↔

          Flower of Life: 132 171 192 120 . . . <231> + <171> + <291> + <021> = **714**.

        714 . . . 71^4 = 2541 1681 . . . 2541 + 1681 = **4222**, Market Forces.

        √714 = 2672 0778 . . . [2672 + <2762> = **5434**] + [0778 + <8770> = **9548**] = **14982**.

          [14982 + **{12}/(85)**, Hay House / manuscript + **1059**, a page in the life of = **17326**

          [Hay House / no, need a literary agent: **10/(6)/13** + **(67)/13** = **17326**.

            and,

            {17}/(326) is **{17}/39**.

        14982 + [<4345> + <8459> = **12804**] = **27786**.

         666, the Heart-Beat grid . . . √6 = 2449 4897

        [2449 + <9442> = **11891**] + [4897 + <7984> = **12881**] = **24772**.

         24772 - **27786** = 3014 . . . 30:14 = 1 day / 6:14 . . . **1614**.

          11/(29) days /8, Cher's passing / 7 = **1614**.

          (1)/6/14, Gina, a literary agent / manuscript

          16:14 = 974 minutes . . . 9 * 74 = **666**.

    1542 = <2451> . . . [2^4 = 16]51 . . . **16/(51)**, it certainly is your Playground.

9/27/5, corporate issues resolved = **(67)/13**, Hay House / no, need literary agent + **2562**.

    2562 + <2652> = 5214 . . . 52:(14) = 3106 minutes . . . 3106.

      3106 minutes + <41> = **3147** . . . **3/1/{47}**, Cher's birthday ↔ 31:47 is 1 day / 7:47 . . . **1747** ↔

        17:47 is 5:47 PM . . . **(54)/{7}**, Cher's funeral ↔ 547 minutes = 9:07 . . . **907**, a marriage

    31:(06) = 1854 minutes . . . 1854

      18:54 = 6:54 PM = 414 minutes . . . 4:14 PM is 16:14 . . . **(1)/6/14**, literary agent / manuscript.

      (1)/6/14, a manuscript + **(54)/{7}**, a funeral + **90/7**, a marriage = **306/8**, a death → 30:68 = 1868

      minutes - <86> = **1782**, Resurrection.

    1854 minutes + <60> = **1914**.

2562 = **144/3**, Robert Loomis / manuscript + **1119** . . . 1119 minutes = 18:39 . . . **18/39** falls on **{17}/8/2**.

6699 . . . 66 * 9 * 9 = **5346**.
   [5346 = <6435>] = **(221)/3**, Robert Loomis / manuscript + **4222**, Market Forces.
   5346 = **1782**, Resurrection + **1782**, the Second Coming + **1782**
      which gives us 1782 . . . 1 day / (782) = 16:18 . . . **1/(6)/18**, being **18/25** ↔
         18:25 = 6:25 PM . . . **625**, Robert needs 14 days to tidy things up,
            and,
               18/25 plus 14 days brings us to **{17}/8/2**.
                  which leads to: **1782** . . . 1 day / 782 = 31:82 = 1942 minutes - <28> = **1914**.

9465, Cher's funeral / 5 = **1893**, rediscover of the Forms of Life ↔ **18/9/3** weeks.
[1893 - <3981> = 2088] - **9/(3)/5**, corporate issues resolved = 1153
   11:53 = 713 minutes . . . **713**, the Season ends.
   [1153 = <3511>] = **1/(6)/18** + **18/9/3** weeks.
      and,
         [**1/(6)/18** + **18/9/3** weeks + **1914 = 5425**] = **31/3/{6}**, a marriage + **2289**.
            22:89 = 1409 minutes . . . **1409**, John Kordupel.

         2289 = **1914** + 375 . . . 375 * 6 = **2250**, New Harmonic Vibrations.

                        and,

[**4/227**, I'll see you tomorrow at 815 + **815** = **5042**] - ([**1409**, John Kordupel + [**1893**, rediscovery F of L - <3981> = 2088] = 3497) = **1545**.
√1545 = 3930 6488 . . .
            [3930 - <0393> = 3537] + <7353> = **10890**.
               [10890 – 9465, Cher's funeral = **1425**] / 5 = 285 = <582> . . . 582 PM is 1782 . . . **1782**.
               [10890 / 2 = **5445**] + **17/82** = **7227**, Book-End.

            [3930 - <0393> = 3537 = <7353>] - 6488 = **1425**.
               1425 . . . 1[4² = 16]5 . . . 1165 . . . 11:(65) = 595 minutes . . . 595.
                  595 - <56> = 539 . . . 5:39 PM is 17:39 . . . **1739**.
                     14/08/4, I'll see you tomorrow at 815 + **815** = **14899** . . .
                        14:899 = 1739 minutes . . . **{17}/39** falls on **{17}/8/2**.
                  595 + <56> = 651 . . . 6:51 PM is 18:51 . . . **18/(51)** falls on **{17}/11/10** ↔
                     17/11/10, I cannot talk with you about your world unless you know about Mine.

            [3930 - <0393> = 3537] - [<8846> - 6488 = **2358**] = **1179** ↔
            Resurrection: 147 147 159 153 . . . <741741> - <351951> = 389790 . . . 389 + 790 = **1179**.

               1877, Mary Magdalene = <7781>
                  77:81 = 3 days / 5:81 . . . 35:81 = 2181 minutes . . . 21:(81) = 1179 minutes . . . **1179**.
                     1179 + [9465, Cher's funeral – 7781, Mary Magdalene = 1684] = **2863**.
                        28:63 = 1 day / 4:63 . . . **1463**, John Kordupel
                        28:(63) = 1617 minutes . . . **1/(6)/{17}** is **18/25**.
                           16:17 is 4:17 PM = <714>
                              7:14 PM is 19:14 . . . **1914**.
                                 714 . . . 71⁴ = 2541 1681 . . . 2541 + <1681> = **4222**.

5745, Jesus . . . 5745 minutes = 95:45 . . . (9545 - [95 * 45 = 4275 + **625**, Isa = 3650] = 5895
5895 / 5 = **1179**, the Lamb.

[3930 - <0393> = 3537 + <7353> = 10890] – [6488 + <8846> = 15334] = **4444**.
and,
9465, Cher's funeral – **4444** = 5021 . . . 50:21 = 2:21 / 2 days . . . **(221)/{2}**, Robert Loomis / manuscript.

[9465, Cher's funeral = <5649>] - [**2358** + **4444** = 6802] = **1153** . . . 11:53 = 713 minutes . . . **713**, a Season ends.

and,
the story so far:
[**4/227**, I'll see you tomorrow at 815 + **815** = **5042**] - ([**1409**, John Kordupel + [**1893**, rediscovery F of L - <3981> = 2088] = 3497) = **1545**.
1545 . . . 1 day / 545 = 29:45 . . . 29:45 = 1785 minutes + <54> = 1839 . . . **18/39** falls on **{17}/8/2**.

1545 . . . 1:54 / 5 days = 121:54 . . . 12:154 = 874 minutes + <451> = 1325
13:25 = 805 minutes . . . **805**, End of Days
1325 = <5231> . . . 52:31 = 2 days / 4:31 . . . 24:(31) = 1409 minutes . . . **1409**, John Kordupel.
1325 . . . [13² = 169]5 . . . **1695**.
1695, the Light → 1695, Lot → [1695 - <5961> = 4266, Jesus] → 1695, Second Coming ↔
1695, the Unlettered Prophet ↔ John Kordupel.

1545 . . . [1:54/ 5 days = 121:54 + <45> = **12605**] – [**14/08/4**, I'll see you tomorrow at 815 + **815** = **14899**] = **2294** ↔
22:94 = 1 day / (106) . . . 1106 . . . 11:06 = 666 minutes . . . **666**, the Heart-Beat grid.

2294, Shroud of Turin.
and,
You have made the bed as far as you could. Now it is up to Me: 13/1/{6}/7 + (18)/7/{6} = **31343**.
13/1/7 . . . 1317 minutes = 21:57 . . . 2157 minutes = 35:57 . . . 3557 minutes = 59:17 . . . 5917 minutes = 97:97 . . . 9797.
9797 = **24/5/3**, Robert Loomis / manuscript + 7344
73:44 = 1:44 / 3 days * 7 = 10101 . . . **{10}/101**, Invitation to Change the Language.
7344 . . . [7³ = 2401]44 . . . 240144 . . . [-2 + 40 = 38 . . . 3 * 8 = 24]144 . . . 24144.
24144 = <44142> = [31343, making of beds = <34313>] + 9829.
98:29 = 2:29 / 4 days . . . **2294**.

22:94 = 1414 minutes + <49> = **1463**, John Kordupel.

2294 . . . [22 * 9 * 4 = 792] * 7 = 5544
5544 . . . 554 weeks / 4 days = 3882 days . . . **3882**, the Unlettered Prophet.
and,
[5544 / 2 = 2772, Know Me] + [<4455>, Untitled One] = **7227**, Book-End.
[5544 = <4455>] = **{13}/6/(1)**, Gina / manuscript + **(3)/09/{4}**, corporate issues resolved.
and,
(3)/09/{4}, corporate issues resolved . . . 3094 minutes = 50:94 = 2 days / 294 . . . **2294**.

and,
7/3/31, a marriage . . . 7[33 past 1 is 2:(27) . . . 227} . . . [**7227**, a marriage, a Book-End * 7 = 50589] - <98505>
= 47916.

177

[50589 = <98505>] - [47916 - <61974> = 14058 = <85041>] = **13464**.

13:464 = 1244 minutes + <464> = 1708 . . . 1 day / 7:08 = 31:08 . . . 3108.

3108 minutes = 50:18 = 3:18 / 2 days . . . 3182.

31:82 = 1 day / 7:82 . . . **1782**.

31:82 = 1942 minutes - <28> = **1914** . . . 19:14 is 7:14 PM . . . **714**.

and,

Cher passed away on 1/11/{7} . . . 1117.

11:17 = 677 minutes . . . 6:77 PM is 18:77 . . . **1877**, Mary Magdalene.

1117 + <776> = **1893**, rediscovery of the Forms of Life.

11:(17) = 643 minutes + <71> = **714**.

23:83 = 1463 minutes . . . **1463**, John Kordupel.

2383 . . . 238 * 3 = **714**.

3108 - <8013> = 4905 = <50:94> = 2 days / 2:94 . . . **2294**.

2294 + **5045** = 7339.

73:39 = 3 days / 1:39 . . . 31:39 = 1 day / 7:39 . . . **1739**.

31:(39) = 1821 minutes + <93> = **1914**.

7339 . . . [7 * 3 = 21]39 . . . 2139 / 3 = **713**, the season ends.

and,

concerning 5045:

[John: 10, 15, 8,14] + [Kordupel: 11,15,18, 4, 21, 16, 5, 12] = 11,151,843,132,326:

we separate 11,151,843,132,326 into two groups of seven, to which we add our birthday:

1115184 . . .1115 + 184 = **1299**.

1299 . . . 12:(99) = 621 minutes . . . **621** . . . 6:21 PM is 18:21 . . . **1821**.

18:(21) = 1059 minutes . . . **1059**, a page in the life of . . .

1299 . . . [12:(99) = 621 minutes - <99> = 522] + <225> = **747**, 2nd. Coming.

3132326 + 34/19{46}, my birth day = 3474272 . . . 3474 + 272 + 1299 = **5045**.

and,

[5045 + <5405> = 10450] – **13464**, see 7227, marriage, Book-End = 3014

30:14 = 1 day / 6:14 . . . **1614** ↔

11/(29) days /8, Cher's passing, M/D/Y . . . 11298 / 7 = **1614**.

5045 . . . 50 * 45 = **2250**, New Harmonic Vibrations.

2250, New Vibrations + **621** = **2871**, Eve ↔ <1782>, the Second Coming.

5045 = **1821** + **974** + 2250, New Harmonic Vibrations

974 minutes = 16:14 . . . **(1)/6/14**, Gina / manuscript.

and,

5045 = **27/9/5**, corporate issues resolved + **2250**, New Harmonic Vibrations.

and,

the story so far:

[**4/227**, I'll see you tomorrow at 815 + **815** = **5042**] - ([**1409**, John Kordupel + [**1893**, rediscovery F of L - <3981> = 2088] = 3497) = **1545**.

1545 . . . (154)/5 days = 118:46 + <451> = 122:97 = 2:97 / 5 days . . . **27/9/5**, corporate issues resolved.

1545 . . . (1:54)/5 days = 118:06 - <451> = 113:55

11355 – ([9465, Cher's funeral = <5649>] + **13/(67)**, Hay House / need literary agent = **7016**) = 4339

    4339 . . . 4[3³ = 27]9 . . . **4279**.

       4279 . . . 42:(79) = 2441 minutes . . . 2441.

        2441 = <1442> . . . **144/{2}**, Robert Loomis / manuscript.

        2441 . . . [2⁴ = 16]41 . . . 1641 = <1461> . . . **14/6/(1)**, Gina / manuscript. 6755 – 3116 = 3639

        24:(41) = 1399 minutes . . . 1399.

          1399 = <9931> . . . 99:31 = 3:31/4 days . . . 33:14 = 1 day / 9:14 . . . **1914**.

          1399 minutes - <14> = 1385 . . . **13/(85)**, Hay House / manuscript.

        [1399 = <9931>] - [(67)/13, Hay House / no, need a literary agent = <3176>] = 6755.

          <5576> - **14/6/(1)**, Gina, literary agent / manuscript + **2299** + **1816**.

           2299 . . . 22 * 9 * 9 = **1782**, the Second Coming.

           2299 + 1463, John Kordupel + 1782, the Second Coming = 5544

             5544 . . . 554 weeks / 4 days = 3882 days . . . **3882**.

               3882, the Unlettered Prophet = <2883>, Maitreya.

               28:83 = 1 day / 4:83 . . . **14/8/{3**, I'll see you.

          2299 = **14/8/4**, I'll see you tomorrow at 8:15 + **815**, Messiah.

          2299 = **974** + 1325 . . . 13:25 = 805 minutes . . . **805**, End of Days.

           974 minutes = 16:14 . . . **(1)/6/14**, Gina, literary agent / manuscript.

          2299 = **1255**, Second Coming + **10/(44)**, know My world to know yours.

          and,

          concerning 1816:

          18/1/(6) is **18/25** ↔

           18:25 = 6:25 PM . . . **625**, Robert starts to tidy things up.

      (18)/1/{6}, You have made the bed as far as you could. Now it is up to Me.

    2441 = <1442> minutes + 79 = 1521 + <97> = **1618** . . . **1/(6)/18** is **18/25** ↔

      18:25 = 6:25 PM . . . **625**, Robert needs a couple of weeks to tidy things up.

    4279 . . . [4 * 2 = 8]79 . . . 879 = <978> . . . 978 minutes = 16:18 = 1 day / (782) . . . **{17}/8/2**.

    and,

    {17}/8/2 is 14 days after 18/25

    4279 . . . **{4}/27/9**, corporate issues resolved ↔

  [4339 = <9334>] = **3/(221)**, Robert Loomis / manuscript + **6113** ↔

6113 = 569, Jesus + 5544 . . . 554 weeks / 4 days = 3882 days . . . **3882**, the Unlettered Prophet.

6113 . . . **6/(1)/{13}**, Gina / manuscript ← **{6}/1/13**, You have made the bed as far as you could. Now it is up to Me.

6113 = <3116>

From the manuscript *The System:*

31/1/6. Yesterday, I recalled thoughts from 29/1.

    Robert needs a couple of weeks to tidy things up.

I didn't give it much thought as there was no starting point. I assumed it was to do with when he comes to Melbourne.

Starting from when?

625.

31/1/6 is 1/31/6 → **{13}/(1)/6**, Gina, a literary agent / manuscript ↔
13/1/{6}, You have made the bed as far as you could. Now it is up to Me.

and,
the story so far:
[**4/227**, I'll see you tomorrow at 815 + **815** = **5042**] - ([**1409**, John Kordupel + [**1893** - <3981> = 2088] = 3497) = **1545**.
1545 . . . (154)/5 days = 118:46 + <451> = 122:97 = 2:97 / 5 days . . . **27/9/5**, corporate issues resolved.
and,
concerning 1893, rediscovery of the Forms of Life:
Daniel [5:1 + 5:2 + 5:3 + 5:4 + 5:5 = 265] + [5:01 + 5:02 + 5:03 + 5:04 + 5:05 = 2515] = 2780.
[265 + <562> + 2515 + <5152> = 8494] + [2780 = <0872>] = **9366**, God's Hand writing
MENE, MENE, TEKEL, UPHARSIN / PERES, God's Hand writing: 297 380 407 270. <792> +
<083> + <704> + <072> = 1651.
Daniel: 16:24 + 16:25 + 16:26 + 16:27 + 16:28 = **8130**, God's Hand writing.
[9366 = <6639>] + [8130 = <0318>] = 6957) - 8130 = **1173**, God's Hand writing.
1173 minutes = 18:93 . . . **1893**, God's Hand writing.

[**4/227**, I'll see you tomorrow at 815 + **815** = **5042**] = <2405> + **1545** = **3950**.
3950 – [15:(45) = 815 minutes . . . **815**] = 3135 . . . 31:(35) = 1825 minutes . . . **18/25**.
3950 / 10 = 395 . . . **(3)/9/5**, corporate issues resolve.
(3)/9/{4}/5, corporate issues resolved = **1173**, God's Hand writing + **2772**, Know Me.

and,
as,
15:(45) = 815 minutes . . . **815**,
then,
the various expressions of 1545 are expressions of 815, I'll see you tomorrow.

9/11/2017.

Two of Disks.
Key Words: change, transformation, progress, constant steps towards the good, growing harmony.

A huge serpent, symbol of renewal, is coiled in a figure 8, the symbol of infinity. This indicates ongoing change. The serpent is wrapped around two disks with the Chinese yin-yang on them, symbols of balance and harmony. The two turn in opposite directions, indicating internal and external change. The triangles – ancient symbols from alchemy – are represented in the colors of the four elements: red = fire; blue = water; grey = earth; yellow = air. The transformation touches all area of being.
Jupiter, the planet of good fortune and expansion, indicates that the transformation goes well and enriches your life. The new will bring more stability and safety (Capricorn) with it.
Necessary change always indicates that the old was no longer suitable. Change wakes us up. The snake's crown is a symbol of awakening to a new, fitting reality.
Violet, the color of warriors, shows how new power emerges from the transformation. The only constant is constant change. The only certainty is the uncertainty and transience of all structures and forms. Tarot – Mirror of the Soul. Gerd B. Ziegler.

and,

306/8, Cher passed away → 30:68 = 1868 minutes - <86> = **1782**, Resurrection ↔ **1782**, Leanne Long.

1782, Leanne Long ↔ 1782 . . . 1 day / 782 = 31:82 . . . 31:82 = 1942 minutes - <28> = **1914** ↔

11/(29) days /8, Cher's passing, M/D/Y . . . 11298 / 7 = **1614** ↔

16:14 = 974 minutes = 15:74 . . . 1day /5:74 = 29:74 . . . **2974**.

2974 = <4792> . . . [4 + 7 = 11] [2 * 9 = 18] . . . 1118 . . . **1/11/8**, Cher passed away.

29:74 = 1814 minutes . . . {18}/14 is **19/14** . . . **1914** ↔

1914 + **3/(7)/5**, Robert Loomis / manuscript = 2289.

22:89 = 1409 minutes . . . **1409**, John Kordupel.

2289 . . . 228 * 9 = 2052

2052 + <2502> = 4554 . . . 4days / 554 weeks = 3882 days . . . **3882**, the Unlettered Prophet.

3882 = **8/(60)**, Cher passes away **1409**, John Kordupel + **(1)/6/{13}**, Gina / manuscript.

3882 . . . [3 * 88 = 264]2 . . . 2642 . . . 26:42 = 1602 minutes + <24> = **1626** ↔

16/2/6, is contact with Robert imminent?

20:(52) = 1148 minutes . . . **1148**.

1148 minutes = 18:68 . . . 1868 minutes = 30:68 . . . **306/8**, Cher passed away.

1148 minutes - <25> = 1123 minutes = 17:103 . . . {17}/1/(03) is **1/(3)/{17}** ↔

13/1/7, You have made the bed as far as you could. Now it is up to Me.

1148 minutes + <25> = **1173** ↔ **1173**, God's Hand writing.

1173 minutes = 18:93 . . . **1893**, God's Hand writing.

1173 . . . [11 * 7 = 77]3 . . . 773 . . . 7[7³ = 343] . . . 73:43 = 3 days / 1:43 . . . 3143.

[3143 + <3413> = 6556] – [1173 = <3711>] = 2845.

2845 / 5 = **569**, Jesus → <965>, Iwan Kordupel / John Kordupel

[2845 = <5482> . . . 548 * 2 = 1096] - <6901> = 5805 = <5085> = 2:85 / 2 days.

28:(52) = 1628 minutes + <25> = 1653.

1653 + 965, Iwan Kordupel / John Kordupel = **2618**.

2618 - <8162> = 5544 = <**4455**>

4455, MENE, MENE, TEKEL, UPHARSIN / PERES.

1653 . . . [165 * 3 = **495** = <594>] * 3 = **1782**, the Second Coming.

2852 / 4 = **713**, the Season ends.

3143 = <3413> . . . [3 + 4 = 7]13 . . . **713**, the Season ends →

<3413> - **495** = 2918 . . . 29:18 = 1758 minutes + <81> = 1839 . . . **18/39** is **{17}/8/2**.

31:(43) = 1817 minutes . . . **(18)/1/7**, You have made the bed as far as you could.

and,

(18)/17, making of beds + 1893, God's Hand writing = 3710] – [15:(45) = 815] = **2895**.

28:95 = 1775 minutes - <59> = **1716** ↔

2289 = **5/(7)/3**, Robert Loomis / manuscript + **{17}/1/(6)**, being **18/25** ↔

18:25 is 6:25 PM . . . **625**, Robert begins to tidy things up.

and,

2289 = <9822> . . . 98:22 = 4 days / 2:22 . . . **4222**.

19:14 is 7:14 PM . . . **714** ↔

the Morgans:	321	433	462	292	the space in-between:	352	29	362
Leanne Long:	99	161	171	89	the space in-between:	78	10	86
	420	594	633	381		430	39	448

we join the numbers: 42059463338143039448 . . . 42059 46333 81430 39448 . . .

[42059 + 46333 + 81430 + 39448 = **209270**] + [<95024> + <33364> + <03418> + <84493> = **216299**] = **425569**.

425569 – [Leanne's birth day: day 5 / week 2 / 07 / {61}] = **95192**.

(425569 – [Leanne's birth day: day 5 / week 2 / 07 / 62] = **95193**) - <39159> = **56034**.

[56034 = <43065>] - [**95192** - <29159> = 66033 = <33066>] = **9999**, the Morgans / Leanne / Leanne's birthday.

9999 . . . 9 * 999 = 8991 = <**1998**> ↔

Mary:	57	47	51	53
Magdalene:	62	172	181	53

we sum the horizontal: 57475153 + 6217218153 = 6,274,693,306 . . .

6274 + <4726> + 693 + <396> + 306 + <603> = 12998.

12998 / 2 = 6499 . . . [6 * 4 = 24][9 + 9 = 18] . . . 2418 . . . [2^4 = 16]18 . . . 16:18 = 1 day / (782) . . . **1782**.

12998 . . . [-1 + 2 = 1]998 . . . **1998** ↔ 1998 / 3 = **666**.

9999 = **7227**, Leanne Long + **2772**, Chain of Rebirth.

9999 + **714** = **10/7/13**, Hay House / manuscript.

714 . . . 71^4 = 2541 1681 . . . 2541 + 1681 = **4222** ↔

Moses and his people spent 40 years in the Wilderness: √40 = 6324 5553 . . . 6324 + 5553 = 11877.

12322, Anakhita = <22321> - 11877 = 10444 / 2 = 5222 . . . 52:22 = 4:22 / 2 days . . . **4222**.

Leanne Long:	99	161	171	89	the space in-between:	78	10	86
High Priestess:	162	176	189	149	the space in-between:	146	13	148
the Morgans:	321	433	462	292	the space in-between:	352	29	362
	582	770	822	530		576	52	596

[**582** + 770 + 822 + 530 = **2704**] + <4072> = **6776**; [<285> + <077> + <228> + <035> = **625**] + <526> = **1151**.

6776 + 1151 = **7927**.

1151, Leanne Long / High Priestess / the Morgans . . . 11:51 = 711 minutes . . . **711**, a Cycle ends.

7927, Leanne Long / High Priestess / the Morgans = <7297> . . . 72:97 = 3 days / 0:97 . . . **3097**.

30:97 = 1897 minutes - <79> = **1818**, Magdalene.

30:(97) = 1703 minutes + <79> = **1782**.

30:(97) = 1703 minutes = <**3071**>

3071 + 1151 = **4222**, Leanne Long / High Priestess / the Morgans ↔

10026, Parousia i.e., (the Second Coming) . . . 10026 days = 1432 weeks / 2 days . . . 14322 . . . [14 * 3 = 42]22 . . . **4222**.

"The price of gold was not always exposed to market forces. Up until November 1973, the price of gold was set, officially fixed, by the government. The practice was to set a price for gold at which a nation's currency would be exchanged for gold. By linking a currency to gold, the financial soundness of a currency was established. Gold gave a currency credibility which was important when trading to the world. The last price of gold set by government was in February 1973 when it was increased from $38 an ounce to **$42.22** an ounce. In November 1973 gold was officially released from government influence and was left to fluctuate according to market forces."

The Elliott Wave Principle. Frost and Prechter.

4222, Market Forces, an expression of the Collective Will . . . 4:22 / 2 days = 52:22 . . . 5222.

5222 + <2225> = 5446 . . . 5[4 * 46 = 184] . . . 51:84 = 3144 minutes . . . **3144**, Earth.

52:22 = 3142 minutes . . . 31:(42) = 1818 minutes + <24> = 1842.

1842 minutes = 30:42 . . . 30:(42) = 1758 minutes + <24> = **1782** ↔

God: 7,15,4 . . . 5√**7154** = 13196374 . . . [1319 = <9131>] + [6374 = <4736>] = 13867

13867 . . . 13 + 867 = 880, God.

13:867 = 1647 minutes - <768> = 879 = <978> . . . 978 minutes = 16:18 = 1 day / (782) . . . **1782**.

and,

11:6. And the Lord said, Behold, the people is one, and they have all one language; and this they begin to do: and now nothing will be restrained from them, which they have imagined to do." Genesis.

√ 116 = 1077 0329 . . . 1077 + 0329 = 1406;

[1406 + <6041> = 7447] + [<7701> + <9230> = **16931**] = **24378** = <87342>

169:31 = 1:31 / 7 days . . . 13/1/7, You have made the bed as far as you could. Now it is up to Me.

√1106 = 3325 6578 . . . [3325 + 6578 = 9903] + [<5233> + <8756> = 13989] = 23892 + <29832> = **53724**.

87342 - 53724 = 33618 . . . 33:618 = 2598 minutes - <816> = **1782**, having the One Language.

10/11/2017.

the time footprint:

it is 17/11/10 ↔ **17/11/10**, I cannot talk with you about your world unless you know about Mine. Get out of My Car.

it is {16}/17/11/10 . . . [20{16} + 2017 = 4033] – 11/10 = 2923 . . . 29:23 = 1763 minutes . . . **1763**, the other Book-End.

it is {16}/(51) ↔ **16/(51)**, it certainly is your Playground

it is 11/10/17 . . . 11:1017 = 1677 . . . 16[7 + 7 = 14] . . . **(1)/6/14**, Gina / manuscript

it is 10/11/{16} . . . 10:1116 = 1716 minutes . . . **1716**.

{17}/1/(6), being **18/25** ↔ 18:25 is 6:25 PM . . . **625**, Robert begins to tidy things up.

1716 + **5/(7)/3**, Robert Loomis / manuscript = **2289** ↔ <9822> . . . 98:22 = 4 days / 2:22 . . . **4222**, Market Forces.

4222, Market Forces + [**625**, the tidying up begins . . . 625 minutes = 10:25] = 5247.

5247 . . . [5 + 2 = 7]47 . . . **747**, 2nd. Coming.

5247 = **24/5/3**, Robert Loomis / manuscript + **27/9/{4}**, corporate issues resolved.

it is 11/10/17 . . . 11:1017 = 1677 + [10/11/{16} . . . 10:1116 = 1716 minutes . . . 1716] = 3393 . . . [3 * 39 117]3 . . . **1173**.

Daniel [5:1 + 5:2 + 5:3 + 5:4 + 5:5 = 265] + [5:01 + 5:02 + 5:03 + 5:04 + 5:05 = 2515] = 2780.

[265 + <562> + 2515 + <5152> = 8494] + [2780 = <0872>] = **9366**, God's Hand writing

MENE, MENE, TEKEL, UPHARSIN / PERES, God's Hand writing: 297 380 407 270. <792> + <083> + <704> + <072> = **1651**.

Daniel: 16:24 + 16:25 + 16:26 + 16:27 + 16:28 = **8130**, God's Hand writing.

[9366 = <6639>] + [8130 = <0318>] = 6957) - 8130 = **1173**, God's Hand writing.

Four of Disks.

Key Words: Strong and set structures; desire for security; manifestation, integrity, character . . .

The four disks are depicted as the four towers of a fort. They bear the signs of the four alchemical elements, which point to stability and strength on all levels of being. The power represented here is expressed in the solid, almost rigid form of the building. Everything is in its place. No superfluous ornaments decorate the fortress walls.

The positive aspects of such adherence to a precise order is the clarity of a structure which has visible boundaries on the outside and solid standards on the inside. A person with these qualities has character and is someone who can be relied upon. This individual remains unshakably true to principle and acts with absolute integrity. He or she belong to the few people who live according to their ideals . . .

Tarot – Mirror of the Soul. Gerd B. Ziegler.

3. Fertility.

Traditional Name: The Empress.
Energy: The Abundance of Mother Nature.
Keyword Meaning: Fruitfulness.

Commentary:

Bountiful Earth Mother springs forth from even the most barren of ground, and with time, will turn it back to rich, fertile land. She is filled with hope, love and joy and uses theses energies to bring new opportunities through the union of opposite and sometimes contradictory forces. She brings abundance in all its forms, from simply having food on your table every day, to possessing the resources to bring your dreams into reality.

Meaning:

This is a time, pregnant with possibilities, when great things can be accomplished. Follow your natural instincts; look to Mother Nature for inspiration and you will know when to sow and when to harvest. This faith applies not only to external ventures but to inner spiritual work also. You can make progress on your path if you align yourself to the energies of the land you live upon.

Reversed Meaning:

Indecision comes when you dwell on a contradiction. One part of you wants to deeply trust what you intuitively know while another part of you fears the unknown. Feel the fear but don't believe in it. Worry and anxiety are no more than projections of your past into the future. It is only through letting the past go and being fully present that we can create a bountiful new life.

Imperial Dragon Oracle. Andy Baggott & Peter Pracownik.

Sugilite.

This is the time for you to trust, whilst keeping an open heart and mind. You are well on your way to achieving your Hearts Desire, and very soon something wonderful is going to happen. Know that you are on the right path, as your life is full of potential.

Be patient, keep focused on your desires and what you want to achieve. Do not be discouraged by any previous setbacks, as this is a time when the universe will assist you with manifesting your dreams.

Divine Inspiration Angelic Crystal Therapy Cards. Danielle Alaina Ellis.

* * * * *

12/11/2017.
the time footprint:
{16}/11/(18) . . . [1 + 6 = 7]1118 . . . 71118 . . . **{7}/1/11/8**, Cher passed away.

17/11/(18) . . . [1 + 7 = 8]11[-1 + 8 = 7] . . . 8117 . . . **8/11/7**, Cher's funeral.

Two of Swords.
　The card shows two swords opposing each other. The Drombeg Stone Circle in Ireland is in the background.

　The Symbolism:
　The two identical bronze swords that oppose each other are equally balanced. Neither has any advantage that would enable it to overcome the other, but neither will back down and a perpetual state of war is maintained.
　In the background is Drombeg Stone Circle in County Cork. It is aligned to the winter solstice sunset in one direction, and therefore the summer solstice in the other, representing the equal and opposing forces of winter and summer, held in eternal balance.

　Divinatory Meanings:
　You find yourself in a stalemate situation and you are neither able to move forward nor retreat. This is not a comfortable situation, but a state of armed truce. Any quarrels you have been involved in have been superficially glossed over, but resentments and tensions still lie under the surface. At present, any efforts you make to resolve the situation will be frustrated. It is best to sit back and wait for things to blow over.

　Reversed Meanings:
　The Two of Swords reversed indicate that you have been given bad advice from a source who is either misguided or malicious. You must carefully consider the consequences of acting on any advice you have been given.
　The Sacred Circle Tarot. Anna Franklin.

Shortly after Cher passed away, I agreed to write *One More Song* on the basis that I would try to complement whatever Know Me was trying to achieve.
Along the way, I came across more than one Know Me – the making of beds.

　This Reading brings *One More Song* to a conclusion.

Forthcoming publications.

Book Three. The Second Coming and I. Her Song Is My Witness. Part One. 336 pages.
3:16. Twin Spirits and Kundalini Energy. (93 pages)
3:17. Twin Cities. (126 pages)
3:18. The Destruction of the Cities. (98 pages)
3:19. Wandjina and the Dreaming. (7 pages)
3:20. Yggdrasil, the World Tree and the Fate-Carving Norns. (12 pages)

Extracts:
Chapter: *Twin Spirits and Kundalini Energy.*

"Listen to what I say next, because it is very important. Every human has a particular entity who inhabits the place of their Spirit Lake. These entities exist within this inner space, waiting at the entrance to Belovodia. I call this entity the Spirit Twin, but its name could also be Spirit Helper, Shadow Watcher, Spirit Guide, or Inner Guardian. They are really many different things.

To begin with, they are intimately connected with the ultimate purpose given to each person at birth. They are also pure observers, set apart and invulnerable to the influences of the outer world. They watch and silently consider everything we do. They are the holders of the primal essence of our natal being. If called upon in the proper way and circumstances, they can be important helpers to us in performing actions that move us in the direction of our correct purpose. And finally, they can be our guide to Belovodia.

There are seven different kinds of these Spirit Twins. Just seven, and no more. The seven types of Spirit Twins that exist for people are these: Healers, Magus, Teacher, Messenger, Protector, Warrior and Executor. Understand that the last is not a person who kills, but one who makes things happen.

One of the most important tasks is to learn the identity of our Spirit Twin and then to integrate ourselves fully with it. In this way we come into unity with the ultimate purpose of our being. When our lives have finally been illuminated by the pure light of our inner observer, everything we do becomes much easier. Only by discovering the nature of one's Spirit Twin, and then by coming into total association with it, can one really find and open the gate to Belovodia." Entering the Circle. Olga Kharitidi.

* * * * *

From the manuscript *The Medicine Wheel.* Chapter: The Tree of Knowledge and Understanding.
24/11/2013; it is 13/(37).
There is a passage in *Conversations with God* that is the key to the relationship between Heaven and Earth. It goes something along the lines of
"I will bring to you the exact right thought or feeling suited to the situation" - and the smoking gun to that relationship is order in price and time of gold futures and the Second Creation.

What that means is that what puppets come off the Cosmic Shelf and when they do so depends on the Puppet Master. Once off the Cosmic Shelf, what dance the puppets perform depends on what gives You the jollies.

This is Your creation, not mine!!!

The spiritual evolution of the puppets is not my problem, it is part and parcel of Your creation!!!
Why should I take responsibility for Your Creation, when, by putting obstructions upon obstructions across my path, You are not? The reply:

In terms of Twin Spirits, the missing ingredient is the Executioner.
Why don't you want to be in the God-Business?

Because I don't like Your current Creation. Not liking this Creation boils down to not liking God.

There is a Goddess.

I see no evidence of a Goddess.
If there is a Goddess, She has been party to this creation.

Not necessarily. It is a matter of different realms.

She will have Her Twin Spirits. I want out!!!

So be it.
. . . There could be a merging of realms.

So the Good-Cop / Bad-Cop Essence, is going to *evolve* to a God / Goddess Essence?

Something like that.

* * * * *

Jesus was born on **2BC / (73)**; it is **19/10/2BC**; it is **(12)/10/2 BC**.
Jesus was born on 2BC/10/19 – 19/10/2 BC = **1917**, the space between a birth day
    1917, Christ ↔ 1917, Crucifixion ↔
        John Kordupel, synthesis from format: 153 159 167 145.
        ([153 + 159 + 167 = 479] + <974> = 1453) + [145 + <541> = 686] = 2139 . . . 213 * 9 = **1917** ↔

        [153:145 – 159:167 = 6022] + [145:153 – 167:159 = 22006] + [159:153 – 167:145 = 7992] + [159:145 – 167:153 = 8008] +
        [159:145 – 153:167 = 5978] + [145:159 – 153:167 = 8008] + [145:159 – 167:153 = 21994] = 80008
           80008 – [gold futures: $10100 + $87300 = 97400, the Collective Will] = 17392.
             173:92 = 7 days / 592 . . . 75:92 = 3 days / 392 . . . 33:(92) = 1888 minutes + <29> = **1917** ↔
    1917, Evolution + <7191> = **9108** → 1287, Leanne Long + <7821> = **9108**.
        ([1917 - <7191> = 5274] - <4725> = 549 = <945>) + ([1917 = <7191>] - [9108 = <8019>] = 828) = **1773**, Leanne Long.
    1917, Evolution ↔ **1/9/17**, Leanne agrees to a Reading ↔
    1917, Evolution . . . 19:17 is 1 day / (483) . . . 1483 . . . **14/8/{3}**, I'll see you tomorrow.
        1483 . . . 1 day / 4:83 = 28:83 . . . **2883**, Maitreya ↔ <3882>, the Unlettered Prophet.
        1917 . . . 1[9* 17 = 153] . . . **1153**, Leanne Long ↔ 11:53 = 713 minutes . . . **713**, the Season ends.

Jesus was born on 2BC / (73) . . . 273 minutes = 4:33 . . . 433 minutes = 7:13 . . . **713**, the Season ends . . . 713 minutes = 11:53 . . . **1153**.

Jesus was born on: [2 BC / 292 + 292 / 2 BC = 5214] – [2883 + <3882> = 6765] = **1551**.
    15:(51) = 849 minutes = 14:09 . . . **1409**, John Kordupel ↔

    {15}/(51), the 1,000 year reign of Jesus has to begin sometime.

and,
Executioner.

E	5	(21)	22	(4)
X	24	(2)	3	(23)
E	5	(21)	22	(4)
C	3	(23)	24	(2)
U	21	(5)	6	(20)
T	20	(6)	7	(19)
I	9	(17)	18	(8)
O	15	(11)	12	(14)
N	14	(12)	13	(13)
E	5	(21)	22	(4)
R	18	(8)	9	(17)
	139	147	158	128

([139 + 147 + 158 + 128 = **572**] + <275> = **847**) + ([<931> + <741> + <851> + <821> = **3344**] + <4433> = **7777**) = **8624**.
    [572 + 3344 = **3916**] + [572 + <4433> = **5005**] + [572 + <4268> = **4840**] = **13761**.
        13761, Executioner + <16731> = 30492 . . . 30:492 = 2292 minutes . . . **2292**, Executioner ↔ **2292**, Mary Magdalene ↔
            2292 minutes - <294> = **1998**, Executioner ↔
                Leanne Long: ([<9991> + <8644> + <3892> + <4452> = 26979] - 11994 = 14985) / 5 = **2997**.
                    [2997 = <7992>, Leanne Long] / 4 = **1998**.

    [<275> + 3344 = **3619**] + [<275> + <4433> = **4708**] + [<275> + <4268> = **4543**] = **12870**.
        13761 + 12870 = **26631**, Executioner . . . [2663 + 1 = 2664, Executioner] / 4 = **666** ↔

        [I Am: 9113] + [God: 7,15,4] + [Allah: 1,12,12,1,8] + [Jahwe: 10,1,8,23,5] = 2155720.
        2155720 . . . <5512> - 2155 = 3357 + 7 + 20 = 3384 . . . [3384 – 720 = 2664] / 4 = **666** ↔

            Leanne Long: ([<9991> + <8644> + <3892> + <4452> = 26979] - 11994 = 14985) / 5 = **2997**.
                [2997 = <7992>, Leanne Long] / 12 = **666** ↔

    12870, Executioner . . . 1 + 2870 = **2871**, Executioner = <1782>, Leanne Long.

    13761 – 12870 = **891**, Executioner ↔ 152241252642, Leanne Long, fig. 3 . . . <251> + <142> + 252 + <246> = **891** ↔
        891, the Day of Resurrection * 2 = **1782** . . . **{17}/82**, instigated publication of an e-book with Hay House.

Executioner: 139 147 158 128

([139 + 147 + 158 + 128 = **572**] + <275> = **847**) + ([<931> + <741> + <851> + <821> = **3344**] + <4433> = **7777**) = **8624**.

[572 + 3344 = **3916**] + [572 + <4433> = **5005**] + [572 + <4268> = **4840**] = **13761**.

([<275> + 3344 = **3619**] + [<275> + <4433> = **4708**] + [<275> + <4268> = **4543**] = **12870**) - 13761 = **891**.

[5005 + 4708 = **9713**] - <3179> = 6534) + <4356> = **10890**, Executioner ↔

9669, John Kordupel, synthesis from format . . . [96 * 69 = **6624**] + <4266>, Jesus = **10890**.

10890 – [**1695**, John Kordupel + <5961> + **3882**, the Unlettered Prophet + <2883> = 14421 = <12441>] = **1551** ↔

{15}/(51), the 1,000 year reign of Jesus has to begin sometime.

Chapter: *Twin Cities.*

We could view Kali Yuga, Earth's dark night of the Soul, with the Essence wearing two hats, as a clash of Cosmic civilizations. In *Notes From the Cosmos*, we are informed that post 2250, those whose vibrations are not in harmony with that of Earth's, will reincarnate onto a different realm.

There you have it!

There is more than one realm, there is more than one Essence.

We are also informed, that should their vibrations subsequently harmonize with those of Earth's, they will be able to reincarnate back on Earth. We could be dealing with a bit of God-Speak.

Setting Satan free would signal a change in Earth's vibrations, and in this time window, the vibrations of those from the other realm could harmonize with Earth's – there is unfinished business from the pre-2250 era to address. The three horsemen from Hell will probably not be revolutionaries. It may be all about power.

Atlantis destructed because the Dark side won; the Dark side won because of the Collective Will.
Jesus was Crucified because the Dark side won; the Dark side won because of the Collective Will.
Satan being let loose is not about the progressive dissipation of negative energies at the individual level, but rather to see how far the Collective Will has evolved and its ability to discern.

The Atlantis legacy may finally be buried.

Under this scenario,
Reconciliation with God entails a Reconciliation between Gods – Satan being let loose for but a short season means one God vacates the realm.

Secondly, post the short season when Satan is let loose, Earth's vibrations will have moved, and who knows what the subsequent matrix will be.

Given this backdrop, it is feasible that, somewhere in the future, there may be another clash of the Titans.

In the meantime,
some of us may reincarnate on their realm, they may reincarnate onto ours – it could be a two way evolutionary street.

The energy grids associated with Leanne Long, High Priestess and the Morgans, provide us with a footprint of the transfer of souls between realms.

If you believe in reincarnation, then the energies of the parties that were party to WWI and WWII did not just fall through a crack in the floor - They had a prior existence!
They were party to a prior matrix and that matrix was sitting on the cosmic shelf, waiting to be dissipated.
How to make sense of all of that?
Was their genesis a result of energies arising from Kali Yuga, Earth's dark night of the Soul,
or,
did it go back further, to previous Big Bangs? - Lemuria, Atlantis, Avalon.

Alliances were formed on those realms – alliances means that some people embraced one Essence, others embraced a different Essence.

Alliances were formed between different Essences and you and I.

We are the meat in the sandwich in the battle between two Essences.

Which Essence do you want to support? - this is about Star Wars.
Don't look to me! Twice you left me hanging.

This is your Playground now.

I am out of the God-business. I have my Chain of Rebirth to break, you have yours.

Who went to bed with the lodestar of the Dark Side on Atlantis?
Who has got into bed with China?

Which Essence, which Lodestar do you want to get into bed with?

It is your Chain of Rebirth.

The U.N. is an expression of an alliance between the lodestar of two Essences.

The lodestar of the Essence of the Dark Side of Atlantis has veto power in the U.N.
Not one,
        but two.

Which lodestar does Planet Earth want to embrace on its World Body?

This is a turf warfare between the God Essence on the one hand, and the Devil Essence on the other.
Between the two of You, You decide on the Product Mix of the Collective Will.

This is Your Playground, not mine!

I am out of the God-Business. I am not going to participate.

You and the Collective Will sort it out amongst yourselves.

I am signing off.

10. Karmic Completion.

This card indicates the end of a karmic lesson or cycle where you have successfully cleared a contract or debt from your past. This could refer to a challenging situation you have recently conquered in your life or a troubling experience with an individual that involved a great deal of effort or pain. Even though there are ongoing lessons to confront throughout the course of your life, you will never have to experience this particular lesson again . . . Numerology Guidance Cards Guidebook. Michelle Buchanan.

Lightworker.

You are a lightworker. You are here to inspire and enlighten yourself and others to move from fear into love. This will be present always in all that you do. You don't have to figure out how you are going to do it, for you have always been doing it. As you allow light to illuminate your inner world, embrace and love all parts of you, you feel yourself shift from fear into love. Today, let us give great thanks to Mother Earth for the incredible privilege of being here. Through co-creation, we anchor our stream of consciousness into her for the joy of creating, expanding and lightworking. This brings love and growth for all, you and I, Mother Earth, this solar system, galaxies, the Universe and beyond. You are spinning light into the web of life. The Flower of Life. Wisdom of Astar. Denise Jarvie.

* * * * *

. . . He who is the Lord of Sirius,[1] that it was He who destroyed 'Ād first and then Thamūd, sparing no one, and before them the people of Noah, who were more wicked and more rebellious. The Mu'tafikah[2] He also ruined, so that they were smitten by the scourge that smote them.
Which then of your Lord's blessings would you deny? He that now warns you is just like those who warned the others before you. That which is coming is near at hand; none but God can disclose the hour. P. 373. The Koran. Translated by N.J. Dawood.
[1]. The Dog Star, worshiped by the pagan Arabs.
[2]. The Ruined Cities, where Lot's people lived.

Chapter: *The Destruction of the Cities.*

A Perfect Storm.
The Mayans prophesied that the beginning of End of Time occurred on 24/10/2007; that Earth entered the Age of Aquarius on 20/12/2012, and that the Age of Aquarius began on 19/2/2013.
Their prophesy was based on a 5,125 year Galactic cycle that began in 3113 BC; [3113 + 5125 = 8238] + <8328> = 16566.

16566 - (8238 . . .[8^2 = 64]38 . . . 6438 + <8346> = **14784**) = **1782**, the Second Coming.
165:66 is 7 days / (234) . . . 7234 + [(234)/7 days . . . **2/3/47**, my birth day] = 9581
14784 – 9581 = 5203 . . . 52:03 = 3123 minutes + <30) = 3153 . . . 31:(53) = 1807 minutes + <35> = **1842**.
1842 minutes = 30:42 . . . 30:(42) = 1758 minutes + <24> = **1782**, the Second Coming.

the beginning of End of Time is linked to the Second Coming.

Second Coming: anticipated return of Jesus Christ: in Christian belief, the anticipated and prophesised return of Jesus Christ *to judge humanity at the end of the world.* Microsoft ® Encarta ® 2008. © 1993-2007 Microsoft Corporation.

19:11. And I saw heaven opened, and behold a white horse; and he that sat on him was called Faithful and True, and in rightness he doth judge and make war.
19:12. His eyes were as a flame of fire, and on his head were many crowns; and he had a name written, that no man knew, but he himself.
19:13. And he was clothed with a vesture dipped in blood: and his name is called the Word of God.
19:14. And the armies which were in heaven followed him upon white horses, clothed in fine linen, white and clean.
19:15. And out of his mouth goeth a sharp sword, that with it he should smite the nations: and he shall rule them with a rod of iron: and he treadeth the winepress of the fierceness and wrath of Almighty God.

19:16. And he hath on his vesture and on his thigh a name written KING OF KINGS, AND LORD OF LORDS.

19:17. And I saw an angel standing in the sun; and he cried with a loud voice, saying to all the fowls that fly in the midst of heaven, Come and gather yourselves together unto the supper of the great God;

19:18. That ye may eat the flesh of kings, and the flesh of captains, and the flesh of mighty men, and the flesh of horses, and of them that sit on them, and the flesh of all men, both free and bond, both small and great.

19:19. And I saw the beast, and the king of the earth, and their armies, gathered together to make war against him that sat on the horse, and against his army.

19:20. And the beast was taken, and with him the false prophet that wrought miracles before him, with which he deceived them that had received the mark of the beast, and them that worshipped his image. These both were cast alive into a lake of fire burning with brimstone.

19:21. And the remnants were slain with the sword of him that sat upon the horse, with sword proceeded out of his mouth: and all the fowl were filled with their flesh.

20:1. And I saw an angel come down from heaven, having the key of the bottomless pit and a great chain in his hand.

20:2. And he laid hold on the dragon, that old serpent, which is the Devil, and Satan, and bound him a thousand years.

20:3. And cast him into the bottomless pit, and shut him up, and set a seal upon him, that he should deceive the nations no more, till the thousand years should be fulfilled: and after that he must be loosed a little season. Revelations. Holy Bible. King James Version.

> 20:1 – 20:3 . . . 201 + <102> + 203 + <302> = 808 . . . 8:08 is 9:(52) . . . 952 minutes = 15:52 . . . 1 day / 5:52 = 29:52
>> 29:52 = 1792 minutes . . . {17}/92 falls on **18/4/2**, Which melds with the Mayan Prediction.

> 20:1 – 20:3 . . . 201203 - <302102> = 100999.
>> 100999 . . . [100 - <001> = 99 . . . 9 * 9 = 81 . . . 8 + 1 = 9] * [999 . . . 9 * 99 = **891** = <198>] = **1782**.
>> 100999 . . . 100 + <001> + 999 + <999> = 2099.
>>> 2099 = <9902> . . . 99:02 = 3:02 / 4 days . . . 30:24 = 1824 minutes - <42> = **1782**, the Second Coming.
>>> 2099 . . . 209 * 9 = 1881 ↔

> (1881 + [(68)/7, beginning of end of time . . . 6:(87) = 273 minutes] = 2154) - <372> = **1782**, the Second Coming

> 1881 / 9 = 209 . . . 2:09 PM is 14:09 . . . **1409**, John Kordupel; 209 + <902> = **1111**, John Eevash Kordupel.

> 1881 . . . 1[8 * 81 = 648] . . . 1648 + <8461> = 10109.
> { ([1881 * 7 = 13167] – 10109 = 3058) - <8503> = 5445 } + **1782**, the Second Coming = **7227**, Book-End.
>> and,
>> **13/1/{6}/7**, You have made the bed as far as you could. Now it is up to Me.

> 1881 . . . 1day / 8:81 = 32:81 . . . 32:(81) = 1839 minutes . . . 1839 ↔
>> 18/39 is **17/8/2** ↔ 18/3/9 is **17/68** ↔ 18/(39) weeks is 18/(273) falls on **18/4/2**.

> 18:81 is (519)/1 days . . . 51:91 = 2 days / 391 . . . 23:(91) = 1289 minutes - <19> = 1270.
>> 1270 minutes = 22:(50) . . . **2250**, New Harmonic Vibrations.

> 1881 . . . 1day / 8:81 = 32:81 . . . 32:(81) = 1839 minutes - <18> = 1821.
>> 18:21. And a mighty angel took up a stone like a great millstone, and cast it into the sea, saying, Thus with violence shall that great city Babylon be thrown down, and shall be found no more. Revelations.
>> and,
>> 18:21. And if thou say in thine heart, How shall we know the word which the Lord hath not spoken?
>> 18:22. When a prophet speaketh in the name of the lord, if the thing follows not, nor come to pass, that is the thing which the Lord hath not spoken, but the prophet hath spoken it presumptuously: though shalt not be afraid of him. Deuteronomy. Holy Bible. King James Version.

The image is one of great social upheaval, which is in line with the Mayan prediction.

To these images we add a cyclic theory that applies to the stock market. R.N. Elliott observed that prices moved up {impulse waves}, retreated {corrective waves} and then advanced again. He also observed that price waves - both impulse and corrective - formed part of an ever increasing larger wave movements.

Elliott Wave theory holds that after the fifth wave of the fifth wave, of the fifth wave, prices fall back to somewhere above wave 1 of the first wave 5 – in practical terms, this means somewhere to where they were prior to the 1929 crash.

 • At time of writing, the Nikkei still has not broken through its 1987 high.
 • In Australia, the All Ordinaries have not broken the pre- GFC high. I am not sure how long it took to break through the 1929 high after that stock market crash, but we are either looking at a corrective wave 4 of the 5th, of the 5th, of the 5th, or Australia is already

experiencing the first leg of a major bear market.

Against this backdrop there is:

14:15. And another angel came out of the temple, crying with a loud voice to him that sat on the cloud, Thrust in thy sickle, and reap: for the time is come for thee to reap; for the harvest of the earth is ripe.

14:16. And he that sat on the cloud thrust in his sickle on the earth; and the earth was reaped. Revelations. Holy Bible. King James Version.

 [1415 + <5141> + 1416 + <6141> = 14113] - <31141> = 17028 . . . 17:028 = 1048 minutes + <820> = 1868 . . . **18/68**.
 14:15 is 2:15 PM = <512>] + [14:16 = 2:16 PM = <612>] = **1124**.
 [14:15 = 855 minutes + <51> = 906] + [14:16 = 856 minutes + <61> = 917] = **1823** + 1124 = 2947 . . . 29:(47) = 1693 minutes . . . **1693**.

 From *The Birth of a New Earth Essence* on 11/4/2011; it is 11/(264); it is {10}/101 . . . 10101, Dual Essence.
 I stepped out of the Car because I was not comfortable with the language between Heaven and Earth.

 So change it.

 it is (19)/4/11 . . . 19411 / 7 = 2773 . . . 27:73 = 1693 minutes . . . **1693** →

 13/07, You have made the bed as far as you could. Now it is up to Me = <7031> . . . 70:31 = (169)/3 days . . . **1693**.

 1693 = <3961>

and,

14:8. And there followed another angel, saying, Babylon is fallen, is fallen, that great city, because she made all nations drink of the wine of the wrath of her fornication.

18:2. And he cried mightily with a strong voice, saying, Babylon the great is fallen, is fallen, and is become the habitation of devils, and the hold of every foul spirit, and a cage of every unclean and hateful bird.

18:10. Standing afar off for the fear of her torment, Alas, alas, that great city Babylon, that mighty city! for in one hour is thy judgement come.

18:21. And a mighty angel took up a stone like a great millstone, and cast it into the sea, saying, Thus with violence shall that great city Babylon be thrown down, and shall be found no more at all. Revelations. Holy Bible. King James Version.

14:8 + 18:2 + 18:10 + 18:21 = **3961**.

An economy based on consumption and speculation / gambling may not be in harmony with the nature of the times.

* * * * *

Sodom and Gomorrah

Sodom and Gomorrah, according to the Old Testament (notably Genesis 18, 19), two ancient cities near the Dead Sea. The Bible almost invariably speaks of them together. With Admah, Zeboiim, and Zoar, they formed the five "cities of the plain", all but the last-named of which are said to have been destroyed by brimstone and fire, perhaps accompanied by an earthquake, because of the indecency and perverse sexual practices of their inhabitants. Some evidence indicates that they did exist, were destroyed and that their sites now lie under the Dead Sea. The biblical story of the destruction of the cities is considered by many critics to be similar to tales found among the Arabs (and other ancient peoples) regarding the sudden disappearance of places; indeed, Lot (or Lut), who in the biblical story survives the destruction with his family, figures prominently in the Koran. Some contend that the desolate character of the land around the Dead Sea, which is fatal to plant and animal life, would naturally suggest the thought of some catastrophe. Microsoft ® Encarta ® 2008. © 1993-2007 Microsoft Corporation.

Reflections on the Fall of the Cities.

Genesis:

18:16. And the men rose up from thence, and looked toward Sodom: and Abraham went with them to bring them on the way.

18:17. And the Lord said, Shall I hide from Abraham that thing which I do;

18:18. Seeing that Abraham shall surely become a great and mighty nation, and all the nations of the earth shall be blessed in him?

18:19. For I know him, that he will command his children and his household after him, and they shall keep the way of the Lord, to do justice and judgment; that the lord may bring upon Abraham that which he hath spoken of him.

18:20. And the Lord said, Because the cry of Sodom and Gomorrah is great, and because their sin is very grievous;

18:21. I will do down now, and see whether they have done altogether according to the cry of it, which is come unto me; and if not, I will know

18:22. And the men turned their faces from thence, and went toward Sodom: but Abraham stood yet before the Lord.

18:23. And Abraham drew near, and said, Wilt thou also destroy the righteous with the wicked?

18:24. Peradventure there be fifty righteous within the city; wilt thou also destroy and not spare the place for the fifty righteous that are therein?

18:25. That be far from thee to do after this manner, to slay the righteous with the wicked: and that the righteous should be as the wicked, that be far from thee: Shall not the Judge of all the earth do right?

18:26. And the Lord said, If I find in Sodom fifty righteous within the city, then I will spare all the place for their sakes.

18:16 + 18:17 + 18:18 + 18:19 + 18:20 + 18:21 + 18:22 + 18:23 + 18:24 + 18:25 + 18:26 = 20031

    20031 = <13002> . . . 13:(002) = 778 + <200> = 978 . . . 978 minutes = 16:18 = 1 day / (782) . . . **1782**, the Second Coming.

<6181> + <7181> + <8181> + <9181> + <0281> + <1281> + <2281> + <3281> + <4281> + <5281> + <6281> = 53691

    53691 . . . [536 * 9 = 4824] + 1 = 4825

        4825 / 5 = **965** ↔

            Redeemer: 73 135 143 65 . . . <37> + <531> + <341> + <56> = **965**.

            5225, Iwan Kordupel + [John Kordupel: 1409 + 1463 + <3641> = 6513]) = 11738.

                11738 – [1539, John Kordupel * 7 = 10773] = **965**.

        4825 + <5284> = **10109** ↔

            Kali Yuga, Earth's dark cycle: 416 + <614> + 1217 + <7121> = 9368 . . .

                [93:68 = 5648 minutes + <86> = 5734] + <4375> = **10109**.

            10109 * 4 = 40436 . . . [40 + 4 = 44 . . . 4 * 4 = 16][3 * 6 = 18] . . . 16:18 is 1 day / (782) . . . **1782**, the Second Coming.

            101:09 = 5:09 / 4 days . . . 5094

                50:94 = 2 days / 2:94 . . . 22:94 = 1414 minutes + <49> = **1463**, John Kordupel

50:94 = 2:94 / 2 days . . . 29:42 = 1782 minutes . . . **1782**, the Second Coming.
[2942 + 2294 = 5236 / 2 = 2618] - <8162> = 5544.
5544 . . . 554 weeks / 4 days = 3882 days . . . **3882**, the Unlettered Prophet.

Chapter: *Wandjina and the Dreaming.*

Understanding "the Dreaming". by Jim Poulter.
. . . When Wandjina saw that human beings understood their responsibilities to the environment and the Dreaming, two more things were done to ensure the Dreaming would be sustained.
First, the spirits of all children ever to be born were seeded into the Dreaming, where they must wait until it is their turn to be born. This happens when a father finds the spirit of the child in a dream and directs it to the body of their mother, who makes their flesh.
One implication of this belief is that every single human being is part of original creation and therefore has a direst, personal connection to God . . .

The Second thing that Wandjina did to sustain the Dreaming was to seed all knowledge and the answer to every question into the Dreaming. We therefore have unfettered access to this knowledge through our own Personal Dreaming. We can find the knowledge and shape the world according to our own Dreaming.
With the understanding and acceptance of this human responsibility, God withdrew from any further involvement in the real world.
Aboriginal people therefore believe there is no divine intervention and everything that happens is due to human agency, either witting or unwitting.
This is why all drawings of Wandjina are shown with eyes but no mouth.
God sees everything, but says nothing. Warrandyte Diary. No, 515. February 2018.

Wandjina

					the space in-between	
W	23	(3)	4	(22)	20	18
A	1	(25)	26	(0)	24	26
N	14	(12)	13	(13)	2	0
D	4	(22)	23	(3)	18	20
J	10	(16)	17	(9)	6	8
I	9	(17)	18	(8)	8	10
N	14	(12)	13	(13)	2	0
A	1	(25)	26	(0)	24	26
	76	132	140	68	104	108

. . . 104 + <401> + 108> + <801> =**1414**, Wandjina ↔ **1414**, Adam.

and,
the space in-between: 104 108 . . . 104 + <401> + 108> + <801> = **1414**, Wandjina ↔ **1414**, Adam ↔

220198, Wandjina . . . [220 + <891> = **1111**] + **1414**, Wandjina = **2525**, Wandjina ↔ **2525**, Eve.

Wandjina: ([76 + 132 + 140 + 68 = 416] + <614> = **1030**) + ([<67> + <231> + <041> + <86> = 425] = **<524>**) = **1554**, Wandjina ↔
1554 / 2 = **777**, Eve.

1414, Wandjina ↔ 1414, Adam; 1554, Wandjina ↔ 1554 / 2 = **777**, Eve.
and,
as,

195

416, Wandjina ↔ **416**, Anakhita, and, **949**, Wandjina ↔ **949**, Anakhita,

and,

1030, Wandjina ↔

Genesis 11:6. And the Lord said, Behold, the people is one, and they have all one language; and this they begin to do: and now nothing will be restrained from them, which they have imagined to do. [116 * 7 = 812] + <218> = **1030**.

and,

as Anakhita is associated with Sirius / Lemuria, the First Medicine Wheel,

then,

the Australian Aborigines are a genetic link to the first People.

Chapter: *Yggdrasil, the World Tree and the Fate-Carving Norns.*

44. Well of Wyrd.

Magic is real – it is a force in the universe. Your power is real – you are a force in your own life. Do not dwell too long on the past, for you will miss your present and, thus, your opportunity to direct your future. Everything is connected. Even apparently external influences may affect us.

> Wyrd flows beneath the great tree
>> Deeply, roots
>> Strengthened
> With the magic of destiny
> I am in a flux and in flow.
>> All circles back
> Choices weaves with fate.

The Well of Wyrd (also known as Well of Urd or Well of Urðarbrunnr) is a holy well at the base of the world tree, Yggdrasil. Anything that touches Wyrd's waters will turn pure white, like the swans that swim upon it. Mentions of the Well of Wyrd are found throughout the *Eddas* and in particular in the poem "Havamal", which says that its waters are spread over the roots of the tree by the Norns, *who set down laws, they choose lives, for the sons of men, the fates of men.*

Connected as they are to the fate-carving Norns, the waters of Wyrd represent the magic of destiny. They flow through Yggdrasil's leaves then drip back into the well, representing a cycle in which the past feeds the present and the future. Since Yggdrasil drips back dew from what has occurred, the dew can circle back and affect the past, which can affect the present, which can affect the future. All is in flux. All circles back.

While all beings receive the blessings and influence of Wyrd, they also have their own life force, which can be used to change the destiny they have been handed. Through this sophisticated, complex approach, the ancient Norse explained how destiny works and even spoke to the nature of time, itself. They have shown us that we always have a choice – even if the Norns have carved us what seems at first to be a difficult destiny. Viking Oracle Guidebook. Stacey Demarco.

1332, Yggdrasil / 2 = **666**, Yggdrasil, the World Tree ↔ **666**, the Number of Man.

2160, Yggdrasil + <0612> = **2772**, Yggdrasil, the World Tree ↔ **2772**, the Chain of Rebirth.

3564, Yggdrasil / 2 = **1782**, Yggdrasil, the World Tree ↔ **1782**, the One Language.

1476, Yggdrasil + 1476, Yggdrasil = 2952 . . . 29:52 = 1792 minutes . . . **1792**, Yggdrasil, the World Tree.

20:1. And I saw an angel come down from heaven, having the key of the bottomless pit and a great chain in his hand.

20:2. And he laid hold on the dragon, that old serpent, which is the Devil, and Satan, and bound him a thousand years.

20:3. And cast him into the bottomless pit, and shut him up, and set a seal upon him, that he should deceive the nations no more, till the thousand years should be fulfilled: and after that he must be loosed a little season. Revelations. Holy Bible. King James Version.

20:1 – 20:3 . . . 201 + <102> + 203 + <302> = 808 . . . 8:08 is 9:(52) . . . 952 minutes = 15:52 . . . 1 day / 5:52 = 29:52

29:52 = 1792 minutes . . . **1792**, Satan bound for a thousand years equates with the beginning of the 1,000 year reign of Jesus

1792 . . . {17} / 92 falls on 18/4/2 . . . 1842 minutes = 30:42 . . . 30:(42) = 1758 minutes - <24> = **1782** ↔
1782, the Second Coming ↔ **{17}/82**, instigated publication of an e-book with Hay House.

and,
the fate-carving Norns:
Norns: 80 50 55 75

75:80 – 50:55 = **2525**, the fate-carving Norns = <5252> ↔
5252, Jesus . . . 52:(52) = 3068 minutes . . . 30:68 = 1868 minutes - <86> = **1782**, the Second Coming.

<602>, Norns + <304>, Norns + <645>, Norns = **1551**, Norns ↔
Fig. 5.
Leanne, alphabet L → R: 12, 5, 1, 14, 14, 5 . . . 125,114,145
Long, alphabet R → L, residual: (11), (14), (13), (6) . . . 1,114,136: 125,114,145 + 1,114,136 = 126,228,281 . . .
([126 + 228 + 281 = **635**] + <536> = **1171**) + ([<621> + <822> + <182> = **1625**] + <5261> = **6886**) = **8057**.
(8057 + [1171 = <1711>] = **9768**) + 8057 = 17825 . . . 17:(825) = 195 minutes . . . 195 = <591>
591 minutes = 9:51 . . . 951 minutes = 15:51 . . . **1551**.

1551, Norns . . . 15:(51) = 849 minutes = 14:09 . . . **1409**, John Kordupel.
1551, Norns . . . **{15}/(51)**, the 1,000 year reign of Jesus has to begin sometime ↔
1551, Norns . . . **{15}/(51)**, it certainly is your playground.

Forthcoming publications.
Book Four. The Second Coming and I. Her Song Is My Witness. Part Two. 375 pages.
4:21. The 1,000 Year Reign of Jesus Begins. (20 pages)
4:22. In Remembrance of Me. The Last Supper. (16 pages)
4:23. The Last Supper, the Crucifixion and the Time Lineage. (6 pages)
4:24. The Times, They Are A'Changing. (50 pages)
4:25. Sending a Prophet Amongst Thee. (5 pages)
4:26. Her Song Is My Witness. (6 pages)
4:27. The Making of Beds and Market Forces.
4:28. My Generation and the Nature of the Times. (26 pages)
4:29. The Space Between Noe and Lot. (17 pages)
4:30. Noe, Lot and a City Like Sodom. (4 pages)
4:31. On the Road to Damascus. (21 pages)
4:32. Judas Iscariot. Changing the Course of History. (29 pages)
4:33. The Last Whisper of a Lost Civilization. (2 pages)
4:34. Energy Healing. (19 pages)
4:35. The Final Battle. (10 pages)
4:36. The Promised Land. (6 pages)
4:37. A Listing of Numerical Names. (138 pages)

Extracts:
Chapter: *The 1,000 Year Reign of Jesus Begins.*

From *A Second Creation. Numerical Names and a Re-orientation. The Maze Run Begins.*

10/11/2016; it is {15}/(51).

Donald Trump, President elect? this is not my playground.

It is very much your Playground!

I look around and You reward those who embrace a moral compass that bears no remembrance to what I have been saying. I see no reason why people should pay any attention to what I have been saying.

Life is not a rip-off!

Tell that to Hillary and her supporters.

With Donald Trump as President, American, the world, will get the Experience it deserves.

I was left hanging. Until your Experience tells you otherwise, don't pay any attention to what I have said.

That about sums it up.
The 1,000 year reign of Jesus has to begin sometime.

it is (51)/{15} . . . 5115 . . . 5 days / (1:15) = 118:45 + <511> = 123:56 = 5 days / 356 . . . 53:56 = 5:56 / 2 days . . . 5562 + <2655> = **8217** ↔

John Eevash Kordupel: 209 153 266 191 . . .
([209 + 153 + 266 + 191 = 819] + [<902> + <351> + <662> + <191> = 2106] = 2925) + <5292> = **8217** ↔
[8217 = <7128>] / 4 = **1782**, John Eevash Kordupel ↔ **1782**, the Second Coming.

51:15 = 3075 minutes . . . 30:(75) = 1725 minutes + <57> = **1782**, the Second Coming.

it is (51)/16, the 1,000 year reign of Jesus has to begin sometime ↔ **8217**, John Eeevash Kordupel; it begins with my birth day ↔
[(25)/2/47/{46}, my birth day . . . 2524746 / 7 = 360678] - <876063> = 515385.
515385 . . . 51[385 - <583> = 198] . . . 51198.
51198 . . . [-1 + 9 + 8 = 16] . . . 5116 . . . **(51)/16**, the 1,000 year reign has to begin sometime, a Playground ↔

51198 . . . [5 − 1 = 4] * [198 = <**891**>, the Day of Resurrection] = **3564** ↔
3564 = **1782**, Leanne Long + **1782**, the Second Coming.

51198, the 1,000 year reign has to begin sometime . . . 51[198 = <**891**>] . . . 51891 / 7 = 7413.
7413 - <3147> = **4266**, Jesus ↔ 42 * 66 = **2772**, the Chain of Rebirth ↔
John Kordupel, synthesis from format: 153 159 167 145
<351> + <951> + <761> = 2063;
[1:45 is 2:(15) . . . 215] + [<5:41> being 6:(19) . . . 619] = 834 + <438> = 1272
([1272 = <2721>] - [2063 = <3602>] = 881 - <188> = 693) * 4 = **2772**.

7413, the 1,000 year reign of Jesus has to begin sometime / 3 = 2471 ↔
24:71 = 1 day / 0:71 . . . 1071 + <1701> = **2772**, the 1,000 year reign has to begin sometime ↔

Jesus Christ: 10,5,19,21,19. 3,8,18,9,19,20; from R to L:

$$19,21,19,5,10 + 20,19,9,18,8,3 = 394,111,393$$
$$394,111,393 \ldots <493> + 111 + 393 = 997 \ldots 99 * 7 = \mathbf{693} \leftrightarrow$$

John Kordupel, synthesis from format: 153 159 167 145
$$<351> + <951> + <761> = 2063;$$
$$[1{:}45 \text{ is } 2{:}(15) \ldots 215] + [<5{:}41> \text{ being } 6{:}(19) \ldots 619] = 834 + <438> = 1272$$
$$[1272 = <2721>] - [2063 = <3602>] = 881 - <188> = \mathbf{693} \leftrightarrow$$
$$693 * 4 = \mathbf{2772}, \text{ Jesus Christ} \rightarrow \mathbf{2772}, \text{ John Kordupel} \leftrightarrow \mathbf{2772}, \text{ the reign begins}$$

* * * * *

Vladimir Putin thinks the Nature of the Times is all about Star Wars and a Death Star.

Given Vladimir Putin's and Xi Jinping lodestar, why should Russia and China have veto power?

If the 1,000 year reign of Jesus is all about the lodestar of the superior wo/man,
what exactly is the nature of your future?
Ragnarok?

Chapter: *In Remembrance of Me. The Last Supper.*

22:19. And he took bread, and gave thanks, and brake it, and gave unto them, saying, This is my body which is given for you: this do in remembrance of me. St. Luke. Holy Bible. King James Version.

22:19, in Remembrance . . . 2 days / (219) = 4581 - <912> = **3669**, in Remembrance
    3669, in Remembrance + <9663> = **13332** ↔

Moses:	71	59	64	66
Moussa:	<u>88</u>	<u>68</u>	<u>72</u>	<u>82</u>
	159	127	136	148

$$([159 + 127 + 136 + 148 = 570] = <075>) + ([<951> + <721> + <631> + <841> = 3144] = <4413>) = 4488.$$
$$4488 + <8844> = \mathbf{13332} \leftrightarrow$$

John Kordupel, Synthesis From Format: 153 159 167 145.
$$([153 + 159 + 167 = 479] + <974> = 1453) + [145 + <541> = 686] = 2139.$$
$$([153 + 159 + 167 + 145 = 624] + <426> = 1050) + ([<351> + <951> + <761> + <541> = 2604] + <4062> = 6666)$$
$$= 7716.$$
$$[1{:}45 \text{ is } 2{:}(15) \ldots 215 = <512>] + [<5{:}41> \text{ being } 6{:}(19) \ldots 619 = <916>] = 1428 + <8241> = 9669 \ldots 9 * 669$$
$$= 6021.$$
$$[6021 - 7716 = 1695, \text{ John Kordupel}] + [6021 - 2139 = \mathbf{3882}, \text{ the Unlettered Prophet}] = 5577$$
$$5577 + <7755> = \mathbf{13332}.$$

3669, in Remembrance . . . 3 * 66 * 9 = **1782**, in Remembrance ↔ **1782**, Resurrection ↔ **1782**, the Second Coming ↔

3669, in Remembrance . . . -3 + 669 = 666 ↔ 666 minutes = 11:06 . . . Genesis **11:06**, the One Language

22:19, in Remembrance . . . 2:21 / 9 days = 218:21 . . . **21821**.
    21821, in Remembrance - <12812> = **9009**, in Remembrance ↔

199

the Six Horsemen, up-dating Scriptures: the Mahdi, the Second Coming, Maitreya, the Unlettered Prophet, Kalki, the Messiah:

720 996 1062 654.

720 + 996 + 1062 + 654 = 3432) + <2343> = 5775; [<027> + <699> + <2601> + <456> = 4783] + <3874> = 8657. [5775 + 8657 = 14432] - <23441> = **9009** ↔

9009 = **1782**, the Second Coming + **7227**, Book-End.

22:19, in Remembrance . . . 2 days / (219) = 4581 - <912> = **3669**, in Remembrance.

22:19, in Remembrance . . . 2:21 / 9 days = 218:21 . . . **21821**, in Remembrance – [3669, in Remembrance + <9663> = **13332**] = 8489.

84:89 = 5129 minutes + <98> = **5227** . . . 52:27 = 3147 minutes . . . 31:(47) = 1813 minutes - <74> = **1739** ↔

14/8/4, I'll see you tomorrow at 815 . . . [14:84 = 924 minutes . . . 924] + 815 = **1739** ↔

1739 . . . 1 day / 7:39 = 31:39 . . . 31:(39) = 1821 minutes + <93> = **1914** ↔

when will the manuscript be published ? 47/06 + (12)/02/{5} = 16731.

167:31 = 7 days / (0:29) . . . 70:29 = 3 days / (171) . . . 31:71 = 1931 minutes - <17> = **1914**.

and,

22:19, in Remembrance . . . 2219 weeks = 15533 days . . . 15533 - <33551> = **18018**

18018 - [when will the manuscript be published ? 47/06 + (12)/02/{5} = **16731**] = **1287** ↔

1287 + <7821> = **9108** ↔

and,

34:25. And I will make with them a covenant of peace, and will cause the evil beasts to cease out of the land: and they shall dwell safely in the wilderness, and sleep in the woods. Ezekiel. Holy Bible. King James Version.

3425 . . . ([3^4 = 81]25 . . . { 8125) + <5218> + (81[2^5 = 32] . . . 8132) + <2318> = 23793 } + <39732> = 63525

[63525 / 25 = 2541 = 1452] * 7 = 10164 = <46101>

{ ([63525 = <52536> – <46101> = 6435) / 5 = **1287** } + <7821> = **9108**.

<46101> . . . [4 + 6 = 10]101 . . . **{10}/101**, invitation to change the language

and,

11:6. And the Lord said, Behold, the people is one, and they have all one language; and this they begin to do: and now nothing will be restrained from them, which they have imagined to do. Genesis. Holy Bible. King James Version.

√ 116 = 1077 0329 . . . [1077 + 0329 = 1406] + <6041> = 7447.

74:47 = 3 days / 2:47 . . . 3/2/47, my birth day.

32:(47) = 1873 minutes - <74> = 1799 . . . [17 * 9 = 153]9 . . . **1539**, John Kordupel.

7447 + [<7701> + <9230> = 16931] = 24378 = <87342>

√1106 = 3325 6578 . . . [3325 + 6578 = 9903] + [<5233> + <8756> = 13989] = 23892 + <29832> = 53724.

87342> - 53724 = 33618 . . . 33:618 = 2598 minutes - <816> = **1782**

1782, evolution of the One Language + 1593, You have made the bed as far as you could. Now it is up to Me = 3375

[3375, One Language / up to Me now + <5733> = **9108**.

9108 = [**3882**, the Unlettered Prophet . . . 3882 days = 4 days / 554 weeks . . . 4554] + 4554.

4554 = **2772**, the Chain of Rebirth + **1782**, the Second Coming.

1287 . . . 12 * 87 = 1044 . . . **10/(44)**, I cannot talk with you about your world unless you know about Mine. Get out of My Car.

Chapter: *The Last Supper, the Crucifixion and the Time Lineage.*

From *A Second Creation. Numerical Names and a Re-Orientation. The Maze Run Begins.*
7/2/2013.
I have been going through the manuscript to see how I arrived at these dates but having had no luck I spoke to Julie from the Jewish Community Council of Victoria who happened to have a calendar for 2009. In 2009 Passover commenced on Wednesday 8/4.
The focus was on 2009 because every 19 years, we come back to the same point in time and 8/4/33 + [19 * 104 = 1976 years] = 8/4/2009.

> **8/4/33 AD**, Passover commenced making **9/4/33**, the Last Supper, the Crucifixion on **10/4/33**, and **12/4/33**, the Resurrection.

10/4/33 AD, a Crucifixion ↔ **10/4/2009**, Easter Friday, a Crucifixion; it is day 100/9/(265) ↔
> 9/(265), a Crucifixion ↔ **14/8/4**, D/M/Y, I'll see you tomorrow at 8:15 . . . 4814 + 815 = **5629** = <9265> . . . **9/(265)**, Easter Friday.
> 9/(265), a Crucifixion + 5629, I'll see you tomorrow = 14894
> [14:894 = 1734 minutes + <498> = 2232] + <2322> = **4554** . . . 4 days / 554 weeks = 3882 days . . . **3882**, the Unlettered Prophet.

* * * * *

23:46. And when Jesus had cried with a loud voice, he said, Father, into thy hands I command my spirit: and having said thus, he gave up the ghost. St. Luke.
23:46, a death ↔ **2/3/{46}**, my birth day . . . a birth.
23:46, a death ↔ 2/3/{46}, a birth . . . 23:(46) = 1334 minutes - <64> = **1270** ↔ 1270 minutes = 22:50 . . . **2250** ↔
> Crucifixion: 3,18,21,3,9,6,9,24,9,15,14 . . . [318 + 21 + 396 + 924 + 91 + 514 = **2264**; 318 + 2139 + 692 + 491 + 514 = **4154**.
>> 4154 = <2363>, Christ + 1791 . . . 17:91 = 1111 minutes . . . **1111**, John Kordupel, synthesis from format.
>>> 1111 + [11:11 = 671 minutes . . . 671] = **1782**, Resurrection ↔ **1782**, the Second Coming.
>>>> You have made the bed as far as you could. Now it is up to Me: [7/13/1 + 7/1/13 = 14244] – 13/1/7 = 12927
>>>>> 12927 . . . [12 * 92 = 1104] + 7 = **1111**.
>> [4154 = <4514>] - 2264 = **2250** ↔

The Second Epistle of Paul the Apostle to the Thessalonians 2:1 to 2:4, re the Second Coming:
> 2:01 + 2:02 + 2:03 + 2:04 = 810 . . . 8:10 = 490 minutes . . . 490.
>> 4:90 = 330 minutes = 5:30 . . . 530 minutes = 8:50 . . . 850 minutes = 13:70 . . . 1370 minutes = 22:50 . . . **2250** ↔

[John: 10, 15, 8,14] + [Kordupel: 11,15,18, 4, 21, 16, 5, 12] = 11,151,843,132,326:
> We separate 11,151,843,132,326 into two groups of seven, to which we add our birthday:
> [1115184 . . .1115 + 184 = 1299] + [34/194{6} + 3132326 = 3474272 . . . 3474 + 272 = 3746] = 5045 . . . 50 * 45 = **2250** ↔

13/1/7, You have made the bed as far as you could. Now it is up to Me . . . 200{6} + 2007 + 13/1 = 4144.
1317 minutes = 21:57 . . . 2157 minutes = 35:57 . . . 3557 minutes = 59:17 . . . 5917 minutes = 97:97 . . . 9797.
[4144 + <4414> = 8558] + 9797 + <7979> = 26334.
26:334 = 1894 minutes . . . 1894 . . . 1:89/4 days = 9789 + <981> = 10770 . . . 10:770 = 1370 minutes . . . 1370.
> 1370 minutes = 22:50 . . . **2250**, New Harmonic Vibrations.

and.

22:19. And he took bread, and gave thanks, and brake it, and gave unto them, saying, This is my body which is given for you: this do in remembrance of me. St. Luke.

23:46. And when Jesus had cried with a loud voice, he said, Father, into thy hands I command my spirit: and having said thus, he gave up the ghost. St. Luke.

[22:19, in Remembrance = <9122>] + [23:46, my spirit into thy hands = <6432>] = **15554** ↔

      John Kordupel, 1409 + 1463 + <9041> + <3641> = **15554** ↔

          15554 . . .[-1 + 5 = 4]554 . . .4554 . . .4 days / 554 weeks is 3882 days . . .**3882**, the Unlettered Prophet.

          15554 – **102/33 AD**, the Resurrection = 5321 . . . 53:(21) = 3159 minutes + <12> = 3171 ↔

            31:71 = 1931 minutes - <17> = **1914** ↔

                1782, Resurrection ↔ **1782**, the Second Coming . . . 1 day / 782 = 31:82 = 1942 minutes - <28> = **1914**.

          15554 . . . 1555 – 4 = **1551** ↔

            {15}/(51), the 1,000 year reign of Jesus has to begin sometime ↔

              [625, Robert begins to tidy things up . . . 625 minutes = 10:25] + <526> = **1551** ↔

and,

16/2/6, when will the manuscript be published ? 47/06 + (12)/02/{5} = 16731.

167:31 = 7 days / (0:29) . . . 70:29 = 3 days / (171) . . . 31:71 = 1931 minutes - <17> = **1914** ↔

      {15}/(51), the 1,000 year reign of Jesus has to begin sometime ↔ {15}/(51), it is certainly your Playground.

        {15}/(51) is: [20{15} + 2016 = 4031 = <1304>] + (20)/11 = 3315 . . . 33:(15) = 1965 minutes - <51> = **1914**.

Chapter: *The Times, They Are A'Changing.*

Walk a Mile In Their Shoes.

Over the course of this manuscript, and in other manuscripts, I have presented images of a Second Creation. I *I Am the Second Coming. This Is My Message* I reveal perfect order in the movement in price and time of gold futures. While the story centers around gold, it is i in fact a story about the buying and selling behaviour of people, so it reveals a Second Creation from a different angle.

        A Second Creation cannot occur unless Spirit presses buttons.

Spirit presses buttons before we manifest, and Spirit presses buttons after we manifest, the result being the Product Mix that comes out of the reincarnational hose. It therefore follows that global warming could have been prevented if Spirit had altered the Product Mix earlier. In not doing that, Spirit has created a matrix, a maze run for us to navigate.

Nuclear V coal generated power? The bigger the stockpile of nuclear waste, the greater the potential for a disaster.

       Spirit is not going to let you – reincarnation means you, not your children - walk away from that issue.

I vote for coal.

Coal power V solar panels / wind / battery.

The reality of the situation is that for many people, solar panels / batteries are too expensive.

      For all you people who are opposing the Adani coal project in Australia, I say, Walk a Mile in their shoes.

For all of you who are living in the lap of luxury, turn off your electricity for six months – not a lifetime, just six months. That means no recharging your mobile phone; it means no recharging your lap-top; it means your children not being able to text anybody. Do you think that they could handle not doing that for just one day? ; it means no Facebook, no Google; it means your children having to do their homework by candle-light. There goes your kid's education.

Armchair moralists living in the lap of luxury.

Things have moved on from the bad old days. Governments get it; big business gets it. People are working to address the issue from a number of angles. You are not the only ones beating the drum. Stop being arrogant know-it-alls.

Walk a mile in their shoes.

Do something practical and sponsor a village.
It could be 20 or 30 years or more, who knows, before battery technology and supply could cater for any demand arising from a viable cost alternative to coal. In addition, the demand for the raw materials that make up the components for batteries will only increase as electric cars take off which could create a significant supply issue all round.
That is the issue – do solar panels / wind/batteries provide a quick fix as a replacement for coal?
My view is that things cannot be turned around overnight; that the main damage has already been done, that the incremental cost to stop the food bowl from shifting is now too high, but that Planet Earth will survive. In the meantime, do you ignore the plight of people living below the poverty line?
Armchair moralists living in the lap of luxury may think that they are pure because they ride their bike to work.

But you are not pure!

You are one dimensional. By relegating people to a lifetime of poverty, you are ignoring the plight of your fellow man.

Political correctness V spiritual correctness.

That is the matrix. To find the correct balance. In my view, the Greens have not found the right balance, that they are still fighting yesterday's war.

The Greens are a party that appeals to the holier than thou mob.

How many safe house does a refugee have to go past before they stop being a refugee?
The Greens are saying we should take in all the refugees that knock on our door, which is addressing the issue after the horse has bolted. To address the refugee issue you need to address the political and the economic environment in which the economic and political refugees live in. Their economic environment is influenced by the availability of electricity.

The Greens are saying one thing out of one corner of their mouth, and a contradictory thing out of the other corner.

While we may have free will – I say 'may', because a Second Creation implies otherwise – it is not free in the sense that no matter what we choose, there is a price to be paid.

As the new vibratory force that is incarnating on Earth wants to live in greater harmony with Earth, whether global warming is man-made or not is not the issue. They are orientated to finding a better balance on how we live, and polluting Planet Earth is the issue *in its own right*. It is this new vibratory force that political parties need to tune into. What is the nature of the collective will? Are you talking to yesterday's collective will or tomorrow's? Is it a superior collective will that you, as a political party, are trying to appeal to, or an inferior one? As the new vibratory force gains traction, the Conservative heartland will be made up of yesterday's wo/men.

That is the matrix that Spirit has created.

Chapter: *The Making of Beds and Market Forces.*
the story so far:
{17}/82, Leanne Long introduced me to Balboa Press ↔
{17}/82, purchased a publication package from Balboa Press for Book One, *The Second Coming and I. A Reading For Leanne Long* ↔

1782, the Second Coming ↔ 1782, Leanne Long ↔ 1782, having the One Language ↔
1782 . . . 1 day / 782 = 31:82 = 1942 minutes - <28> = **1914** ↔

when will the manuscript be published ? 47/06 + (12)/02/{5} = **16731**.
167:31 = 7 days / (0:29) . . . 70:29 = 3 days / (171) . . . 31:71 = 1931 minutes - <17> = **1914** ↔
19:14 is 7:14 PM . . . **714** ↔

√714 = 2672 0778 . . . [2672 + <2762> = 5434] + [0778 + <8770> = 9548] = **14982**.
[14982 + {12}/(85), Hay House / manuscript + **1059**, a page in the life of = **17326** ↔
[Hay House / no, need a literary agent: 10/(6)/13 + (67)/13 = **17326**.

714 . . . 71⁴ = 2541 1681 . . . 2541 + 1681 = **4222**, Market Forces.
4222, Market Forces + **17326**, a page in the life of Hay Publishing = **21548**

21548, page in the life of Hay Publishing / Market Forces . . . 215:48 = 9 days /(0:52) . . . [7069 - <9607> = 2538] - <8352> = **5814**.
16731, when will the manuscript be published? . . . 167:31 = 7 days /(0:69) . . . [9052 - <2509> = 6543] - <3456> = **3087**.
[5814 = <4185>] + [3087 = <7803>] = 11988 ↔
11988 / 4 = **2997** ↔
the Five Horsemen updating the Scriptures: the Mahdi / the Second Coming / Maitreya / the Messiah / Kalki: 465 731 777 419
[465 + 731 + 777 + 419 = 2392] + <2932> = 5324;
[<564> + <137> + 777 + <914> = 2392] + <2932> = 5324.
[2392 + 2392 = 4784 = <4874>] + [2392 + 5324 = 7716 = <6177>] = 11051.
11051 + ([2932 + 2932 = 5864 = <4685>] + [2932 + 5324 = 8256 = <6528>] = 11213) = **22264**.
and,
22264, updating the Scriptures + **713** = 22977 . . . [2 + 297 = 299]7 . . . **2997**) = <7992> ↔
2139, John Kordupel / 3 = **713**, the Season ends
Redeemer: 73 135 143 65 . . . 73:135 − 65:143 = **7992**.
John Kordupel (format ↔ synthesis): 153 159 167 145 . . . 159:153 − 167:145 = **7992**.
7992 . . . [7 + 9 = 16][9 * 2 = 18] . . . 16:18 = 1 day / (782) . . . **1782**, the Second Coming ↔

Lao Tzu's lifetime c. 570-c. 490 BC or c. 4th century BC:
([570 + <075> + 490 + <094> = 1229] - <9221> = **7992**.

11988 . . . [1 + 198 = 199]8 . . . 1998 = 19/14 weeks . . . **1914**.
and.
21548, page in the life of Hay Publishing / Market Forces . . . 215:48 = 9 days /(0:52) . . . 9052 + <2509> = **11561**.
16731, when will the manuscript be published? . . . 167:31 = 7 days /(0:69) . . . 7069 + <9607> = **16676**.
16676, when will the manuscript be published = 11561, a page in the life of Hay Publishing / Market forces = **5115** ↔

(51)/{15}, the 1,000 year reign of Jesus has to begin sometime ↔

(51)/{15}, it is most certainly your Playground ↔
51:15 = 3:15 / 2 days . . . 31:(52) = 1808 minutes - <25> = 1783 . . . {17}/(8)/3 is **{17}/82**.

Lao Tzu: 95 61 67 89 . . . 95:61 . . . ([9 + 5 = 14]61 . . . 1461] + <1641> = 3102) + <2013> = **5115** ↔
5115 . . . 5[1:15 is 2:(45) . . . 245] . . . 5245 / 5 = 1049 . . . 10:49 is 11:(11) . . . **1111**, Lao Tzu ↔
1111, John Kordupel
1111, Lao Tzu + [11:11 = 671 minutes . . . 671] = **1782**, Lao Tzu ↔

[51:15 = 2 days / 3:15 . . . 2315 + <5132> = 7447] - [51:15 = 3:15 / 2 days . . . 3152 + <2513> = 5665] = **1782**.
1782, Lao Tzu ↔ **1782**, the Second Coming.

24. When carrying on your head your perplexed bodily soul can you embrace in your arms the One
    And not let go?
    In concentrating your breath can you become as supple
    As a babe?
    Can you polish your mysterious mirror
    And leave no blemish?
    Can you love the people and govern the state
    Without resorting to action?
    When the gates of heaven open and shut
    Are you capable of keeping to the role of the female?
    When your discernments penetrate the four quarters
    Are you capable of not knowing anything? Tao Te Ching. Lao Tzu.

Chapter: *My Generation and the Nature of the Times.*

The End Game.
20:1. And I saw an angel come down from heaven, having the key of the bottomless pit and a great chain in his hand.
20:2. And he laid hold on the dragon, that old serpent, which is the Devil, and Satan, and bound him a thousand years,
20:3. And cast him into the bottomless pit, and shut him up, and set a seal upon him, that he should deceive the nations no more, till the thousand years be fulfilled: and after that he must be loosed a little season. Revelations. Holy Bible. King James Version.

When Satan is bound for 1,000 years, does that mean that during those 1,000 years, You are our keeper?

Definitely not.

So for all practical purposes, Satan is footloose and fancy free.

Basically, yes.
There can be no rite of passage if I am your keeper. A rite of passage means that there must be a maze run.

11:6. And the Lord said, Behold, the people is one, and they have all one language; and this they begin to do: and now nothing will be
restrained from them, which they have imagined to do. Genesis.

The key words there are 'restrained' and 'imagined' – what you imagine is there, but it is not going to be handed to you on a plate.

A Family Tree.

3:23. And Jesus himself began to be about thirty years of age, being (as was supposed) the son of Joseph, which was the son of Heli,

3:24. Which was the son of Matthat, which was the son of Levi, which was the son of Melchi, which was the son of Janna, which was the son of Joseph,

3:25. Which was the son of Mattathias, which was the son of Amos, which was the son of Naum, which was the son of Esli, which was the son of Nagge,

3:26. Which was the son of Maath, which was the son of Mattathias, which was the son of Semei, which was the son of Joseph, which was the son of Jude,

3:27. Which was the son of Joanna, which was the son of Rhesa, which was the son of Zorobabel, which was the son of Salathiel, which was the son of Nerri,

3:28. Which was the son of Melchi, which was the son of Addi, which was the son of Cosam, which was the son of Elmodam, which was the son of Er,

3:29. Which was the son of Jose, which was the son of Eliezer, which was the son of Jorim, which was the son of Matthat, which was the son of Levi,

3:30. Which was the son of Simeon, which was the son of Juda, which was the son of Joseph, which was the son of Jonan, which was the son of Eliakim,

3:31. Which was the son of Melea, which was the son of Menen, which was the son of Mattatha, which was the son of Nathan, which was the son of David,

3:32. Which was the son of Jesse, which was the son of Obed, which was the son of Booz, which was the son of Salmon, which was the son of Nasssson,

3:33. Which was the son of Aminadah, which was the son of Aram, which was the son of Esrom, which was the son of Phares, which was the son of Juda,

3:34. Which was the son of Jacob, which was the son of Isaac, which was the son of Abraham, which was the son of Thara, which was the son of Nachor,

3:35. Which was the son of Saruch, which was the son of Ragau, which was the son of Phalec, which was the son of Heber, which was the son of Sala,

3:36. Which was the son of Cainan, which was the son of Arphaxad, which was the son of Sem, which was the son of Noe, which was the son of Lamech,

3:37. Which was the son of Matthusala, which was the son of Enoch, which was the son of Jared, which was the son of Maleleel, which was the son of Cainan,

3:38. Which was the son of Enos, which was the son of Seth, which was the son of Adam, which was the son of God.

Luke. The Holy Bible. King James Version.

$$3:23 + 3:24 + 3:25 + 3:26 + 3:27 + 3:28 + 3:29 + 3:30 + 3:31 + 3:32 + 3:33 + 3:34 + 3:35 + 3:36 + 3:37 + 3:38 = \textbf{5288}.$$

$$<323> + <423> + <523> + <623> + <723> + <823> + <923> + <033> + <133> + <233> + <333> + <433> + <533> + <633> + <733> = <833> = \textbf{8258}.$$

$8258 + 5288 = \textbf{13546} \leftrightarrow$

    $135:46 = (854) / 6$ days $\ldots$ **8546**.

        $85:46 = 5146$ minutes $\ldots 51:46 = 2$ days $/ 346 \ldots$ **2346** $\leftrightarrow$

            23:46. And when Jesus had cried with a loud voice, he said, Father, into thy hands I command my spirit: and having said thus, he gave up the ghost. St. Luke.

                23:46, into thy hands $\leftrightarrow$ **2/3/{46}**, my birthday, a leg in a family tree.

        $85:(46) = 5054$ minutes $+ <64> = \textbf{5118} \leftrightarrow \textbf{5/1/18} \leftrightarrow$

            $51:18 = 3:18 / 2$ days $\ldots 3182 \ldots 31:82 = 1$ day $/ 7:82 \ldots$ **1782**, the Second Coming, a leg in the family tree $\leftrightarrow$

            and,

            the family tree finished with Adam, the son of God $\leftrightarrow$

            5238, God $\ldots 52:(38) = 3082$ minutes $- <83> = 2999 \ldots 2999 \ldots 2 * 9 * 99 = \textbf{1782}$.

Anakhita: 65 143 151 57 . . .([151:57 − 143:65 = 792] * 4 = 3168) + 8613 = 11781
11781 . . . 1 + 1781 = **1782**.

8613, the Hero / the Truth / the Light + <3168> = 11781 . . . 1 + 1781 = **1782**.

Fo-Hi / Krishna / Buddha / Lao Tzu / Confucius: 364 468 500 243 . . . 500:364 − 243:468 = 256896
256896 . . . ([2 + 56 = 58] + 8 = 66) * 9 * 6 = 3564; 3564 / 2 = **1782**.

Moses / Isiah / Jeremiah / Ezekiel / Jesus Christ / the Prophet Muhammad: 616 814 869 561.
[<616> + <418> + <969> + <165> = 2167] + <7612> = 9779 . . . [97 * 79 = 7663] - <3667> = 3996.
3996 . . . 3 * 99 * 6 = **1782**.

2192, Christ + <2912> = 5104 ↔ **1463**, John Kordupel + <3641> = 5104 ↔
51:04 = 3:04 / 2 days . . . 30:(42) = 1758 minutes + <24> = **1782**.

and,

11:06. And the Lord said, Behold, the people is one, and they have all one language; and this they begin
to do: and now nothing will be restrained from them, which they have imagined to do.
Genesis. Holy Bible. King James Version.
√1106 = 3325 6578 . . . [3325 + 6578 = 9903] + [<5233> + <8756> = 13989] = 23892.

√ 116 = 1077 0329 . . . <7701> + <9230> = **16931** . . . 169:31 = 1:31 / 7 days . . . **1317** ↔
13/1/7, You have made the bed as far as you could. Now it is up to Me.

√ 116 = 1077 0329 . . . ([1077 + 0329 = 1406] + <6041> = 7447) + 16931 = 24378.
[24378 = <87342>] - [23892 + <29832> = 53724] = **33618**.
33:618 = 2598 minutes - <816> = **1782**, having the one language.

1782, having the one language + **1593**, You have made the bed as far as you could. Now it is up to Me = 3375
[3375, one language / up to Me now + <5733> = **9108**, Earth / metamorphosis
and,
3375, one language / up to Me . . . 3 days / 375 = 7575.
     7575 + <573> = 8148;   7575 - <573> = 7002.
     7575 + 8148 = 15723;   7575 + 7002 = 14577

3375, one language / up to Me . . . 337 / 5 days = 12337;
     12337 + <733> = 13070;   12337 - <733> = 11604.
     12337 + 13070 = 25407;   12337 + 11604 = 23941

[15723 + 25407 = 41130] − [14577 + 23941 = 38518] = **2612**, One Language / up to Me.
26:12 = 1572 minutes - <21> = **1551** ↔

{15}/(51), the 1,000 year reign of Jesus has to begin sometime.

[20{15} + 2016 = 4031 = <1304>] + (20)/11 = 3315 . . . 33:(15) = 1965 minutes - <51> = **1914**.

Chapter: *The Space Between Noe and Lot.*

Noe and Lot.

17:26. And as it was in the days of Noe, so shall it be also in the days of the Son of man.
17:27. They did eat, they drank, they married wives, they were given in marriage, until the day that Noe entered into the ark, and the flood came, and destroyed them all.
17:28. Likewise also as it was in the days of Lot; they did eat, they drank, they bought, they sold, they planted, they builded:
17:29. But in the same day that Lot went out of Sodom it rained fire and brimstone from heaven, and destroyed them all.
17:30. Even thus shall it be in the day when the Son of man is revealed. Luke. The Holy Bible. King James Version.

17:26 + 17:27 + 17:28 + 17:29 + 17:30 = **8640**; <6271> + <7271> + <8271> + <9271> + <0371> = **31455**.
([8640 + <0468> = **9108**] + <8019> = **17127**) +([31455 + <55413> = **86868**] + <86868> = **173736**) = **190863**.

8640 + <0468> = **9108** ↔
Luke. 1:76 + 1:77 + 1:78 + 1:79 + 1:80 + 2:11 + 4:24 + 13:34 + 13:35 = **4194**, preparing the Way.
4194 + <4914> = **9108**.
Crucifixion: 3,18,21,3,9,6,9,24,9,15,14 - Crucifixion R to L: 14,15,9,24,9,6,9,3,21,18,3 = 1,766,214,723,170,331 . . .
[1 + 766 + 214 + 723 + 170 + 331 = 2205] + [176 + 621 + 472 + 317 + 033 + 1 = 1620] = 3825.
3825 + <5283> = **9108** = **4554** + **4554**.
4554 . . . 4 days / 554 weeks = 3882 days . . . **3882**, Messiah ↔
John Kordupel, 1409 + 1463 + <9041> + <3641> = 15554 . . . [-1 + 5 = 4]554 . . . **4554**.

31455, the space between Noe and Lot . . . [3 + 1 = 4]455 . . . **4455** ↔
[John: 10, 15, 8,14] + [Kordupel: 11,15,18, 4, 21, 16, 5, 12] = 11,151,843,132,326
[1115 + 184 + 313 + 2326 = 3938] - <8393> = **4455** ↔ 4455 . . . [4 * 4 * 5 = 80]5 . . . **805**, End of Days.
4455 / 5 = **891** ↔

4455 + 9108 = **13563** ↔
135:63 = (837) / 6 days . . . **8376**; it is 6 days / (837> . . . **6837**.
8376 – 6837 = **1539**, John Kordupel
83:76 = 5056 minutes + <67> = **5123** . . . 51:23 = 2 days / 3:23 . . . **2323**, 2nd. Coming.
[8376 + <6738> = 15114] – [6837 + <7386> = 14223] = **891** ↔
God: 7,15,4 . . . 5√<4517> = 13008105 . . . 1300 + 8105 = 9405.
God: 7,15,4 . . . [5√7154 = 13196374] + [5√<4517> = 13008105 = 26204479 . . . 2620 + 4479 = 7099.
[7099, God = <9907>] - ([9405, God = <5049>] + [7693, God = <3967>] = 9016) = **891**.
and,
Anakhita: 65 143 151 57 . . . ([151:57 – 143:65 = 792] * 7 = 5544 = <4455) / 5 = **891**.

the space between Noe and Lot is Spirit,

Mary Magdalene & Jesus Christ:
Mary Magdalene: 13,1,18,25. 13,1,7,4,1,12,5,14,5: 1311825 + 131,741,125,145 = 131,742,436,970
Jesus Christ: 10,5,19,21,19. 3,8,18,9,19,20. 105,192,119 + 381,891,920 = 487,084,039.
131,742,436,970, Mary Magdalene + 487,084,039, Jesus Christ = 13222 952 1009.
132,229,521,009 . . . 13 + 222 + 952 + 1009 = 2196 . . . 21:96 = 1356 minutes - <69> = 1287.
1287 . . . 12 * 87 = 1044 . . . **10/(44)**, know My world to know yours.
132,229,521,009 . . . 132 + 229 + 521 + 009 = **891**.

[2093, Christ + <3902> = 5995] – [2192, Christ + <2912> = 5104] = **891**.

the Second Epistle of Paul the Apostle to the Thessalonians 2:1 to 2:4 re the Second Coming:
[21 + 22 + 23 + 24 = 90] + [<12> + <22> + <32> + <42> = 108] = 198 = <**891**>

891, the Day of Resurrection . . . 8√91 = 1017 7766.

[1017 + 7766 = 8783] - [<7101> + <6677> = 13778] = 4995.

[1017 + <6677> = 7694] - [<7101> + 7766 = 14867] = 7173.

[7173 = <3717>] + [4995 = <5994> = 9711.

[9711 - <1179> = 8532] = **4266**, Jesus + [**6624**, John Kordupel = <4266>]

97:11 = 4 days / 1:11 . . . 4111 + [1:11 / 4 days . . . 1114] = **5225** ↔

and,

Iwan; 9,23,1,14 + (Kordupel: 11,15,18, 4, 21, 16, 5, 12 . . . [1115184 + 2116512 = 3231696]) = 4154810 . . .

4154810 . . . 415 + 4810 = **5225**

13563 . . . 1 + 3563 = **3564** ↔

3564 . . . [3 * 5 = 15][6 * 4 = 24] . . . 1524 . . . 15:24 = 924 minutes = 14:84 . . . **14/8/4**, I'll see you tomorrow.

3564 = **1782**, the Second Coming + **1782**, the One Language ↔

3564 . . . [3 + 5 = 8]64 . . . 864 * 10 = **8640** ↔

Luke. 17:26 + 17:27 + 17:28 + 17:29 + 17:30 = **8640**, the space between Noe and Lot.

4455 . . . [4 * 455 = 1820] + **805**, End of Days = 2625) - [**1716**, Anakhita . . .17:16 = 5:16 PM = <6:15> = 375 minutes . . . 375] = **2250**.

2250, Planet Earth, Our World buzzing to New Vibrations.

190863, the space between Noe and Lot - <368091> = 177228 . . . 177 + <771> + 228 + <822> = **1998** ↔

John (Eeevash) Kordupel . . . the space in-between: 400 546 . . . 400546 - <645004> = 244458 . . . 244 + <442> + 458 + <854> = **1998**.

1998 . . . 19/98 = 19/14 weeks . . . **1914** ↔

1782, the One Language . . . 1 day / 782 = 31:82 = 1942 minutes - <28> = **1914**.

Chapter: *Noe, Lot and a City Like Sodom.*

10:11. Even the very dust of your city, which cleaveth on us, we do wipe off against you: notwithstanding be ye sure of this, that the kingdom of God is come nigh unto you.

10:12. But I say unto you, that it shall be more tolerable on that day for Sodom, than for that city. The Holy Bible. King James Version.

1011 + <1101> + 1012 + <2101> = **5225**.

Iwan; 9,23,1,14 + (Kordupel: 11,15,18, 4, 21, 16, 5, 12: . . . [1115184 + 2116512 = 3231696]) = 4154810.

415 + 4810 = **5225** → [5² = 25]25 . . . 2525 = <5252>, Jesus.

Chapter: *On the Road to Damascus.*

20:1. And I saw an angel come down from heaven, having a key of the bottomless pit and a great chain in his hand.

20:2. And he laid hold on the dragon, that old serpent, which is the Devil, and Satan, and bound him a thousand years. Revelations. Holy Bible King James Version.

20:1 + 20:2 = 403 . . . 4:03 is 5:(57) . . . 557 minutes = 9:17 . . . 917 minutes = 15: 17 . . . **1/5/{17}** ↔

15:17 = 3:17 PM = <**713**>, the Season Ends.

[20:1 + 20:2 = 403 + <304> = 707] + [20:01 + 20:02 = 4003 + <3004> = 7007] = **7714**, Satan chained

7714, Satan chained 77:14 = 5:14 / 3 days . . . 51:(43) = 3017 minutes . . . 30:17 = 1 day / 6:17 . . . **1617 ↔ 1/6/{17} ↔ (1)/6/{17} ↔**

16:17 = 4:17 PM . . . 417 = <714>, Satan chained ↔ **714**, the One Language ↔

John: 10, 15, 8,14 + Kordupel: 11,15,18, 4, 21, 16, 5, 12 = 11,151,843,132,326:
We separate 11,151,843,132,326 into two groups of seven, to which we add our birthday:
1115184 . . .1115 + 184 = 1299; 2/03/194{6} + 3132326 = 5164272 . . . 5164 + 272 = 5436
[1299 + 5436 = <5376>] - [**1593**, making of beds . . . 1 day / 5:93 = 29:93 . . . 2993] = 2383. 23:(83) = 1297
minutes + <38> = 1335 . . . 13:35 = 815 minutes . . . **815**, Messiah.
23:83 = 1463 minutes . . . **1463**, John Kordupel.
2383 . . . 238 * 3 = **714**.

the Mahdi,: 20,8,5 13,1,8,4,9 . . . [2085131849 . . .20 * 8 * 5 = 800] + [13 * 1 * 8 * 4 * 9 = 3744] = **4544**.
4544 . . .4 * 54 * 4 = **864** = <468> . . . 46 to 8 is 7:14 . . . **714**.

7714, Satan chained . . . [7 * 714 = 4998] - <8994> = 3996 . . . 3 * 99 * 6 = **1782**.
11:06. And the Lord said, Behold, the people is one, and they have all one language; and this they begin to do: and now nothing will be restrained from them, which they have imagined to do." Genesis. Holy Bible. King James Version.
$\sqrt{1106}$ = 3325 6578 . . . [3325 + 6578 = 9903] + [<5233> + <8756> = 13989] = 23892.
$\sqrt{116}$ = 1077 0329 . . . <7701> + <9230> = **16931**
169:31 = 1:31 / 7 days . . . **13/1/7**, You have made the bed as far as you could. Now it is up to Me.

$\sqrt{116}$ = 1077 0329 . . . ([1077 + 0329 = 1406] + <6041> = 7447) + 16931 = 24378.
[24378 = <87342>] - [23892 + <29832> = 53724] = **33618**.
33:618 = 2598 minutes - <816> = **1782**, having one language.

1782 . . . 1 day / 782 = 31:82 = 1942 minutes - <28> = **1914** ↔

19:14 is 7:14 PM . . . **714**, the One Language ↔

and,
You have made the bed as far as you could. Now it is up to Me: 13/1/{6}/7 + (18)/7/{6} = **31343**.
31343, making of beds . . . [3 + 1343 = 4029 + <9204> = 13233] - [7714, Satan chained + <4177> = **11891**] = **1342** ↔
1342, the Mahdi ↔ **1342**, Second Coming.

[**4222**, Market Forces + <2224> = 6446] – [**3641**, Lord + **1463**, John Kordupel = 5104] = **1342** ↔
4222, Market Forces . . . 42:(22) = 2498 minutes . . . 24:(98) = 1342 minutes . . . **1342**.
and,
714, the One Language ↔ 71⁴ = 2541 1681 . . . 2541 + 1681 = **4222**, Market Forces.

Chapter: *Judas Iscariot. Changing the Course of History.*

Judas Iscariot

J	10	(16)	17	(9)
U	21	(5)	6	(20)

D	4	(22)	23	(3)
A	1	(25)	26	(0)
S	19	(7)	8	(18)
	55	75	80	50

I	9	(17)	18	(8)
S	19	(7)	8	(18)
C	3	(23)	24	(2)
A	1	(25)	26	(0)
R	18	(8)	9	(17)
I	9	(17)	18	(8)
O	15	(11)	12	(14)
T	20	(6)	7	(19)
	94	114	122	86

Judas:	55	75	80	50
Iscariot:	94	114	122	86
	149	189	202	136

202:149 – 189:136 = 13013 . . . 13:(013) = 1077 minutes - <7701> = **6624**, Judas Iscariot ↔

   John Kordupel, synthesis from format: 153 159 167 145

   ([1:45 is 2:(15) = <512>] + [<5:41> being 6:(19) = <916>] = 1428) + <8241> = 9669 . . . 96 * 69 = **6624** ↔

6624 = <**4266**>, Jesus ↔ 42:66 = 2586 minutes . . . 25:86 = 1414 minutes . . . **1414**, Adam ↔

6624 . . . [66² = 4356]4 . . . 43564 . . . [435 + 6 = 441]4 . . . **4414** ↔

   13/1/7, You have made the bed as far as you could. Now it is up to Me: 200{6} + 2007 + 13/1 = 4144 = <**4414**>

Chapter: *Energy Healing.*

A Reading For Leanne Long has a number of underlying themes:

- The Second Coming ushers in the 1,000 year reign of Jesus which is associated with an update of the various Scriptures. This in turn is associated with the Day of Resurrection, the consequence of which is the destruction of the Cities.
- Bring to a conclusion the Conversation started in *A Second Creation, I Am the Second Coming. This is My Message, One More Song, The Birth of a New Essence, Reflections on a New Language, and, The Medicine Wheel.* If this was all about the Second Coming, I could have commissioned someone to set up the above titles for publication as an e-book.

   However,
      we are not dealing with a solo act, but a joint communication. Which brings us to the next underlying theme.

- The existence of previous realms, Medicine Wheel One, Two and Three, were evolutionary stepping stones for the fourth Medicine

211

Wheel, Kali Yuga, Earth's Dark Night of the Soul.

- The transition through the Borderlands between the Fourth Medicine Wheel and the Fifth, i.e., the Promised Land, requires the ability to navigate a rite of passage. Specifically, the dissipation of negative energies accumulated during the journey through the previous

Medicine Wheels which have now been expressed as a dis-ease.

In relation to the last theme, Western medicine is not going to do the trick. Which leads into the final theme, identifying the tools that will. The first step in that process is to *give credibility to Leanne Long as well as the healing approach Leanne has adopted.*

To that end, a key theme of *A Reading* was the endorsement of Leanne Long by Heaven.

Chapter: *The Final Battle.*

Ragnarok – Site For the Battle at the End of Days.
38. The Halls (Valhalla and Folkvangr)
You will be rewarded for your work. Be brave, even if you are afraid. Now is time to work for the greater good – volunteer.

I am content.
For I have passed from the world
With a sword in my hand,
Blood spilled in your name.
With honour in my heart,
I join the Allfather,
Or is it the golden-haired Freyja?
I am carried by the winged women
Screaming my name.

To the Vikings, dying, weapon in hand, fighting to save one's community was considered the most honourable of deaths. Such warriors were rewarded in the Norse afterlife with admittance to either Freyja's hall, Sessrúmnir (seat roomer), in Fólkvangr, (people's field) or Odin's hall, Valhalla, in Asgard.
It was told that Freyja had the first pick of the dead, even above Odin. Those whom Freyja selected were carried to Sessrúmnir by the mighty, winged Valkyries, who served her. Freyja's chosen dead included brave warriors as well as women who had died an honourable death – either those who fought on the battlefield or those who had committed suicide rather than endure rape or a life of dishonour. Freyj's hall was known as a hospitable and wondrous place, described as "large and beautiful" in the *Eddas*. Those who joined Freyja were free to do nothing more than practise their fighting skills in preparation for *the battle at the end of days at Ragnarok.*
Odin's hall, situated in Asgard, was described in ancient texts as being impressively built, guarded by eagles and wolves and containing long tables groaning with food and mead. Like those chosen by Freyja, the exemplary men that Odin selected to join him in his hall also trained to stand besides Odin at Ragnarok.
Do not confuse these halls with the Christian idea of heaven, though. The halls are not places where spirits lay idle or ready to be reborn. There, life continued in ways the Vikings found ideal – celebrating, fighting and training in happy, purposeful companionship. Admittance to one of the halls was seen as a reward for honour, for courage, for giving up one's life for the community. The halls remind us to step outside our own needs and consider the greater good. Viking Oracle Guidebook. Stacey Demarco.

The Lord also said to me: "Son of man, will you judge Oholah and Oholibah? Then declare to them their abominations. For they have committed adultery, and blood is on their hands. They have committed adultery with their idols, and even sacrificed their sons whom they bore to Me, passing them through the fire, to devour them. Moreover they have done this to Me: They have defiled My sanctuary on the same day and profaned My Sabbaths. For after they had slain their children for their idols, on the same day they came into My sanctuary to profane it; and indeed thus they have done in the midst of My house. Book of Ezekiel. P. 1183 – 1184. The MacArthur Study Bible. New King James Version.

1183 + <3811> + 1184 + <4811> = 10989 = **7992**, John Kordupel (format ↔ synthesis) + **<2997>**

The Eight Amigos: Isaiah / Jeremiah / Ezekiel / Jesus Christ / the Prophet Muhammad / Krishna / Buddha / Fo-Hi.
705 1039 1106 636

[705 + 1039 + 1106 + 636 = 3486] - <6843> = **2997**; 3339, Resurrection . . .333 * 9 = **2997**, Resurrection ↔

2997 = <7992> . . . [7 + 9 = 16][9 * 2 = 18] . . . 1618 . . . 16:18 is 1 day / (7:82) . . . **1782**, the Second Coming.

23:1. The word of the Lord came again unto me, saying,

23:2. Son of man, there were two women, the daughters of one mother;

23:3. And they committed whoredoms in Egypt; they committed whoredoms in their youth: there were there breasts pressed, and there they bruised the teats of their virginity.

23:4. And the names of them were Aholah the elder, and Aholibah her sister: and they were mine, and they bare sons and daughters. Thus were their names; Samaria is Aholah, and Jerusalem Aholibah.

   Comment: the key passage is "and they were mine, and they bare sons and daughters." - part of the story of evolution of the species.

23:36. The Lord said moreover unto me; Son of man, wilt thou judge Aholah and Aholibah? yea, declare unto them their abonimations;

23:37. That they have committed adultery, and blood is in their hands, and with their idols have they committed adultery, and have also caused their sons, whom they bare unto me, to pass for them through the fire, to devour them.

23:38. Moreover this they have done unto me: they have defiled my sanctuary in the same day, and have profaned my sabbaths.

23:39. For when they had slain their children to their idols, then they came the same day into my sanctuary to profane it; and, lo, thus they have done in the midst of mine house. Book of Ezekiel. Holy Bible. King James Version.

   Comment: If you believe in reincarnation, then "their sons" and "their children", would refer to their different aspects.

23:1 → 23:4 . . . [231 + <132> + 234 + <432> = 1029] + <9201> = **10230** . . . 10:230 = 830 minutes = 13:50 . . . **1350**, the Untitled One.

23:36 → 23:39 . . . 2336 + <6332> + 2339 + <9332> = 20339

   20:339 = 1539 minutes . . . **1539** ↔

      Thessalonians 2:1 to 2:4, re the Second Coming . . . [2¹ = 2] [2² = 4] [2³ = 8] [2⁴ = 16] . . . 24816.

         24816 . . . [-2 + 4 = 2]816 . . . 2816 . . . 28:(16) = 1664 minutes . . . 1 day / 664 = 30:64 . . . 3064 - <4603> = **1539**.

      [John: 10, 15, 8,14] + [Kordupel: 11,15,18, 4, 21, 16, 5, 12] = 11,151,843,132,326.

         [1115184 . . .1115 + 184 = 1299] + [3132326 . . . 313 + 2326 = 2639] = 3938.

            3938 - <8393> = 4455 = <5544> . . . 554 weeks / 4 days = 3882 days . . . **3882**, the Unlettered Prophet.

            39:38 = 2378 minutes + <83> = 2461.

               2461 + <1642> = 4103 . . . 41:03 = 2463 minutes . . . 24:63 = 1503 minutes + <36> = **1539**.

   20339 – 10230 = **10109** ↔

      Kali Yuga, Earth's dark cycle: 416 + <614> + 1217 + <7121> = 9368 . . .

         [93:68 = 5648 minutes + <86> = 5734] + <4375> = **10109**.

      101:09 = 5:09 / 4 days . . . 5094

50:94 = 2 days / 2:94 . . . 22:94 = 1414 minutes . . . **1414**, Adam → 1414 + <49> = **1463**, John Kordupel
50:94 = 2:94 / 2 days . . . 29:42 = 1782 minutes . . . **1782**, the Second Coming.
    ([2942 + 2294 = 5236] / 2 = 2618) - <8162> = 5544.
    the Day Of Resurrection: 249 271 191 229
([249 + 271 + 191 + 229 = 940] + [<942> + <172> + <191> + <922> = 2227 = <7222>] = 8162) - <2618> = **5544**.
    5544 . . . 554 weeks / 4 days = 3882 days . . . **3882**, the Unlettered Prophet.

and,

the Five Horsemen: the Mahdi / the Second Coming / Maitreya / the Unlettered Prophet / Kalki, updating the Scriptures:
    613 843 899 557 . . . 613 + <348> = 961.
  961 + <169> + <998> + <755> = **2883**, Maitreya ↔ <**3882**>, the Unlettered Prophet.
    28:83 is 1 day / 4:83 . . . **14/8/{3}**, I'll see you tomorrow ↔

and,

3882, the Day of Resurrection . . . [3 * 88 = 264]2 . . . 26:42 = 1602 minutes + <24> = **1626** ↔
5935, the Day of Resurrection – 3118, the Day of Resurrection = 2817 . . . 28:17 = 1697 minutes - <71> = **1626**.
16/2/6, when will the manuscript be published? . . . is 6/(318> . . . 63:18 = 3 days / (882) . . . **3882** →
    16/2/6, when will the manuscript be published ? 47/06 + (12)/02/{5} = 16731.
    16731 . . . [167 - <761> = 592] ([3 * 1 = 3] = 1782, the Second Coming ↔ {17}/82.
        17:82 = 5:82 PM . . . 582 + [582 minutes = 9:42] + [58 to 2 is 1:02] = **1626**.
        1782, the One Language . . . 1 day / 782 = 31:82 = 1942 minutes - <28> = **1914** ↔

    167:31 = 7 days / (0:29) . . . 70:29 = 3 days / (171) . . . 31:71 = 1931 minutes - <17> = **1914**.

    16731 . . . 16 + [7:31 is 8:(29) . . . 829 = <928>] = **944** ↔
        √944 = 3072 4582
        30:72 is 672 / 1 day . . . 6721 - <1276> = 5445 . . . 54:45 = 2 days / 645 . . . 2645.
      45:82 = 2 days / (218) . . . 2218; it is (218)/2 days . . . 2182.
      [2645 + 2218 = 4863] – 2182 = 2681 = 1862 . . . 18/6/2;
        it is 2/6/18 . . . 2618 - <8162> = **5544**.

{9}/ (44), I cannot talk with you about your world unless you know about Mine. Get out of My Car

Book Two: Back Cover.

"Your soul (subconscious id, spirit, past, etc.) is the sum total of every feeling you've ever had (created)." P. 74.

" . . . there is no coincidence in the universe – only a grand design; an incredible "snowflake." P. 54.

Emotion is energy in motion. When you move energy, you create effect. If you move enough energy, you create matter. Matter is energy conglomerated. Moved around. Shoved together. If you manipulate energy long enough in a certain way, you get matter. Every Master understands this law. It is the alchemy of the universe. It is the secret of all life. Thought is pure energy. Every thought you have, have ever had, and ever will have is creative. The energy of your thought never ever dies. Ever. It leaves your being and heads out into the universe, extending forever. A thought is forever.

All thoughts congeal; all thoughts meet other thoughts, crisscrossing in an incredible maze of energy, forming an ever-changing pattern of unspeakable beauty and unbelievable complexity.

Like energy attracts like energy – forming (to use simple words) "clumps" of energy of like kind. When enough "clumps" crisscross each other – run into each other – they "stick to" each other (to use another simple term) it takes an incomprehensibly huge amount of similar energy "sticking together," thusly, to form matter. But matter will form out of pure energy. In fact, that is the only way it can form. Once energy becomes matter, it remains matter for a very long time – unless its construction is disrupted by an opposing, of dissimilar, form of energy. This dissimilar energy acting upon matter, actually dismembers the matter, releasing the raw energy of which it was composed . . . P. 54 – 55. Conversations with God. Neale Donald Walsch.

"No soul shall bear another's burden." P.176. The Koran. Translated by N. J. Darwood.

That being the case, you cannot inherit an illness from your parents.

In her previous life, Cherryl, my wife, was Mary Magdalene. When I told her that I was the Second Coming, the soul said 'Shit. Here we go again'.
Mary Magdalene's emotional baggage resulting fro the Crucifixion came off the Cosmic Shelf, and Cher came down with scleroderma, which would be the cause of her death.
So began my odyssey – how do you cure an dis-ease that had its genesis in a previous lifetime.

In order to break your Chain of Rebirth, that is what you need to do.

A Spiritual Master can be defined as someone who has broken their Chain of Rebirth.

Back cover for Book Three:
The Nature of the Times.
19:20. Behold now, this city is near to flee unto, and it is a little one: Oh, let me escape thither, (is it not a little one?) and **my soul shall live**.
19:21. And he said unto him, See, I have accepted thee concerning this thing also, and I will not overthrow this city, for the which thou hast spoken.

19:22. Haste thee, escape thither; for I cannot do anything till thou be come thither. Therefore the name of the city was Zoar. Genesis.

       19:20 + 19:21 = 3841 = <1483> . . . **14/8/{3}**, I'll see you tomorrow at 815.

       19:20 = 1160 minutes + <02> = 1162 minutes = 18:82 . . . 18/82 is **{17}/82** ↔ **1782**, the Second Coming.

       [1920 = <0291>] + [1921 = <1291>] = 1582.

          15:82 = 982 minutes . . . 982 + <289> = **1271** ↔

            Lot / Lut: 90 56 62 94.

              ([90 + 56 + 62 + 94 = 302] + <203> = 505) + ([<09> + <65> + <62> + <49> = 185] + <581> = 766) = **1271**.

           [15:82 = 982 minutes - <289> = 693] * 4 = **2772**, the Chain of Rebirth ↔

          1582 . . . [1 + 5 = 6]82 . . . 6:82 PM is 18:82 . . . 18/82 is **{17}/82** ↔ **1782**, the Second Coming.

          15:(82) = 818 minutes - <28> = 790 minutes = 12:70 . . . 1270 minutes = 22:(50) . . . **2250**, New Harmonic Vibrations.

19:22, I cannot do anything till thou be come thither . . . [19² = 361]2 . . . 3612 + <2163> = **5775** ↔

       the Mandi / the Second Coming / Maitreya / the Unlettered Prophet / Kalki / the Messiah: 720 996 1062 654. the Six

Horsemen updating the Scriptures ([720 + 996 = 1716] + [1062 + 654 = 1716] = 3432) + <2343> = **5775** ↔

       [Hay Publishing / manuscript: **{12}/(85)** + **(85)/13** = **9798**] – [Hay Publishing: no, need literary agent **13/(67)** + **(67)/13**

= **8080**] = **1718** [17:18 = 1038 minutes . . . 1038] + [17:18 = <81:71> = 3 days / 9:71 . . . 3971] = 5009

          50:09 = 2 days / 2:09 . . . . . . 2209 = **(139)/4**, I'll see you tomorrow at 815 + **815**.

       17:18 = 5:18 PM = 318 minutes . . . 3:18 PM is 15:18 . . . week **1/5/18** ↔

          it is **5/1** week/18 . . . 51:18 is 3:18 / 2 days . . . 31:82 is 1 day / 782 . . . **1782**, the One Language.

       [17:18 = 1038 minutes . . . 1038] - [2209 - <9022> = 6813] = **5775** ↔

          5775 = **3882**, the Unlettered Prophet + **1893** . . . 18:93 = 6:93 PM . . . **693**, John Kordupel ↔

            693 * 8 = 5544 . . . 554 weeks / 4 days = 3882 days . . . **3882**, the Unlettered Prophet.

       1718, Hay Publishing / manuscript / no, need literary agent + **5775**, Six Horsemen updating Scriptures = 7493

          74:93 = 3 days /293 . . . 32:93 = 1893 minutes . . . **1893**, rediscovery of the Forms of Life.

          74:93 = 293 / 3 days . . . 29:33 = 1773 minutes . . . **1773** ↔

            Leanne Long: 99 (161) 171 (89) . . . 99:171 – (89):(161) = 10010 . . . 100:10 = 4:10 / 4 days . . . **4104**.

            4104 – [171:99 – (161):(89) = **1010**] = 3094 . . . 30:94 = 1 day / 6:94 . . . **1694**, Leanne Long

              ([1694 + <4961> = **6655**] / 11 = 605) + [6655 / 5 = 1331] = 1936) - <6391> = **4455**.

            4455, Leanne Long + [<5544> / 2 = **2772**, Know Me] = **7227**, Leanne Long ↔ **7227**, Book-End.

              72:27 = 3 days / 0:27 . . . 30:(27) = 1773 minutes . . . **1773**, Leanne Long.

                1773, Leanne Long . . . [17:73 is 5:73 PM = <375>] * 6 = **2250**, New Harmonic Vibrations.

                (continued on inside of back cover)

Inside back cover:

Lot was concerned for his soul to live:

Your soul (subconscious id, spirit, past, etc.) is the sum total of every feeling you've ever had (created). P. 74.

       74, sum soul's creation ↔ **74**, Christ . . . 7⁴ = 2401 . . . 2 days / 4:01 = 52:01 . . . 5 days / 2:01 = 122:01 + <102>

       = **12303**.

      12:(303) = 417 minutes = <**714**>

          [John: 10, 15, 8,14] + [Kordupel: 11,15,18, 4, 21, 16, 5, 12] = 11,151,843,132,326:

            We separate 11,151,843,132,326 into two groups of seven, to which we add our birthday:

            [1115184 . . .1115 + 184 = 1299] + [2/03/194{6} + 3132326 = 5164272 . . . 5164 + 272 = 5436] = 6735.

[6735 = <5376>] - [**1593** . . . 1 day / 5:93 = 29:93 . . . 2993] = 2383 . . . 238 * 3 = **714**.

13/1/{6} . . . 13/1/7, You have made the bed as far as you could. Now it is up to Me →

[13:16 = 796 minutes . . . 796] + [13:17 = 797 minutes . . . 797] = **1593**.

7:14 PM is 19:14 . . . **1914** ↔

12:303 = 1023 minutes + <303> = 1326 . . . ([13² = 169] * 6 = 1014) + <4101> = **5115** ↔

51:15 = 3075 minutes . . . 30:(75) = 1725 minutes + <57> = **1782**, the Second Coming ↔

1782, the Second Coming . . . 1 day / 782 = 31:82 = 1942 minutes - <28> = **1914** ↔

[12303 / 3 = 4101] + <1014> = **5115** . . . (51)/{15}, the 1,000 year reign of Jesus has to begin sometime; it is {15}/
(51) ↔

{15}/(51) is: [20{15} + 2016 = 4031 = <1304>] + (20)/11 = 3315 . . . 33:(15) = 1965 minutes - <51> = **1914**.

The destruction of Sodom and Gomorrah is about bringing the fourth Medicine Wheel, Kali Yuga, Earth's dark night of the Soul, to an end.

Zoar is the fifth Medicine Wheel, the Promised Land.

Back cover. Book Four:

20:1. And I saw an angel come down from heaven, having the key to the bottomless pit and a great chain in his hand.
20:2. And he laid hold on the dragon, that old serpent, which is the Devil, and Satan, and bound him a thousand years.
20:3. And cast him into the bottomless pit, and shut him up, and set a seal upon him, that he should deceive the nations no more, till the

thousand years should be fulfilled: and after that he must be loosed a little season. Revelations. Holy Bible. King James Version.

the time of the 1,000 years:
17:9. The heart is deceitful above all things, and desperately wicked: who can know it?
17:10. I the Lord search the heart, I try the reins, even to give to every man according to his ways, and according to the fruits of his

doing. Holy Bible. King James Version.

([17:9 + 17:10 = 1889] - <9881> = 7992) / 12 = 666 . . . 666 minutes = 11:06 . . . **1106** ↔

11:6. And the Lord said, Behold, the people is one, and they have all one language; and this they begin to do: and now nothing will be restrained from them, which they have imagined to do." Genesis. Holy Bible. King James Version.

√ 116 = 1077 0329 . . . [1077 + 0329 = 1406] + <6041> + [<7701> + <9230> = 16931] = 24378.

169:31 = 1:31 / 7 days . . . 13/1/7, You have made the bed as far as you could. Now it is up to Me.

√1106 = 3325 6578 . . . [3325 + 6578 = 9903] + [<5233> + <8756> = 13989] = 23892

[24378 = <87342>] - [23892 + <29832> = 53724] = 33:618 = 2598 minutes - <816> = **1782**, having One Language.

God: 7,15,4: 7 + 154 = 161; 715 + 4 = 719: 161 + 719 = 880.
Devil: 4, 5, 22, 9,12 . . . ([4 + 522 + 912 = 1438] + [452 + 291 + 2 = 745] + [4522 + 912 = 5434] + [452 + 2912 = 3364] = 10981.
10981, Devil – 880, God = 10101, the Dual Essence.

[880, God * 10 = 8800] + 10101, Dual Essence = 18901 = <10981>, Devil.

This equation reads that God and the Devil are one and the same.

18901, God / Devil . . . 18:901 = 1981 minutes = <1891> - <109> = **1782** ↔

As the Devil shall be let loose for but "a little season", after that "little Season", we are left with just God ↔

Without the Devil component, we are facing a different Matrix,

We are dealing with a New Essence, a New God.

Is that not so?

Printed in the United States
By Bookmasters